Africa's Islamic Experience

History, Culture, and Politics

Africa's Islamic Experience

History, Culture, and Politics

Edited by

Ali A. Mazrui
Patrick M. Dikirr
Robert Ostergard Jr.
Michael Toler & Paul Macharia

STERLING PUBLISHERS PRIVATE LIMITED

STERLING PUBLISHERS PRIVATE LIMITED
A-59, Okhla Industrial Area, Phase-II, New Delhi-110020.
Tel: 26387070, 26386209; Fax: 91-11-26383788
e-mail: sterlingpublishers@airtelmail.in
www.sterlingpublishers.com

Africa's Islamic Experience: History, Culture, and Politics
© 2009, Sterling Publishers Pvt. Ltd.
ISBN 978- 81-207-4085-3

All rights are reserved. No part of this publication may be reproduced, stored in a retrieval system or transmitted, in any form or by any means, mechanical, photocopying, recording or otherwise, without prior written permission of the publisher.

Index by **Abdul Samed Bemath**

PRINTED IN INDIA

Printed and Published by Sterling Publishers Pvt. Ltd., New Delhi-110020.

Contents

Preface and Acknowledgments   vii

Introduction: The African Impact on Muslim History: A Prelude
Ali A. Mazrui ix

AFRICA'S RELIGIOUS CANVAS: AN OVERVIEW

1. Islam, Christianity, and Africa's Indigenous Faiths:
   Demographic Introduction
   Amadu Jacky Kaba 3

HISTORY AND SPREAD OF ISLAM IN AFRICA

2. Islam in Africa's Experience: Expansion, Revival, and
   Radicalization
   Ali A. Mazrui 13

3. The Spread of Islam and Arab Culture in West Africa in the
   Eleventh Century: Impact on African-European Relations
   Brahim El Kadiri Boutchich 31

4. Islam and Christianity in Uganda: Conflict, Dialogue, and
   Search for Partnership
   James Ndyabahika 47

5. Indian Muslims in South Africa's History: Continuity and Change
   Goolam Vahed 73

POLITICAL ISLAM AND AFRICAN POLITICS

6. Afrabia: Evolutionary Convergence between Africa and the
   Arab World
   Ali A. Mazrui 109

7. Ethnoreligious Pluralism and Democratization in Nigeria:
   The Politics of the Shari'a
   Siraj Abdulkarim Barau 124

8. Structuring Islam and the Culture of Democratization:
   The Case of Niger
   Abdoulaye Sounaye 147

9. Globalization and the Assertive Ummah: The Case of Islam
   in Kenya
   Gimode A. Edwin 165

ISLAM AND COMPARATIVE CULTURE

10. Islam and Acculturation in East Africa's Experience
    Ali A. Mazrui 189

11. To Veil or not to Veil: Faces of Islam in Comparative Literature
    Abd el Kader Cheref 206

12. Cultural Interaction and Comparative Architecture:
    The Colonial Experience in Francophone Africa
    Lione Moshe 236

13. Comparative Human Values: African and Islamic
    Ali A. Mazrui 244

    Subject Index   259

    Author Index   266

Preface and Acknowledgments

The Institute of Global Cultural Studies (IGCS) at Binghamton University is basically interested in all cultural phenomenons across the world — from Tokyo to Timbuktu, from Mumbai to Mombasa, and from Harlem to The Hague. But the Institute has specialized in the study of three particular and very influential civilizations: the West, Islam, and what we call "Global Africa." The idea of Global Africa encompasses the African continent itself and the people of African descent, worldwide.

The convergence of these three civilizations — the West, Islam, and Global Africa — constitutes what Ali A. Mazrui has called "the Triple Heritage." Much of Professor Mazrui's own work has focused on how the three civilizations have interacted on the African continent. But this Institute has treated those three legacies as *global* phenomena and not just Africa's own experience. The triple heritage should, therefore, be counted as the inheritance of humankind.

Arising out of this agenda of the Institute of Global Cultural Studies, several projects have been promoted. One project posed the question of whether globalization was a dialogue of civilizations. A book by multiple authors on the theme has already been published (2008). Another book, focusing more narrowly on *Africa and Asia* in the postcolonial era, is in preparation. A book on *Africa and Other Civilizations* has already been published; so has a book on *Islam between Globalization and Counterterrorism*.

This particular Afro-Islamic volume, by multiple authors, focuses on *Islam in Africa*. Some of the chapters included here originated in an IGCS workshop on that subject held at Binghamton, while the other chapters are based on papers specially commissioned for this volume. It is hoped that the collection will illustrate not just the impact of Islam upon Africa but also the impact of Africa on Muslim history.

This particular volume is indebted to a wide range of benefactors. Binghamton University has financed many of the preparatory activities, ranging from a workshop on the theme to additional research and manuscript preparation.

There were oral participants at the workshops who did not have papers. This volume is also grateful to them for their contribution of ideas. For the earlier phases of the editing of this volume, we are particularly grateful to Michael Toler, Robert Ostergard, Fouad Kalouche, Tracia Leacock Seghatolislami, Thomas Uthup, and Ruzima Sebuharara. For secretarial services we are truly obliged to Nancy Levis, Barbara Tierno, AnnaMarie Palombaro, and Nancy Hall.

For computer and website support we are especially indebted to Senthilkumar Mehalingam as the technical graduate assistant. Needless to say, the editors are particularly obliged to the authors for their patience and cooperation over a long period.

Ali A. Mazrui, Binghamton University (SUNY)
Patrick M. Dikirr, Binghamton University (SUNY)

INTRODUCTION

The African Impact on Muslim History: A Prelude

ALI A. MAZRUI

There have been many books about the impact of Islam on Africa's history but very few studies about the impact of Africa on the history of Islam.[1] While the chapters in this collection are still primarily about Islamic influence in Africa, the chapters should also be read with the reverse impact in mind.

Muslims regard their religion as being partly a refinement and elaboration of the messages of Moses and Jesus. Islam is also regarded as being solidly based on the principle of *tawheed* — the singularity of God. Where does Africa feature in this initial configuration?

The Origins of Monotheism

It is arguable that Africa is not only the cradle of monotheism in world history, it also provided asylum to the three Abrahamic religions in their infancy.[2] While sub-Saharan Africa is the mother of the earliest forms of religion in human experience, North Africa later became the mother of monotheism. Since Eastern and Southern Africa were, on present evidence, the area of the world where the human species originated,[3] this sub-Saharan area must also have been the birthplace of such basic elements of human culture as language, religion, and family. Early humans adopted gods of thunder, of floods, of earthquakes, and of war and fertility. Ancestral Africa was preparing the ground for the human experience of worship, awe, and belief in the supernatural.

It took a millennia before another part of Africa — the North — singularized the deity. The Pharaoh Akhenaton (1369 – 1332 B.C.) is widely regarded as the father of monotheism, and monotheism later became the most globalizing of all religious principles. Was the Pharaoh Akhenaton a *rasul* (apostle) or *nabi* (prophet) or neither? The *Qur'an* tells us that to each Umma, God sends a *rasul*.[4] Was Akhenaton the *rasul* to ancient Egypt?[5]

Egypt was also where Moses was born. So Egypt was, in that sense, also the cradle of Judaism, even if one does not accept the thesis that Moses himself was an Egyptian (a thesis made famous in the twentieth century by Sigmund Freud's theories about Jewish identity).[6] Judaism became another monotheistic tradition born in Egypt. If Egypt was the country from which Moses later fled, Egypt subsequently became the country in which the infant Jesus later found asylum from the deadly machinations of King Herod.

> ...the angel of the Lord appeared to Joseph [Mary's husband] and said, "Rise, take the child and his mother to Egypt, and stay there until I tell you. Herod is going to search for the child to destroy him. (Matthew, 2:13)

The underlying logic of the story is that without the asylum in North Africa, there would have been no Christianity — for the infant Jesus would have been 'crucified' in the cradle. Was North Africa therefore the savior of Christianity? If North Africa was the birthplace of historical monotheism and the birthplace of Moses and if North Africa was also the asylum of the infant Jesus, what is Egypt's historic destiny for Islam?

Starting with Egypt, North Africa was the first grand clash between Christian power and Muslim challenge. This was the Arab military conquest of Egypt away from the Byzantine Empire. Some would argue that this was the first blow which set in motion a process which culminated in the fall of Constantinople to the Muslim invaders several centuries later. The conquest of Constantinople (now Istanbul) in 1453 by the Turks, inaugurated the Ottoman Empire.[7]

But Islam had a humbler arrival in Africa than its triumphant arrival in Egypt. Just as North Africa had played a part as the cradle of the gospel of Moses, Egypt also played a part as a political refuge of the infant Jesus, and Ethiopia played a part as a place of refuge for persecuted Muslims on the run from pre-Islamic Arabia. The Prophet Muhammad had just begun to preach his own new gospel. Muhammad was protected for a while by his tribe; but when, in desperation and anger, Muhammad's tribe (the Hashemites and Kureish) withdrew their protection, it became open season to hunt down Muslims. That was when Muhammad authorized some of his followers to cross the Red Sea and seek asylum in Christian Ethiopia.[8] It was hoped that the monotheistic Ethiopian Christians would be sympathetic to the new monotheists from Arabia. These Muslim asylum seekers in Ethiopia were led by Uthman bin Affan, who subsequently became the third Caliph of Islam and a major preserver of a single version of the Qur'an.[9]

The subsequent Arab conquest of Egypt and the Maghreb also fertilized the flowering of an Islamic civilization on African soil, one of whose institution is Al-Azhar University, a centre of learning which has lasted a thousand years.[10] Can we describe Al-Azhar as the first global university, attracting as it does, students from all corners of the Muslim world? Another North African university in Fez, Morocco, is even older than Al-Azhar.

We have referred elsewhere to technology as another engine of globalization across time. Were ancient Egyptians the first to use technology for grand constructions of eternal durability? Long before the construction of the Aswan Dam, by Soviet engineers, in the 1950s and 1960s, there was the construction of the great pyramids, linking the living with the dead. Ancient Egypt was arguably among the first grand civilizations. Technology and empire were linked in anticipation of new worlds to conquer.

Much closer to our own day was a different kind of construction in Egypt — the building of the Suez Canal in the nineteenth century, led by the French engineer Ferdinand de Lesseps. Hundreds of lives of Egyptian and other African workers were lost in the construction of the canal. The Canal was a product, not just of Western expertise and capital but also of the sweat and blood of the Nile Valley workers. The Canal was a major contribution to globalization since it helped to connect Europe, Africa, and Asia in new ways. But the canal was also a monument to technology and economy as the engine of globalization.[11]

By the second half of the twentieth century, Abdul Nasser, Egypt's President (reign 1953 – 1970) saw Egypt as a center of three circles: Arab, Islamic, and African (a triad of cultures).[12] Egypt had, indeed, become a bridge across three continents: Africa, Asia, and Europe (a triad of continents). In one way or another, Egypt had nursed four different traditions of monotheism: Akhenaton, Judaism, Christianity, and Islam (a monotheistic quadrangle).

Between Islamization and Arabization

The Arab conquest of North Africa unleashed two processes, which subsequently gave Africa a special significance in the history of Islam. The more obvious process was the Islamization of Egypt and the rest of North Africa, as more and more of their populations became converts to Islam. While Egypt and much of the rest of North Africa were Christian in religious affiliation in the seventh century C.E., North Africa has since become overwhelmingly Muslim.[13]

In addition to Islamization (the spread of the Islamic religion), North Africa underwent Arabization (the spread of the Arabic language). Today, the great majority of North Africans are native speakers of the Arabic language. The big exceptions are the Berber minorities of the Maghreb and the Black Nuba minority of the upper Nile, who all speak different tongues of their own.

The process of Islamization in Africa went well beyond the borders of North African states and penetrated further and further south of the Sahara. In fact, Islam arrived in many African societies in different guises. We have already referred to its arrival in Ethiopia as asylum seeker and in Egypt and North Africa as conqueror. In Eastern Africa (from Harar in Ethiopia to the city states of Coastal Kenya and Coastal Tanzania) Islam arrived partly as an Arab settler and partly as a missionary. Across the Sahara and across the Indian Ocean, Islam also arrived as an Arab trader — including trade in slaves.[14]

On the other hand, Islam arrived in Southern Africa enslaved in chains. These were the enslaved Muslim Malays, who were captured by the Dutch — in or near what is today Indonesia — and imported into South Africa three hundred years ago as slaves and serfs.[15]

In West Africa, Islam was also spread by *jihadists* and religious revivalists, such as the nineteenth century jihad of Ousmane Dan Fodio, in what later became Nigeria.[16] Much more common was the spread of Islam by evangelization, proselytism, and missionary work.

By the end of the twentieth century, Muslims in Africa constituted either a plurality or an absolute majority of the population of the continent.[17] Nigeria alone contained more Muslims than the Muslim population of any Arab country, including Egypt.[18] Africa was emerging as the first continent in the world with perhaps a preponderance of Muslims in its population. Is such preponderance a kind of climax for the process of Islamization, which began to unfold after the Arab conquest of Egypt in the seventh century C.E.?

As for the process of Arabization, the language initially spread westwards from Egypt and southwards up the Nile Valley. Over the centuries, more and more people not only learned the Arabic language, but eventually identified themselves as Arabs. Arabization came to mean the making of more and more Arabs on the African continent.

Today, the African members of the League of Arab States include Egypt, Sudan, Tunisia, Libya, Algeria, Morocco, Mauritania, and such semi-Arabized members as Somalia and the Comoro Islands. Within these countries resides the majority of the population of the Arab world.[19]

Islam does not have a doctrine of the Chosen People. But it does have a *de facto* doctrine of the Chosen Language — Arabic. It is the language of the five compulsory prayers of each day, the original language of the Qur'an recited by millions every twenty-four hours, the language of the rituals of the Hajj or pilgrimage to Mecca. It is also the language of ritual ceremonies of birth, marriage, sickness and health, and funeral services.

Of the total native speakers of this sacred language, the majority are in Africa. What is more, the making of newer and newer Arabs continues as countries with a majority of Arabs assimilate more and more of their minorities into the fold of Arab identity. This includes the assimilation of non-Arab populations of countries like Sudan (Arabizing Blacks), Algeria and Morocco (Arabizing Berbers), and Egypt (Arabizing the Nuba mountains).

If Arabic is the Chosen Language of God, it has made its most spectacular spread on the African continent. This is quite apart from those Africans who have learned the Arabic language as a medium of their Islamic rituals rather than in pursuit of acquiring a new Arab identity.

The spread of the Arabic language in Africa is partly a consequence of the spread of Islam. But the spread of the Arabic language in turn helped to stimulate the rise of new African indigenous languages. Perhaps the most successful African language on the continent is Kiswahili, dominant mainly in countries of Eastern Africa. Just as the English language, as we know it today, is inconceivable without the impact of Latin, so Kiswahili (as we know it) would not have happened at all without the impact of both Islam and the Arabic language.[20]

The most influential African language in West Africa is Hausa. The impact of Arabic and Islam on Hausa is of comparable magnitude to their impact on Kiswahili.[21] What this means is that three out of the five subregions of Africa have a neo-Islamic language as the major medium of indigenous discourse. Arabic dominates North Africa, Hausa towers over other African languages in West Africa, and Kiswahili continues to expand in Tanzania, Kenya, Uganda, Rwanda, and Burundi in Eastern Africa.

Other neo-Islamic languages in Eastern Africa include Somali and Oromo, while other neo-Islamic languages in West Africa include Wolof, Fulfulde, Tuareg, and Malinke.

Southern Africa is the fourth subregion of the continent. There is no highly prominent neo-Islamic language in Southern Africa, but Kiswahili has already substantially penetrated Mozambique, Malawi, and elsewhere in the South.

If Central Africa is the fifth subregion of the continent, it is also without a prominent neo-Islamic language. However, Kiswahili has already become a major rival to Lingala in the indigenous discourse of the Democratic Republic of the Congo. All evidence indicates a continuing expansion of the Swahili language in both Southern and Central Africa in the generations to come.

Islam and Ancient African Diasporas

Is there a sixth subregion of Africa? Does it have a prominent neo-Islamic language or some other aspect of culture? The African Union in this twenty-first century has considered recognizing the African Diaspora as the sixth subregion of African solidarity. Is there an Islamic factor in relation to this Diasporic experience? If language is not relevant here, what other aspect of culture is?

One factor to be taken into account is that there was an African Diaspora in Arabia long before the birth of the Prophet Muhammad. The proximity of the Horn of Africa had resulted in different forms of contact between the Arabian peninsula and countries in the Horn. For example, there is passionate disagreement to the present day as to whether the Queen of Sheba was Ethiopian or Yemeni. Biblical and Qur'anic scholars place her in Yemen. African historians and cultural nationalists place her in Ethiopia.[22]

The Qur'an also refers to an invasion of Arabia by "people of the elephant," *(as-habil feel)*.[23] It is almost certain that this is a reference to a fighting force from Ethiopia led by commanders riding two or three elephants. The Qur'an implies a divine intervention which thwarted the invaders on elephants. Did a pestilence break out among the invading foreigners, which resulted in their retreat? Again, this was a pre-Islamic conflict between Arabia and an African fighting force, seemingly long before Muhammad was born.

Another compelling testimony that relations between Arabia and Africa are older than Islam concerns Bilal, son of Rabah. He was a Black Ethiopian, enslaved by Arabs before Islam. In fact, it was the early Muslims (probably the Prophet's disciple, Abubakar) who bought Bilal in order to emancipate him. Bilal was converted early to the new religion of Islam, and he then developed into one of the closest disciples of the Prophet Muhammad.[24] When the Muslims peacefully re-conquered Mecca in the year 620 C.E., Bilal was the first Muezzin to call believers to prayer at the newly re-constituted mosque of the Kaaba — the first Islamic call to prayer from the holiest place in the Muslim world. Bilal symbolized the Diaspora of Eastern Africa in Arabia.

A few generations later, there began to develop a Diaspora of Northern Africa in the Iberian Peninsula. Spain was Europe's nearest point to Africa. Across the centuries there developed a constant movement of people, goods, wealth, and ideas between North Africa and Spain. Such historic Moroccan religious and political movements as Mourabiteen and Almoravids eventually bestowed the name 'Moors' to the darker-skinned North African Muslims. They were among the very first Africans ever to exercise sovereignty over the Europeans in Europe itself.

Muslims were in power in Spain for eight centuries. Some of the most spectacularly built monuments to Islamic civilization were constructed in Muslim Spain, Al-Andalus. The most dazzling are the gardens, palace, and the citadel of Alhambra.

Granada fell to the Christian onslaught on January 2, 1492. Thousands of masterpieces of poetry, philosophy, science, history, maps, and atlases were condemned to the bonfires of the Catholic Inquisition. Over a period of time, three million Moors were expelled from Spain or burnt alive or forcibly forced to convert to Christianity.[25] In the words of Jan Carew:

> The burning of thousands of books and the expulsion of the Moors was a terrible loss to the Renaissance... And the glaring irony is that the Renaissance would not have been possible without the seminal-cultural infusions of Moorish scholarship.[26]

Islam's dazzling impact on medieval Europe was disproportionately through Muslim Spain. The achievements of Muslim Spain are not only a part of European history, they are also inseparable from North African history.

Ivan Van Sertima has argued that it was not an accident that nearly all major European universities of the Middle Ages came into being during the flowering of Moorish science and the widespread translation of Moorish treatises from Arabic into Latin. This intellectually fertile period was from the twelfth century right through the thirteenth.

> In Italy we have Bologna, Padua, Naples, and Rome; in France, Montpelier and Toulouse; in Portugal, Lisbon and Coimbra; in England, Oxford. Several of the Moorish works in mathematics, astronomy, and medicine became standard texts at these universities.[27]

Shakespeare's Othello is a Moor of courage and physical heroism, rather than a Moor of learning and intellectual prowess. In any case, to avoid complications of an interfaith marriage, Shakespeare did not make his Moor a Muslim. On the contrary, Othello was anti-Muslim — as evidenced by his description of a Turk as "a circumcised dog" whose throat was worth slitting!

It was, nevertheless, significant that Shakespeare could deal with so sensitive a subject as inter-racial sexual mating — and still make the murderous Black man a tragic hero.[28] The idea of a Moor as a dignified and authoritative figure must have been wholly credible to Elizabethan audiences. The reputation of Moorish Spain must have contributed to such an image.

If Ethiopians in Arabia constituted the earliest Diaspora of Eastern Africa and if Andalusia was the earliest Diaspora of North Africa, what is the earliest Diaspora of West Africa? It would be totally defensible to regard the Atlantic slave trade as the major force which created the West African Diaspora in the Americas and the Caribbean. This was the Diaspora of enslavement — of survivors of the Middle Passage.

In the twentieth century there followed the Diaspora created by European colonialism in Africa and its disruptions. Hundreds of thousands of Africans migrated to the Western world to escape the economic and political dislocations of postcolonial Africa.

And yet, long before the Atlantic slave trade, there might have been more voluntary African attempts to cross the Atlantic. The Senegalese scholar, Pathé Diagne, initiated a project in the 1980s to research jointly with Cornell University, the role of Bakari II of ancient Mali in crossing the Atlantic, ostensibly before the year 1312. (Columbus' achievement across the Atlantic is normally dated as 1492, the same year as the expulsion of the Moors from Spain.) Pathé Diagne's thesis was that the expeditions of Bakari II (a West African Muslim) and Christopher Columbus were inter-related.

Both Bakari II and Christopher Columbus learned from the African navigators of Senegambia and the Gulf of Guinea about (1) transoceanic traffic and trade, (2) the existence of a corridor fed by North Equatorial winds, and (3) the existence of a current that was easy to navigate during the summer and autumn and that led to the rich Maya, Olmeque, Aztec, and Inca Kingdoms and civilizations. Neither Bakari II nor Christopher Columbus were ready to share this geographical secret with rivals... [29]

The case for a pre-Columbian African crossing of the Atlantic is far from complete and may never be fully proven.[30] But alternative explanations of the pre-Christ Negroid stone heads in Mexico have not been convincingly argued either. If the fleet of Mensa Bakari (Abubakar) II did succeed in reaching the New World, this was the earliest post-Christ Black Diaspora originating from West Africa; and the Kingdom of Bakari II was, of course, also Muslim.[31]

While Islam and adventurous Africans had gone out of Africa to create new Diasporas abroad, other races and ideologies came into Africa to create new social forces. We have already referred to the arrival of Arab asylum seekers, conquerors, traders, and settlers. We have already referred to the Atlantic slave trade and the arrival of European traders and adventurers. Even more pervasive were, the arrival of European colonizers and the establishment of new empires in Africa.

But from the point of view of the fortunes of Islam in Africa, the most relevant new force was the arrival of Christianity, especially in its European versions. Egyptian Christianity goes back to the first century of the Christian era — the Coptic Church. Ethiopian Christianity goes back to the fourth century C.E. But most of the rest of Africa got its Christianity from the nineteenth century onwards, mainly through European colonization. It is this twin arrival of European imperialism and Euro-Christianity which set the stage for the Seventh Act in this historical drama. The concluding Act now unfolding is Africa's Triple Heritage.

The arrival of these new Western forces on the African continent carried wide-ranging implications for both Islam and the ancestral religions of African societies. Sub-Saharan Africa became, almost for the first time, a theater of rivalry between contending religious forces on an almost unprecedented scale. Indigenous African religions did not compete with each other, but Christianity and Islam had competitive universalistic ambitions.[32]

However, is this phase a case of 'Islam in Africa' or a phase of 'Africa in the history of Islam?' The phase qualified for both descriptions. While the two monotheistic religions have co-existed and/or competed in other parts of the world, going back to at least the Christian crusades and continuing in places like modern-day Lebanon and Bosnia and Albania, Africa as a theater of comparative religious experience became very distinctive. Let us look more closely at Africa as a unique religious arena in the modern history of both Christianity and Islam, interacting with the indigenous culture to create a vibrant Triple Heritage.

Between Faith and Friction

Relations between Islam and Christianity can be conflictual as they currently seem to be in parts of the Nile Valley or competitive as they seem to be in East Africa or ecumenical as they have often been in countries like Senegal and Tanzania. Christianity and Islam are in conflictual relations when hostilities are aroused, and the two great religions re-enact in Africa a shadow of the Crusades. Christianity and Islam are in competition, when they are rivals in the free market of values and ideals, scrambling for converts without edging towards hostility.

Christianity and Islam are in an ecumenical relationship when they appear to accept each other as divergent paths towards a convergent truth — different means towards a shared ultimate end. Minimally, the ecumenical spirit is a spirit of 'Live and Let Live.' Maximally, the ecumenical spirit is a spirit of interfaith cooperation.

Whether it is conflict, competition, or ecumenicalism, it is a matter determined by three other forces — the import of doctrine, the sociological balance in a given society, and the legacy of history in that particular society.

Doctrinal, sociological, and historical forces help to shape relations between Christians and Muslims in a given part of the world.

In Africa, these two triads (conflict, competition, and cooperation on one side and doctrine, sociology, and history on the other) operate within yet another triad — the triple heritage of twentieth century Africa: Indigenous, Islamic, and Western civilizations.

Africa since the twentieth century has been a confluence of these three civilizations. The Muslim populations of Nigeria, Egypt, and Ethiopia together account for about a quarter (180 million) of the total population of the African continent as a whole. Nigeria may have more Muslims than any Arab country, including Egypt.[33] In the 1990s, the Republic of South Africa celebrated not only its first multiracial democratic elections, but also the 300th anniversary of the arrival of Islam in the country — a minority religion which has proven more historically resilient than anyone would have expected.[34] The Republic of Malawi elected its first Muslim President in 1994; in 1996 Sierra Leone elected its Muslim President.

Africa's triple heritage of indigenous culture, Islam, and Western culture sometimes is a source of cultural enrichment and at other times a cause of social and political tensions. Within the context of this triple heritage, Christianity and Islam have sometimes been in conflict, sometimes been in gracious competition, and have increasingly sought areas of ecumenical cooperation.

Apart from the Atlantic slave trade, the impact of the West came initially through colonization and this impact had a direct bearing on the fortunes of Christianity, Islam, and Indigenous culture in Africa. The cornerstone of British colonial policy in Africa became Lord Lugard's doctrine of Indirect Rule — a strategy of ruling people subjected primarily through their own "native authorities and institutions," [comparable to the Maharajahs in India were the Emirs in Northern Nigeria and the Kabaka (king) of Buganda].[35]

In its application in Africa, Indirect Rule favored Islam in those areas which were already Islamized before the British came — but the British favored Christianity in areas where traditional African religion still prevailed. Thus, Indirect Rule favored Islam in Northern Nigeria (which owed its Islam to precolonial times), but favored Christianity in South Nigeria, Buganda, and Southern Sudan where the prevailing mores and beliefs were indigenous.

But in what ways did the British Indirect Rule favor either Islam or Christianity? One extreme pro-Christian strategy was to keep Islam out of a particular area altogether. This was true of British policy for Southern Sudan during the colonial period. Both the Arabs of Northern Sudan and any Muslim missionary activity were kept out of the South.

In Northern Nigeria, on the other hand, the British rulers discouraged Christian missionary work in the most Islamized parts of the North, such as Sokoto and Zaria, but permitted Christianization in parts of the North, which were not yet under the sway of Islam.

In most other parts of their African empire, the British helped spread Christianity by facilitating and subsidizing Christian missionary schools and Christian missionary clinics. Even the British language policy in the colonies favored Christianity more than Islam. The British helped to promote a number of African languages and to create orthographies for them. Missionaries became allies in this enterprise. The Bible has been translated into many more African languages than the Qur'an.

Have the consequences of Indirect Rule after independence promoted conflict, competition, or cooperation between Christianity and Islam? Some would argue that the most dramatic postcolonial consequences have been conflictual. In Sudan, the colonial policies of ethnoreligious apartheid, separating north from south were a major cause of the first Sudanese civil war (1955 – 1972) and a contributory factor to the Second Sudanese Civil War which started in 1983 and lasted for twenty years.[36]

British policies of Indirect Rule in Nigeria might also have deepened the North-South divide in the country and aggravated ethnic and sectarian tensions. British policies were more respectful of Islam and indigenous culture than the policies of any other European power in Africa, but nevertheless British concessions to Islamic institutions did carry a postcolonial cost within the artificial boundaries which colonialism had created.

The French colonial authorities, on the other hand, had put great emphasis on a policy of assimilation. At its most ambitious, French colonialism sought to turn Africans into Black French men and French women. And since, for most of their history the French people had not been Muslim, the assimilation policy was implicitly a rejection of Islam and a declaration of cultural war on indigenous African traditions.

However, outside North Africa, French assimilationist policy hurt indigenous cultures more deeply than it hurt Islam. Paradoxically, assimilationist policies weakened indigenous resistance to Islamization and, therefore, helped the spread of Islam in West Africa.

French assimilationist policy made Africans ashamed of their own native cultures and of their Islam — but that did not necessarily make them French. Islam, therefore, continued to thrive even in such long-established French colonies as Senegal, which the French regarded as their own cultural showpiece, a part of which they had colonized for well over a century.

Other Muslim countries in French West Africa included Western Soudan (now Mali), Nigeria, Guinea (Conakry), parts of the Ivory Coast and Mauritania in the north-west. In all of them, Islam survived French assimilation policy and was sometimes even inadvertently helped by it.

This configuration of doctrine, sociology, and history during the colonial period had consequences for the postcolonial era. Some of these consequences were dialectical, replete with contradictions and paradoxes. Especially significant are the consequences in postcolonial political experience. It is to this political experience that we must now turn, with all its paradoxes.

The Postcolonial Balance

What is the balance between conflict, competition, and cooperation between Islam and Christianity as we approach the twenty-first century? In Africa, Christianity and Islam are divisive only if they reinforce pre-existing divisions of other kinds. Thus, in Nigeria, almost all Hausa are Muslims; almost all Igbo are Christians; and Yoruba are split between the two religions. Thus, Islam reinforces Hausa identity; Christianity reinforces Igbo identity; and the Yoruba people are caught in between.

In Sudan, the degree of Islamization is not the only difference between the north and south of the country. The two subregions differ in a whole range of other cultural and historical differentiations.

But where Islam and Christianity do not reinforce prior divisions (as in Senegal), these two religions are not conflictual. It is in this way that sociology and history help to moderate the consequences of doctrine.

Leveling the field of missionary work between Islam and Christianity also helps to diffuse conflict and turn it into peaceful competition for the soul of Africa. The petrowealth of parts of the Muslim world has made available resources for *tabligh da'wa* and levels of propagation unheard of for hundreds of years.

Muslim missionary work is still less efficient, less well-organized, less imaginative, and less well-endowed than Christian missionary work. But the gap has narrowed as a result of *petro-da'wa*. The sacred playing field is being slowly leveled.

A third factor which helps in reducing conflict and even promoting cooperation is an important change in the nature of the Christian missionaries in Africa. Many Christian groups have decided to concentrate on saving lives rather than saving souls, focusing more on service now than salvation for the hereafter. Such Christian groups will even go to help in devastated Muslim areas like Somalia to save Somali lives rather than Somali souls. They would concentrate on easing pain rather than spreading the Gospel.

In Africa, such service-oriented activists have their Muslim counterparts. An Association of Muslim Doctors in South Africa spends a lot of medical hours and resources helping the poor in South Africa regardless of religious affiliation. They build clinics and give their time to the sick.

Between these two universalistic religions, these three tendencies are often there:

- the risk of conflict
- the inherent competitive tendency
- the potential for ecumenical cooperation

In Africa, the worst days of religious conflict north of the Sahara may, unfortunately, not be over, but south of the Sahara those worst days are probably receding in history. The days of rivalry between Christianity and Islam in Africa are alive and well, but the competition is getting more gracious and more considerate.

The days of ecumenical cooperation between Christianity and Islam in Africa are now unfolding, and Africa may be the best setting in the world for such Christo-Islamic ecumenicalism in the twenty-first century.

In distribution, Christianity is an Afro-Western religion, since almost all Christian nations are either in the Western World or in Africa. Asia, the largest continent in the world, has been far less receptive to Christianity. There are hardly any Christian nations in Asia apart from the Philippines.

In distribution, Islam is an Afro-Asian religion, since most Muslim nations are either in Asia or in Africa. Apart from small Albania and Bosnia, there are no Muslim countries in the Western world. Turkey is divided between Asia and Europe.

If Christianity is primarily Afro-Western and Islam is primarily Afro-Asian, what the two religions have in common geographically is mainly the

'Afro' part. Afro is, therefore, the pre-eminent theater for ecumenical cooperation between these two great religions — moderated by the traditional doctrines, the sociology of religion, and the history of the African people themselves.

Concluding Summary

As indicated, most of the literature about Islam and Africa focuses upon the influence of Islam in Africa. This particular book is no different. But our present introductory chapter to the volume has sought to redress the imbalance, however minimally. Our focus has been on how Africa has influenced directions of Muslim history instead of how Islam has impacted upon Africa.

If this Prelude was a whole play in seven distinct acts, we would count as the first chapter — "Africa as the birthplace of human religious experience." Since Africa is where the human species began, it must also be the birthplace of the first basic elements of human culture. These earliest formations of human cultural evolution would surely include language, the family, and 'primitive religion.' There emerged gods of thunder, floods, fire, war, and fertility.

The second Act of Africa's impact on the origins of Islam concerns Africa's role in the origins of monotheism. Theologically, Jews, Christians, and Muslims believe that monotheism began with Adam and Eve as the first humans. But this is theology rather than history. From the point of view of the first historically documented monotheist, we have to turn to Akhenaton, King of Egypt of the 18th dynasty. His reign was from 1379 – 1362 B.C.E. Pharaoh Akhenaton is widely regarded as the first real monotheist confirmed by recorded history.

The question has arisen among historians whether Akhenaton's reign, however brief, subsequently influenced the monotheistic ideas of the Hebrews in Egypt. Did they influence Moses before the Exodus? If Islam was born out of Judaism and Christianity, was it therefore, not born out of the womb of the Nile Valley? It is to the role of Africa in protecting the infancy of the Abrahamic religions that we must now turn.

If sub-Saharan Africa gave birth to human beliefs in deities and the supernatural, and Egypt gave birth to monotheism, what was the more direct link between the African and the Abrahamic religions? This is Act III of this great unfolding drama.

We have already referred to the African origins of Moses. Was he a Hebrew baby who was brought up by the Pharaoh's court in Egypt? Or was he an Egyptian who empathized with the Hebrews, helped them cross the

Sea of Reeds, and accompanied them towards the Promised Land? Whether Moses was an Egyptian by birth or by upbringing, there is little doubt that the origins of Judaism were linked to Pharaonic Egypt.

What part did Africa play in protecting nascent Christianity? King Harod had passed a sentence of death on baby Jesus and sent out a search party for the infant. The angel of God tipped off Joseph, Mary's husband that the child's life was in danger. Joseph was to take Jesus to Egypt for safety. Asylum in Egypt saved baby Jesus from premature execution.

What part did Africa play in protecting Islam? Early converts to Islam in pre-Islamic Arabia were being persecuted and in danger of their lives in pre-Islamic Mecca. The Prophet Muhammad authorized some of his followers to cross the Red Sea and seek asylum in Christian Ethiopia — among fellow monotheists. This group of asylum seekers was led by Uthman bin Affan, who much later became the Third Caliph of Islam after the death of the Prophet Muhammad.

This early asylum for Islam in Ethiopia gave the nascent religion a breathing space. As its converts multiplied, they later had to secretly migrate from Mecca to Medina in larger numbers. This second migration (the Hijjra) became the starting point of the Islamic calendar.

After the death of Muhammad, Islam became more territorially expansionist. The Arabs entered Egypt in 641 C.E., not as asylum seekers but as conquerors. Two massive historical processes began to unfold in Africa. One process was Islamization, the spread of the Islamic religion; the second process was Arabization, the spread of the Arabic language and the making of new Arabs.

With the pace of Islamization we enter Act IV of this momentous historical drama. Islam arrived in Africa not just as an asylum seeker (Ethiopia in 615 C.E.) or as a conqueror (Egypt from 641 C.E.), but also as a trader (trans-Saharan for centuries), for settlement as an immigrant (across the Indian Ocean), enslaved by Europeans (enslaved Malays in South Africa), as a slave-trader (in Eastern Africa), as a jihadist (like Ousmane Dan Fodio in West Africa), and as a missionary and evangelizer (across the centuries all over Africa). By the end of the twentieth century, Africa had become the first continent in the world with a plurality, if not majority, of Muslims.

The Fifth Act in this drama is Arabization, meaning not just the spread of the Arabic language but also the making of new Arabs. Arabic swept across North Africa and became the mother tongue of majorities in Egypt, Libya, Tunisia, Algeria, Morocco and, to a lesser extent, Sudan and Mauritania. There are now more native speakers of Arabic in Africa than in the rest of the Arab world.

But Arabic was not the only neo-Islamic language which triumphed in Africa. The Swahili language (strongly influenced by Arabic and Islam) is continuing to expand in Eastern Africa and elsewhere. In West Africa, the Hausa language (equally impacted by Islam and Arabic) is spoken more widely than any other African indigenous language.

The Sixth Act of this historic drama is the gradual formation of African Diasporas. Arabia had an African Diaspora long before the birth of Muhammad and of Islam. The Ethiopian Bilal was enslaved in precolonial times, but emancipated by the Islamized Abubakar. Bilal later became a strong disciple of the Prophet Muhammad.

The earliest North African Diaspora produced some of the rulers of Muslim Spain over a period which added up to eight centuries. The Moors produced some of the most spectacular architectural wonders of Muslim Spain, such as Alhambra. And Moorish scholarship contributed to both the Renaissance and the Enlightenment in Europe.

The most important West African Diaspora was to the Americas, consisting of millions of survivors of the Middle Passage in the course of the Atlantic slave trade. But there were earlier Afro-Islamic attempts to cross the Atlantic. The most famous is the fleet assembled by Mensah Abubakar (Bakari) II, the ruler of ancient Mali. There may be more evidence of the beginning of the expedition than of its arrival in the New World. But the huge Olmeque sculptures with 'Negroid features,' found in Mexico, are not only pre-Columbian, they are also pre-Christ. Were there other African trans-Atlantic travelers long before Bakari II? In that case, Bakari II would count as the first African Muslim to assemble an expedition, rather than the first African.

The Seventh Act of this historic drama of Africa in the history of Islam is the birth of Africa's Triple Heritage as a continental phenomenon. Until the nineteenth century, a dual heritage was more common in Africa — either a combination of indigenous and Islamic cultures (as in classical Timbuktu) or a combination of indigenous and Western cultures (as in Southern Africa after the arrival of the white man).

But the arrival of full-scale European colonization in Africa and the rapid spread of Christianity in sub-Saharan Africa, began to transform Africa into a theater of three civilizations — indigenous, Islamic, and Western. Africa became a laboratory of newer forms of interfaith relations.

When the boundaries of Christianity and Islam coincided with prior divisions between ethnic groups, the two Abrahamic religions reinforced those prior ethnic divisions (as in the divide between Northern and Southern Sudan). But when Christianity and Islam crisscrossed ethnic boundaries, the two Abrahamic religions could be unifying and ecumenical — as in the case of the Senegalese experience of a Christian Head of State presiding over an overwhelmingly Muslim society.

New patterns of relationships between Christianity and Islam developed which were sometimes conflictual, sometimes cooperative and, most remarkable of all, periodically ecumenical. The doctrines of these two religions, the sociology of the countries in which they have operated, and the history of the African people have placed Islam in a unique comparative perspective in this African theater of religious experience.

Egypt and Morocco have served Islam with two of the oldest universities in the world. Modern Egypt has also served Islam by being the most prolific publishing country in Islamic literature in history. Africa has served Islam by generating the majority of the native Arabic speakers of the world. Eastern Africa has served Islam by endowing it with the most important neo-Islamic language on the continent — Kiswahili. West Africa has served Islam by endowing it with the most widespread indigenous language in the Western subregion — Hausa. Poets of Muslim Africa have enriched the poetic heritage in Islamic literature — in languages which have ranged from Somali to Wolof, from Berber languages to Hausa, from Oromo to Kiswahili.

Above all, Africa has served Islam well by being on its way towards becoming the first continent in the world with a Muslim plurality and potentially a Muslim majority.

Endnotes

1. Some relevant works include, for example, J. Spencer Trimingham, *The Influence of Islam Upon Africa* (New York: Praeger, 1968); Mervyn Hiskett, *The Course of Islam in Africa* (Edinburgh: Edinbugh University Press, 1994); *The History of Islam in Africa*, ed. Nehemia Levitzion and Randall L. Pouwels (Athens, Ohio, and Cape Town: Ohio University Press; James Currey; and David Philip, 2000); Charlotte A. Quinn and Frederick Quinn, *Pride, Faith and Fear: Islam in Sub-Saharan Africa* (New York: Oxford University Press, 2003); and also see Chapter 4, "The Africanization of Islam" in David Robinson's *Muslim Societies in African History* (Cambridge, UK, and New York: Cambridge Univeristy Press, 2004).
2. Relatedly, see Julian Baldick, *Black God: The Afro-Asiatic Roots of Jewish, Christian, and Muslim Religions* (London; New York: IB. Tauris, 1997) p. 29.
3. Consult Christopher Stringer, *African Exodus: The Origins of Modern Humanity* (New York: Henry Holt, 1997).
4. See Sura 10: 47 and Sura 16: 36, for example.
5. For profiles of this king see C. Nicholas Reeves, *Akhenaten, Egypt's False Prophet* (New York: Thames & Hudson, 2001) and Donald B. Redford,

Akhenaten, The Heretic King (Princeton, NJ: Princeton University Press, 1984).

6. A recent discussion of this thesis may be found in Richard J. Bernstein, *Freud and the Legacy of Moses* (Cambridge and New York: Cambridge University Press, 1998).
7. A brief account of the conquest of Constantinople may be found in Judith Herrin, "The Fall of Constantinople," *History Today* (June 2003) Volume 53, Issue 6, pp. 12–17.
8. For a discussion of this journey see, W. Montgomery Watt, *Muhammad at Mecca*, (Oxford: Clarendon Press, 1953), pp. 101–117 and for a general overview of Islam in Ethiopia see Hiskett, *The Course of Islam in Africa*, pp. 135–150.
9. See, for instance, Paul Grieve, *A Brief Guide to Islam—History, Faith, and Politics: The Complete Introduction* (New York: Carroll and Graf Publishers, 2006) pp. 51–52.
10. On this venerable University, consult Bayard Dodge, *Al-Azhar: A Millennium of Muslim Learning* (Washington, DC: Middle East Institute, 1961).
11. A history of this canal may be found in Hugh J. Schonfeld, *The Suez Canal in Peace and War, 1869–1969* (Coral Gables, FL: University of Miami Press, 1969) and also see Ferdinand de Lesseps, *The Suez Canal: Letters and Documents Descriptive of its Rise and Progress in 1854–1856*, trans., N. D. Ánvers (Wilmington, DE: Delaware Scholarly Resources, 1976, reprint of 1876, edition published by Henry S. King).
12. A handy bibliographical guide on Nasser may be found in Faysal Mikdadi, *Shorter Notices — Gamal Abdul Nasser: A Bibliography, Journal of Palestine Studies* (Spring 1993) Volume 22, Number 3, pp. 134–135.
13. Thus, for instance, the percentage of Muslims in North African countries like Algeria, Morocco, Tunisia, and Libya is over 90 percent; see the respective entries in the *CIA World Factbook* available at <www.odci.gov/cia/publications/factbook/index.html>
14. See Ira M. Lapidus, *A History of Islamic Societies* (Cambridge and New York: Cambridge University Press, 2002), pp. 400–442; and for a discussion on Islam and slavery, consult John R. Willis, *Slaves and Slavery in Muslim Africa: Islam and the Ideology of Slavery, Volume I* (Totowa, NJ, and London: Frank Cass, 1985).
15. For a description of the three waves of Muslims — exiles from South East Asia, slaves from other areas of Africa, and indentured laborers from the Indian subcontinent — who came to South Africa, see Quinn and Quinn, *Pride, Faith, and Fear*, pp. 127–135 and Hiskett, *The Course of Islam in Africa*, p. 174.
16. For a biography of this important figure in Nigerian history, see M. Hiskett, *The Sword of Truth: The Life and Times of the Shehu Usuman Dan Fodio* (New York: Oxford University Press, 1973).
17. According to an estimate of the UAE Ministry of Islamic Affairs and Awaqf, 59 percent of Africa's population (in 1996) was Muslim; see http://www.fedfin.gov.ae/moia/english/e_growingreligion.htm, accessed May 28, 2004

Introduction: The African Impact on Muslim History: A Prelude xxvii

18. There are, of course, varying estimates on Muslim populations in these countries. For instance, the estimation of the numbers of Muslims in Nigeria is somewhat controversial because of political issues over the census. According to an Associated Press report, "Muslim Mobs, Seeking Vengeance, Attack Christians in Nigeria," *New York Times* (May 13, 2004), "Many of Nigeria's 126 million people, [are] split almost evenly between Muslims and Christians ..." However, another report estimates the percentage of Muslims in Nigeria at 75 percent; see http://www.islamicweb.com/begin/population.htm, accessed May 28, 2004. On the other hand, if we were to go by the *CIA World Factbook* July 2006, estimate of Nigeria's population at 131 million (50 percent Muslim) and that of Egypt at 78.8 million (90 percent Muslim), Egypt may still have a slight edge.
19. The population of current African members of the Arab League, according to the *CIA World Factbook 2006* estimates is: Egypt (79 million), Libya (5.9 million), Sudan (41 million), Morocco (33 million), Tunisia (10.1 million), Algeria (33 million), Mauritania (3.2 million), Somalia (8 million estimate), Djibouti (487 thousand), and Comoros (690 thousand), leading to a total of 213-214 million. It must be remembered that population figures in many of these countries is not accurate.
20. Consult Ali A. Mazrui and Pio Zirimu, "The Secularization of an Afro-Islamic Language: Church, State, and Marketplace in the Spread of Kiswahili," in Ali A. Mazrui and Alamin A. Mazrui, *The Power of Babel: Language and Governance in the African Experience* (Oxford, Nairobi, Kampala, Cape Town, Chicago: James Currey, E.A.E.P, Fountain, David Philip, and the University of Chicago Press, 1998) pp. 169–171.
21. Relatedly, see the discussion by Louis Brenner and Murray Last, "The Role of Language in West African Islam," *Africa* (1985), Vol. 55 Issue 4, pp. 432–446
22. The importance of the Queen of Sheba in various traditions is described in Lou Silberman, "The Queen of Sheba in Judaic Tradition;" W. Montgomery Watt, "The Queen of Sheba in Islamic Tradition;" Edward Ullendorf, "The Queen of Sheba in Ethiopian Tradition;" and Paul F. Watson, "The Queen of Sheba in Christian Tradition," in *Solomon and Sheba,* ed. James B. Pritchard (London: Phaidon, 1974) pp. 65–145.
23. See Sura 105 in the Qur'an.
24. An unusual account of this African Muslim's life may be found in H. A. L. Craig, *Bilal* (London and New York: Quartet Books, 1977).
25. On the mistreatment of the Moors in Christian Spain, see Charles Melville and Ahmed Ubaydli, *Christians and Moors in Spain, Arabic Sources, 711–1501,* Vol. III, (Warminster: Aris & Phillips, 1992, esp. pp. 186–191.
26. See Jan Carew, "Moorish Culture-Bringers: Bearers of Enlightenment," in *Golden Age of the Moor,* ed. Ivan Van Sertima (New Brunswick and London: Transaction Publishers, 1999, third printing) pp. 248–49.
27. Van Sertima, "The Moor in Africa and Europe: Origins and Definitions," *Golden Age of the Moor,* p. 10.

28. For analyses of Shakespeare's treatment of the racial aspects of Othello, consult, for example, J. Adelman, "Iago's Alter Ego: Race as Projection in *Othello*," *Shakespeare Quarterly* (Summer 1997), Volume 48, Number 2, pp. 125–144, and M. Neill, "Unproper Beds: Race, Adultery, and the Hideous" in *Othello, Shakespeare Quarterly* (Winter 1989), Volume 40, Number 4, pp. 383–412.
29. See Ali A. Mazrui and J. F. Ade Ajayi, et al. "Trends in Philosophy and Science in Africa", Chapter 21, *Africa Since 1935*, ed. Ali A. Mazrui and C. Wondji (Oxford, Berkeley and Paris: Heinemann, California, and UNSCO, 1993), pp. 660–61.
30. Consult Ivan Van Sertima, *They Came Before Columbus: The African Presence in the Ancient Americas* (New York: Random House, 1976) and Harold G. Lawrence, "African Explorers of the New World," *The Crisis* (June–July 1962) Volume 69, No. 6, pp. 322–323.
31. One scholar has argued that pre-Columbian history of the Caribbean includes evidence of considerable contacts with Islam both north and south of the Sahara; see Abdullah Hakim Quick, "Islam in the Caribbean: Past, Present, and the Future," chapter 28 in *Islam in Africa: Proceedings of the Islam in Africa Conference* ed. Nur Alkali, Adamu Adamu et al. (Ibadan ad Lagos: Spectrum Books, 1993) pp. 388–417.
32. Relatedly, see Ali A. Mazrui, "African Islam and Competitive Religion: Between Revivalism and Expansion," *Third World Quarterly* (1988), Vol. 10, No. 2, pp. 499–518.
33. See Note 18 above.
34. Relatedly, see Shamil Jeppie, "Commemorations and Identities: The 1994 Tercentenary of Islam in South Africa," and Tamara Sonn, *Islam and the Question of Minorities* (Atlanta, GA: Scholars Press, 1996), pp. 73–92.
35. For specific cases and discussions of 'indirect rule' in Nigeria, see *Nigerian History, Politics, and Affairs: The Collected Essays of Adiele Afigbo*, ed. Toyin Falola (Trenton, NJ: Africa World Press, 2005) pp. 253–295; Olufemi Vaughan, *Nigerian Chiefs: Traditional Power in Modern Politics, 1890s–1990s* (Rochester, NY: University of Rochester Press, 2000), pp. 22–68; J. A. Atanda, *The New Oyo Empire: Indirect Rule and Change in Western Nigeria, 1894–1934* (London: Longman, 1973); and A. E. Afigbo, *The Warrant Chiefs: Indirect Rule in Southeastern Nigeria, 1891–1929* (New York: Humanities Press, 1972).
36. For overviews of these Sudan conflicts, consult Douglas H. Johnson, *The Root Causes of Sudan's Civil Wars* (Oxford; Bloomington, IN; Kampala: James Currey; Indiana University Press; Fountain Publishers, 2003); and Catherine Jendia, *The Sudanese Civil Conflict, 1969–1985* (New York: Peter Lang, 2002).

AFRICA'S RELIGIOUS CANVAS: AN OVERVIEW

1

Islam, Christianity, and Africa's Indigenous Faiths: Demographic Introduction

AMADU JACKY KABA

The world's largest religions, Christianity and Islam, both of which originated in the Middle East, have deep roots in Africa (Blyden 1887, Mazrui 1986, Sundkler & Steed 2000, and Brenner 2001) and continue to have profound cultural and philosophical impact on the lives of majority of the people in Africa. That impact is due to the fact that both religions, Christianity and Islam, require a convert to abandon most or all of his or her traditional beliefs or cultural practices. For example, Goody (2003) points out that "...Muslim missionaries spread forms of restrained behavior..." (p. 68).

This chapter presents a brief statistical overview of the numbers and percentages of Christians, Muslims, and those who continue to practice traditional religions in Africa as of 2001. Utilizing the regional classification of the United Nation's Population Division, the chapter presents figures (gathered from the 2002 *New York Times Almanac*) for all of Africa and its five geographic regions (East Africa, Middle Africa, North Africa, Southern Africa, and West Africa). This chapter also presents a breakdown of the number of Christians, Muslims, and Africans who practice traditional religions in the former African colonies of Belgium, England, France, Portugal, and a group of countries categorized as 'Other.'

Let me begin by examining the distribution of Christians, Muslims, and those who practice traditional religions in Africa.

THE RISING NUMBERS OF CHRISTIANS AND MUSLIMS IN AFRICA

In a work on Africa, entitled *Africa: A Biography of the Continent,* author John Reader points out that about 100,000 years ago, of the estimated less than one million people that lived in the entire world, 900,000 lived on the continent of Africa (p. 130). It is apparent that if there were any religions practiced within Africa, at that time, they had to be traditional or indigenous African religions, since, for a long time after that, Christianity and Islam did not exist. Ali A. Mazrui (1986) also writes: "Long before the religion of the crescent or the religion of the cross arrived on the African continent, Africa was at worship and its sons and daughters were at prayer," (p. 135).

Today, however, we see a reverse — of not only the religious breakdown of the continent but also a reverse of a world population shift. For example, as of July 2003, out of the estimated 6.3 billion people in the world, 857 million (13.6%) live in Africa.[1] In the beginning of the twenty-first century, Christians and Muslims comprised over 50 percent of the world's population. According to figures presented in the *Encyclopedia Britannica 2003 Book of the Year*, as of mid-2002, of the 6.2 billion people in the world, Christians comprised 2,038,905,000 (32.9%), Muslims comprised 1,226,403,000 (19.8%), and Hindus comprised 828,130,000 (13.3%) (p. 306).

Africa has been a big contributor to the large numbers of Christians and Muslims in the world. In the past half century, while the populations of Christians and Muslims in Africa have increased substantially, the total number of Africans who practice indigenous religions has increased in absolute numbers but declined in proportion to the continent's total population. For example, Mazrui (1986) points out that:

> Between 1931 and 1951, the number of Muslims in the whole of Africa had risen from 40 million to 80 million in comparison with a Roman Catholic rise from 5 million to 15 million. Of the total Black population, estimated at the time as being 130 million in Africa south of the Sahara, 28 million were Muslim, 13 million were Catholics, 4 million were Protestants, and 85 million still followed their own indigenous religions, even though some of these traditionalists were nominally Muslim or Christian. Islam in Africa as a whole, including Arab Africa, commanded the allegiance of approximately 40 percent of the continent's population (pp. 135–136).

Within the continent, of the estimated 823 million Africans in 2001, those who practiced traditional or indigenous religions were 137.8 million (16.7%). Christianity has been very successful in converting Africans. In 2001, there was an estimated 304.3 million (36.9%) Christians in Africa. Indeed, as of 2004, statistics show that there were as many Catholics alone in Africa as there were Africans who continued to practice traditional religions in 2001. There are an estimated 130 million Catholics in Africa, comprising 16% of the continent's population (*Conscience* 2004: 34). Simon Robinson writes for *Time* magazine that:

> In mud huts and giant tabernacles, city parks and suburban halls, Christianity is growing faster in sub-Saharan Africa than anywhere else on earth. Adherents to the world's largest religion are increasing at 3.5% a year in Africa, compared with 2.5% in Latin America and Asia, and less than 1% in Europe and North America. The proportion of African Christians to all Christians has grown from one in 10 in 1970 to one in five today. On current trends, African Christians will soon outnumber European believers, leaving them second only to those in Latin America.[2]

As for the total estimates of Muslims in Africa in 2001, they comprised 371.4 million (45.1%) of the total 823.4, thus making Africa the only continent in the world where proportionally Islam has the largest number of followers. The religious group categorized as 'Other' comprised 9.8 million (1.2%). People who practice the Hindu religion are among those in the 'Other' category. For example, according to figures presented in the *Encyclopedia Britannica 2003 Book of the Year,* there were an estimated 2.4 million Hindus in Africa in mid-2002 (p. 306).

Below, I provide the distribution of the religious breakdown of the five regions of Africa and also of the former colonies of the United Kingdom, France, Belgium, and Portugal.

REGIONAL DISTRIBUTION OF CHRISTIANS, MUSLIMS, AND THOSE WHO PRACTICE TRADITIONAL RELIGIONS

Muslims are the majority in Northern Africa. Of the estimated 183 million North Africans in 2001, 166.9 million (91.2%) were Muslims. The indigenous population, all from Sudan, made up 9 million (4.9%) of the North African population. Christians comprised 6.4 million (3.5%) of the total population, while the religious group classified as 'Other' made up 632,920 (0.34%).

In Western Africa also, Muslims comprised the majority in 2001, although their proportion was not as high as that of Northern Africa. In the 17 countries and territories that comprised Western Africa, of the estimated 240.7 million people in 2001, Muslims constituted 131 million (54.4%); the Christian population was estimated at 66.7 million (27.7%) of the total population of Western Africa; and Africans who practiced traditional religions comprised 41.6 million (17.3%). The people in that region of the continent who practiced other religions made up 1.6 million (0.6%) of the total population.

In Middle Africa, Christians constituted the highest proportion in 2001. Christians made up 61.8 million (64%) of the estimated 96.8 million people in Middle Africa. Africans who practiced indigenous religions comprised 21 million (21.6%). The estimated number of Middle Africans who practiced Islam was 13.5 million (14%). The people with other religious beliefs made up 437,688 (0.4%).

Christians constituted the highest proportion of the total population of Southern Africa. Of the total population of 50.25 million in Southern Africa, an estimated 34.2 million (68%) were Christians. Southern Africans who practiced indigenous religions comprised 14.1 million (27.9%). In Southern Africa, the Muslim population was 871,722 million (1.7%). Southern Africans who practiced other religions comprised 1.09 million (2.1%).

Christians again comprised the highest proportion of the total population of Eastern Africa. Of the 252.5 million people in Eastern Africa in 2001, an estimated 135.1 million (53.5%) were Christians. The total Muslim population in Eastern Africa was 59.1 million (23.4%). An estimated 52.1 million (21%) East Africans practiced indigenous African religions. The estimated total number of people in Eastern Africa who practiced other religions was 6 million (2.3%).

RELIGIOUS BREAKDOWN OF FORMER AFRICAN COLONIES OF EUROPEAN POWER

There are significant differences in the numbers and percentages of Christians, Muslims, and Africans who practice indigenous religions. In the African countries that were at one time partly or fully colonized by France, Muslims were the majority in 2001. Of the total estimated population of 203.7 million people in the former African colonies of France, Muslims comprised an estimated 137.2 million (67.2%). Africans who practiced indigenous religions made up 36.9 million (18.1%), Christians comprised 28.7 million (14%), and Africans who practiced other religions made up 879,514 million (0.4%).

In the African countries that were partly or fully colonized by the United Kingdom, Muslims again comprised the highest proportion. In 2001, the Muslim population in the former African colonies of the United Kingdom was estimated at 194.6 million (44.3%) of the total 438.8 million. The Christian population constituted 165 million (37.6%). Africans who practiced indigenous religions comprised 72 million (16.4%). The people who practiced other religions constituted 7.2 million (1.6%).

Christianity and Islam appeared not to have penetrated deeply into the former African colonies of Portugal as they did in other former African colonies. Of the total estimated population of 31.6 million in the former African colonies of Portugal in 2001, 15.2 million (48.1%) practiced indigenous religions, an estimated 11.9 million people (37.7%) were Christians, and Muslims made up 4.4 million (14.1%).

It appears as if Christianity penetrated more deeply into the former African colonies of Belgium than the other former African colonies. Of an estimated total population of 67.1 million, Christians comprised 52.4 million (78.1%). The people who practiced indigenous African religions constituted 8.6 million (12.8%), and Muslims comprised 6 million (9%).

Christians comprised the highest proportion of the six countries (Eritrea, Ethiopia, Liberia, Libya, Namibia, and Equatorial Guinea) that were grouped as 'Other.' Of the total estimated population of 80.9 million Africans who live in countries categorized as 'Other' in 2001, Muslims comprised 29.3 million (36.2%) and Christians made up 45.4 million (56.1%). Africans who practiced indigenous religions comprised 4.5 million (5.6%). Those who practiced other religions comprised 1.6 million (1.9%) (Data compiled and computed based on figures in the 2002 *New York Times Almanac*).

CONCLUSION

This chapter has illustrated that, in the post World War II era, Christianity and Islam have grown rapidly in numbers in Africa. Both religions have been successful in spreading all across the continent.[3] There is the potential that the number of Africans who practice indigenous religions will continue to decline, but we may see more African Christians and Muslims who will continue to incorporate some of their traditional and philosophical beliefs in their religious practices.

The study has also shown that both Christianity and Islam are having an important impact on the lives of most Africans on the continent. By the beginning of the twenty-first century, Africa had become the only continent on the planet where there were more Muslim adherents than any other single religion. The growing numbers of Africans within the two world's largest religions are also resulting in African religious leaders beginning to have significant influence when dealing with important world issues.

This study has attempted to only discuss the influence of Christianity and Islam in Africa and to describe the parts of the continent where they could be found. More future research is required to better understand the current and future implications of this massive increase in the proportion of Christians and Muslims in Africa.

Endnotes

1. Compiled and calculated by the author, based on data in the 2004 *New York Times Almanac*, pp. 517–707.
2. Simon Robinson, "The Lord's Business," *Time* (Europe), February 7, 2000 Vol. 155, No. 5.
3. However, with the exception of South Africa, Islam has not spread or has not been accepted to any appreciable extent in Southern Africa.

Appendix

Classifications of Regions of Africa (N=57)

Eastern Africa (n=19)
Burundi, Comoros, Djibouti, Eritrea, Ethiopia, Kenya, Madagascar, Malawi, Mauritius, Mozambique, Reunion, Rwanda, Seychelles, Somalia, Tanzania, Uganda, Zambia, Zimbabwe, and Mayotte.

Middle/Central Africa (n=9)
Angola, Cameroon, Central African Republic, Chad, Republic of Congo, Democratic Republic of Congo, Equatorial Guinea, Gabon, and Sao Tome & Principe.

Northern Africa (n=7)
Algeria, Egypt, Libya, Morocco, Sudan, Tunisia, and Western Sahara.

Southern Africa (n=5)
Botswana, Lesotho, Namibia, South Africa, and Swaziland.

Western Africa (n=17)
Benin, Burkina Faso, Cape Verde, Cote d'Ivoire, The Gambia, Ghana, Guinea, Guinea-Bissau, Liberia, Mali, Mauritania, Niger, Nigeria, Senegal, Sierra Leone, Togo, and Saint Helena.

Source: Country/regional classifications by the United Nations Statistics Division, Department of Economic and Social Affairs, from <http://unstats.un.org/unsd/methods/m49/m49regin.htm>. Accessed on July 12, 2004.

References

"A World View; Catholic Attitudes on Sexual Behavior & Reproductive Health," 2004. *Conscience*, Vol. XXIV, Issue 4. p. 37.
Blyden, Edward W. 1887. *Christianity, Islam and the Negro Race*. London: Whittingham Press.
Brenner, Louis. 2001. *Controlling Knowledge: Religion, Power and Schooling in a West African Muslim Society*. Bloomington: Indiana University Press.
Central Intelligence Agency (CIA): *World Factbook*. 2001.
Global Support Imaging & Publishing Support. <http://bookstore.gpo.gov/>

Encyclopedia Britannica 2003 Book of the Year. Chicago: Encyclopedia Britannica, Inc.
Goody, Jack. 2003. "The 'Civilizing Process' in Ghana," Arch. Europe, Sociology. XLIV, 1, 61–73.
Mazrui, Ali A. 1986. *The Africans: A Triple Heritage*. Boston: Little, Brown and Company.
The New York Times Almanac. 2002, ed. John W. Wright. New York: Penguin Group.
Reader, J. 1998. *Africa: A Biography of the Continent*. New York: Alfred A. Knopf.
Sundkler, Bengt and Christopher Steed. 2000. *A History of the Church in Africa*. New York: Cambridge University Press.

HISTORY AND SPREAD OF ISLAM IN AFRICA

2

Islam in Africa's Experience: Expansion, Revival, and Radicalization

ALI A. MAZRUI

The history of Islam in Africa is almost as old as the history of the religion itself. There is reason to believe that in Ethiopia, Islam arrived before the beginning of the Islamic calendar itself — before the *Hijjra*: the era the Prophet Muhammad migrated to Medina. A few believers, persecuted in Mecca, finally crossed the Red Sea and found their way to the *Habash* of Abyssinia in search of asylum. Ethiopian records claim and celebrate that event to the present day.

Islam's earliest conversion of an African probably took place in the Arabian Peninsula itself. It seems probable that Bilal, the slave who was freed as a result of the Prophet's intervention, was the first great African convert to Islam. Bilal became the first outstanding *muezzin* (a person who calls Muslim faithful to prayer) in Islamic history. As a person, Bilal was one of the Prophet Muhammad's favorites.

While Islam in sub-Saharan Africa first arrived as a victim in search of asylum, in North Africa it first arrived as a victor in search of new worlds to conquer. The Arabs, from Byzantium, conquered Egypt in the year 639 A.D. The victors then moved further west, conquering more and more of North Africa.

With the Arab conquest of North Africa, two processes were set in motion, which were of relevance for Africa as a whole in the modern period — the processes of Islamization and Arabization. Islamization was the gradual transmission of the Islamic religion, as more and more of the conquered people embraced the faith. Arabization was the transmission of the Arabic language, as more and more North Africans became, over the centuries, native speakers of Arabic. In North Africa, Arabization took much longer than Islamization. But when North Africans became native speakers of Arabic, it was only a matter of time before they would see themselves as indeed Arabs. It was not just their language; it was also their very identity.

Up the Nile Valley, the twin processes of Islamization and Arabization continued. Together, the two processes constituted the making of new Arabs along the valley of the great river. More and more Northern Sudanese were not only converted to Islam but increasingly saw themselves as part of the Arab world. The Arabic language became their mother tongue, long after the Islamic religion had indeed become their faith.

More recently, we can say that there is only one place in Africa where the Arabic language is spreading faster than the Islamic religion. And that place is Southern Sudan. The Arabic language is needed by Southern Sudanese not just to communicate with the more Arabized Northern Sudan, but as *a lingua franca* among Southern Sudanese tribes themselves. Elsewhere in Africa, Islam has been undergoing three processes — the process of geographical expansion, the process of cultural revival, and the process of political radicalization. Let us look at these three processes more closely.

AGENTS OF ISLAMIC EXPANSION

Underlying the whole saga about religion and society are the five modes by which Islam has spread in Africa — expansion by conquest, migration and settlement in non-Muslim areas, trade, actual purposeful missionary work, and periodic revivalist movements. The most spectacular mode is expansion by conquest. Paradoxically, this affects mainly Arab Africa in the north of the continent that was indeed Islamized initially by the sword. Sub-Saharan examples of Islamization by conquest are few and far between. Some conquests did take place, as in the case of the Almoravids' devastating incursions into West Africa from 1052 to 1076.[1] Ibn Khaldun, the great Arab historian and philosopher of history, confirms that the conquerors did force the Blacks to become Muslims. But today's historians affirm that, since the Almoravids did not maintain a continuing presence, their short-term atrocities harmed the image of Islam rather than helping it. Such invasions were therefore not relevant for explaining the spread of Islam. People were subsequently converted, in spite of the memory of the Almoravids.

The second agency for the expansion of Islam was Muslim migration and settlement in non-Muslim areas. Arabs from Yemen and Oman who settled in East Africa were among the co-founders of the Swahili civilization in what is today Tanzania and Kenya. The rapid Islamization and

Arabization of North Africa was not only achieved through conquest, but also through migration and settlement. Doctrinally, this mode of transmission of the *Message* goes back to the great *Hijjra* itself — the Prophet Muhammad's own migration mid-career from Mecca to Medina.

As indicated earlier, migration may sometimes be of victims rather than victors. This is true of the Malay slaves and laborers imported into South Africa. Islam arrived in chains in what later became the land of apartheid. These ex-slaves, now among the 'Coloreds' of South Africa, have kept the flame of Islam burning in South Africa for three hundred years.

The third agency for the spread of Islam was trade. By far, the best illustration was once again the Trans-Saharan trade. The camels which crossed the great desert carried varied commodities in each direction. Perhaps the greatest commodity of all was cultural diffusion, the spread of Islam from Northern Africa to Western Africa especially. Today, countries like Guinea, modern Mali, Senegal, and Niger are overwhelmingly Muslim in population.

Arab and Swahili traders in Eastern, Central, and Southern Africa also played a part in carrying the torch of Islam to parts of what are today Uganda, Zaire, Malawi, and Mozambique. The commodities involved in the trade included ivory, copper, gold, manufactured goods from abroad and, tragically also, slaves.

The fourth agency for the spread of Islam was actual purposeful missionary work, *D'awa*. In the earlier centuries, this took the form of traveling imams, healers, and teachers. Muslim leaders acquired such a reputation that to the present day a large proportion of their patients in Africa are non-Muslims, including Christians. Their healing techniques have included the use of verses of the *Qur'an*, including the popular prescription of writing out the verse in washable ink on a slate and then washing it into a bowl and having the patient "drink the sacred verse." Grateful patients were sometimes converted to the faith.

In more recent times, Islamic missionary work has included material for use in *madrassa* and schools. Special books or pamphlets have been written in African languages to explain the religion not only to students but also to non-Muslims. Pamphlets in the Swahili language have poured forth from Zanzibar, the Kenyan Coast, and the Coast of mainland Tanzania. And, in the twentieth century, the Qur'an was at last translated into Kiswahili — first by the controversial *Ahmadiyya* movement and later by Sunni scholars from Tanzania and Kenya. As the twentieth century drew to a close, there were three different Swahili editions of the Qur'an, though the third one was published only in part.

Some Muslims believed that translations of the Qur'an into other languages were a form of sinful imitation of the Holy Book. The Chief Muslim jurists of East Africa have given *fatwas* (legal rulings) contradicting that doctrine. They have argued that if it was not sinful to translate the Qur'an orally in a sermon in a mosque, it was not sinful to translate it into writing.

Sunni and Shiite missionary work entered a new stage in the second half of the twentieth century with the arrival of petro-wealth in Saudi Arabia, Iran, Libya, and other parts of the oil-producing Muslim world. At last, it was possible for the cause of Islam in Africa to command considerable financial resources. Schools could be built, as well as mosques. Clinics were subsidized, and scholarships to study abroad were offered.

On the whole, the petro-wealth was used not so much to attract new converts into the Muslim fold, as much as to support the welfare and well-being of those who were already Muslims. But there were reparations favoring new conversions. Sunni Islam is still by far the main beneficiary of such conversions. Iran has sometimes been ready, although it is itself Shiite, to subsidize Sunni missionary work in Africa in a spirit of Muslim unity. As for the Ismailia movement, under the leadership of His Highness the Aga Khan (who himself is more Shiite than Sunni), it sometimes explicitly committed its missionaries to the propagation of Sunni Islam rather than to its own denomination. Expanding the size of the Muslim *ummah* (the totality of all Muslims) in Africa was more important than creating more followers for His Highness the Aga Khan. That was the rationale.

The fifth agency in Africa's historical experience has been the periodic revivalist movements. These sometimes take the form of an internal 'morally purifying *jihad*,' or are under the leadership of a *Mahdi* (the Guided one).

Among the most spectacular of these revivalist movements were those which unleashed the *jihad* led by Ousmane Dan Fodio, in what is today Nigeria. Until this upheaval, the Hausa states were at best an informal and loose confederation — sometimes allies, sometimes rivals. Katsina, Gobir, Zaria, and Kano vied with each other from about the fourteenth century. The north-south trade across the Sahara was at the core of much of their rivalry.

It was in the nineteenth century that the revivalist jihads led by Ousmane Dan Fodio, and partly inspired by a glorified vision of the Abbasid dynasty centuries earlier, burst onto the stage of West African history. Was it merely revivalism or was it conquest? In reality, it was both. The long-term consequence was the relative unification of much of Hausaland under a single overarching sovereign. Ousmane's son,

Muhammad Bello, became the first *Amir al Mu'minin* of Hausaland — Commander of the Faithful. Islam expanded as the Hausa got integrated.

Also, as spectacular was the movement in Eastern Sudan, led by Muhammad Ahmad Ibn Abdullah. This Muslim Reformation in Eastern Sudan started in 1881, in the wake of many years of Turco-Egyptian rule compounded by British manipulations. Unlike the jihad of Ousmane Dan Fodio, that of Muhammad Ahmad was also a struggle for national independence — religious revivalism intertwined with political nationalism.

Muhammad Ahmad went further than Ousmane Dan Fodio. The Sudanese leader declared himself the Mahdi appointed by God to re-unite the Muslim *ummah*. His vision extended well beyond his own ancestral Sudan. In a sense, he wanted to fuse Pan-Islam with Pan-Africanism and Pan-Arabism. His dream was too big for his base and too vulnerable to the new European imperialism. He was indeed defeated. But Islam did take one more step forward in Sudanese history. And, to the present day, the Mahdi's religious and political legacy lives on in the political configuration of Sudan. Indeed, the country's last elected prime minister of the twentieth century was Sadiq el Mahdi, Muhammad Ahmad's grandson.

In Africa, since independence, two issues have been central to religious speculation — Islamic expansion and Islamic revivalism. Expansion is about the spread of religion and its scale of new conversions. Revivalism is about the rebirth of faith, among those who are already converted. Expansion is a matter of geography and populations, in search of new worlds to conquer. Revivalism is a matter of history and nostalgia, in search of ancient worlds to re-enact. The spread of Islam in postcolonial Africa is basically a peaceful process of persuasion and consent. The revival of Islam is often an angry process of re-discovered fundamentalism.

Outside Arab Africa, the central issue concerning Islam is not merely its revival, it is also the speed of its expansion. It is not often realized that there are more Muslims in Nigeria than there are Muslims in any Arab country, including Egypt. Muslims in Ethiopia are not a small minority; they are nearly half the population. Islam elsewhere in Africa has spread, however unevenly, all the way down to the Cape of Good Hope. Islam in South Africa is three hundred years old — having first arrived not directly from Arabia but from South East Asia with Malay immigrants, as earlier indicated.

The largest countries in Africa in population are Nigeria, Egypt, Ethiopia, and the Democratic Republic of Congo (formally known as Zaire). Between them, these four countries account for well over 200 million Muslims. The Islamic part of former Zaire is mainly in the east. More than half the population of the continent is probably now Muslim.

But Islam in Africa does not, of course, exist in isolation. The world of religious experience in Africa is rich in diversity. Let us look at Islam in this wider religious context.

INDIGENOUS ECUMENICALISM AND SEMITIC COMPETITIVENESS

Of the three principal religious legacies of Africa — indigenous, Islamic and Christian, perhaps the most tolerant is the indigenous tradition. It is even arguable that Africa did not have religious wars before Christianity and Islam arrived. Precisely because these two latter faiths were universalistic in aspiration, seeking to convert the whole of humankind, they were inherently competitive. In Africa, Christianity and Islam have often been in competition for the soul of the continent. Rivalry has sometimes resulted in conflict.

Indigenous African religions, on the other hand, are basically communal rather than universalistic. Like Hinduism and modern Judaism, and unlike Christianity and Islam, indigenous African religions have not sought to convert the whole of humankind. By not being universalistic in that sense, African traditions have not been in competition with each other for the souls of other people. The Yoruba do not seek to convert the Igbo to Yoruba religion or vice versa. Nor do, either the Yoruba or the Igbo compete with each other for the souls of a third group like the Hausa. By not being proselytizing religions, indigenous African creeds have not fought with each other. Over the centuries, Africans have waged many kinds of wars with each other but hardly ever religious ones before the universalistic creeds arrived.

But what has this to do with contemporary Africa? The indigenous toleration today has often mitigated the competitiveness of the imported Semitic religions — Christianity and Islam. Let us illustrate with Senegal, which is over eighty percent Muslim. The founder president of this predominantly Islamic society was Leopold Sedar Senghor. He presided over the fortunes of postcolonial Senegal for two decades, in basic political partnership with the Muslim leaders of the country — the Marabouts.

His successor, as President, partly sponsored by him, was Abdou Diouf; at last a Muslim ruler of a Muslim society. But the tradition of ecumenical tolerance continued in Senegal. The first lady of the country, Madame Elizabeth Diouf, was Roman Catholic, and several of the Ministers of the new President were also Christians.

Senegalese religious tolerance has continued in other spheres since then. What in other Islamic countries elsewhere in the world might be regarded as provocative, in Senegal it has been tolerated. There have been occasions when a Christian festival, like the First Communion, with a lot of feasting, merrymaking, and singing has been publicly held in Dakar right in the middle of the Islamic fast of Ramadhan, and the Christian merrymakers were left undisturbed.[2]

To summarize the argument so far, predominantly Muslim countries south of the Sahara have been above average in religious toleration. The capacity to accommodate other faiths may, to some extent, be part of the historical Islamic tradition in multi-religious empires. But far, more religiously tolerant than either Islam or Christianity, have been the indigenous African traditions — especially since these do not aspire to universalism and are not inherently competitive. In Black Africa, this indigenous tolerance has often moderated the competitive propensities of Christianity and Islam.

In his first administration as President of Uganda, Milton Obote (a Protestant) used to boast that his extended family in Lango consisted of Muslims, Catholics, and Protestants "at peace with each other." Obote's successor, Idi Amin Dada (a Muslim), also had a similarly multi-religious extended family. He once even declared that he planned to have at least one of his sons trained for Christian priesthood. Amin may have reconsidered the matter when, upon losing office, he found political refuge in Saudi Arabia as a guest of the custodians of the Islamic holy cities of Mecca and Medina. And, as earlier indicated, the first Muslim president of Senegal, Abdou Diouf, had a Roman Catholic wife.

BETWEEN REVIVALISM AND DOMESTIC RADICALIZATION

In Cote d'Ivoire, there is a similar North-South divide, which coincides with religious differences. Under the Presidency of Felix Houphouet-Boigny, the North-South divide was softened by wise power-sharing. Cote d'Ivoire has more Muslims than Christians. But Christians dominated both the economy and the political system. From 1990 to 1993, Felix Houphouet-Boigny made Alassane Dramane Ouattara (a Northern Muslim) the Prime Minister.

Ouattara had a break in his political career, from 1994 to 1999, when he joined the International Monetary Fund as Deputy Managing Director. He returned to the Ivory Coast to bid for Presidency. Liberalization, however, did not translate into real democratization. The Muslim plurality in the Ivory Coast is at last re-asserting its claim to a fair share of power.

The coming of the Nobel Prize to West Africa, in 1986, was a symptom of yet another major force — the force of cultural globalization, which has recently coincided with the digital revolution. Globalization, it should be noted on the onset, consists of the forces that are leading the human race towards a global village. But, since the 1990s, globalization has also carried the seeds of cultural revivalism — ranging from ethnic resurgence to religious revivalism. In Northern Nigeria, globalization has converged with the legacy of Lord Lugard.

Nigeria, as earlier indicated, has the largest concentration of Muslims on the African continent. It has more Muslims than any Arab country, including Egypt. Since Olusegun Obasanjo became President in May 1999, some predominantly Muslim states in the Nigerian federation have taken steps towards implementing the *Shari'a* in their own states, although the country as a whole is supposed to be a secular republic. This has caused consternation among non-Muslim Nigerians. Indeed, in Lord Lugard's own Kaduna state, this Christian consternation exploded into intercommunal riots, which cost hundreds of lives, in early 2000. But the momentum for *shariacracy* still continues. Is *Shariacracy* an inevitable part of the legacy of Lord Lugard?

Many different reasons have been advanced for the rise of *Shari'a* advocacy and *Shari'a* implementation in Northern Nigeria. One explanation is that the Nigerian federation is becoming more decentralized, and part of the decentralization is taking the form of cultural self-determination and revivalism. In Yorubaland, this cultural self-determination is taking the form of Yoruba nationalism and re-tribalization. In Igboland, it is taking the form of new demands for confederation. In the Muslim North, cultural self-determination is taking the form of *shariacracy*. Did Lord Lugard's Indirect Rule, during the British colonial era, lay the foundation of *Shariacracy* in the year 2000?

Another explanation for the rise of *Shari'a* militancy is to regard it as a political bargaining chip. As the North is losing political influence in the Nigerian federation, it is asserting new forms of autonomy in preparation for a new national compact among the contending forces which Indirect Rule helped to democratize.

What has not been discussed is whether the rise of *Shari'a* militancy itself is a consequence of globalization. One of the repercussions of globalization worldwide, has been to arouse cultural insecurity and uncertainty about identities. Indeed, the paradox of globalization is that it promotes both enlargement of economic scale and stimulates fragmentation of ethnic and cultural scale. The enlargement of economic scale is illustrated by the rise of the European Union (EU), and by the North American Free Trade Agreement (NAFTA).

The fragmentation of ethnic and cultural scale is illustrated by the disintegration of the Soviet Union, the collapse of Czechoslovakia into two countries, the rise of Hindu fundamentalism in India, the rise and fall of the Taliban and Islamic fundamentalism in Afghanistan, the collapse of Somalia after penetration by the Soviet Union and the United States, and the re-activation of genocidal behavior among the Hutu and Tutsi in Rwanda and Burundi.

Because globalization is a special scale of Westernization, it has triggered off identity crises from Uzbekistan to Somalia and from Afghanistan to Northern Nigeria. Fragile ethnic identities and endangered cultures are forced into new forms of resistance. Resisting Westernization becomes indistinguishable from resisting globalization. In Nigeria, the South is part of the vanguard of Westernization and therefore the first to respond to globalization. When, in addition, the South appears to be politically triumphant within Nigeria under Obasanjo's presidency, alarm bells are sounded in parts of the North. This may not necessarily be Northern distrust of Yoruba or Igbo cultures, it may be Northern distrust of Westernization. Is Southern Nigeria a Trojan horse for globalization? And is globalization, in turn, a Trojan horse for Westernization? Paradoxically, a Westerner named Lord Lugard had helped to nurse the Northern distrust of cultural Westernization.

The *Shari'a*, under this paradigm, becomes a form of Northern resistance — not to Southern Nigeria but to the forces of globalization and to their Westernizing consequences. Even the policy of privatization of public enterprises and liberalization of the economy is probably an aspect of the new globalizing ideology. Privatization in Nigeria may either lead to new transnational corporations establishing their roots, or to private Southern entrepreneurs outsmarting Northerners and deepening the economic divide between North and South. Again, the *Shari'a* may be a Northern gut response to these looming clouds of globalization and the *de-facto* structural adjustment.

In Nigeria, the *Shari'a* is caught between the forces of domestic democratization and the forces of wider globalization. On the one hand, Lord Lugard had helped to protect Islam in Northern Nigeria; Islam had been an earlier form of cultural globalization within a worldwide community of believers. On the other hand, the Legacy of Lord Lugard had helped to heighten Hausa-Fulani identity and was therefore a parochializing force. Both globalization and *Lugardization* in Northern Nigeria had, therefore, contributed to the rise of *Shariacracy*.

In Uganda, the North-South divide does not coincide with the religious divide, in spite of the fact that one arm of Northern resistance calls itself "the Lord's Resistance Army."

In Sudan, the North-South divide does coincide with a religious divide. But unlike in Nigeria, the South in Sudan does not lead in economic skills. Southern Sudan is beginning to lead in economic resources. The discovery of oil in Southern Sudan has compounded the civil war between the North and South. In Sudan, the North had previously tried to monopolize both political power and economic control. But a new 'gold rush' has been precipitated by the discovery of oil. Piety and politics have now been compounded by petroleum.

THE FIRES OF INTERNATIONAL RADICALIZATION

When, in October 2001, the United States' State Department released its list of the 22 most wanted terrorists, twelve were Africans, including two Kenyans, one Tanzanian, one Cameroonian, one Libyan, and seven Egyptians.

As already indicated, the largest concentration of Muslims in Africa is in Nigeria — some of whom have embraced the *Shari'a,* but there is no evidence of affiliation to *Al-Qaeda.* There are more Muslims in Nigeria than in any Arab country, including Egypt.

Indeed, there are more Muslims in Black Africa than in the Middle East. And 27 out of the 57 members of the worldwide organization of the Islamic Conference are from Africa. Will Africa therefore be turned into a major battlefield of the war against terrorism?

The war initiated by Osama bin Laden and *Al-Qaeda* was geographically targeted and specific in the countries chosen. Its primary targets were the United States and Israel.

The war against *Al-Qaeda* is less geographically specific and more global. The American-led war, against terrorism, may turn out to be more globally destabilizing than the terrorism of *Al-Qaeda* itself.

Much of the world is in favor of attempting, once again, the process of nation building in Somalia, but the United States has virtually vetoed the idea, in spite of all the assurances that Somali nation building would be a protection against infiltration by *Al-Qaeda* rather than an invitation to it.

The aftermath of September 11, 2001, may begin to undermine the multiracial solidarity of post-apartheid South Africa. It has already deepened the cleavage between the Christian-led central government of Tanzania, in Dar es Salaam, and the overwhelmingly Muslim separatist islands of Zanzibar and Pemba.

While globalization and structural liberalization have indeed been major causes of cultural revivalism and re-tribalization, the latest such force of re-tribalization is the new Cold War of counterterrorism.

International terrorism is one more area of intermingling between the policies of the Middle East and the politics of Africa. Before the end of colonialism and the end of apartheid in Africa, what was described as 'terrorism' was as common in Africa as in the Middle East. Since the collapse of political apartheid in the 1990s, the term 'terrorism' has been more narrowly focused on the politics of the Middle East. We shall explore the reasons more fully.

Much of the old anti-colonial and anti-apartheid terrorism in Africa, in the second half of the twentieth century, was targeted against Europeans and the colonial powers. Much of the Middle Eastern terrorism of more recent times has been targeted against the United States and Israel.

In the retrospect of history, Africa gained from its own guerrilla movements and terrorist activities against European powers. The Mau Mau war in Kenya did result in Kenya's independence in 1963; the Algerian revolution did result in the liberation of Algeria in 1962; the anti-colonial wars in Angola, Mozambique, and Guinea-Bissau did destroy the Portuguese empire in 1974; the anti-UDI struggle in Zimbabwe ended Ian Smith's Unilateral Declaration of Independence; and the anti-apartheid struggle in South Africa finally triumphed against the racial order. Terrorism and guerilla war by Africans against European powers did yield positive results. Terrorism was a form of warfare and had to be judged in its total political and moral context, as well as by its ultimate results.[3]

What is more, all forms of warfare kill overwhelmingly more civilians than combatants. The American War in Vietnam killed over three million Vietnamese civilians, against less than sixty thousand American combatants.[4]

However, if anti-European and anti-colonial terrorism in Africa had in the end produced good results for Africa, anti-American and anti-Zionist terrorism in the Middle East has not yet found its moment of triumph. Both the Middle East and Africa have been paying the price for anti-American terrorism. The violent price which the Middle East is paying is obvious, especially in Palestine, Iraq, and in neighboring Afghanistan. But what is the price which Africa is paying for terrorism against the United States?

First, there is the issue of being caught in the crossfire. Africa has been the victim of violent action intended by the terrorists for the United States. Africa has also been a victim of violent action taken by the United States which was intended for the terrorists.

In order to kill twelve Americans, Middle Eastern terrorists killed about two hundred Kenyans in the streets of Nairobi a few years ago. This was the attack on the U.S. Embassy in Nairobi, in August 1998. There were also Tanzanian casualties when the U.S. Embassy in Dar es Salaam was targeted at the same time.[5]

On the other hand, Sudan was caught in the crossfire soon after President Bill Clinton ordered the bombing of an apparently harmless pharmacy near Khartoum.[6] President Ronald Reagan had, before Clinton, ordered the bombing of Tripoli and Benghazi in Libya because Reagan thought the Libyans were responsible for a bomb in a German bar which had killed Americans.[7] Violence between the Americans and Middle Easterners and from both Middle Easterners and the Americans, had been spilling over into Africa for decades. This may politicize African Muslims faster than African Christians.

An unknown number of Africans — Senegalese hawkers, Nigerian investors, Ethiopian or Eritrean drivers or professionals, Ghanaian students, Egyptian and South African tourists, and others were killed at the World Trade Center in New York on September 11, 2001. For Africa, September 11, 2001 has had other consequences. The Security Forces of Africa have opened their doors to the United States' Federal Bureau of Investigation (FBI) and the Central Intelligence Agency (CIA). Today, Africa has fewer secrets (if it ever had any) from the Americans. Many African Muslims become suspect just by being at the same time anti-American (a common stance in the Third World).

The FBI reportedly arrived in Tanzania, after September 11, with 60 Muslim names for interrogation and potential action. A few officials of the Kenyan authorities have been so eager to help the Americans that they are sometimes tempted to repatriate their own Kenyan citizens to the United States if they are *Al-Qaeda* suspects. Fortunately, the American Embassy in Nairobi is sometimes more cautious. And will Ethiopia collaborate with the Bush administration in the hunt for *Al-Qaeda* in Somalia? Will Ethiopia be a neighbor like Musharraf's Pakistan has been to Afghanistan?

The now retired President of Kenya, Daniel Toroitich Arap Moi, marched in sympathy with the victims of September 11. The Muslims of Kenya marched against the American bombing of Afghanistan. A Presidential spokesman asked, "Why didn't the Kenyan Muslims march when Nairobi was bombed by terrorists in August of 1998?" The Kenyan Muslims turned the tables on their President: "Why didn't President Moi lead a march when Nairobi was bombed in August 1998?"[8] Kenyans were quarreling with each other over the policies of the United States.

The also now retired third President of Tanzania, Benjamin W. Mkapa, declared a day of mourning in Tanzania for the victims of September 11 in the United States. His critics apparently retorted that they did not remember a day of public mourning in Tanzania when 800,000 Rwandans were killed in the genocide of 1994. Africans grieve when Americans are massacred, but do we grieve as much when Africans are massacred? Tanzanians were quarrelling with each other over U.S. policies.

There is some anxiety that September 11 and its aftermath has exacerbated tensions not only between pro-Western and anti-Western schools of thought in the African continent, but also between Christians and Muslims in Africa. A demonstration by Nigerian Muslims in Kano against the American war in Afghanistan, late in October 2001, provoked stone throwing by Nigerian Christians in Kano, which flared up communal riots. Churches and mosques were burnt down, and at least 200 people were killed.[9] President Olusegun Obasanjo had to rush to Kano to contain the tensions before they spilled over into sectarian riots all over Nigeria.

The United States is trying to unite African governments against terrorism. But is there a risk of dividing African people among themselves — a coalition of elites resulting in a contestation at the grassroots?

U.S. pressure on many African governments, to enact new legislation against terrorism may pose newer threats to civil liberties in Africa, just at the time when democratization has begun gathering momentum in some African states. Nor must we forget that if America's own democracy decays, it makes it easier for Africa's own dictators to justify their own tyranny.[10] Are we witnessing the decline of the United States as a democratic role model? Indeed, the aftermath of September 11 has already been compromising some civil liberties in the United States itself.

I: There have been hundreds of people in detention without trial,[11] and with no access to lawyers. Pro-democracy activists in Africa are dismayed.

II: The great majority of those in detention are not publicly announced as being in detention. It is a bad example to less mature African democracies.

III: Out of the hundreds in detention, less than a dozen show any evidence of knowing any particular terrorist suspect or being associated with any movement or charity accused of terrorism. Pro-democracy activists in Africa are alarmed that detention with little evidence can be used against them in Africa.

IV: Out of the millions of illegal immigrants in the United States and those whose visas have expired, the people chosen for detention without trial are almost certainly those with Muslim names, or who come from the Middle East. Is this a new version of Western tribalism?

V: The President of the United States, George Walker Bush, goes to a mosque to proclaim that the war on terrorism is not a war on Islam and, then, the Federal government goes ahead and raids two dozen Muslim educational and cultural institutions, to search and seizure them, with being Muslim as the only probable cause.

VI: The United States is actually planning to have military tribunals and has even considered secret trials for those suspected of terrorism.[12] Even the leaders of Nazi Germany were given a public trial at Nuremberg after World War II, with access to counsel and proper representation. Some of those tried at Nuremberg had been responsible for the death of millions of people.[13]

VII: Israel continues to look for old Nazi militants so that they can be tried today in a court of law in Israel. Yet Israel feels free to kill Palestinian militants, instead of capturing them for trial. Israel tried Adolf Eichmann in 1961 and protected him at the trial with a bulletproof glass cage so that he would not be assassinated. Yet, both the U.S. and Israel, in 2001, openly talked about killing terrorist suspects instead of capturing them. And even when Israel has illegally captured Palestinian or Lebanese suspects from across its own borders, the purpose has almost never been to give them a fair trial (Adolf Eichmann style) but to detain those suspects indefinitely without trial.

VIII: The United States, as a democratic role model has been compromised. Former U.S. Attorney General, John Ashcroft, even attempted to empower the FBI to spy on churches, mosques, and other sacred places to an extent not envisaged in the country for a long time. Places of prayer were once protected from close police scrutiny. However, mosques especially may soon be fair game for police raids in American cities, while synagogues may enjoy *de facto* protection even if there is militant Zionism or fundamentalist Judaism being preached inside.

When African countries like Uganda consider new anti-terrorist legislation, their governments have to resist the temptation to use such legislation against their own political opponents, especially opponents who happen to be Muslim. Other postcolonial African regimes inherited Preventive Detention Acts from British colonial rule and were not slow to use such colonial repressive legislation against their own opponents. Will the new war on terrorism provide cover for African dictators?

Fortunately, American democracy is stronger than any particular American administration in any particular year. While the United States has declined as a democratic role model, both because of how the Presidential election of the year 2000 was decided and because of the erosion of civil liberties since September 11, 2001, civil society in the United States is still too democratic to accept repression for long. There may still be a role for the United States as a model for Africa when the present American anti-terrorist frenzy has subsided.

Meanwhile, Africa should be on the alert that the new cold war of counterterrorism does not exacerbate old divisions between Christians and Muslims in Africa or precipitate the military victimization of Muslims in countries like Somalia, Sudan, and Libya.

Globalization and structural adjustment have already damaged Africa. Africa does not deserve further damage, threatened by the new cold war of counterterrorism. The latest report about Press freedom worldwide, already indicates that many governments are using September 11 as an excuse for new Press curbs.

CONCLUSION: IN SEARCH OF THE SACRED ADJUSTMENT

We have argued that three forces — globalization, the legacy of structural adjustment programs, and the unfolding cold war of counterterrorism — have forced many Africans to look afresh at their own cultural identities. This has sometimes taken the form of clan identities, as in Somalia, sometimes ethnic nationalism, as among the Yoruba, and sometimes the rise of religious consciousness, as in the Northern states of Nigeria and the north-south divides of Sudan and Cote d'Ivoire.

Islam in Africa has been undergoing three inter-related processes — geographical expansion, cultural revivalism, and political radicalization. The political radicalization is sometimes domestic and sometimes international.

But is this re-tribalizaiton and cultural revival necessarily a bad thing? Should we not look more closely at the pluses as well as the minuses of re-tribalization?

When serving on the World Bank's Council of African Advisors, in the 1980s–1990s, I had the occasion to say to the president of the bank at the time, Barber B. Conable, that the World Bank had been crowned King of Africa. I then quoted to him a Motion passed in the House of Commons in London in 1780: "The power of the crown has increased, is increasing, and ought to be diminished."

The Bank's President conceded that the power of the Bank in Africa had increased, was increasing, and ought to be diminished. But he insisted that the Bank was struggling hard to be less needed by Africa. The Bank would be proud of its own contribution if its power diminished because Africa needed the Bank much less. If the World Bank became a Constitutional Monarch without great power, would International Monetary Fund still be the Queen-Consort? While I do not here want to emphasize this monarchical role of the Bank, I will, nevertheless, stress the Bank's role as an oracle, as a source of what Muslims call *fatwas*.

In Islam, a *fatwa* is a guide to action based on the *Shari'a*. The World Bank's *fatwas* have been economic. They have often become sacred conditionalities to guide the actions of governments in Africa. If the President of the World Bank is an *Imam*, rather than a king, he may insist on formulating his own *fatwas* soon after assuming office. The shorthand used for these *fatwas* may be the slogans of "Basic Needs" or "Structural Adjustment" or "Poverty Reduction Strategy" or "Comprehensive Development."

But, surely, religious revivalism in places like Nigeria and Sudan was bound to harm prospects for development, one might argue. Yet, in reality that need not follow. We need to be reminded that England led the Industrial Revolution of the world, in the eighteenth and nineteenth centuries, when England was still a quasi-theocracy. The monarch as Head of State was also Head of the Church of England. The Prime Minister appointed the Archbishop of Canterbury, and major doctrinal changes in the Church of England needed the approval of the British Parliament.

In spite of this link between the state and the church, England became 'the workshop of the world' and blazed a technological trail for the human race. Indeed, very religious people sometimes led the industrial revolution in England. England did not confuse science with secularism. But while the British experience in the nineteenth century had less secularism and more science, British educational policies in their African colonies resulted in more secularism and less science.

Secularism is the decline of religion; it does not necessarily mean the rise of science. In spite of the influence of European missionaries, and sometimes because of that influence, the overall impact of Western education on Africa was to reduce religious values (of all creeds) rather than enhance the scientific spirit.

Does Africa need to recover some of its spirituality in order to become a new scientific force? If Western capitalism was born out of the Protestant reformation, and British science was born out of nonconformist

Christianity, perhaps Africa needs to experience its own Protestant revolution — rather than merely imitate somebody else's Reformation. Africa's re-tribalization may be a precondition for Africa's re-modernization.

There is little doubt that the short-term consequences of globalization, of the legacy of structural adjustment, and of the new cold war of counterterrorism are painful and sometimes devastating for Africa. But if those three forces are also forcing Africa back to the cultural drawing board, they are giving an opportunity to Africa to correct the false start with which it inaugurated its postcolonial era. One day, Africa will find a system of government that works, the economic *fatwa* that truly delivers, and a cultural response to globalization that is not destabilizing. To paraphrase the English poet, Alexander Pope (1688-1744):

> For forms of government, let fools contest;
> Whate'er is best-administered is best;
> For modes of faith, let graceless zealots fight;
> He can't be wrong whose life is in the right;
> In faith and hope the world will disagree;
> *But all mankind's concern is liberty.*
> [Pope, *An Essay on Man* Ep. iii I].

In reality, Pope was championing political and cultural systems that could genuinely deliver desired goods. The search continues in the Africa of today.

Endnotes

1. The Almoravids were a group of zealous Muslims, originating in southern Mauritania.
2. Consult Susan MacDonald, "Senegal: Islam on the March," *West Africa*, (London), No. 3494, August 6, 1984, p. 1570.
3. For a general discussion of terrorism in international politics, see *Violence, Terrorism, And Justice*, Eds. R. G. Frey and C. W. Morris, (Cambridge, NY: Cambridge University Press, 1991); Heather A. Wilson, *International Law And The Use Of Force By National Liberation Movements* (Oxford and New York: Clarendon Press and Oxford University Press,1988); and with specific reference to Africa, see Aquino De Bragança and Immanuel Wallerstein, *The African Liberation Reader*, 3 volumes (London: Zed Press, 1982).
4. The Vietnamese numbers are controversial. One study has a lower estimate; Charles Hirschmann, Samuel Preston, Manh Loi Vu, "Vietnamese Casualties during the American War: A New Estimate," *Population And Development Review* 21, 4 (December 1995), pp. 783–812, estimates the combined Vietnamese toll as approximately one million, with a margin of error of about 175000 between 1965–1975; the lowest figure is about 415,000 while Hanoi

claims there were two million deaths between 1954–1975. In contrast, there were about 58,000 American military fatalities; also see Spencer C. Tucker, Ed., *Encyclopedia of the Vietnam War*, Volume One, (Santa Barbara, CA: ABC-CLIO, 1998), p. 106.
5. For the report lamenting the end of the African 'safe haven,' see *New African*, 367 (October 1998), pp. 16–17.
6. Consult *Middle East International*, Issue 582 (September 4, 1998), pp. 4–5.
7. This action is discussed in P. Wapner, "Problems of US Counter-Terrorism: The Case of Libya," *Alternatives*, Volume 13, Number 2 (April 1988), pp. 271–289.
8. See the report in *The Nation* (Kenya), October 21, 2001 reported in the Africa News Service on-line at http://allafrica.com/eastafrica/.
9. This was reported in *The Washington Post* (October 15, 2001), p. 9.
10. A Human Rights Watch report pointed out that country leaders were taking advantage of the antiterror campaign to suppress, dissent, and abuse human rights; see *The Washington Post* (January 18, 2002), p. 12.
11. *New York Times* (November 29, 2001), p. 1.
12. See the concerns raised by critics in a report in the *New York Times* (December 29, 2001), p. B7.
13. For a discussion of the issues at Nuremberg, consult Alan S. Rosenbaum, *Prosecuting Nazi War Criminals* (Boulder: Westview Press, 1993).

3

The Spread of Islam and Arab Culture in West Africa in the Eleventh Century: Impact on African-European Relations*

BRAHIM EL KADIRI BOUTCHICH

Despite the large number of historical studies written about the spread of Islam in West Africa[1], it is still unclear how Islam first spread in this area. This lack of clarity calls for more research, in order to discover the first roots of Islam in West Africa. Arabic sources use the term "Bilad Sùdan" to refer to the region ranging west from the northern borders of the Great African Sahara to the borders of South Ghana. Various ethnic groups, speaking different languages, lived in this area, which was dominated by a type of desert pastoral activity and livestock breeding.

THE EARLY STEPS IN THE SPREAD OF ISLAM IN WEST AFRICA BEFORE THE XI CENTURY

According to Ibn Khaldoun[2], paganism and magianism were predominant in sub-Saharan Africa before the Muslims first arrived in the region. This has been confirmed by archeological studies, which discovered that every West African city had its own protecting sacred animals and human-like gods. Trees also were worshipped, as they were related to fertility and production.[3] According to some historians, Christianity experienced some spread in sub-Saharan Africa[4], but it seems that it remained limited in an area where paganism was the dominant religious belief.

Islam, however, first appeared in this region in the second half of the seventh Century when the Arab commander, Oqba Ibn Nafi, conquered North Africa. Since then, Islam began to penetrate into West Africa.

---

* I would like to thank Abdelmonim Karam, a sworn translator of English, who translated this research from Arabic into English.

However, I do not agree with historians who overestimated the influence of Oqba Ibn Nafi's military expedition to North-West Africa, when they say that he succeeded in spreading Islam among the tribes of the *Sanhadja alitham* in the Mauritanian Sahara and Senegal, and that he reached the land of Tikrour and Ghana in this early stage.[5] They refer to Al-Bakri who argues that, after Oqba Ibn Nafi's conquest of the city of Gadames in 666 (64 of the Hegira), he marched deep South until he reached the province of Kouar.[6] Had he continued his march, he would have reached Nigeria. Such an achievement seems unlikely, given the limited means that were available to him since he had not yet completely subjugated North Africa by spreading Islam there on a large extent.[7] It is more likely that he made swift tours aimed at spreading Islam in those areas, but that he could not deepen its roots. This goal was later attempted by the *Idrisid* dynasty, which failed to achieve it either. Islam, therefore, remained superficial in those areas, a situation we can understand from a conversation that took place in Qairawane between Abù Imrane al Fassi and Yahya bin Ibrahim El Jùdali, leader of the Sanhadja tribe who told the former that his own tribe does not know anything about Islam apart from the two *shahada* — that there is no God but Allah and that Mohamed is His Messenger.[8] This tribe reigned over the kingdoms of West Africa, which regularly paid taxes to it since the formation of the first Sanhadji Alliance.[9] Therefore, what were the new developments which contributed to the spread of Islam during the Almoravid era in the eleventh century?

MEANS BY WHICH ISLAM SPREAD IN WEST AFRICA DURING THE ALMORAVID ERA IN THE XI CENTURY

Jihad: The Almoravids' role in spreading Islam in West Africa

Stage 1: The Jihad led by Abdùllah Ibn Yassine
Some historic sources content that Abdùllah Ibn Yassine, the founder of the Almoravid dynasty, established a *ribat* (hospice) on the valley of the river Senegal,[10] yet others argue that he founded the hospice along the Niger river.[11] The establishment of this *ribat* in West Africa is regarded as a focal point in the project aimed at spreading Islam in the region. In addition to its strategic position, as a cross point for trade caravans, it was also a center of practical and theoretical training for preachers and had a clear-cut mission of mobilizing the community for permanent Jihad against the remnants of paganism.[12]

It is still unknown how much time Abdùllah Ibn Yassine and his supporters spent in this *ribat*, but they may have stayed there for seven to twelve years. This period enabled him to give ideological and military training to up to 3,000 members of the *ribat*.

Jihad was first launched by the Almoravids who, having become "a war machine" according to Marçais's own words,[13] led by Abdùllah Ibn Yassine and his supporters set off on a military expedition. His strategy aimed at tackling the tribes of *Lamtùna, Masùfa, Jùdala* and all the West African tribes that opposed his mission. This expedition supplied him with the money he needed for the continuation of Jihad against the tribes of West Sudan. Abdùllah Ibn Yassine succeeded in subjugating *Ùdaghusht* and attacked the pagan kingdom of Ghana in 1056. When African tribes that had converted into Islam through him joined his army, he was able to subjugate the other West African tribes as well. Thus, Islam began to spread in this region, even though Abdùllah Ibn Yassine imposed it by the force of the sword, as expressed by some historians: "He subjugated all Bilad Sahara."[14]

Stage 2: Emir Abù Bakr Ben Omar Lamtùni Spreads Islam in West Africa

After the Almoravid troops led by Abù Bakr Ben Omar Lamtùni marched toward Morocco in order to unify it and fight against the Berber tribes, an uprising against the Almoravid authority occurred in some West African kingdoms. Therefore, Abù Bakr Ben Omar Lamtùni returned in those kingdoms and re-unified the region under his authority once again. He appointed his cousin Yoùssef Ibn Tachfine as his deputy in the continuation of Jihad in Morocco. Then he set for *Ùdaghusht* where he gathered a military force and marched toward the *Sunanki* black tribes,[15] who were under the rule of the kingdom of Ghana. He subjugated a number of West African kingdoms and gave them the right to choose either to convert to Islam or pay the *jizya* (a tax imposed on free non-Muslims under Muslim rule).

Interestingly, historical sources do not tell exactly which way Abù Bakr Ben Omar marched in his Jihad expedition to spread Islam, whether toward the South West or the South East. Some argue in favor of the latter since the Islamic kingdom of Tikrour already ruled the South West as well as some Muslim areas in Bilad Sudan such as "Kouga" and "Sala." Since pagan tribes governed the South East, it is more likely that Abù Bakr Ben Omar marched towards them, subjugated them, and spread Islam in their lands.[16]

However, the Jihad came to a sudden halt in Bilad Sùdan when the news reached the Almoravid Emir that his deputy, Yoùssef Ibn Tachfine, had seized power. Abù Bakr Ben Omar hurried back toward Morocco, but finally surrendered power to his cousin and headed back to Bilad Sùdan in order to continue the mission of spreading Islam. This time he targeted the kingdom of Ghana, then regarded as the oldest and the most outstanding of the West African kingdoms. Since its foundation, between the third and fourth centuries,[17] it underwent rapid development — thanks to its control of gold mines and roads, so much so that the capital city of Ghana became one of the biggest cities in Bilad Sùdan. Al-Bakri, a geographer who witnessed the beginning of the Almoravid dynasty, says that Islam spread in this region thanks to the previous work of Abdùllah Ibn Yassine. However, some pockets retained their traditional faith, which explains Al-Bakri's division of the capital of Ghana into two parts — "A city with a Muslim population and twelve mosques" and a second city which he called the "City of the King," known as the "Jungle," where wizards lived and worshiped statues.[18]

Historical sources fail to provide details, apart from some hints, of the expedition launched by Abù Bakr Ben Omar on Ghana, although he spent 14 years in this region engaging in Jihad. He finally brought Ghana under his authority. His army consisted of two divisions: he led the first one himself while his son, Abù Yahya, commanded the other. The latter apparently played a major role in subjugating Ghana, according to the author of *Al Hùlal Al Mawshiyya*, who says, "The people of Ghana entered Islam in 469 of the Hegira, when they were surrounded by the troops of Emir Abù Yahya, son of Abù Bakr Ben Omar."[19] He was later killed by the local population, some of whom later converted to Islam. Thus, the banner of Islam was raised high on the entire kingdom of Ghana.[20] The king of Ghana himself converted to the Muslim faith, otherwise Emir Abù Bakr would not have allowed him to continue reigning in the name of the Almoravids.[21]

The Emir was himself, however, assassinated in a plot mounted by a leader of the *Mùssa* tribes in South Dahomi in 480 H. West African tribes became angry and called for revenge and, as a result, war broke out between the Muslims and the pagans. Later, the tribes that fought against the *Saracola* Muslim tribe, which called for avenging of Emir Abù Bakr's death, converted to Islam as well. Islam thus gained momentum in this region, propelled by the killing of the Almoravid Emir.[22] Emir Abù Bakr Ben Omar was thus instrumental in spreading Islam on a larger scale in West Africa, a fact which historian Ibn Abi Zar'e described, saying: "He reigned over the Sahara until the Gold Mountain in Bilad Sùdan."[23]

Stage 3: Jihad of Yoùssef Ibn Tachafine
After Emir Abù Bakr Ben Omar was killed, his son returned from Ghana to claim the throne of his father. Then, the kingdom of Ghana rebelled against the Almoravids and tried to break free of their rule, as other kingdoms

related to Ghana had successfully done, such as *Anbara, Diara*, and *Kaniga*. These kingdoms played an expansionist role under the leadership of *Fulani* tribes, which succeeded in annexing some emirates and founding the *Susu* emirate.[24]

However, Emir Yoùssef Ibn Tachfine responded swiftly to these uprisings, brought stability to the Sudanese tribes and Ghana under the rule of the Almoravids, and spread Islam in the region once again. The mission of the Jihad led by Yoùssef Ibn Tachfine was a success, because Islam prevailed again in the Kingdoms of West Africa. This was confirmed by a letter Yoùssef Ibn Tachfine sent to the Abbassid Caliphate, Al Mùstadhir Billah, through the Judge of Seville, Abù Mohamed Ben El Arabi Al Maafiri, who said during his meeting with the Abbassid Caliphate in Baghdad that the rule of Yoùssef Ibn Tachafine ranged southward beyond Bilad Ghana.[25]

Yoùssef Ibn Tachafine organized the Jihad with the cooperation of the black tribes, who were motivated to spread Islam. Thus, Islam spread from the Atlantic Ocean in the west to *Kanem* and *Borno* in the east. Later, the kingdom of *Songhai* also converted to Islam. The first among its kings to convert to Islam was *Zakassi* in 400 H (1009 A.C), that is, shortly before the beginning of the Almoravid Jihad. The kingdoms of Kanem and Borno then joined them.[26] New Muslim converts increased in number during the expeditions of Abù Bakr Ben Omar and Yoùssef Ibn Tachafine.

THE ROLE OF TRADE IN SPREADING ISLAM IN WEST AFRICA

The Islamic conquest of North Africa and, subsequently, the Islamic emirates of the Khawarij, the Idrisid, and the Fatimid heralded a new era for trade and exchange with the West African people. Trade tours provided an opportunity to spread Islam. However, in the eleventh century, a major change affected trade roads, which had strengthened relations between the North African Muslims and the people of Sudan. In fact, sandstorms had rendered the trade road linking Ghana to Egypt impassable. Trade caravans, thus, changed their direction and took the Atlantic coastal road from West Africa to *Sidjilmassa*, then Morocco's main gate. Since the eleventh century, trans-Saharan trade had been concentrated in West Africa, which became a "useful area" according to Terrasse's own words.[27] The road network consisted of three axes:
- The coastal road linking Taroudant to Nùl Lamta towards Oulil Island. [28]

- The medium road linking Sidjilmassa to Ùdaghusht and Niger via Azki.
- The road linking Bilad Sùdan to Mount Nafoussa and Tripoli.

The new roads were a key element in trade relations between North African Muslims and West African people. Islam could easily spread among the local population, particularly because they needed products and goods such as salt and copper, just as much as North Africans needed slaves and gold for trade with Europe. *Ùdaghusht* became both a central post in trade with Ghana from the north and a center of Islamic preaching.[29] Islam and trade were so interlinked that Trimingham ascertained its verity.[30] The West African populace and their Muslim conquerors enjoyed close contacts. Unlike the Romans who preferred to live along the coast, the Muslims lived interior of the country. These relations were strengthened through trans-Saharan trade. [31]

In their trade travels, Muslims encountered various groups of West African traders — the Fulani, Hausa, Dioula, Mandju, and other Tikrour traders.[32] Lamtùna, Jùdala, and Tùareg tribes were quite active as commercial intermediaries and seized the opportunity of their presence in West African cities to spread Islam. The control exercised by the Almoravids over the trade road to Sùdan strengthened their trade relations with the local population.[33] The Southern Moroccan city of Aghmat had an important role in West African trade and was described by a historian as "the equipping house toward the Sahara."[34] Traders entered it loaded with bronze, clothes, wool, turbans, glass, sea shells, steel, utensils, salt, Chinese pottery, and copper[35] and left laden with Tikrour goods, particularly slaves and gold.[36]

Traders often had administrative and financial experience. They exploited it in reaching senior positions at the Court of West African kings, who helped them to establish new trade markets where they could perform their prayers and preach the teachings of Islam. Through close contacts and influence, traders convinced West African kings to embrace Islam, and once they did, their subjects would also follow suit.[37] Whenever a trader entered a pagan village, he would be noticed by the local population because of his frequent ablutions, prayers, and high morals. Such behavior had an impact on the local people and it did somewhat persuade them to convert to Islam.[38]

The author of *Tarikh al Fattach*, when talking about the kingdom of Songhai, quotes an outstanding example of the role of Arab traders in spreading Islam in West Africa. He says that the people of this kingdom converted to Islam through the influence of traders from Jawa, whose presence on the crossroads of trade caravans in the north provided them with a prominent trade center and the ability to introduce change in the Songhai people's faith.[39] The historian, Assaadi explained that the ruler of Songhai was known in the local language as "Muslim dam," which means that he willingly embraced Islam in 1009.[40]

Other West African communities converted to Islam in the same way, and, in turn, contributed in spreading Islam. The Dioula traders' community, in particular, set up trade centers which enabled them to build up a highly organized network. Thanks to the establishment of these trade groups, Islam penetrated these areas on a larger scale, as the traders reached interior cities through trade roads, spreading Islam.[41]

These first contacts, between Muslim and the West African traders, may have led to setting up of businesses engaged in trade and the spread of Islam. One of these businesses was "Al-Makkari Brothers." Formed in the late eleventh century, it spread its activities in the following century when the sons of Abdurrahman Al-Makkari agreed, after their father's death, to found a company. One of the five brothers settled in Bilad Sùdan.[42] No doubt, this company brought Islamic spiritual values to West Africa.

The traders' role in spreading Islam in West Africa is confirmed by a letter reported by the author of *Al Istibsar* to have been sent from the King of Sùdan to Yoùssef Ibn Tachafine. This letter confirms the existence of strong relations between the two Emirs that were not based on military power. Additionally, some epitaphs discovered during archeological research were found to have been made in Andalusia in the twelfth century. They were later carried through the Sahara and put on the tombs of some Emirs from the city of Coco, who were said to have converted to Islam.[43] This finding confirms that Coco's leadership converted to Islam.

THE ROLE OF SCHOLARS AND PREACHERS IN SPREADING ISLAM IN WEST AFRICA

As far as preaching of Islam was concerned, Muslim traders and preachers were two faces of the same coin.[44] The preacher, with his religious affinity and knowledge of Islam, used to file trade registers (regarding the adequate date for caravan departures) and to offer blessings to departing caravans. Sometimes, he acted as a judge, resolving disputes that arose during the caravan journey.

When the Almoravids seized the city of Ùdaghusht, many of their preachers set for Bilad Sùdan.[45] From the outset, Abdùllah Ibn Yassine sent preachers trained in the *ribat* of Senegal to the black tribes hoping to persuade them to convert to Islam. As a result, Ahrabi Ben Rabis, the king of Tikrour and his people entered Islam through these preachers. He then began to send preachers to other regions, as well, such as the city of Sala. The mission was successful — the king of Sala converted to the Muslim faith and, he too, sent preachers to neighboring areas, particularly pagans of *Qalambu*.[46] He invited Almoravid preachers into his palace in order to teach Islamic law, reading, and writing.[47] A group of preachers from *Wùluf, Fùlbi,* and *Mandjù* tribes were trained in Bilad Tikrour. They accompanied troops in order to teach Islam to people in the conquered areas of West Africa. In this respect, Al Bakri[48] says that when Bilad Mali was beset by drought, its king called on a senior righteous Muslim preacher. The preacher asked the king to convert to Islam, and so he did. They prayed together in the *Istisqaa* prayer (prayer for rain) until rain began to fall. The king then destroyed all statues and gave up his pagan faith. However, other historical sources say that the king's subjects became Muslims before the king himself, who was nonetheless the first to perform Hajj (pilgrimage) to the Holy lands.[49]

This senior preacher settled in the king's country where he began teaching the Qur'an and Hadith. The historian Assaadi[50] says that when the king of Jana decided to convert to Islam, he gathered all of his kingdoms' 4,200 scholars or so and embraced Islam in their presence. A large number of scholars confirm that Islam had been widely spread in Jana since the eleventh century. Preachers were respected by kings. In some West African tribes, each village had a house for their accommodation.

THE ROLE OF MUSLIM COMMUNITIES IN SPREADING ISLAM IN WEST AFRICA

West Africa served as a migratory destination for many Muslims who settled there and set up a cornerstone for trade and cultural relations. In this respect, Al-Bakri says that in Ghana lived a community called *Al Hùnaihin*, who were the offspring of the army sent by the Umayyad to Ghana. He also says that some of them, known as *Al Ghaman*, populated the city of Sala.[51]

Ùdaghusht, in particular, after its conquest by the Almoravids, received a group of North African Berbers from the tribes of Zenata, Nafusa, Lùwata, and Nafzawa among others, which constituted an important community in this city.[52] However, it was the Sanhadja Alitham tribe, which settled between River Senegal and River Niger, that spread Islam in those areas.[53]

Historical sources cite, among other Islamic communities that spread Islam in West Africa, were a group of Arabs and Berbers who settled in the city of Jana and turned it into an Islamic center.[54] When Ibn Battùta later visited Mali, he found a group of Arab Muslims known as *Al Bidane* (the whites) who lived in their own area.[55] Some other Muslims also immigrated to the city of Coco. They settled there and built a mosque which served as a center for spreading the Muslim faith.[56]

In the same context, Al-Bakri says that, while the Muslim Sanhadja tribe of *Beni Medassa* reached the coast of the River Niger and settled there, the Muslim Berber tribe of Ghùmara reached the south coast of the River Niger. These communities did not live separated from the local population. Indeed, they lived among them and married their women. Islamic law even became a means of providing justice among them.[57]

Therefore, various means contributed in spreading Islam in West Africa — Jihad by the Almoravids, the role of traders and preachers, and the contribution of Muslim communities in West Africa. The rapid spread of Islam in West Africa is additionally explained by the following factors:

- The peaceful approach followed by both preachers and traders led some West African Emirs to let them preach Islam as long as they did not jeopardize the country's stability.
- Islam's simple rules suited the nature of black Africans, who were considered by Muslims as equals and Masters of their own lands. Muslims even married black women.
- Spiritual beliefs were deeply rooted in black Africans. Even if paganism was widely spread, they could easily embrace Islam's monotheist faith because their religious consciousness occupied a major place in their beliefs.

THE SPREAD OF ARAB-ISLAMIC CULTURE IN WEST AFRICA

The cultural field was clearly marked by Islamic presence in West Africa. Even today, West African culture has retained some Arab and Islamic aspects. In the Almoravid era, Arab-Islamic culture spread in West Africa as follows:

The Spread of the Arabic Language in West Africa

On the one hand, the Arabic language was the language of the Holy Qur'an and Islamic law; on the other hand, it served as the language of business transactions and correspondence, and most of the time, as a means of communication. Its spread was also facilitated by the establishment of Islamic schools, where sciences were taught in Arabic. Moreover, some African languages, such as Fulani and Hausa, were written in the Arabic alphabet. Naim Kaddah provides a good example of the acquisition of the

Arabic language by the people of West Africa, when he cites a letter written by Sultan Ahmed Ben El Hadj in Farsi calligraphy.[58] This letter, even though it was written at a later date compared to the period of this research, demonstrates a typical example of Arabic fluency among the elite in West Africa.

The Spread of Arab Cultural Centers in West Africa
In his book, *Al Mùghrib fi Bilad Ifrikia wal maghrib,* Al-Bakri recorded some invaluable information on cultural centers in the region, such as:
Ûdaghusht: This city was one of the main cultural centers in West Africa in the Almoravid era. Al-Bakri, who himself was a contemporary of the Almoravids, says that the city held many mosques, as well as many children's schools where the Qur'an and Islamic law courses were taught.[59]
Ghana: This was the capital of the kingdom of Ghana. Al-Bakri says that preachers and scholars from North Africa flocked here and that it had 12 mosques where prayers were performed and Islamic law courses taught. When Abù Bakr Ibn Umar seized the city in 1076, he set up besides every mosque a school for teaching the Qur'an, rules of Islam and Arabic language and sciences.[60] The Ghanaian people appreciated the Arab-Islamic civilization. Their kings invited preachers and scholars into their palaces and made them responsible for translating works or supervising some of the positions requiring a certain degree of culture and knowledge, such as the treasury.[61] Thus, Ghana became a destination for scholars and students.
Jana: This city had become an important center of Islamic culture and sciences since the city's Emir "Kanbaru" converted to Islam in the eleventh century. Scholars and students flocked to it from everywhere.[62] The historian Assaadi says that scientific debates were held in the city from midnight until the morning prayer. After the prayers, students listened to scholar's courses until midday. After the midday prayer, another scientific session was held until the afternoon prayer.[63]
Timbuktu: Since Yoùssef Ibn Tachafine founded it in 1096, it had remained an Islamic city where "statues have never been worshipped," according to the historian Assaadi.[64] Many mosques were built which increased its outstanding position as a cultural center. Scholars came to it from the East and the West. Students were encouraged and cared for. Mosques that were built in the city increased its cultural prominence.[65] Having completed learning the Qur'an by heart, they came to the mosque of Timbuktu and remained there until they finished their studies.

The Emir of Timbuktu, who highly respected religious scholars, used to name them by decree and buy very expensive manuscripts.[66] Timbuktu's own scholars used to travel to Fez and Marrakech to study and teach. After they had acquired experience, they returned to their city, which became an intellectual lighthouse in West Africa.

THE FOUNDING OF SCHOOLS IN WEST AFRICA

The *ribat* of Abdùllah Ibn Yassine in Senegal may be considered as the first school in West Africa. The *ribat* served as a space for teaching the Qur'an, the Sunna (Prophet's tradition), Islamic law, and the rules of the Malikite School of theology. When the Almoravids conquered a city, they used to build mosques and schools. Students benefited from the mosques' religious endowment (wakf), as it was the case for the mosque of Sankore in Timbuktu.[67]

Moreover, courses were not exclusively given in schools but in mosques as well; discussions and debates were held on issues pertaining to religion, worship, and behavior. Al-Bakri says that in Ghana there were 12 mosques where scholars and students used to meet.[68] The presence of scholars and students in those mosques shows the importance of the mosque as a place for study.

Furthermore, even palaces of Emirs and rulers served as schools. In the kingdom of Borno, Sheikh Muhammad Ben Mani, whose name had been linked with Borno's conversion to Islam in the eleventh century, used to teach Sultans of this emirate in their own palaces. One of them, Umi Jùlmi (1086–1096), who admired this teacher, issued a decree by which he granted him (and his offspring as well) lifetime privileges.[69] In African tribes where there were no schools, children used to learn from one preacher in a small square or in a room of some wealthy man's house.[70]

There was not a fixed period for study in West African schools. However, students would learn and understand a certain number of books pertaining to law, Hadith, logic, and grammar.[71] Some students spent more than three years reading the *Muwataa* by Imam Malik and the science of Hadith.[72] When African students graduated from these schools, having learnt the various fields of study, they received a degree, qualifying them to practice a religious job, such as literacy teacher, *khatib* (preacher), *imam* (prayer leader), or judge.[73]

The people of West Africa imitated these kinds of schools. Every religious *zaouia* (a Sufi institution) had its own children's school. They grew respectful of scholars and teachers and granted them money. In the beginning, most teachers were from North Africa, but they were soon afterwards replaced by a generation of West Africans who, having received proper education, began teaching their own people and gathering books into public libraries in mosques.

The child first used to learn chosen *surate,* verses of the Qur'an, and then he studied Qur'an-issued Islamic sciences, such as commentary of Qur'an (*tafsir*), grammar, rhetoric, conjugation, fikh (Muslim doctrine), and the law of descent and distribution. Those wishing to undertake higher studies traveled to Fez or Cairo. Courses included explanations and dialectic and doctrinal debates. Grammar courses consisted of conclusion and analysis; students read the literary text, discussed some grammatical issues, then sort out the rule.[74]

THE INFLUENCE OF ISLAM IN WEST AFRICA ON ECONOMIC RELATIONS BETWEEN AFRICA AND EUROPE

I will conclude this study with an analysis of economic consequences resulting from the spread of Islam in Africa, particularly in trade, and the influence it had on African-European relations in the eleventh century. Thanks to Islam, the people of West Africa were no longer isolated and commercial centers and markets emerged, such as Timbuktu, Ùdaghusht, and Jana. Since the introduction of the Arabic language in the region, West African trade ceased to be 'silent.' Business instruments were written in Arabic. With the introduction of checks and the multiplication of roads and markets, trade no longer relied on barter.

However, the most important result is the unification of the markets of North Africa and West Africa by the Almoravids. As the Almoravids extended their political authority from Andalusia to Bilad Sùdan, their economy became stronger. Trade with Europe increased, particularly in slaves and gold trade, which resulted in a development of ports — as described by geographers.[75]

Because of the unification of West African markets and goods with the Almoravids' markets in North Africa and due to the gold trade monopoly, the Almoravid dinar became a widely appreciated currency in international trade. It was used as far a field as Constantinople[76] and Northern Spain where it was known as *metical* or *metcal*, which are derivatives of the Arabic word *mithcal*.[77] In the *Al Hawliyat Al Qachtalia*, it was known as "El moravididoro," the Almoravid gold dinar. It was also found in Portuguese texts.[78] Among documents found in the *Delcamps* monastery in South Toulouse, were Almoravid dinars.[79] A study which analyzed many Almoravid coins dating back between 1050 and 1200, showed that the Almoravids played a major role in the distribution of West African gold in the Mediterranean Sea and Europe.[80]

It is unlikely that popularity of the Almoravid dinar in the eleventh century occurred without the contribution of West African gold. A researcher even called it "the Middle Ages dollar,"[81] because of the radical change caused by West African gold on trade relations between Africa and Europe,[82] as the monetary system in Mediterranean exchanges between Western Europe and Africa shifted to a gold standard instead of a silver standard.[83] This confirms the emergence of Africa in the eleventh century and the eminent role that it began to play in relations with Europe, thanks to West African gold and the unification of West African markets with North African markets. This was a result of the introduction of Islam in West Africa and its unification under the Almoravid authority.

Endnotes

1. See, for example:
    - P. Clark, *West Africa and Islam*, (London, 1982).
    - J. C. Froelich, *Essai sur les causes et les methodes de l'Islamisation de l'Afrique de l'ouest du IX au XX siècle*, (Oxford University Press, 1969).
    - Gouilly, *L'Islam dans l'Afrique occidentale*. (Paris, 1912).
    - J. S. Trimingham, *A History of Islam in West Africa*. (Oxford, 1970).
2. Ibn Khaldùn. *Kitab al I'bar*, (Dar al-fikr, Beyrouth, 1981), T6, p. 142.
3. N. Kadah, *Ifrikia al- gharbia fi zili al-Islam*, Alger (second edition), p. 48.
4. *Kitab al-hùlal al mawshiyya* (Dar al-rachad al-haditha, Casablanca, 1979)), p. 17.
5. F. DeLachapelle, "Esquisse d'une histoire du sahara occidentale", Hes., (1990), T: XI, Fas I-II, p. 24.
6. Al-Bakri. *Al-Mùghrib fi dhikr bilad Ifrikia wal-maghrib*. (Alger, 1911), p. 13.
7. H. A. Mahmoud, *Al-Islam wa thakafa al-Arabia fi Ifrikia*. (Cairo, 1984), pp. 202–206
8. Ibn Abi Zar'e, *Rawad al-kirtas* (Dar al Mansùr, Rabat, 1973), p. 172; Ibn Idari, *Al bayn-al Mughrib fi akhbar al-Andalùs wal-maghrib*, (Beyrouth, 1980), T1, p. 7.
9. Ibn al Khalib, *A'emal al-'elam*. (Casablanca, 1964), T3, pp. 225–226.
10. A. Ch'ira, *Al-Murabitùn: Tarikhùhùm assïassi*. (Cairo, 1969), p. 39.
11. M. A. Inan, *A'sr al-mùrabitine wal Mùahidine fi al-maghrib wal Andalùs*. (Cairo, 1964), T1, p. 302.
12. I. M. Al-Jamal, "Al-Imam Abdùllah ben yassine fi ribat a sinighal" *Madjalat al-bahth el I'lmi*, no: 10, (1967), p. 253.
13. J. Marçais, *La berberie Musulmane et l'orient au moyen âge*, (Paris, 1946), p. 74.
14. Al-Bakri, op. cit. p. 17.
15. E. W. Bovill, *The golden trade of the Moors*, (Oxford University Press, London, 1958), p. 74.
16. I. A. Dandash, *Dawr al-Mùrabitine fi nashr al Islam fi gharb Ifrikia* (Dar al-gharb al Islami, Beyrouth, 1988), p. 103.
17. Awe Bolantie, *Empires of Western Sudan*, (Ibadan University Press, 1967), p. 35.

18. Al-Bakri, op. cit., pp. 172–175.
19. *Al-hùlal al mawshiyya*, p. 7.
20. Anta Diop, *l'Afrique noire pre-coloniale*, p. 69.
21. Dandash, op.cit., p. 114.
22. Ibid., p. 116.
23. Ibn Abi Zar'e, op. cit., p. 136.
24. Anta Diop, op. cit., p. 69.
25. Dandash, *Rihlat Abù Bakr al-Maafiri*, op. cit., p. 106.
26. Dandash, op. cit., p. 127.
27. H. Terrasse, *Histoire du Maroc* (Casablanca, 1946) T1, p. 213.
28. Oulil is today the city of Saint Etienne in Senegal.
29. A. Zaki, *Al Islam wal Mùslimùne fi gharb Ifrikia* (Cairo, 1969), p. 6.
30. Trimingham, *A History of Islam in West Africa*, (Oxford University, London, 1962), p. 31.
31. Mahdi Razq Allah, *Harakat attidjara wal Islam wa ta'lim al Islami fi gharb Ifrikia kabl al Isti'mar wa atharùha al hadaria*, (Riyadh, 1998), p. 67
32. Ibid., p. 67.
33. C. Vanacker, *Géographie économique de l'Afrique du Nord selon les auteurs Arabes du IXe siècle J'usqu'au milieu du XIIe siècle*, Annales E.S.C, (1973), p. 667.
34. *Kitab Al Istibsar*, (Casablanca, 1985), p. 207.
35. Al-Omari, *Masalik al-absar*, (manuscript of Rabat library, no 2642), T3, p. 110
36. Al-Idrissi. *Nùzhat al mùshtak*, (Alger, 1957), p. 3.
37. Froelish, op. cit., p. 169.
38. T. Arnold, *Adda'ewa lil Islam*, (Cairo, 1971), Translated by Hassan Ibrahim Hassan, pp. 391–461.
39. Mahmoud Kaàt, *Tarikh al fattach*, (Berdin, Angi, 1913), p. 17.
40. A. Assaadi, *Tarich assoudan*, (Angi, Paris, 1898), p. 2, ch: 1.
41. Ibid., pp. 81–82.
42. Z. Riadh, *Al-mamalik al-Islamia fi gharb Ifrikia*, p. 129.
43. A. I. Taïbi, *Dirasat wa Bùhùth fi tarikh al-Maghrib wal Andalùs*, p. 308.
44. Mahdi Razq Allah, op. cit., p. 48.
45. H. A. Mahmoud, op. cit., pp. 223–235.

46. Al-Bakri, op. cit., p. 172.
47. Dandash, op. cit., p. 150.
48. Al-Bakri, op. cit., pp. 175–76.
49. Ibn Khaldùn, *Kitab al I'bar* (Dar al kitab alùbnani, Beyrouth, 1956), p. 413.
50. Tarikh Assoudan, p. 12.
51. *Kitab al-Mùghrib*, pp. 168–179.
52. Ibid., p. 158.
53. Ibn Khaldùn, op. cit., p. 181.
54. Assaadi, op. cit., p. 30.
55. *Rihlat Abù Bakr al-Maafiri*, p. 680.
56. Al-Bakri, op. cit., p. 164.
57. Assaadi, op. cit., p. 18.
58. *Ifrikia al-gharbia fi zili al Islam*, p. 167.
59. Al-Bakri, op. cit., p. 158.
60. Ibid., p. 175.
61. Assaadi, op. cit, p. 16.
62. Ibid., 18
63. Ibid., p. 21.
64. Ibid., pp. 62–63.
65. H. A. Mahmoud, op. cit, pp. 85–86.
66. Froelich, op. cit, p. 163.
67. H. A. Mahmoud, op. cit., p. 86.
68. Al-Bakri, op. cit., p. 175.
69. Mahdi Razq Allah (A), op. cit., p. 294.
70. Trimingham, *The Influence of Islam Upon Africa*, (Lùbnane, 1986), p. 60.
71. Assaadi, op. cit., pp. 23–25.
72. I. A. Dandash, op. cit., p. 94.
73. Mahmoud Kaàt, op. cit., p. 94.
74. N. Kaddah, op. cit., p. 161.
75. Ibn Said, *Kitab al-djùrafia*, (Beyrouth, 1970), p. 139; Al-Bakri, op. cit., p. 109.

76. H. A. Mahmoud, *Kiam dawlat al Mùrabitine,* (Cairo, 1957), p. 403.
77. A. T. Taïbi, op. cit., p. 309.
78. J. Devisse, "Routes de commerce et échanges en Afrique occidentale en relation avec la mediterranée : un essai sur le commerce Africain Médiéval du XIe au XVI e siecle," RHES, vol : l, no: 1, 1972, p. 57.
79. Lopez, "Le facteur economique dans la politique africaine," RH, 1974, p. 178, 18.
80. Messier. "Quantitative analysis of Almoravid dinars," JESHO, 1980, p. 8.
81. S. D. Goitein, *Letters of medieval Jewish traders,* (Princeton University Press), p. 325.
82. J. Devisse, op. cit., p. 52.
83. A. Luis, *al-kiwa al Bahria wa tidjaria fi hawd al bahr al Mùtawasit,* translated into Arabic by Ahmed Mohamed Aissa, (Dar annahda al Misria, Cairo, n.d.), p. 393.

Hes. = hesperis

RH = Revue d'Histoire

JESHO = Journal of the Economic and Social History of the Orient.

RHES = Revue d'Histoire Economique et Sociale.

Vol. = volume.

T = tome

4

Islam and Christianity in Uganda: Conflict, Dialogue, and Search for Partnership

JAMES NDYABAHIKA

This chapter attempts to quantify the quality and quantity of Islam and Christianity, which Ugandans have been able to imbed since the two historical religions penetrated the nation. Both Islam and Christianity have "east" as their birthplace and emerged from almost the same area. Both are foreign to Uganda. No wonder the faithful are still discussing ways and means of making these two religions part and parcel of their culture, customs, religious faith, and way of life.

Within this context, reference needs to be made that there is lack of serious investigation that treats the idea of Muslim-Christian relations and dialogue as a topic worthy of study in its own right.[1] This unfortunately has been mercilessly overlooked. The topic is significant as it relates to men and women in the mainline Churches, Islam, new religious movements, and people of other faith or no faith. All these suggest the need to compare and contrast the claims of numerous religious uprisings, but with much more substance and without Christian polemics. It is from this vantage point that an impartial, balanced, and empirical assessment is paramount.[2]

In the light of this perspective, I may be excused if I approach this topic from a slightly different perspective. I will begin with two observations before I give a résumé on the advent of Islam and Christianity. This will be followed by the centrality of this chapter, which is "confrontation, tolerance and dialogue towards a better understanding." I will conclude with areas of genuine dialogue without compromise. The reason for this is clear; "Muslim-Christian dialogue" will form a new agenda for the twenty-first century — not only in our nation, Uganda but also in Africa, South of the Sahara.

CRITICAL OBSERVATION

Today, when people are traveling in Uganda they see the old guesthouses that once served as night camps for the governors and their entourage. The one time symbol of colonial rule is starting to crumble. White ants and tropical vegetation overwhelm them. Several questions are raised, although this chapter will not answer them directly. Will the Church be the next to meet its fate as it happened in North Africa, where the one time vibrant church of Tertullian, Cyprian, and Augustine disappeared without a trace during the eighth century and Islam reigns to this day?[3] Will the worshipping community indulge in a fruitful dialogue with Muslims and continue to act as an activating leaven at the grassroots level? Will the prophetic voice of 'interfaith relations' address the prevailing issues relating to corruption, social injustices, religious disharmony, ethnic strife, and backwardness?

The second observation relates to pluralism. At the present time, most Ugandans live in a nation that is religiously diverse. It would, therefore, be naïve to minimize the growth of a number of people adhering to faiths other than Islam and Christianity. Due to the influence of globalization, pluralism has been pre-eminently advancing in the nation during the second half of the last century. Pluralism can mean many things. It can mean the proliferation of different religions not as isolated or self-contained or inferior to one's own. It can also mean the presence of diverse ideologies and openness to receive from other religious traditions something of their experiences of "one and the same God" — Allah, the Supreme Being.

To avoid a false start, it is significant to affirm that the age of considering other faiths as inferior to one's own is over. The uniqueness of one religion, as opposed to other religions, does not arise any more. Natural interaction is the music of the day. Accordingly, different religions receive insight and contribute to the growth of each other in order to arrive at the content of faith — experience geared to concrete reality.

THE COMING OF ISLAM AND CHRISTIANITY TO UGANDA

The rise of Islam, as a powerful religion, was a turning point in the history of the world.[4] When it penetrated the continent of Africa, in the seventh century, it deeply influenced and radically transformed the political, social, and religious structures of the countries it came into contact with. In some states, it is the predominant religion — the only universal religion to rise after Christianity. In East Africa, Islamic influence came from the Arabian Peninsula. From the tenth century onwards, some Arab traders settled at the Coast and formed Islamic communities up to the coming of the Portuguese in 1498.⁵ Apart from these intruders (Portuguese), who introduced Christianity and established political control on the coast of East Africa, Muslims had more than twelve hundred years of unparalleled opportunity to spread the Islamic faith. One of the obstacles was that they lacked missionary cadres. From 1500–1700, more missionaries came and built churches and established monasteries. As they did not gain many converts, by mid-seventeenth century, they had lost total control of East Africa. On November 26, 1729, their flag was lowered down for the last time. The Arabs regained control of the East African coast and held undisputed monopoly. Their trading centers became the bases for teaching the Islamic faith. This venture came to an end in the 1840s, when the missionaries of the Church Missionary Society came on the scene. Islam again faced Christianity. It also faced other challenges, such as religious competitiveness and the concomitant decline of its membership. It was by no accident, therefore, in the same year, Muslim traders began to penetrate the hinterland of East Africa.

Next, Islam spearheaded by Muslim traders, who exchanged material and spiritual goods, was the first foreign religion to reach Uganda (1844).⁶ The Islamists firmly believed that *Allah* (God) had sent them to a specific nation, at a specific time, to proclaim a specific message through teaching and preaching. Progressively, they were assisted by the technological superiority of the coastal Swahili people. Their contacts were regular and unbroken. Ahmad bin Ibrahim started to teach the indigenous people some tenets of Islamic faith.⁷ Together with his team they introduced new patterns of thought, new material products, and commerce which altered the socio-economic and religious relationships of the Baganda people. Despite their zeal in stressing that a Muslim cannot live his/her religious life alone, by the time King Suuna died, fifteen valuable years had passed and Islamic influence had not taken root. During the reign of Mutesa I, the successor of Sunna (1856), Arabs continued to come to Uganda. The King was taught the alphabet and privately given instructions in various chapters of the Qur'an. Although uncircumcised, he led *Juma* prayers in a Mosque, which he had built at the palace. In the 1860s, he ordered all his subjects to observe Islamic rites, customs, and traditions. It is no secret that some of the indigenous people, instead of being fetish worshippers, suddenly became incurably religious and accepted *Allah* as the Supreme Being. The king forbade his subjects from eating meat not butchered according to Islamic law. He also prohibited the possession of dogs, although his subjects were very fond of hunting. He even went to the extent of sending missionaries to other parts of Uganda.⁸

It is because of this reality that Islam not only made a psychological revolution, which made it possible for the indigenous people to listen to and later embrace other foreign religious beliefs, but also awakened certain aspirations *par excellence* among the untutored indigenous people. Examples abound — an idea of a holy book, a holy day, a moral life, a religious calendar, the resurrection of the body, and the judgment after death. The notion of paradise, prayers for specific purposes, and of God who is above all gods (the Supreme Being — the compassionate ruler of the universe) became the cornerstone of their religious life. The missionaries equated *Allah* with God, the Father of Jesus Christ. These were some of the religious concepts pioneered by Islam, which received further emphasis by the Christian missionaries.[9] But circumcision *(khitan)* was a real barrier to most 'truth seekers' who hated any kind of mutilation. The Baganda culture rejected circumcision and prohibited the shedding of royal blood. That said, however, the king remained uncircumcised despite his zeal in Islamic faith. All this indicates that he only added *Allah* to the hierarchy of Baganda's traditional gods. If the Arabs and younger Islamic converts understood this, they diplomatically and culturally kept their mouths shut.

As the century progressed, new developments took place. The Anglican missionaries of the Church Missionary Society (CMS) followed Muslims in the religious field in 1877. They registered a high degree of dedication, seldom equaled and never surpassed.[10] Two years later, in 1879, they were joined by the Catholic missionaries of the Society of African Missions who are commonly known as the French "White Fathers" (WF).[11] Initially, the Roman Catholics dedicated their missionary enterprise to a powerful patron — the Blessed Virgin Mary. To the faithful Catholics, Uganda became truly the kingdom of Mary — *"regnum Ugandae, regnum Mariae."* More significantly, both missions (the Anglicans and Roman Catholics) did not function haphazardly. They had clear-cut philosophical objectives, administrative policies, and religious practices. Their theory and practice in the humanitarian service effected social formations and transformations of the indigenous people in the areas of educational programmes, medical services, literature, planting of mission stations, and other forms of spiritual, moral, and social development. More often than not, they encouraged their followers to think for themselves, to reflect on their own religious experiences, to cultivate positive moral values, and to open their minds in search of a meaningful purpose in life.[12] The most salient features of the two historical religions were accepted as supplement rather than substitute of the indigenous religious obligations and code of conduct.

This scenario sets a useful stage to highlight some points that contributed to the failure of Islam to penetrate Uganda. First was the small number of Arab traders in Buganda who could teach the Islamic faith. The reasons for this small number remain a mystery. Secondly, the Baganda were opposed to the Arabs trading directly with other kingdoms around Lake Victoria (currently the Great Lakes Region). Lastly, the Arabs were finding it extremely difficult and unprofitable to come to Buganda because they were paying heavy taxes to the chiefs in Central Tanganyika (present Tanzania). In all seriousness, the absence of a big number of Arabs was the main cause of the decline of Islamic influence.

RELIGIOUS CONFRONTATIONS AND TOLERANCE

Between 1870–1880, the religio-political situation changed more drastically.[13] The climax came in 1874 when the king, who observed the month of *Ramadan*, led *Juma* prayers and was well-versed in some Qur'anic tenets, turned against the young Muslims and more than seventy were executed.[14] The most hit were the royal pages (*Bagalagala*). The oasis of peace and tranquility at the palace suddenly became the focus of terror and death. In fact, more than three hundred pages escaped with Arabs to the Coast of East of Africa.[15] The question, one might ask is, was the king a truth seeker or an adventure seeker? Several reasons are advanced as to why he executed the *Bagalagala*. First, the *Bagalagala* had developed a separate loyalty, which challenged (among other things) his political, cultural, and religious rights. Secondly, they refused to eat pork saying that it was unclean. Lastly, they disobeyed the king when he accorded them numerous opportunities of grace to recant. For these acts of treason, they were either executed or burnt to death.

On religious grounds, their martyrdom served as an inspiration to the Muslim community in the nation ever since. Muslims woke up; their trading centers enhanced not only legitimate trade with the outside world, which supplanted the indigenous practices, but also became the propagating stations. Furthermore, the blood of the martyrs became the seed of Islamic growth. In the same regard, a number of people who had joined the Islamic faith for convenience rather than out of conviction became stronger in their religious commitment. In retrospect, the Islamic faith continued unabated, and by the 1880s there were more Muslim chiefs than in any other religion. This was a victory to Islam. Although, in 1886 some Christians (who were later known as the Uganda martyrs) were massacred,[16] the fact remains that the Muslims proved to be stronger, better organized, and the most formidable group militarily.

To make the aforementioned points more explicit, within a period of four years (1888), they re-organized themselves, staged a coup, and installed a new King. After swearing to pay allegiance to the Islamic code of conduct, King Kalema was circumcised, took an Islamic name (Nuhu), and re-ordered the kingdom along Islamic theocratic lines.[17] This marked the climax of the religious and political ascendancy of Islam. At best, the Muslim *Junta* convinced Christians to believe that theocracy was the only government possible for all true believers. But the general public was, for the most part, unaware of, and unconcerned about foreign, bizarre, or Islamic beliefs and practices. At worst, the new Muslim *junta* ravaged the country, caused much misery, political turmoil, and moral decay. Surprisingly, Muslim scholars hardly admit this today.[18] Besides, King Nuhu Kalema initiated a policy of forced conversion. Accordingly, circumcision was obligatory. Nothing is more striking than the fact that after his victory, the fanatical Muslims preached a *jihad* message against Christians and the traditionalists. They made unsuccessful attempts to convert the whole country. They saw Christian missionaries as opportunists and political intruders to their gained territory. The result was suspicion and confrontation. Hence, all Catholic and Anglican missionaries were forced to leave.[19] Nuhu Kalema's reign was cut short in 1890 by his death. This gruesome and tragic end of his life marked the climax of the religious and political ascendancy of Islam.

Between the years 1890–1893, a combined force of Christians and Traditionalists mounted aggressive counterattacks. They first cut short the Muslim military supply before they destroyed the Arab shops. It cannot be denied; thick clouds over-shadowed their bright future. Facing gun-armed Christians and a spear-handed revamped force of the Traditionalists, the Muslims were defeated ignominiously and retreated northward into exile. Christians and the Baganda Traditionalists won the day. From the 1890s onwards, Muslims were a defeated people, a small scattered disadvantaged minority, politically discriminated, socially ostracized, and have remained ever since peripheral to Ugandan life.[20] Narrowing down the scope of our argument, by the turn of the century, the nation had gone through several phases of revolutions — a Muslim revolution (1888–1889), a Christian revolution (1889–1892), a Nubian revolution (1893), and a British revolution, which culminated into the British takeover (1894).[21] Although the colonial government enhanced religious liberty and political hope, by 1900 the Islamic faith was not advancing. On the contrary, it was retreating. Muslims entered the twentieth century as a defeated party — relegated to three poor counties of Gomba, Busuju, and Butambala, where they have stayed ever since.²² It was difficult for them, as spreaders of Islamic faith, to call upon masses to join them. They could only teach people on an individual basis. Under these circumstances, they had no outside body that could help them to initiate a mass conversion campaign in any way. Weeks led to months and months led to years. With no other foreseeable way out of this dilemma, Muslims remained in the three counties preserving their Islamic heritage with their strange manner of dressing (*turbans*) that made them look foreign to most Ugandans.

Between 1901 and 1960, nothing more significant happened, except that the British government was anxious to maintain the political balance of power by keeping the Protestants and Catholics in good positions. Under these conditions, the Baganda Muslims and a few Swahili (or Arab) traders introduced the Islamic faith to other areas outside Buganda. Without the aid of those in power, the Islamic team failed to make impressive headway. There is also a related point here. Chieftainships and other appointments continued to be made on religious grounds. As the years went by, both religions taught their followers, logically and consistently, what it was that divided them rather than what they had in common. These are sad facts of the past, which make a sorry reading.²³

During the 1960s and the first half of the 1970s, religio-political competitions, sectarianism, and rival sentiments of the nineteenth century surfaced after Uganda attained independence. They served to undermine rather than to attract new converts to their respective denominations.²⁴ This was a cause of regret and embarrassment to any true believer. Muslims, at this material time, were looked upon as political commodities to assist the ruling regime. The story of their involvement in politics, social services, and public life is a complex one, the details of which should not detain us here. However, one of the major setbacks of their failure to be involved in policy matters resulted into the formulation of laws that were repugnant or not favorable to their ways of life. Some intelligent Muslims resented this because the reciprocal benefits were very minimum and limited. Sadly, there were very few Muslims in top political positions. This feeling of imbalance persisted on for some time. Such tendencies retarded the religious programmes, health services, and educational systems of Uganda for the following decades. At worst, when these unhappy relationships were institutionalized in the politics of the 1960s, they culminated into internal strife and wars. To make our argument more forceful, in 1971 when Idi Amin overthrew the Obote regime in a bloodless coup, the total population of Muslims was less than two percent. Amin Dada's outrageous reign of tyranny — characterized by scanty respect of human rights — lead to unspeakable atrocities and sporadic killings. As if that was not enough, he enticed people to become Muslims. It is in this respect that the kingdom of *Allah* locked horns with the kingdom of Christ. Muslims saw the Christians as a threat to their goal of building an Islamic community. By the time Amin was overthrown (1979), the population of Muslims had swelled (Muslims claim) to six percent.

There is also a related point. Idi Amin Dada wished to transform Uganda into an Islamic state. To fulfill his dream, in the 1970s he unilaterally forced the nation to become a member of an Islamic world cooperation. He was convinced that "the religion of the ruler should be the religion of the state" (*cujus regio, ejus religio*).[25] Accordingly, his rule culminated into anarchy and the nation experienced social change, rampant corruption, economic inefficiency, ethnic strife, and widespread infringement of human rights. This amounted to genocide and political disharmony.[26] Most Ugandans felt that they had reached the bottom line of misery. Amin's lack of formal education contributed to his inability to realize the limits of changing religious practices and social services in a single generation. The idea of peaceful co-existence, natural respect, and genuine dialogue did not exist in his vocabulary. Those who sought to build bridges of mutual respect and understanding were in short supply. It was not easy to see a way out of this dilemma. As far as the writer was able to understand, the subsequent history of religious involvement in politics was a cause of regret and embarrassment for any true believer. This was far from bringing the gospel of love, unity, and peace. It is just recently that some religious people began to realize the foolishness and backwardness of inheriting imported negative attitudes.[27]

With these sentiments in mind, it should be pointed out that from 1980–2000 and particularly during the reign of Yoweri Kaguta Museveni, there has been a change for the better. The Muslim-Christian relations changed gears from confrontation to tolerance and dialogue. Today, there are healthy signs within the local communities. Muslims (Sunni, Tabliqs, Juma-Zukuri, Sufi, Shia, and Ahmadiyya) and Christians (Anglicans, Catholics, Orthodox, Pentecostals, and Seventh-day Adventists) live in villages as neighbors. They have collectively built health centers, dispensaries, maternity homes, and schools in their localities. Their co-operation and co-existence cement their relationship. In the government sector, they are offering good leadership. There is little doubt that they are tirelessly contributing to the developmental projects and cultivating religious morals in terms of social ethics and discipline. In so far as truth abides with power, Muslims are now having a fair share of the loaf of the national political power. Ugandans witness trucks on the streets with Islamic labels — Islamic Medical Association of Uganda or Islamic African Relief Agency. As if this is not enough, in 1988, the Muslims founded their own University in Mbale. Recently, due to promises of educational bursaries and financial economic assistance, a number of Christians are crossing over to Islam.[28]

One may ask why the writer has referred to the historical growth of Islam and Christianity. He is of the view that history is a sure guide for the present and for the future. The present is a consequence of the past, and the future is the result of the present. To put the matter simply, any attempt to explain the present without reference to the past remains superficial and misleading. In a multireligious milieu of our nation, most Ugandans are aware that knowledge of the past is precisely the key that unlocks new possibilities for the future. In this vein, the historical growth of Islam and Christianity has been studied objectively and analyzed subjectively.

It is fitting to end this subsection by stressing that the age of confrontation has passed. Lasting peace is on the horizon. The ominous clouds looming are signaling that the era of dialogue is the beginning of a new age and the religious history of confrontation (between Islam and Christianity) may end up as a footnote in the third millennium. Fruitful dialogue, supported by rational proof, clears the way for truth and truth in turn becomes a verification mode. Thus, dialogue is an essential feature and a solemn sign of religious concern. This concern is a new phenomenon that shuns any manner of particularism. The faithful believers are tired of wars, fragile democracies, religious bigotry, oppression of women, and seeing displaced people in their neighbourhoods. Ugandans take their religions seriously; their relation with each other is an important point that will contribute to the slow emergence of national religious identity. It is now possible to secure areas of common recognition. This is in conformity with an indigenous proverb, which says, "if the rhythm of the drum changes, the dancer must change his/her dancing steps as well." Armed with such rebuttals, we now turn to the discussion about tolerance between Muslims and Christians.

DIALOGUE WITHOUT COMPROMISE AND INTERFAITH RELATIONS

No discussion of religious dialogue can avoid the following questions — How do the major religions in Uganda handle the facts of diversity and conflicting truth-claims? Does tolerance require the abandonment of one's religious commitment to universal truth? What is the distinctiveness of the

Christian or Islamic message in a nation of diverse faiths? What can Christians learn from Muslims through their struggle to live with integrity and faithfulness as a minority in a nation?

This subsection is an attempt to address such challenging issues. For the sake of clarity, dialogue[29] is a religious interaction that brushes aside any encumbrance and determines one's knowledge. It enhances a religious meeting place that has new agendas, new values, and new attitudes. The characteristic thing to note, therefore, is that dialogue deals with tensions, eschews past prejudices, and avoids confusion. It is a healthy conversation between two or more persons, who exchange views and distinguish the truth from error and good from evil. It is a type of reflection, which by right belongs to the universality of all people beyond geographical and religious frontiers. It is a commitment to overcome misunderstandings that might have been built up between communities. Some misunderstandings may relate to the past colonial rule or to the ludicrous theological stereotypes or to the inherited hermeneutic paradigms. Instead of, for example, criticizing, ridiculing, or creating barriers of language and defensiveness, the faithful have to forge ahead and share some important religious beliefs and inspirations that make mutual conversation possible.

To maintain a floor of meaningful dialogue, improved demands between different sides of believers have to be considered and these largely take the form of issues to be overcome. Each partner, in the fruitful dialogue, has to listen with a sincere desire to understand and articulate within his or her heart, what the other is saying, although with critical tolerance and moral compassion. The implication here is that those who have no room for dialogue can only be regarded as fanatics.

Fruitful dialogue is impeded when one side sees the other as a threat. Dialogue should be free from superiority and chauvinism. It does not entertain confessionalism or proclamatory elements. This is a challenge to be taken seriously. A chorus of voices claims that efforts should be made to engage in genuine and meaningful communication that will enable both sides to accept with courage and humility the possibility of taking risks, which involve undergoing change. There is no room for isolation. The faithful Christians should not compromise their religious principals or sacrifice their religious commitment. This is in conformity with an indigenous proverb, which says: *"even if a log remains in a river for one hundred years, it will not become a crocodile."* Today, dialogue takes on different forms — the witness of mutual respect, spiritual sharing, doctrinal discussion, and active collaboration in life. At another level, it is accepted as a primary tool for reconciliation. In this context, there are no longer shortages of topics for serious considerations. For example, at the grassroots level, the faithful can reclaim and sanctify the kind of possibilities that come to them, everyday, in market places, waiting for the buses (taxis), working in gardens, walking on the way, or chatting in their sitting rooms. This kind of dialogue sometimes involves a conversation or an advice or a word of encouragement.

Dialogue can also be carried out through informal meetings. Muslims and Christians can sit around a table and exchange views on the use of spiritual concepts like peace and God, religious healing, dreams, prophesy speaking in tongues, and prayers as points of contact.[30] Furthermore, it is important to mention that the story of Jesus Christ as Son of Mary, Messiah, Servant of God, Spirit of God, or Mary, the mother of Jesus, who is used in the Qur'an as a symbol of purity, perfection, and righteousness, could be discussed.[31] On the same platform, the idea of Allah (God) could be developed. Such a forum of dialogue will keep the faithful from unwelcome triumphalism and offer the way forward. To ignore them is to confine Muslims and Christians into religious ghettos. On this note, the words of Bishop Taylor, written over twenty years ago, are still timely as he made a balanced and forward-looking comment when he said:

> Dialogue, as I understand it, means a sustained conversation between parties who are not saying the same thing and who recognize and respect the differences, the contradictions, and the mutual exclusions between various ways of thinking. The object of this dialogue is understanding and appreciation, leading to further reflection upon the implication for one's own position of the convictions and sensitivities of other traditions.[32]

While concurring with Taylor and admitting that fruitful dialogue will be impeded if one side sees the other as a threat, the writer is of the view that efforts should be made by the faithful to engage in genuine and meaningful communication. If public meetings for dialogue are of no avail or they fail to attract an audience, printed materials should be used and distributed (or radios and television programmes could fill the gaps). This will enable both sides to accept with courage and humility the possibility of taking risks, which involve undergoing changes. To put it differently, radical change does not mean that one should give up his or her position and accept the other religious ethos in *toto* (or unconditionally), without critical analysis and evaluation. These are examples worthy of being followed. In fact, dialogue demands "the faithful must listen to each other carefully and more respectfully without ceasing to be conscious of the tenets of his or her respective religion."

Now, the point to be stressed is that, as we face the third millennium, dialogue should not fizzle out or lose some of its steam. In fact, new topics for discussions should be re-framed which will enable Muslims and Christians not to indulge in accusations against or condemnation of one another, but to cherish lessons that can be learned from the successes and failures of each other. It is only at the platform of fruitful dialogue where Muslims and Christians will cherish that they are brothers and sisters. Besides, there are now several areas where they will participate and rub shoulders together — in marriage celebrations, funeral rites, burials, and other *rites de passage*. In the light of these cultural realities, dialogue will bridge the gap, broaden horizons, and guide the faithful to find ways of drawing nearer to each other and establishing new principles of co-existence in spite of their doctrinal and liturgical differences. The analysis of Namwera on this matter is very helpful. Writing from a Christian perspective, he succinctly declares: [33]

- Christians should actively collaborate with Muslims, wherever possible, to conscientize the faithful on basic human rights and the values shared by both religions.

- Muslims studying in Christian Schools should be welcomed; this may be seen as an occasion to impart the national values, such as justice, love, forgiveness, without formal preaching.

- At all levels, Christian pupils should be taught the basic doctrine and precepts of Islam.

- Christian women should support other groups that bring together women of various religions to fight for equality with men.

- Social services sponsored by the Church should be rendered without religious discrimination like health services, distribution of food to the needy, services for refugees, and rehabilitation programmes.

From these five points, it is clear that dialogue is a pre-condition for true conversation of hearts that promote fellowship. Efforts should therefore be made to continue genuine and meaningful communication as a pre-requisite for true fellowship.[34] In this respect, dialogue will heal the wounds of past divisions and hatred. But this would not be possible unless and until parties involved in dialogue are ready to dialogue as equals.

In the light of these realities, we now look at viable areas of interfaith relations at a community and national level. Nevertheless, an undeniable rift has been brought to or created on the soil of our nation by the contemporary 'global village,' which has brought about mingling of religions on a scale that our parents never imagined. What this entails is that Christians and

Muslims must charter new avenues, which will enrich their relations and enhance cooperation. To fulfill this mission, they have to discover new resources, which will enhance cooperation without compromise. They have to be aware of the inherited, often unconscious attitudes which lurk under the surface. More often than not, conflicts over the truth may boil down or erupt into hatred and sometimes even into violence. Families have been torn apart and brothers or sisters cast asunder with wounds, which linger and fester, long after they have been made. From time to time conflicts break up, and morass confusion enhances "new crusades" and endeavors to spoil the good atmosphere of understanding that may have temporarily prevailed. The conflict of that magnitude is not easy to resolve and may require religious ethicists to stretch into the realm of apologetics in order to effectively influence those involved. It is therefore paramount that in their struggle for religious or economic or political justice, both religious groups must advance the teachings of the Qur'an and the prophetic messages of the Bible.[35] Whatever religious traditions they belong to and whatever religious convictions they hold, they must teach that the whole life belongs to God, to whom all people are responsible for their entire social, political, economic, and religious actions. To say this, is not to advance that they should surrender their holistic religious commitments.

CHRISTIAN ATTITUDE

Christians of every shade of belief — from the die-hards to the fundamentalists — teach that salvation is deliverance from the consequences of sin (spiritual) and social injustices and backwardness (physical). They outrightly advance that "biblical truth cannot be watered down." This kind of teaching rests entirely on God's merciful action in Christ. The faithful call this teaching, saving knowledge. Directly or indirectly, this calculated teaching is repeated every Sunday or every day to those who study the Bible. To both classes, it cements their commitment and permeates all the departments of their spiritual lives.[36] Christians have come to believe that there is no trace of Christianity's salvific perspective in Islam or other New Religious Movements and their adherents (who have attracted a sizeable working class or the unemployed youth or the inner city down-and-outs) will be judged unless they renounce and abandon their religious beliefs and turn to Jesus Christ.[37] It is for these reasons that the objective call of the faithful Christians is not, as the crusaders believed, the repossession of what the Christendom had lost, but for the restoration to Muslims of Christ whom they have missed.[38] In a nutshell, the Christian approach to all aspects of disciplines of education, and not only theological or spiritual, is a great task that awaits the faithful in this century. All truth is God's truth. Thus, to the faithful the twenty-first century is not a time to shrink from fruitful dialogue.

MUSLIM ATTITUDE

On the other hand, Muslims advance that the chief yardstick to determine faithfulness to Islamic faith, a believer had to confess that there is no god besides *Allah* (God) and Muhammad is his prophet. This confession is the core of Islamic faith and it occupies a central position in every respect of the faithful Muslims because *Allah* is the first and the *last*, All knowing and All wise.[39] Accordingly, Islam articulates that its doctrines are easy to grasp. Muslims also articulate that the demands of their faith are not different from those which are common in the indigenous traditional setting. In the light of this awareness, they stressed that the new converts would not have to undergo substantial and rigorous cultural transformations; that joining Islam was a voluntary decision, although like other religious groups some people could be pressured in varying degrees. A holistic understanding behind Islamic traditions, customs, moral actions, and social relations is that — to be is to be religious, in a religious community. Furthermore, it advocates community orientation characterized by friendly co-operation, communal sharing, and charges its adherents to help one another in all fields. It should be pointed out here, more specifically, Muslims uphold that Christians are good neighbors and are the people of the book who became spoilt when the western world instilled in them a message that Christianity is superior and therefore it must be emulated by all. For these reasons, Muslims believe that Christians can be converted to believe in the only true religion, which is Islam. In this vein, it is paramount to draw up some areas in which Christians and Muslims have interacted, tolerated, cooperated, and are continuing to do so in the nation. It is therefore in this context that the following are but a few areas (among many others), which depict serious and strong feelings at the community level. Such feelings are beginning to traverse boundaries, which used to separate Christians and Muslims. They are, however, mentioned primarily as areas of opportunities, which demand Christian-Muslim cooperation, enhancement, and development.[40]

MEDICAL MINISTRIES AND SERVICES [41]

Religious Institutions pioneered medical services, when both the Colonial Government and the Native Authorities had no adequate medical institutions for their subjects especially in the rural areas. They built health centers, dispensaries, and maternity homes. They also established Leprosy services as well as eye clinics and hospitals. Just as in the field of education, the Colonial Government and the Native Authorities needed the help of Religious Institutions in this area. Religious institutions contributed immensely to the state of health, demography, and social well-being of the people. This led to the dichotomy between the 'word' and the 'deed' or the 'spiritual' and the 'social,' which somewhat affected holistic message approach. If Religious Institutions are to serve and meet men and women's total needs, in the twenty first century, they must go beyond this dualistic worldview and the religious expansionism legacy. This is exemplified clearly by the fact that diseases such as AIDS,[42] Ebola, malaria, cholera, typhoid and other epidemics do not discriminate between Christians, Muslims, or followers of other faiths. Christians and Muslims face similar demands everyday. They find themselves as displaced or uprooted people, either due to political or natural resurgence or due to other calamities. This offers them many opportunities that challenge them for concerted efforts of how they should cooperate when they face overwhelming odds or how they should collectively assist those who live at the bottom line of the social strata. The life entrusted to them is precisely in this area of health. This is in conformity with an indigenous proverb, which states categorically that "prevention is better than cure." Failure to cooperate can give rise to misunderstandings or prejudices unless the healing ministry is carried out in an integrated manner.

EDUCATION

For a long time Christian Missionaries held a dominant position as leading pioneers in the fight against illiteracy, ignorance, physical human ailment, and other epidemics. It suffices to say that they used education as a decisive tool in evangelism. Their educational programs included literacy classes, religious instructions, social development, and moral as well as spiritual upbringing. The bulk of the educated civil servants and professionals had their humble beginnings from missionary education programmes and institutions. It is interesting to look back and realize how education was not only the most potent for the transformation of Ugandan societies but also the most effective tool of evangelism. Most people became Christians than by any other means. Consequently, education and Christianity became so intrinsically inseparable that the local people simply came to refer to the Christians as readers or educated. From this very understanding, Muslims saw 'Christian' education as a means of assimilating their followers into the 'Christian' orbit. To protect themselves Muslims took precautions to safeguard their children even to the extent of keeping them out of schools.

Christians also feared to enroll their children in the Qur'anic Schools for fear of disdaining them. Interestingly, Muslims came to realize that by 'neglecting' the opportunity of sending their children to 'Christian' schools they were running the risk of allowing Christians to occupy all prestigious positions of power and responsibility. Through the Qur'anic Schools, Muslims sought to retain their children in the faith, only to discover that Qur'anic recitation did not enable the young people to play their role in the shaping of their destiny. They did not heed to the indigenous proverb, which states that *you were forced to learn but when you finally understood be grateful.* The inescapable conclusion is that there is a great shortage of educated Muslims who are able to guide their fellow Muslims in a rapidly changing society. At the same time Christians have allowed secularism to creep into their education, so that although the vast numbers of educated elite are 'Christians,' they are not capable of dealing with the prevailing situations as 'Christians,' but only as 'professionals.' Christians and Muslims face the challenge of developing education in such a manner that it prepares the nationals to play their part in the growth of their nation.[43]

CONCLUSION AND THE WAY FORWARD

While it is true that Islamic institutions and mosques are multiplying and that Islam is using the mass media much more than before, there is no cause for alarm. This is a process of Islamization that has been going on slowly but surely since Amin became the President of Uganda. The decision to implement this came to him as a celestial communication while he was in Mecca performing a holy pilgrimage. To fulfill his dream, he established the Muslim Supreme Council, made Friday a public holiday, banned a number of Christian denominations, killed some prominent Christians, and forced others into exile. Islamic faith, which was burnished to the margin of political and religious discussions by Christian propaganda at the end of the Victorian Age (1832–1900), seized the central stage during Amin's era. In fact, the process of Islamization increased in the areas where Islamic faith had already been planted. To understand the unfolding significance of Islamic expansionism, it is important to note that its adherents are busy re-assessing their past failures (a history with still open wounds) and injecting new messages of reconciliation, moral sensitivity, and unity; a unit based on the truth lived in love.

It is reassuring to note that the Christians and Muslims are now aware that without religious unity and peaceful co-existence no political, economic, or social ethics can solve the prevailing tribal divisions, corruption, backwardness, and disintegration of the local communities. In order for the faithful Ugandans to have complete peace, justice, and tranquility, they are challenged to know that this is the time to build bridges and allow the spirit of forgiveness to permeate all sections of their lives. New walls of love, speaking the truth, and boundaries of reconciliation will need to be invoked. The holistic approach will stimulate discussions and create new incisive moods for dialogue. More significantly, the faithful should teach and accept the Supreme Being (*Allah*) whose existence is well known. In fact, God (*Allah*) should be invited not only to guide them in their balanced dialogue but also to participate in their respective day-to-day activities.

From the foregoing points, Ugandans should not be surprised at the current upward trend of Islamic expansionism. Islam is a missionary religion. Muslims are commanded in the Qur'an to invite "all" to the way of *Allah*. The centre of gravity of Christianity, too, is shifting from the north to the south especially in Uganda. New Religious Movements and other Oriental Religions (Hinduism, Buddhism, Jainism, or Brahma Kumaris) are invading the nation. All these are universal religions and they would be failing their missionary obligation if they neglect any means and methods of proselytization. All are impelled to share the good news and to invite others to their fellowships. When they are witness to God's converting power, they point to him and not to themselves. These are examples worth being followed. In fact, as the faithful people proceed into the twenty-first century, they must 'listen' to other religions more carefully and more respectfully without a hidden evangelistic agenda. Their religious commitment must be absolute. Never before in the history of Uganda has there been so much contact between adherents of different religions as is today. This said, however, they should hear the sound that rings loud and clear in their ears — *we have come this far by faith, leaning on God.* I beg to conclude this paper with a prayer of St Francis of Assisi:

> Lord, make us instruments of Thy peace:
> Where there is hatred, let us sow love;
> Where there is injury, pardon;
> Where there is discord, union;
> Where there is doubt, faith;
> Where there is despair, hope;
> Where there is darkness, light;
> Where there is sadness, joy;
> For thy mercy and
> Truth' sake. Amen

Endnotes

1. It should be noted that, historically, there has been very little or no dialogue at all between Islam and Christianity. This can easily be exemplified and demonstrated by looking at the recent jihads and crusades waged against each other.

2. Although the writer is handicapped by the fact that this topic has been overlooked, he will do what a detective has to do who is sent out to investigate a crime and of which there are no eyewitnesses. A good detective knows to look for evidence in the shape of the prevailing data (fingerprints, footmarks, and things like that). When he has collected and examined everything very carefully and which may possibly have some connection with the crime, he may be able to prove beyond doubt that the crime was committed and who committed it. Similarly, a historian has to find the piece of evidence that exists; he collects it, examines it very closely, and then by careful comparison and sifting may be able to say what happened and who did it. There are various kinds of evidence for which a historian is always on the lookout. The writer is not going to enumerate them all.

3. These ideas are very well-expressed and enhanced by Stephen C. Neill, *A History of Christian Mission*, (Grand Rapids: Wm. B. Eerdmans Publishing Co., 1964), pp. 62–65; J. B. Webster and Ikime Obero, *Tarikh*, (1967), pp. 16–28; Herbert J. Kane, *A Global View of Christian Muslims from Pentecost to Present*, (Grand Rapids: Baker Book House, 1971), pp 384–385; and Johatnan Hilderbrandt, *History of Christianity in Africa* (Achimota, Ghana: Africa Christian Press, 1981), p. 20.

4. The word "Islam" means to surrender, to seek peace, and to make complete submission (aslam) to the will of Allah. The followers of Islam are called by the corresponding adjective "Muslim," which comes from the same word that suggests a degree of surrender to Allah and his commandments. For further studies see Donald S. Tingle, *Islam and Christianity*, (Downers Grove: Inter-Varsity Press, 1985) pp. 3–12; *A Southern Africa Guide to World Religions*, ed. John W. de Crunchy and Martin Prozesky, (Cape Town: David Philip, 1994), p. 203; Abd-ul-Masih, *Islam and Christianity: Ninety Questions and Answers*, (Ibadan: Daystar Press, 1967), p. 6; and Norman Anderson, *Islam in the Modern World*, (London: Apollos, 1990), pp. 3–42.

5. Some historians of Islam believe that some Arab refugees came from the Arabian Peninsula and settled along the Coast of East of Africa after having fled their homeland following the religious dispute over the

issue of who should be the rightful successor of Prophet Muhammad. For a detailed study, see Samuel G. Ayany, *A History of Zanzibar*, (Nairobi: East Africa Literature Bureau, 1970), especially chapter one; *The first incursion of Europeans (Portuguese) into the Indian Ocean* and particularly "The Coast of East Africa;" *History of East Africa: The Early Period*, ed. Roland Oliver and Gervase Mathew, (Nairobi: Oxford University Press, 1963) pp. 129–168; Spensor J. Trimingham, *Islam in East Africa*, (Oxford: Oxford University Press, 1963), p. 3; J. Allen, "Muslims in East Africa," *Afer* (1965), pp. 255–262; *From Mission to Church*, ed. Z. Nthamburi, (Nairobi: Uzima Press, 1991), pp. 4–12; John S. Pobee, *AD 2000 and After, The Future of God's Mission in Africa*, (Accra: Asempa Publishers, 1991), pp. 4–28. Pobee states that Prince Henry, the Navigator's flag which the explorers from Portugal hosted on their ship, bore the inscription *infideles debent subjuci fidelibus* i.e., the infidel (Muslims) must be subjected to the faithful (Christians). The Pope blessed their imperialistic mission. Rome had granted Portugal both the spiritual-cultural and politico-economic monopoly of Africa. In 1436, Pope Eugene IV gave the king the right to make war against the "heathens" and reduce them to embrace the Christian faith. The Bull Romanus Pontifex by whom the "heathen" Africa was to be brought under the Portuguese jurisdiction force reinforced this. Thereafter, the building of churches and monasteries was an integral part of Portuguese expansionism.

6. One can see Sir J. M. Gray, "Ahmad bin Ibrahim, the first Arab to reach Buganda," *Uganda Journal*, (1947), pp. 80–97; Roland Oliver, *Missionary Factors in East-Africa*, (London: Longmans, 1952), p. 203; A. B. K. Kasozi, *The Spread of Islam in Uganda, 1844–1945*, (unpublished PhD Thesis, University of California, 1974), pp. 90–98; and Abasi Kiyimba, "Muslim Community in Uganda Through 140 years," *Journal of African Religion and Philosophy*, (1990), pp. 86–87.

7. Note especially the five pillars of Islam: (1) Recitation of the creed (shahada); (2) Prayers (salat); (3) almsgiving (Zakat) as an offering to God or act of piety; (4) Fasting (sawm) during the month of Ramadan; and (5) Pilgrimage (hajj) to Mecca once in one's lifetime. A. B. K. Kasozi, "The Process of Islamization in Uganda," *Uganda Journal*, (1976), pp. 83–108; Michael Twaddle, *Kakungulu and the Creation of Uganda*, (Kampala: Fountain Publishers, 1993), p. 25; and Sir Norman Anderson, *Christianity and World Religions*, (Downers Group: Inter-Varsity Press, 1970), pp. 64–68. See also Ebrahim

Moosa, "Islam" in *A Southern African Guide to World Religions*, ed. Crunchy and Prozesky, (1991), pp. 203–237. Moosa makes it clear that Islamic teachings and social views are based on four primary sources of knowledge: the *Qur'an*, the *Sunnah* (traditions), the *ijma* (consensus), and *qiyas* (analogy). When these sources are employed to explicate theology, they are known as the source of theology; when used to elaborate the moral and social low, they are termed the science of jurisprudence.

8. A. B. K. Kasozi, "Impact of Koran Schools in Education of African Muslims in Uganda," *Dini na Mila*, (1970), pp. 1–21; Kateregga, pp. 3–4; Arye Oded, *Islam in Uganda: Islamization Through a Central State in Pre-Colonial Africa*, (New York: 1974), pp. 65–72; James Ndyabahika, "The Understanding of Islam in Uganda: A Historical Review," *Asia Journal of Theology* (1993), pp. 136–148; and A. B. K Kasozi, "The Impact of Islam on Baganda Culture (1844-1894)," *Journal of Religion of Africa*, (1981), pp. 127–135.

9. Kevin Ward, "A History of Christianity in Uganda," in *From Mission to Church*, ed. Z. Nthamburi, (Nairobi: Uzima Press, 1991), pp. 81–88. Kevin, for one, is very clear when he drew our attention to the fact that Christianity was able to build on Islamic religious concepts. With a CMS printing press reinforced by the distribution of Christian literature in the indigenous language, Christianity was able to accomplish to a larger extent what Islam was unable to do (Ward 1991:81).

10. William B. Anderson, *The Church in East Africa 1840-1974*, (Nairobi: Uzima Press, 1977), p. 48; Samuel R. Karugire, *A Political History of Uganda*, (Nairobi: Heinemannn Educational Books, 1980), pp. 61–64; Brian Stanley, *The Bible and the Flag*, (London: Inter-Varsity Press, 1990), pp. 127–132. For a recent survey on the historical growth of Christianity in Uganda, see Paul Gifford, *African Christianity: Its Public Role in Uganda and Other African Countries*, (Kampala: Fountain Publishers, 1999), pp. 57–125.

11. Adrian Hastings, *African Christianity*, (London: Geoffrey Chapman, 1976), pp. 21–40; Yves Tourigny, *So Abundant a Harvest: The History of the Catholic Church in Uganda 1879-1977*, (London: Longmans, 1979), pp. 21–40; and John Baur, *Two thousand years of Christianity in Africa*, (Nairobi: Pauline Publications, 1994), pp. 230–240.

12. J. D. Y. Peel, "Conversion and Tradition in two African Societies: Ijebu and Buganda," *Past and Present, 77 (1977)*, pp. 108–141; Adrian

Hastings, "From Mission to Church in Buganda," *Zeitischrift fur Missionswissenscaft*, 53 (1969), pp. 206–228; John Mary Waliggo, "The Religio-Political Context of the Uganda Martyrs," *African Christian Studies*, 2; 1 (1986), pp. 3–40; Louise Pirouet, "Traditional Religion and the Response to Christianity," *Geographia Religioner*, 6 (1989), pp. 191–200; and Kevin Ward, "The Church of Ugandan Amidst Conflict," in Religion and Politics in East Africa, ed. Holger Bernt Hansen and Michael Twaddle, (Kampala: Fountain Publishers, 1995), pp. 72–105.

13. From that time up to now, the relationship between Religion and Politics or Church and State has been an age long controversial one. For the situation relating to other parts of Africa, see U. R. Onunwa, "Church and Politics in Africa: A quest for stable democracy," *African Christian Studies*, 11:4 (1995), pp. 14–26.

14. Ahmed Katumba and F. B. Welbourn, "Muslim Martyrs of Buganda," *Uganda Journal*, (1964), pp. 151–163; Gideon S. Were and Derek A. Wilson, *East Africa Through a Thousand Years*, (Ibadan: Evans Brothers, Nigeria Publishers Limited, 1968), pp. 174–175. The Bagalagala were taught the political systems of the kingdom and the traditional setup of the country. Then, the musicians, craftsmen, and all people of talents in every field were attracted to serve at the palace in order to be noticed by the king. Through him, they could rise or fall. Future leaders as well as servants of the state used the court as a training ground. From all counties, the chiefs and their subjects came regularly to pay homage. A. B. K. Kasozi, *The Spread of Islam in Uganda*, (Nairobi: Oxford University Press, 1986), pp. 51–56.

15. The multiplication of loyalties: ethnic, cultural, ideological, and religious ethos reduced the risk of "confrontation" between "We" and "They."

16. R. Barnett, *Uganda Holocaust*, (1980), p. 58; J. A. Rowe, "The Purge of Christians at Mwanga's Court," *Journal of African History*, 5 (1964), pp. 55–72; John Mary Waliggo, "The Religio-Political Context of Uganda Martyrs and its Significance," *African Christian Studies*, (1986), pp. 3–40. The clash of May 1886 between the faithful Christians and the Kabaka (king) Mwanga can be understood in the light of the 1870s Muslim martyrs. In the two incidents, there were common factors. To begin with, the King was not happy the way his subjects were behaving. Secondly, the King was not attempting to eliminate all professed religions or to take them as forbidden religions.

He only carried out a few executions to teach a lesson to other Christians how they should respect his rule.

17. A. D. Low, *Religion and Society in Uganda, 1875-1900*, (Kampala: East African Institute of Social Research, 1955), p. 14; M. S. Kiwanuka, *A History of Buganda: From the Foundation of the Kingdom to 1900*, (London: 1971), pp. 204–205; John Mary Waliggo, "The Catholic Church and the Root Cause of Political Instability in Uganda" in Religion and Politics in East Africa, ed. H. B. Hansen and M. Twaddle, (Kampala: Fountain Publishers, 1995), pp. 106–119. One thing seems fairly evident to observe here — conversion to Islam during this decade was often a strategic decision.

18. Kasozi (1976), pp. 87–95; H. B. Kakunguru and A. B. K. Kasozi, *Abasimba Obuyisilamu mu Uganda*, (Kampala, 1977), pp. 32-42; Katelega (1978), p. 10.

19. T. W. Gee, "A Century of Muhammadan Influence in Buganda, 1952-1951," *Uganda Journal*, 20 (1958), pp. 139–207; James Ndyabahika, *The Attitude of the Anglican Church of Uganda: To the New Religious Movements and in particular the Bacwezi Bashomi in South-Western Uganda*, (unpublished PhD Thesis, University of Cape Town – South Africa, 1998), pp. 19–24.

20. John A. Rowe "Islam under Idi-Amin" in *Uganda Now: Between Decay and Development*, ed. H. B Hansen and M. Twaddle, (Kampala, Fountain Publishers 1995), pp. 267, 279. Kasozi recalls that in 1893, an intermittent battle between the Muslims and Christians was fought till the Muslims were decisively defeated at Bulwayi. From then on, Muslims became a second-class citizen and a despised minority in Uganda, as they lacked facilities to educate their young. Most Muslims were reduced to the position of taxi drivers, butchers, hewers of wood, and drawers of water (Kasozi, 1976), pp. 95–103.

21. At the time the colonial agents arrived in Uganda in 1894 — with their foreign culture, superior organization, new economic systems, and new forms of laws — religious conflicts were almost at their worst. There is concrete evidence to substantiate that each religion was still making war-like noises and the colonial agents too, fuelled such conflicts. For a detailed explanation, see R. W. Beachey, *A History of East Africa 1592-1902*, (London: I. B. Taurus Publishers, 1996), pp. 272–275.

22 *Islam and the Confluence of Religion in Uganda 1840-1966*, ed. A. B. K. Kasozi, Noel King, and Arye Oded, (Florida: 1973), p. 81.

23. F. B. Welbourn, *Religion and Politics in Uganda 1952-1962* (Nairobi: East African Publishing House, 1965), p. 3; John S. Mbiti, "Church and State: A Neglected element of Christianity in contemporary Africa," *African Theological Journal*, (December, 1972) pp. 31–45; R. Moloney, "Religious, Politics, and the Uganda martyrs," *Afer*, (1987), p. 15; and A. B. T. Byaruhanga-Akiiki, "Religious Rehabilitation in Uganda," in *Uganda: A Century of Existence*, ed. Okoth, (Kampala: Fountain Publishers, 1995), p. 252.

24. Elizabeth Isichei, *A History of Christianity in Africa* (London: SPCK, 1995), pp. 145–150; Adonia Tiberondwa, *Missionary Teachers as Agents of Colonialism in Uganda* (Kampala: Fountain Publishers, 1998), pp. 16–17; The most unfortunate episode in the history of the two Christian religions in Uganda is that once CMS and WF Missionaries arrived in the nation, the old enmities exported from Canterbury and Rome surfaced and dangerously slipped out of control and were passed on to the new converts. Hence, their followers were at the crossroads.

25. Ali A. Mazrui, "Religious Strangers in Uganda: From Emin Pasha to Amin Dada," *African Affairs*, (1977), pp. 21–38.

26. Margaret Ford, *Janoni: The Making of a Marty*, (London Marshall and Scott, 1978) pp. 20–25; Kefa Ssempangi and Barbara Thompson, *Reign of Terror, Reign of Love*, (London: Aslan Lim Books, 1979), p. 89; Louise Pirouet, "Religion in Uganda under Amin," *Journal of Religion in Africa*, (1990), p. 1; R. Edward Bakeitwako Muhima, *The Fellowship of Suffering: A Theological Interpretation of Christian Suffering Under Idi Amin*, (Unpublished Ph.D. Thesis, North-Western University, 1981), pp. 35–55; and Emmanuel Twesigye, "When God and Caesar come into conflict: Idi Amin kills the Archbishop of Uganda," *The Ohio Academy of Religion Papers*, (1999), pp. 51–74.

27. Suffice it to say that in 1991, more than 85% of the total population of Uganda professed to be Christians, more than 10% Muslims, and the rest were either Indigenous religious believers or members of the New Religious Movements or people of no faith. For more information, see Uganda Census 1991: compiled by E. Tumusime Mutebile, Statistics Department, Ministry of Finance and Economic Planning, (Entebbe, 1992), p.7 which gives a detailed explanation as follows:

Name	Mid 1980 (Census)	1991	Percentage	2000 (Prediction)
Christians	10,353,000	14,913,600		20,417,900
RomanCatholics	6,558,000	7,426,500	44.5%	9,804,800
Protestant (Anglican)	3,473,000	6,541,800	39.2%	8,761,800
Other Christian denominations	266,000	545,200	1.7%	1,682,300
Muslims	872,700	1,758,100	10.5%	3,787,800
Indigenous Religionists	330,600	400,100	4%	724,800
Total		13,220,000	16,671,700	23,561,500

28. Leonard Namwera, "A Historical Search for Dialogue between Islam and Christianity in East Africa," *African Christian Studies*, (1994), pp. 33–51. This article makes it clear that a lot of change has taken place since Abiya Conference, which was held in Nigeria in 1989. Eyewitness accounts prove the crossover from Christianity to Islam but statistical data is not given so far.

29. In the twentieth century, this topic was discussed by Zurich Consultation "Christians in Dialogue with Men of Other Faith," *International Review of Missions*, (1970), pp. 282–391; L. O. Sanneh, "The Christian-Moslem encounter in Africa," in African Challenge, ed. Kenneth Y. Best (Nairobi: Transafrica Publishers, 1975), pp. 101–110; Badru Katelegga, "Islam Relations with African Traditional Religion and with Christianity," *Occasional Research Papers*, Makerere University, (1978), pp. 1–10.

30. Bruce J. Nichollas, "The witnessing church in dialogue," *Evangelical Review of Theology*, (1992), pp. 48–65; Vinoth Ramachandra, *Faith in Conflicts?* (Leicester: Inter-Varsity Press, 1999), pp. 9–46; Ramachandra draws our attention to the fact that although "Islamophobia" or "Christophobia" are ugly words, they draw out attention to ugly realities, because all phobias are the result of ignorance and the inability to look critically at oneself. He went on to say that there is room for "listening, humility, and respect" — tenets necessary for genuine dialogue — with others in pluralistic nations.

31. One provoking example of a focus on Mary is given by Amnah Rabiatu, "The Islamic Understanding of Creation: The Place of Women," in Where God Reigns: Reflections on Women in God's World, ed. Elizabeth Amoah (Accra; Sam–Woode Ltd., 1997), pp. 26–38. See also A. B. K. Kasozi, "Christian-Muslim inputs into Public Policy Formation in Kenya, Tanzania, and Uganda," in Religion and Politics in East Africa, ed. Holger B. Hansen and Michael Twaddle (Kampala: Fountain Publishers, 1995), pp. 223–246.

32. John V. Taylor "The Theological Basis of Inter-faith Dialogue," in *Mission Trend No. 5: Faith Meets Faith*, ed. Gerald H. Anderson (New York: Paulist Press, 1981), pp. 91–110; see also John A. Saliba, "Dialogue with New Religious Movements: Issues and Prospects," *Journal of Ecumenical Studies*, (1993), pp. 51–80; H. W. Kinoti, "The Challenge of New Age Movement and Oriental Mysticism" in *Mission in African Christianity*, ed. A. Nasimiyu and D. W. Waruta (Nairobi: Uzima Press, 1993), pp. 89–107.
33. Namwera, (1994), pp. 47–48.
34. On the theological platform, religion must be rooted in the heart of the faithful. However, the belief in Jesus Christ that distinguishes Christians from Muslims should not separate them but rather press them in their right religious perspective. Faithful Christians enhance, that in Christ, God did not become a Christian but rather a human being. In Christ, God loved the whole world and reconciled it to himself. In this regard, dialogue is not the opposite of Mission. On the contrary, dialogue includes mutual witness to ones faith rather than excluding it. In a nutshell, a desirable dialogue between Muslims and Christians is paramount.
35. There has been a wealth of scholarship on Islamic teaching and history and Christians have often been in the forefront of such scholarship. The writings of Richard Bell, Constance Padwick, Sir Norman Anderson, and Keneth Cragg (among many others) have greatly enriched our understanding of many important topics, from the calling and preaching of Muhammad. In contrast, it is extremely rare to meet a Muslim who has made a serious study of the New Testament and no one among the nearly one billion professing Muslims in the world has been recognized as having made a contribution to the study of the Bible or of early church history. As long as this situation continues, the claim of Islamic apologists to be well-read, respectful, and tolerant in their dealings with Christians must be treated with considerable skepticism.
36. The faithful Christians advance that the Christian faith is never "grown up," it is always growing. To keep it growing, the faithful must always search and search everywhere for the truth.
37. James P. Dretke, *A Christian Approach to Muslims: Reflection from West Africa* (Pasadena: William Carey Library, 1979), pp. 203–206; see also Marston R. Speight, "Some Bases for a Christian Apologetic to Islam," *International Review of Missions*, (1965) pp. 191–205; Ralph E. Brown, "How dialogue can be used to witness to Muslims," *Evangelical Missions Quarterly*, (1971), pp. 65–78.
38. Kenneth Cragg, *The call of the Minaret*, (London: Collins, 1986), pp. 219–220.
39. E. Dada Adelowo, "Islamic Monotheism and the Christian and Traditional African Concepts of Godhead," *African Theological Journal*, (1980), pp. 62–76; A. B. K. Kasozi, *The Spread of Islam in Uganda* (Nairobi: Oxford University Press, 1986), p. 21; see also Jacob S. Dharmaraj and Glory E. Dharmaraj, "Christian-Muslim Relationship, A Theological Debate over Prophethood and Scriptutres," *Asia Journal of Theology*, (1998), pp. 295–302.

40. Louse Pirouet, "Refugees in and from Uganda in the Post-Colonial Period," in *Uganda Now: Between Decay and Development*, ed. H. B. Hansen and Edward Twaddle (Kampala: Fountain Publishers, 1995), pp. 239–253.
41. *A Century of Christianity in Uganda 1877–1977*, ed. Tom Tuma (Nairobi: Uzima Press, 1978), pp. 122–124. It is expedient to state one fact of interest. Muslim or Christian Health Centers have made an impact and produced immeasurable results at the grassroots level.
42. Human Immunodeficiency Virus (HIV) is a virus that breaks down the immune system of the body and essentially causes AIDS (acquired immunodeficiency syndrome). As it is so well known in Uganda, it is a physical condition resulting from the progressive destruction of immunity in the body by the Human Immunodeficiency Virus. See Laurenti Magesa "AIDS and survival in Africa: A tentative Reflection," in Moral Ethical Issues in African Christianity ed. J. N. K. Mugambi and A. Nasimiyu-Wasike (Nairobi: Initiatives Publishers, 1992) pp. 197-216.
43. James Katorobo, *Education for Public Services in Uganda* (New York: Vantage Press, 1982), p. 13; Deogratius M. Byabazaire, *The Contribution of the Christian Churches to the Development of Western Uganda 1894-1974*, (Frankfurt: Peter Lang, 1979), pp. 63–78; A Wandera, *Early Missionary Education in Uganda: A Study of the Practice and Purpose of Indigenous Education in Uganda* (Kampala: 1971), pp. 130–142; A. R. Nsibambi, "The Politics of Education in Uganda 1964 -1970," *Uganda Journal* (1976), pp. 58-82; D. W. Waruta, "The Educational Mission of the Church: An African Perspective," in *Mission in African Christianity*, A. Nasimiyu-Wasike et el., (Nairobi: Uzima Press, 1993), pp. 110–111.

5
Indian Muslims in South Africa's History: Continuity and Change

GOOLAM VAHED

The majority of Indian Muslims arrived in Natal between 1860 and 1911 as contract indentured workers or pioneer traders. Indentured migration lasted between 1860 and 1911, by which time 152,641 Indians had come to Natal. Approximately seven to ten percent (10, 000–15,000) were Muslim.[1]

The indentured Muslim population was characterized by diversity of religious tradition, caste, language, ethnicity, and culture as migrants were drawn from a range of ecologies and modes of production. Traders from Gujarat, on the west coast of India, began arriving in Natal from the mid-1870s, at their own expense and of their own volition. The majority of traders were Muslims, either Memons from Porbandar in Kathiawar or Sunni Bohras from Surat, who spoke Gujarati. While the exact number of traders is not certain, the Wragg Commission approximated their number to be around one thousand in 1887, while Maureen Swan (1985: 2) estimated it to average around 2,000 between 1890 and 1910.

Indian Muslims were a minority within a minority. According to the 1904 Census, of 100,918 Indians in Natal, 9,992 (9.901 per cent) were Muslim, the overwhelming majority (72 per cent) of whom were male. There was a great degree of internal differentiation among Natal Muslims. While the most obvious distinction was between traders and indentured migrants, neither of these two groups comprised a homogenous group.

Muslims traders were incorrectly called "Arabs," because most adopted the Middle Eastern mode of dress. They themselves emphasized this distinction to obtain equality with whites on the basis of Queen Victoria's 1858 Proclamation, which asserted the equality of British subjects (Bhana and Brain, 1990: 65). This class distinction among Indians was evident to the authorities. In a confidential report to the Durban Town Council

(DTC) in 1885, police inspector Richard Alexander (1885) pointed out that the "Arabs will only associate with Indians so far as trade compels them to." In fact, Gujarati Muslims had more in common with Gujarati Hindus than they had with indentured Muslims. George Mutukistna, a free Indian, testified before the Wragg Commission that "caste feeling ... is kept up by the Indian merchants, who think themselves better because they are rich. By observing caste distinctions they can set themselves apart from the Natal Indian people." (Wragg Commission, 1885: 393). Muslim traders considered themselves 'high-class.' They were largely endogamous and did not intermarry with Muslims from an indentured background, whom they disparagingly referred to as 'Calcutteas'— Calcutta being one of the ports from which indentured Indians departed for Natal.

INDENTURED INDIANS AND ISLAM

In terms of the contract that they signed, indentured workers agreed to work for five years for the employer to whom they were allocated. Swan (1985), Tayal (1977), and Henning (1993) have chronicled the appalling conditions that indentured workers were subjected to. Swan concludes that "there is a solid weight of evidence, in the Protector's[2] files, to suggest that overwork, malnourishment, and squalid living conditions formed the pattern of daily life for most agricultural workers" (1985: 26).

The experience of indenture militated against maintenance of culture, religion, and caste. The long wait at the depot in India, the cramped journey to Natal, and delays in Natal while immigrants were inspected, would have made it difficult to observe the many everyday rules and rituals that are part of Islam (Buijs, 1992: 7). In the absence of oral or written histories, it is difficult to be precise about the form and content of Islam practiced by indentured Muslims. However, there is evidence in the files of the Protector that, on an individual level, many Muslims displayed 'Islamic awareness.'

The most important 'religious' activity of indentured Muslims was the *Muharram* festival. It was held on the tenth of *Muharram*, the first month in the Islamic calendar, to commemorate the martyrdom of Imam Hussein, the grandson of the Prophet Muhammad, who was killed in battle on this day. Hindus also participated in large numbers. Deputy Protector Dunning noted in his 1910 Annual Report that "the festival is always well attended by Hindu indentured workers, although it is a Mohammedan occasion of mourning." In fact, the three days annual leave to which indentured Indians were entitled by law, was granted to all Indians during this festival. Preparations began at least two weeks prior to the festival as bamboo and other materials were collected to build the *tazzia*, a miniature mausoleum constructed in wood and covered in colored paper and gold and silver tinsels. On the tenth, groups of people pulled *tazzias* by hand, all the while singing songs to the memory of Hussein, beating on drums, dancing wildly, or carrying out stick fights. There was always a strong police presence, because the festival often ended with the spilling of blood. Despite strong disapproval from the local state, as well as middle class Indians, *Muharram* remained a central part of the Islam of indentured workers and their descendants. *Muharram* provided an opportunity for developing and expressing a self-conscious local community identity. But *Muharram* also signaled the participation of Indians in a larger collective by drawing them together, and played an important role in fostering a wider common identity — 'Indianness,' in relation to whites and Africans. Social and economic conditions would have made it difficult for indentured Muslims to fulfill the many requirements of Islam. For example, because of the shortage of Muslim women, the Protector registered 115 marriages between Muslims and Hindus in the years between 1872 and 1887 (Wragg Commission, 261). Muslims and Hindus lived on the same plantations, shared the same housing, experienced the same difficulties, and reacted in the same manner to oppressive social and economic conditions. The files of Resident Magistrates and the Protector are replete with examples of Muslims engaging in crime — desertion, rape, adultery, and so on. Indentured Muslims were widely dispersed, hence the task of establishing mosques, *madrassas,* and other aspects of institutional Islam were difficult, given the long hours, oppressive conditions, and meager wages. The files of the Protector make no reference to Muslims fasting, praying, or observing the festivals of *Eid*. In the absence of contemporary records, or oral history, it is not possible to construct with certainty these aspects of the indentured Muslim experience in Natal.

The arrival of Soofie Saheb, in 1895, had important consequences for indentured Muslims and their descendants. Soofie Saheb, full name Shah Goolam Mohamed, traced his genealogy to Abu Bakr Siddique, the first Caliph of Islam (Soofie and Soofie, 1999: 45). Soofie Saheb was born in 1850 in Ratnagir, about 200 kilometers from Bombay. He studied under his father and qualified as an *alim* (scholar of Islamic law). When his father died in 1872, Soofie Saheb was appointed to succeed him. In 1892, he became the *murid* of Habib Ali Shah — a Sufi in the Chisti order (Abbas Rizvi, 1978: 114). In 1894, Ali Shah sent Soofie Saheb to South Africa to propagate the *Chisti Silsila* (tradition). According to oral tradition, shortly after he arrived in Durban in 1895, Soofie Saheb proceeded to the Brook Street cemetery where he meditated until he located the grave of a 'holy man,' who was given the title *Badsha Pir* (king of the guides), around which a tomb was built (Soofie and Soofie, 1999: 56). Despite Badsha Pir's underdeveloped biographical profile and unclear biological genealogy, his tomb continues to attract large numbers of Muslims and Hindus who believe that praying in the presence of a saint was 'much more likely to be efficacious' (Robinson, 1983: 189). The promptness with which Soofie Saheb erected the shrine is consonant with Sufi practice. As Bayly has pointed out, migrating devotees build "new shrines inspired by the belief that each was an equally potent repository of *barkat.*" Migration results in a 'widening and intensification' of the original cult tradition, and certainly not a turn towards a more 'universal' or transcendent faith devoid of shrines, magical intercessory power, and all other features of the pir cult (Bayly, 1989: 93–94).

Soofie Saheb purchased land in Riverside on the banks of the Umgeni River where he built a mosque, *khanqah* (teaching hospice), *madrassa*, cemetery, orphanage, and a residential home. Between 1898 and his death in 1911, Soofie Saheb built mosques, madrassas, and cemeteries all over Natal — in Springfield and Westville in 1904, in Overport in 1905, in Kenville and Sherwood in 1906, in Tongaat in 1907, Ladysmith and Colenso in 1908, and Verulam and Pietermaritzburg in 1909 (Mahida, 1993: 44). These were situated mainly in rural areas and provided access to large numbers of working class Muslims. Soofie Saheb was instrumental in raising the levels of Islamic knowledge and consciousness among indentured Muslims and their descendants. As a result of Soofie Saheb, the practice of *pir-muridi* became an established part of Indian Islam in Natal. Local Muslims believed that Badsha Pir and Soofie Saheb had special attributes of divinity and could bless the childless with children, cure diseases, prevent calamity, and so on. Soofie Saheb also organized activities throughout the lunar year. The birth and death of the Prophet and great saints were commemorated at the shrine of Badsha Pir. Soofie Saheb's methodology was one adopted by religious leaders elsewhere in India, who accommodated themselves "to local needs and customs ... gradually building a position from which they might draw people into an Islamic milieu and slowly educating them in Islamic behavior" (Robinson, 1983: 192). Soofie Saheb created an environment that resonated with the beliefs of his constituency. It was on the basis of these common practices that an Islamic tradition eventually took shape amongst working class Muslims in Natal.

THE ISLAM OF TRADERS

The situation was different with traders who set about building mosques shortly after their arrival in Natal. The Juma Musjid in Grey Street, built in 1881, remains the largest mosque in the southern hemisphere. It was built on the initiative of Aboobakr Amod, a Memon from Porbander who settled in Durban in 1874. The Juma Musjid has come to be known among Muslims as the "Memon Mosque," because the majority trustees have been Memons who financed the building and the upkeep of the mosque. Since 1905, trustees have comprised of five Memons, two Surtis, one Kokan and one 'colonial-born,' that is, a descendant of indentured Indians (Sulliman, 1985: 10). This is an indication of the depth of ethnic and caste differences among Muslims. Sectionalism explains the decision of Surti traders to build a separate mosque in 1885, just half a kilometer away in West Street (Jamal, 1987: 13). The first trustees were Ahmed Mohammed Tilly and Hoosen Meeran who, as per the constitution, were 'natives from Rander, Surat, in the Presidency of Bombay.' This indicates the corporate outlook of the Surtis.[3] The amended constitution of 1899 stipulated that the mosque was for the use of 'Sunni Mohammedan worshippers from the District of Surat.' It broadened the base from which trustees could be drawn. While at least two had to be from each Rander and Kathor, other trustees could originate from other parts of Surat as long as they were Sunni Muslims, a storekeeper having a business in the Colony of Natal, or were connected with any such business in the capacity of General Manager and had subscribed at least £25 pounds to the Mosque Trust.[4] Mosque committees appointed imams. As their paid employees, they led the prayer and taught Islam but exercised limited authority over the Muslim community.

In addition to language and culture, religious practices also divided the Memons and Surtis. Memons placed great emphasis on visitation of shrines. In India, those with wealth visited Baghdad to pray at the shrine of Abdul Qadir Jailani (d. 1165), considered the greatest saint in Islam. Those who could not go to Baghdad, visited the shrines of Shah Alam at Ahmedabad or Miran Sayad Ali Dattar at Unja, 50 miles north of Ahmedabad.[5] According to an elder Memon, their strong faith in *pirs* is an expression of gratitude to saints for converting them to Islam (Moomal, 1996: vi). Memons trace their origins to Sayad Kadiri of Baghdad, fifth in descent from Abdul Kadir Jailani. They believe that Kadiri was ordered in a miraculous dream in 1421 to set sail for Sindh and guide its people to Islam and that this blessing is responsible for their success in trade (Gazatteer, 1899: 50-51). While the Surti's were also Sunnis of the *Hanafi* inclination, contemporary reports in India suggest that the influence of nineteenth century reform movements in

India were filtering down to them. An 1899 report noted that they were "rapidly shedding remnants of Hindu practices as a result of the activity of missionaries" (Gazatteer, 1899: 61). They were transferring their reverence to the new preachers who became the leaders in religious matters; women were changing their dress to 'Muslim fashion;' there were fewer public dinners; less extravagant expenditures on marriage, death, and other ceremonies; and music was no longer played at weddings.[6] The Islam of traders centered on the mosque and two festivals of *Eid*. Aboobakr Amod told the Wragg Commission that 'the two Eids of *Ramadan* and *Hajj*' were the 'only' festivals observed by Muslims and that these days should be set-aside as public holidays (Wragg Commission, 389). The boisterous festival of Muharram did not have the same importance for traders as it did for the working class Muslims. In comparison, Eid was a sober and temperate affair.

RACE, CLASS, AND RELIGION

Natal's Muslims developed along separate trajectories. Traders did not attempt to forge a broader Muslim community on the basis of Islam. Their concern was to protect their economic and political rights in Natal and they forged class alliances with Hindu traders who were similarly affected. Indian traders who threatened their dominance of local trade, aroused the hostility of Natal's whites (Wragg Commission, 131). Once Natal achieved self-government in 1893, laws were passed to regulate Indian access to trading licenses, deny Indians the municipal vote and control Indian entry into Natal; merchants formed the Natal Indian Congress (NIC) in August 1894, whose strategy was primarily constitutional and it dominated Indian politics. Each of the NIC's six presidents between 1894 and 1913 was a prominent Muslim merchant (Bhana, 1997: 12). The NIC was a tool of the Indian elite and concentrated on protecting their economic and political interests. While the Memons and the Surtis disagreed on religious matters, they worked closely in political affairs as a result of their common class interests.

Politically and socially, Muslim merchants mingled with their Hindu counterparts rather than working-class Muslims. For example, Muslims attended the middle-class Hindu festival of *Diwali*. In 1907, Hindu merchants arranged a *Diwali* celebration at the premises of a Muslim, Abdool Latif, which was attended by non-Hindus like Sheth Rustomjee and Dada Osman (Indian Opinion, 16 November 1907). In 1911, Muslims like Dawad Mahomed, M.C. Anglia, and Ismail Gora attended the *Diwali* celebrations. Mahomed considered the unity and 'happy gatherings' between Hindus and Muslims 'an excellent thing' (Indian Opinion, 21 October 1911). When a dinner was held to bid farewell to Omar Jhaveri, a Muslim intimately involved in local politics, who was departing to India on account of ill-health, the reception was attended by Muslim, Hindu, and Christian elites. In his speech, A. Christopher "bore testimony to his (Mr Jhaveri's) catholicity of spirit in the community life of the Indians in this country, making no distinction against any of his countrymen on the grounds of religion and working for the upliftment of them all" (Indian Opinion, 2 September 1914). The relationship between Muslim traders and workers was mainly economic, causing the *African Chronicle* (14 October, 1914) to chide merchants for "hugging to themselves the delusion that their fate is not bound up with the ordinary laborer ... Many are indifferent to the sufferings of the laboring class."

A similar tendency developed among working-class Hindus and Muslims who shared a history of indentured labor. Both were recruited to work on plantations, came from the same districts of India, spoke the same languages, shared local traditions in India, and had similar backgrounds as peasants, tenant farmers, artisans and agricultural workers. In Natal, the behavior of working-class Muslims was not much different from that of their Hindu counterparts. The files of the Protector of Indian Immigrants and Magistrates' Reports are replete with examples of Muslims guilty of assault, rape, and other crimes. The list is endless and illustrates the fact that traders and indentured Muslims came for different reasons, from different social and economic backgrounds, and established themselves in different milieus in the local colonial setting, which affected their understanding and observance of Islam. The Indian Muslim society in Natal was dominated by elites and riven by cleavages due to class, the urban/rural dichotomy, language, variance in modes of migration, and the region of origin. There were fundamental differences in practice, belief, and definitions of 'true' Islam. The identities of Muslims were left in tension because of the difficulty to assert a transcendent Islamic identity.

While Indian Muslims had 'hybrid' identities relating to language, class, ethnicity, and religion, the most important identity in the political realm was race. The emergent white state was felt economically, socially, and politically, by threatened Indians, who were consequently treated legislatively as a homogenous entity, separated into a discrete racial category and subdued on the basis of that category. Use of the appellation 'Indians' inferred that the attribute 'Indianness' united them as a collectivity, in opposition to whites and Africans. According to Bhana, in the "unique circumstances in which the notion of 'Indianness' became crystallized in

South Africa, it became racialized in the creation of White supremacist rule" (Bhana, 1997: 100). Community formation was a complex construction, historically fashioned out of disparate people, discursively constituted by struggles among Indians between them and Whites and Africans. The privileged economic position of Indian traders was neutralized by racist policies that placed them in the same situation as workers. Politically, this forced a 'made-in-Natal' consciousness, a fact emphasized by Imam Bawazeer, a Muslim priest, when he was departing for India in 1915:

> We are all Indians in the eyes of the Europeans in this country. We have never drawn distinctions between Mohammedans and Hindus in public matters. Mohammedans, like the Hindus, look upon India as our Motherland, and so it is a matter of fact, and when it is a matter of serving India, we must set aside any differences and be united (Indian Opinion, 3 December 1915).

URBANIZATION, POVERTY, AND COMMUNITY: PRE-APARTHEID SOUTH AFRICA, 1910–1948

The four decades after 1910 were witness to important developments. These included the rapid urbanization of Indians, extensive poverty among them, formation of education and social welfare institutions by traders to take care of their working-class counterparts, and increasing hostility by the state. The overwhelming majority of Indians remained Hindu. According to the 1936 Population Census, for example, 81% of Natal's Indians were Hindu and 14% Muslim. In Durban, 70,272 (79.64%) Indians were Hindus and 13,009 (14.74%) were Muslims out of a total Indian population of 88,226 in 1946 (SAIRR, 1946). It is therefore difficult to separate the Muslim experience from the Indian one. By and large, Muslims existed as Indians; being Indian was the primary identity in the public sphere.

The availability of African labor rendered Indians superfluous in farming, mining, and the public sector. When the Indian Legislative Council banned indentured emigration to Natal from July 1911, employers turned to African labor and the numbers of Indians dropped on Natal's mines, the railways, in general farming, and on sugar estates. This spurred the 'urban-ward' migration of dispensable Indian labor. In Durban, for example, the number of Indians increased from 17,015 in 1911 to 123,165 in 1949. As a percentage of Durban's population, Indians increased, from 23 to 33 per cent (Housing Survey, 1952: 35), unemployment and low pay resulted in wide-scale poverty among Indians. While the depression of 1929–1933 was a significant cause, the situation was exacerbated by the

White Labor Policy, which resulted in a drop in Indian employment in industry and the municipality. The majority of Muslims, being descendants of indentured Indians, experienced difficult conditions in the urban milieu. Extensive poverty was a pervasive feature of Indian life in Durban. A 1941 survey found that 36% of Indian families in Clairwood were in debt, 38% barely made ends meet, and only 26% were able to save money (Sykes, 1941: 54). The University of Natal reported in 1943–44 that 70.6% of Indians were living below the poverty datum line and that 40% were destitute. A 6-year study of the clothing industry reported in 1944 that 90% of Indians suffered from malnutrition (Daily News, 8 June 1944). Poverty also manifested itself in the diseases that afflicted Indians. For example, G. H. Gunn, Durban's Medical Officer of Health, reported in 1935 that higher disease and death rates among Indians were due to the "low standard of living conditions, which poverty imposes upon those sections of the population. Slum housing, overcrowding, and defective nutrition combined to create a favorable climate for the spread of disease" (Indian Opinion, 31 January 1936).

Throughout this period, the government focused on repatriating Indians. A round-table conference between South African Indians and Imperial governments in 1927 introduced a system of voluntary repatriation. At the same time, an agent was appointed by the Indian government to oversee the upliftment of Indians who remained in South Africa (Pachai, 1971: 108). The policy failed because few Indians were willing to repatriate. The government, for its part, did nothing to improve the condition of Indians. This was left to private agencies administered by Indians. Muslim traders were prominent in a wide number of organizations that cut across religious and ethnic lines. Haji Dawood Mohamed, for example, was secretary of the NIC, trustee of the West Street Mosque, member of the Rice Advisory Committee formed during the First World War rice shortages, as well as a member of the 1917 Floods Committee. When he died, Hindu and Muslim businesses shut for the day as a mark of respect. An obituary in a Hindu newspaper pointed out that "his heart ever pulsated for the welfare of the entire Indian community. He was a truly and thoroughly patriotic man; ... his genuinely ardent patriotic zeal to lift up his compatriots ever commenced him to the community" (Dharma Vir, 29 August 1919). When M. E. Lakhi, another Muslim trader heavily involved in community work, died in 1941, Sorabjee Rustomjee noted in his eulogy, "he knew no communalism. He was first an Indian and always an Indian ... The vast concourse of Muslim, Hindu, Parsee, and Christian Indians that followed the funeral was a striking testimony to the esteem and respect that he was held by all" (Leader, 25 October 1941).

M. A. Motala, who arrived from India in 1903 and started out as a small retailer, was one of the richest merchants by the time of his death in 1957. In 1922, he founded a school for the children of employees of the Durban Corporation. In 1939, he established the M. A. Motala Boys Hostel near Pinetown for delinquent Indian boys between twelve and eighteen. He was also the second largest contributor to the Sastri College and donated land to the Natal Indian Blind Society in 1945 for the building of a Home and Vocational Training Centre (Mahida, 1993: 68–69). The R. K. Khan Hospital treated large numbers of patients annually at clinics in Somtseu Road, Clairwood, and Sea Cow Lake from the mid-1930s. In 1943, for example, 43,917 Indians were given free treatment (Leader, 6 February 1943). This was made possible by the philanthropic gesture of Advocate R. K. Khan who was born in Bombay in 1874, educated in England, and brought to South Africa in 1895 by Gandhi. During his stay in Natal, he acted as leader of the Ambulance Corps during the Anglo-Boer war, was joint-secretary of the NIC for many years until his death in 1932, president of the Orient Club, trustee in educational and Charity Trusts, and a generous contributor to educational projects. He bequeathed £40,000 for establishing hospitals and dispensaries for Indians (Indian Opinion, 14 October 1932). The clinics evolved into a fully-fledged hospital, which was opened in Chatsworth in 1969, with facilities for training doctors and nurses as well as conducting medical research. One Muslim who played a critical role in education was Malukmahomed Lappa (M. L.) Sultan, who was born in Malabar, South India, in 1874 and came to Natal as an indentured laborer in 1890. He worked as a railway porter for the Natal Government Railways. When he completed his indenture in 1895, he went to the Transvaal where he worked as a waiter. After his marriage in 1905, he took up banana and tobacco farming in Natal. When his wife died in 1933, Sultan established the Mariam Bee Charitable and Educational Trust in her memory with a contribution of £100,000 to promote cultural, educational, spiritual, and economic activities among Indians in Natal — irrespective of creed, caste, or religion (Leader, 27 August 1949). Sultan was also responsible for the first tangible development in technical education among Indians as a result of his donation of £17,500 in January 1942. He doubled this just prior to his death in 1953. The M. L. Sultan Technical College is one of the largest in South Africa (Mahida, 1993: 81).

As far as education was concerned, religious training rather than secular education was a priority. Muslims received formal religious education from a young age at *madrassas* attached to mosques. For example, the Durban Anjuman Islam School, attached to the West Street Mosque, was opened in 1909 (Indian Opinion, 5 February 1910). Similarly, a *madrassa* attached to the May Street Mosque had an average daily attendance of 79 in 1920 (Indian Opinion, 15 April 1921). A. M. Lockhat, proprietor of a large wholesale and import business, established the Hajee Ahmed Mohammed Lockhat Wakuff (Trust) in 1922, which founded *madrassas* in many parts of Durban. According to Bawa, *madrassas* taught Gujarati, Urdu and Arabic in addition to the tenets of Islam. For example, the Stanger Madrassa had three teachers — who taught these languages to 124 pupils.[7] Very few Indian children had access to secular education. In 1930, for example, only 30.9 per cent of children of school-going age attended school (Henning, 1995: 138). It was only during the 1940s and 1950s that leaders like A. I. Kajee and A. M. Moolla attempted to combine religious and secular education and opened the *South Coast Madrassa State Aided School*, *Ahmedia State Aided Indian School*, *Anjuman Islam State Aided School*, and *Orient Islamic High School* for this purpose.

MUSLIM ORGANIZATIONS

For most of this period, Muslim organizations remained confined to localized areas and took care of parochial needs. These included bodies such as the *Iqbal Study Group, Orient Islamic Educational Institute, Young Mens Muslim Association, May Street Muslim Jamaat, Isipingo Muslim Social Group*, and *Ahmedia Madrassa*. The first umbrella Muslim organization, the *Natal Muslim Council (NMC)*, formed in April 1943, was the brainchild of Advocate Ibrahim Bawa who was born in India in 1915 and came to South Africa at the age of four. He completed a BA degree at Wits University in 1938, a rarity for an Indian at that time, and qualified as a barrister at Lincoln's Inn, England, in 1941. According to Bawa, when he returned to Durban he "was struck by the lack of common vision and properly trained hafiz and *ulema* among Muslims," and was determined to form an organization to attend to the needs of Muslims in a coherent manner. Together with A. I. Kajee, the most prominent moderate Indian politician during the 1930s and 1940s, Bawa traveled all over Natal to drum up support for a body, which would speak with one voice for Muslims. The NMC eventually represented 22 organizations. At the first meeting chaired by Bawa, an Executive Committee comprising of A. I. Kajee as president; Bawa and M. S. Badat as secretaries; and M. A. Motala, A. M. Moolla, E. I. Haffejee, and A. B. Moosa as vice-presidents, was formed. There was only one Mawlana on the committee, Mohammed Bashir Siddiqui. The others were traders, who were also involved in sports and community organizations. The Council focused on propagation, culture, social welfare, secular and Islamic education, and finance (Interview, 20 January 1999).

That the NMC, dominated by traders and professionals, was the main voice of Muslims is indicative of the lack of power of ulema. A. I. Kajee, president of the NMC, was a moderate politician who served on many charitable organizations and mosque committees. He was secretary of the NIC and SAIC, manager of the May Street Indian School, secretary of the Indian Child Welfare Society, and was connected to virtually every public movement in relation to Indians. According to Mr G. M. R., Kajee was a regular at the Salisbury Club in Umgeni Road where his favorite pastime was snooker. Writing about Kajee, Pauline Podbrey (1993: 94-95), a white member of the Communist Party in Durban, recalled that during the 1930s and 1940s:

> One place where H. A., [his fiancée], and I might have gone together, was A. I. Kajee's luxurious house. His candle-lit dinner parties were posh affairs, with damask tablecloths, sparkling wine glasses, polished silver. One dressed up to go there and the men behaved with courtesy and charm ... But H. A. would not hear of it. Kajee was his political adversary. More than that, he did not trust his intentions towards me. H.A.'s distrust of Kajee expressed itself in other ways too. Kajee employed me; afterwards he would invite me for a drink or offer me a lift to wherever I wanted to go. H. A. was not happy so he took to dropping in at Kajee's office and waiting for me to finish my work.

Kajee was not the exception; E. I. Haffejee, a committee member of the NMC, was the president of the Durban and District Football Association and helped to form the Muslim Youth Brigade in 1934 with Mawlana Abdul Aleem Siddiqui. The brigade included girls and music, both of which the ulema would later proscribe. According to Mr O. V., a band member, they performed on numerous occasions — during the Prophet's birthday, when Muslims departed for pilgrimage to Mecca, when prominent personalities visited Durban, and during weddings. On festive occasions, the streets of Durban were decorated with flags, buntings, and decorative streamers. Thousands of Muslims lined the streets to watch the brigade march to the Grey Street mosque where the Mayor of Durban or other prominent whites, local Mawlanas, and community leaders addressed the gathering from a podium especially erected outside the Juma Mosque in Grey Street.

Muslim leaders were involved in a host of activities running the gamut from sports and social welfare to education. According to one informant, Mr G. M. R., a regular at West Street mosque from the 1920s, E. M. Paruk, a prominent trader, made decisions affecting Muslims, such as when to celebrate Eid. To cite another example, in 1949, the Durban City Council (DCC) prohibited the slaughter of animals in private premises during the festival of Eid, a tradition practiced by Durban's Muslims since 1860. Trader elites rather than the religious clergy took up the fight against the DCC by agitated Muslims resisting against what they considered a wanton attack on their religious freedom. The split over this issue among Durban's Muslims reflected political divisions. A. M. Moolla and moderate traders preferred to negotiate with the DCC, while A. I. Meer and the ANC-aligned NIC called for a boycott of the abattoir and for Muslims to send monies abroad to India or Saudi Arabia to slaughter animals until the DCC changed its attitude (Indian Views, 5 October 1949). While the DCC only changed its position in 1953, this incident demonstrates that traders rather than traditional ulema provided leadership. The little that is known about the ulema, suggests that they were very orthodox in their thinking. This is illustrated, for example, in their attitude towards the sighting of the new moon. The observance of the Eid festival is determined by the sighting of the new moon even though science accurately calculates the birth of the moon. Thirteen leading ulema decreed in Durban on 4 November 1934 that news of the sighting of the moon received via the telephone, telegram, or wireless message could not be accepted. Such information had to be conveyed personally by the individuals sighting the moon.[8]

Formally-trained ulema were in a weak position because they operated as individual employees of mosque committees. The South African government prohibited Indian immigration from 1914, except for ten "Exempted Educated Entrants" annually. Mosque committees had to apply for permission from the Immigration Department to import religious educators. Successful applicants were allowed into the country for a probationary period of twelve months, which was renewable annually. Permission was only granted when it was shown that a suitable person could not be obtained locally. For example, when seeking a replacement for the deceased Maulvi Matiola Amanulla, the Stanger Madrassa emphasized that advertisements had been placed in *Indian Views* — an Indian newspaper printed and circulated in Natal, but there was no response.[9] The West Street Mosque, likewise, imported Shaik Saith Nagar from the Cape in May 1919.[10] The Immigration Department insisted that permission be confirmed before the individual departed from India. For example, Moobin-ul-Hak and Ahmed Mohammed Vahed departed from India, in November 1917, before they even received permission from the Immigration Department. They were stranded at Delagoa Bay because G.

W. Dick, Principal Immigration Officer, in Natal, refused to allow them into the country.[11] The ulema were dependent on their employers to renew their permission annually. In June 1917, for example, the trustees of the West Street mosque appealed to the Minister of Interior to renew the visiting pass of Tajammal Hoosen.[12] These India-educated ulema, with minimal command of English and in foreign surroundings, were completely dependent on their employers and too weak to organize to protect their interests or articulate a coherent position.

Islam was a taken-for-granted aspect of the lives of most Muslims who were tolerant and broad-minded in their practices. Muslims accommodated a wide range of practices, including those associated with folk Islam, which was the Islam of the majority of Durban's Muslims. Muslims who did not partake directly in activities such as Muharram engaged as observers. Muharram remained a pivotal part of Islamic practice. There were literally hundreds of applications each year from Durban's Muslims to organize the festival, which was spread over several days. Essop Khan's October 1949 application was typical. He requested permission to hold the Muharram festival from 18 to 23 October. Festivities included nightly street processions from until 11 p. m., a fire-walking ceremony at Khan's home in Sea Cow Lake, and the final procession that made its way to Umgeni River.[13] Opposition to Muharram did not come from ulema who considered these practices contrary to Islam, as would be the case later, but from educated and trader elites embarrassed by the raucous processions. Chief Constable Graham interviewed seven 'better class Indian persons' in July 1949, all traders, who told him that the procession was "definitely against the Mahommedan Religion" and that they would give the police their 'whole-hearted' support in stopping it.[14] A letter followed the meeting from E. I. Haffejee and the NMC that stated:

> To our utter dismay and concern we note that some people instead of actually mourning the event actually rejoice. Pagodas, brightly decorated are conveyed through the streets of Durban. Usually music, the beating of tom toms, and tiger dancing accompany the procession and this generally initiates drunkenness, fighting, and rowdiness. Most of the participants in these celebrations are Africans, Coloureds, Hindus, and Muslims of the ignorant type ... We strongly feel that the Islamic religion is being ridiculed and the Moslem community disgraced before the eyes of others. We now appeal to you to refuse to issue these permits and thus do away with this religious farce.[15]

The call for action was in vain, Muharram remained a central part of the lives of the majority of Muslims until education, economic mobility, and a concerted crusade from reform-minded ulema in the 1970s reduced and/or changed the form of participation in the festival.

For the most part, however, Hindus and Muslims lived in harmony. Recalling life in Durban in the 1930s and 1940s, Harry Sewlall recalled "what was remarkable was the camaraderie that existed between Muslims and Hindus, who lived cheek-by-jowl with one another. I was not aware of any differences between us. In my family, we referred to our elderly Muslim neighbors as "mausi" (aunt) and "mausa" (uncle), (*Sunday Times Extra*, 12 December 1999). Muslim leaders largely overlooked religious distinctions. For example, at a meeting to mark the Indian Independence Day, A. I. Kajee, a Muslim, made it clear that they "were not assembled as Hindus, Christians and Muslims, but as Indians. The religious politics of India has not been imported into South Africa. Indians in this country must be Indians alone and not Mussulmans and Hindus" (Leader, 30 January 1948). At the same time, Muslims celebrated Jinnah's birthday annually and sent funds to him in his attempt to create Pakistan. At the 1946 celebration, for example, Kajee regarded Jinnah as a "leader of the entire Muslim world." Jinnah thanked them for the aid and emphasized that "as far as South Africa is concerned it will be treated as an all-Indian problem and I will help the Indians as Indians and not as Hindus or Muslims" (Leader, 5 January 1946). While Muslims celebrated the creation of Pakistan, Muslims and Hindus together celebrated the independence of India. At the 1947 Indian Independence celebrations in Durban, the NIC held a meeting in Durban at which the flags of both India and Pakistan were unfurled side-by-side with photographs of major leaders, including Jinnah (Leader, 2 September 1947).

During the period 1910–1950, the majority of working-class Indians moved from agricultural work into the rapidly growing manufacturing sector of Durban. As a result of the role that traders played in forming welfare and education bodies, the gap between them and the working-class Indians closed. While a multitude of regional and sectarian identities coexisted, they were all 'Indians' in relation to Africans and whites. From the 1930s, the focus of the state was on segregating Indians. The struggle over land was protracted and culminated in a passive resistance campaign by Indians during the period 1946 to 1948 (Bugwandeen, 1991). This increased the distance between Indians and the [white] state. At the same time, the growing tension between Indians and Africans during the 1940s culminated in riots between Africans and Indians following a minor altercation between an Indian man and an African youth on 13 January 1949. In three days of rioting, 142 lives were lost and 1087 people were injured. That a minor incident escalated into a major riot was an indication of the depth of antagonism Africans felt against Indians in a climate where they competed for scarce resources in trade, housing, and transport (Edwards and Nuttall, 1990). Tension with Africans and the purely Indian political parties, formed to fight wholly Indian struggles, brought Indian Muslims and Hindus together in the public sphere, and helped to foster Indianness. This racial identity was cemented after the National Party (NP) came to power in 1948.

INSTITUTIONS AND EXEMPLARS: THE APARTHEID PERIOD, 1948–1994

The coming to power of the National Party (NP) government in 1948 had paradoxical consequences for Indians. On the one hand, segregation intensified socially, politically, and economically. At the same time, Indians were finally recognized as permanent citizens, and there was an expansion of educational opportunities and economic mobility. These socio-economic changes affected the form and practice of Islam. Younger, better-educated Muslims challenged traditional conceptions of Islam, while, at the same time, interpretations that were more conservative of Islam were introduced. The latter laid the basis for the emergence of traditional Ulema as an influential factor shaping local Muslim communities. In 1951, there were 367,000 Indians in South Africa. Of these, 79,000 were Muslims who mostly resided in Durban. Only 6 per cent of Indians regarded English as their home language. Around twenty five per cent of Muslims spoke Gujarati and the rest primarily Urdu. Economic mobility and residential segregation were the main features of Indian life after 1960 (Brijlal, 1989: 29).

Residential clustering played a pivotal role in consolidating Muslim values. Indian traders, who began arriving from the 1870s, could not compete with the established white businesses. Therefore, they established their shops on swampy land at the northwestern periphery of the city. When the Indian and white business areas impinged, whites used the 1897 Dealer's License Act to restrict the further expansion of Indian traders (Davies, 1963: 23). Residential areas, in most parts of Durban, too were segregated according to race. Clearly defined residential areas emerged, either because whites were dissatisfied with the climate or topography, or because of deliberate attempts by the local state to implement segregation. There was 91% residential segregation between Indians and whites in Durban, in 1951 (Davies, 1963: 37). Segregation was consolidated after 1948 through the Group Areas Act. In Durban, 140,000 Indians had to move from their original homes to new residential areas between 1950 and 1978. They were segregated into two large townships — Chatsworth and Phoenix, while areas like Reservoir Hills, La Mercy, and Westville were made available for middle-class housing (Butler Adma and Venter, 1984: 18). Segregation led to population density that allowed Muslims to build mosques, madrassas, and community halls, where Islam was practiced in a value-friendly environment.

Education played an important role in transforming Indian Muslims. Literacy levels in 1950, were very low. The majority of Muslim children attended ordinary government secular schools. After the control of Indian education shifted to the Department of Indian Affairs, in 1965, free and compulsory education was available from 1970. The rapid increase in the building of schools resulted in adequate space for all children by 1983. This was reflected in the number of children attending school. For example, the number of candidates who wrote the final year examination at secondary school level increased from 2,623 in 1968 to 10,449 in 1984 (Naidoo, 1989: 116), which was coupled with the opening of the University of Durban-Westville (1963) and the expansion of the M. L. Sultan Technical College. The advantage taken by Indians of these opportunities was reflected in the fact that the number of Indians who regarded English as their home language increased from six per cent in 1951 to ninety-three per cent in 1996. Mass education was critical in re-shaping conceptions of self and religion. It gave Muslims direct access to the printed word, thus threatening the special position of traditional ulema; it marked a shift from religion being 'taken-for-granted' to Islam being thought of as a self-contained system that could be distinguished from other systems; it cultivated debate among Muslims and the formulation of clear statements of belief in order to illuminate sectarian distinctions. Islam became a subject that had to be 'explained' and 'understood,' rather than 'assumed.' This brought differences among Muslims to the surface (See Eickelman, 1992).

ISLAMIC REVIVALISM

There was a gradual change in the manner in which Muslims understood and practiced Islam. Islamic revivalism manifested itself among all sectors of Muslim society in Durban. It resulted in larger numbers of Muslims introducing Islam into their lives in a more systematic way, propagating and/or contesting the hegemony of their version of Islam, and reconstructing the relationship between faith, community, and society.

Let me explain this further by focusing on three broad traditions, which were influential in Durban — the modernist, Deobandi, and Barelwi. The resurgence of Islam among younger Muslims drew inspiration from the ideas of thinkers such as Muhammad Iqbal (d. 1938) and Sayyad Qutb (d. 1966), who attempted to marry Islamic knowledge with modern secular knowledge in order to engage Western culture and thought. A forerunner of later movements was the Arabic Study Circle, which began operating informally in 1950 and constituted itself into a formal body in 1954 with Dr Daud Saleh Mall as president. The social base of Circle members comprised mainly of the descendants of Gujarati trading class families who could afford secular education locally and abroad. Further, these individuals also traveled to the Middle East for Hajj (pilgrimage), which brought them into contact with Muslims from other parts of the world. The Circle promoted the study of Arabic so that Muslims could consult the Qur'an and formulate their own interpretations without passively relying on the analysis of ulema. The Circle introduced annual speech contests for school children, trained madrassa teachers, established an Islamic library, introduced Arabic in schools from 1975, introduced Arabic (1963) and Islamic Studies (1974) as academic disciplines at the University of Durban-Westville, sent young students abroad to expose them to new ideas, and invited dynamic non-Ulema Muslim thinkers such as Joseph Perdue, an English convert to Islam, to live and lecture in Durban. For these actions, the Circle was heavily criticized by traditional ulema (Mahida, 1993: 71–74). The Circle also promoted religious tolerance and organized regular seminars on Judaism, Christianity, Hinduism, and African faiths. Speakers included luminaries such as Professor Adrianus van Selms, of the Department of Semitic Studies at the University of Pretoria; Rabbi Swift, the then chief Rabbi of South Africa; and author, Alan Paton (Bhayat, 1992: 8–9).

There were several other organizations with a similarly broad perspective. The Durban and District Muslim Association attempted to narrow the gap between Muslims and non-Muslims, and Indians and whites. E. H. Ismail, a trader who was also heavily involved in soccer administration, led it. For example, when the annual celebration to commemorate the birthday of the Prophet was organized, on 31 October 1955, Ismail invited speakers such as the Vernon Essery, the Mayor of Durban; Professor Leo Kuper, of Natal University; and M. B. Naidoo, vice-principal of Sastri College. After garlanding the Mayor, Ismail told the audience, "Our desire is to live in peace and to share our heritage with our fellow subjects who sympathize with these" (Indian Views, 23 November 1955). The Iqbal Study Group, named after the great Muslim thinker, Sir Mohamed Iqbal, was made up of young Muslims who met to discuss issues affecting the Muslim world. They were especially critical of rich Muslims and the ulema. At the 1965 Iqbal Day celebrations, G. H. Bhabha was shocked that one of the speakers, Abdullah Deedat, had stated, "Mawlanas are good for nothing. How can we expect our children to respect the Mawlanas when such slanders are being hurled by mature men?" Cassim Abdullah also complained, that "the day was a monotonous singsong of hurling abuses at the rich and slurring the maulvis" (Indian Views, 30 August 1965). A. S. K. Joomal, who organized the event, was unrepentant. He pointed out that Iqbal has said "many things against the ways, manners, preaching, and peculiar brand of the mullahs' Islam and also the brutal, ruthless manner in which the affluent class has always exploited the poor. If the speakers have quoted from the Doctor's work on these topics, thus showing the Doctor up as the defender of the poor and a crusader for *true* Islam, what crime did these speakers commit?" (Indian Views, 23 August 1965). Other groups included the African Muslim Society and Kemal Study Group.

While these organizations were critical of stagnant thinking among Muslims, they were conservative politically. In comparison, the Muslim Youth Movement (1970) and Muslim Students Association (1974) actively challenged apartheid (Tayob, 1995). Young professionals and businessmen such as Hafiz Abu Bakr, an advocate who had memorized the Qur'an and who was one of the main spokesmen during the formative years, founded these two associations. It is no coincidence that he had spent a year in Cape Town, where he was in close contact with the Cape Muslim Youth Movement (Tayob, 1995: 107). The emergence of these organizations must be viewed in the context of the changing international Islamic environment where events such as the 1973 oil crisis, the 1978 Iranian revolution, the ongoing Palestinian problem, and the Russian invasion of Afghanistan in 1980 radicalized many Muslims. Like the Arabic Study Circle, the MYM too invited Black and women speakers to its conferences. They included Fatima Heeran, a German convert to Islam; Dr Rushud Din Malik, a black American Muslim; and intellectuals like Dr Ahmed Sakr and Ismail Faruqi from Temple University (Tayob, 1995: 108-9). The MYM spawned a host of organizations such as the South African National Zakaat Fund (1977), Islamic Dawah Movement (1981), Association of Muslim Accountants and Lawyers (AMAL), Islamic Medical Association of South Africa (1981), and Islamic Relief Agency (1987), which attempted to make Islam meaningful in the day-to-day lives of Muslims in an organized, coherent, and systematic manner.

The MYM's support was confined to the rapidly growing student and professional population. Among the mass of Muslims, there was a growth of conservative tendencies that came to be termed 'Deobandi' and 'Barelwi.' The year 1968 probably marks the apogee of a tolerant and liberal Islam in Durban. In that year, Durban's Muslims celebrated the 1400th anniversary of the revelation of the Qur'an. Over 20,000 Muslims gathered at Curries Fountain in August 1968 where the likes of Dr Mall of the Arabic Study Circle and A. M. Moolla, moderate politician and community leader, addressed the gathering. Muslim children dressed in gorgeous, colorful costumes that represented the dress of fourteen different Muslim countries including Pakistan, Burma, Kashmir, Moghul India, and Egypt recited *kasidas* (songs) in honor of the Prophet. The Durban and Overport Muslim Brigades lent a special glamour to the occasion as they rendered a military display and led the thousands of Muslims in a procession through the streets of Durban. Men, women, and children performed their Friday prayers in the open at Curries Fountain and joined in lunch, singing, and speeches (Indian News and Views, 15 August 1968). In subsequent years, activities such as singing, music, brigades, and men and women praying together were proscribed because of the growing influence of conservative ulema.

DEOBANDI ISLAM

Deobandi and Barelwi institutions have played an important role in shaping Indian Muslim opinion. Deobandi Islam became a force in India from the 1860s, when certain ulema responded to British dominance by renewing spiritual life through teaching principles of early Islam. They targeted popular behavior and claimed the right to interpret Islam for ordinary Muslims on the basis that only they had access to original Islamic sources. Deobandi schools remained aloof from political activity and the state, focusing instead on ministering to the educational and religious needs of Muslims in an attempt to create a sense of cultural community (Metcalf, 1982). Deobandi ulema were closely allied to the Gujarati trading class. According to Robinson, the conflict between popular and reformist Islam was between an intercessory and otherworldly Islam, and one which is 'this-worldly' in which the human conscience is brought into full play for man to act on earth to achieve salvation. Reformist Islam required Muslims to be literate, and most who embraced reformism were located within the middle class and engaged in aspects of the modern economy (Robinson, 1997). Institutionally, this tradition was represented by the Jamiatul Ulama Natal (hereafter Jamiat), established in 1952 to "guide generally the Muslim public in complete consonance with the laws of Islam" (Mahida, 1993: 71). Deobandi Islam focused on eradicating practices associated with Muharram and the visitation of saints' shrines, as well as reforming Indian customs related to marriage, funeral rites, dress, and so on which had become part of Muslim practice.

Closely allied was the role of the Tabligh Jamaat, the transnational religious movement founded in India by Muhammad Ilyas (1885-1944) (See Anwarul Haq, 1972). This movement was committed "to the fundamentals of faith and an unquestioning loyalty to a literal interpretation of Prophetic authority proclaimed to be Sunna" (Moosa, 1997: 31). The movement first made inroads in South Africa in the early 1960s among Gujarati traders. Later, however, it attracted support from Memons as well as some Urdu-speaking descendants of indentured Muslims (Moosa, 1997: 33). The main methods of propagation are *Gusht* (going from Muslim door-to-door), an annual *ijtima* over Easter (nationwide mass gathering), and *kitaab* (book) reading. The latter involved reading extracts from the works of Mawlana Zakariyya of India. Gusht involves moving from Muslim house-to-house, city-to-city, and country-to-country to impress on Muslims the need to live a righteous life by following the commandments of God and the example of the Prophet. An indication of the growth of the movement is that whereas the first ijtima attracted 300 people to Ladysmith in 1966, the gathering in Durban over Easter in 1999 attracted at least 25,000 people. The ijtima provides common group identity and reinforces Muslim perceptions that they belong to a larger international entity. While the putative right of Deobandi Islam to convey what it meant to be a good Muslim was very strong and it exerted a powerful influence over local Muslims, the diversity of Indian Muslims meant that no group could claim hegemony. In particular, Barelwi Islam has challenged this tradition.

BARELWI ISLAM

The Barelwi tradition has its origins in the work of Ahmad Raza Khan (1856–1922) of Bareilly in Uttar Pradesh, India (Sanyal, 1996). In South Africa, this tradition found expression through Soofie Saheb and his descendants. The main following is among descendants of indentured Muslims who followed this more populist form of Islam, which centered around sheikhs and shrines. This tradition was given organizational expression through the Sunni Jamiatul Ulama of South Africa, established in 1978 and Imam Ahmad Raza Academy, which was formed in 1986 (Mahida, 1993: 114, 133). Differences between Deobandis and Barelwis are due to class (trader against indentured), regional origins (western India against North and South), ethnicity (Gujarati against Urdu), as well as differences in belief and practice. As descendants of indentured Muslims acquired education and economic mobility, a professional class emerged from the 1970s that challenged the hegemony of traders, leading to numerous violent altercations. Barelwis were scathing of reform-minded Deobandis. The Badsha Pir Mazaar Committee, for example, described them as "white ants, eating away at the foundation of Islam." They were seen as following in the "footsteps of Christians." The long white robes of tablighis were equated with the dress worn by followers of the Carmelite Order, the veil was equated with the headdress of nuns, the chilla (forty days devotion) was equated with Lent, and so on. The annual Ijtima was described as a 'picnic;' their only enjoyment in life was to hold this annual Ijtima where they put up huge *degs* (pots) of food. "They have their four days of enjoyment, all under the pretence of propagating Islam." Tablighis were also accused of being CIA agents because their members were granted visas more easily than other Indian South Africans ("The Tableegh," 1 May 1976).

There were many instances of violence. In July 1977, the chairman of the Grey Street Trust, Aboobaker Ismail, terminated a special meeting to elect a new trustee after accusing Mawlana Omarjee, the tabligh-inclined candidate, of having brought supporters from outlying areas like Verulam, Tongaat, and Stanger to vote on his behalf (Mercury, 27 July 1977). In January 1980, twenty men entered the Sparks Road Musjid in Overport and stabbed Mawlana Tauhid of India to prevent him from speaking because he was allegedly pro-tabligh. A lecture scheduled for Grey Street mosque the following evening was canceled. According to one of the attackers, tablighi's controlled mosques in Newcastle, Port Shepstone, Ladysmith, Stanger, and all over the Transvaal. "We do not wish to go to their mosques and they must not come to ours" (Sunday Times, 13 January 1980). When the Grey Street mosque allowed tabligh-aligned ulema to speak, *Militant Sunni Musallees* distributed pamphlets, warning 'fence-sitting' trustees that unless they stopped *kitaab* reading, they would be responsible for "lighting a fuse that would eventually explode into an inferno."[16] An altercation on 7 March 1987 between Deobandis and Barelwis in Azaadville resulted in the death of Sheik Mohideen Saib, a Barelwi (Sunday Times, 8 March 1987). Hajee A. Jabbaar and three other worshippers were hit outside a mosque in Chatsworth in April 1988 (Daily News, 27 April 1988).

There were many other similar altercations as each group tried to prevent the other from carrying out its practices. While Barelwis wanted to end practices like kitaab (book reading), tablighi's prohibited Salaami, a practice in which members of the congregation stand and communally sent salutation to the Prophet. The tabligh program entailed reading extracts from *Hikayaat-e-Sahaabah* (*Stories of the Companions of the Prophet*), by the late Mawlana Muhammad Zakariyya of India, after each prayer. While this might seem an innocuous exercise, together the stories portrayed a picture of what the companions of the Prophet were like and provided an ideal for which Muslims should strive. This included things like, men wearing a beard, women wearing a veil, shunning the visitation of tombs, wearing of the pants above the ankles, and so on. Many of these practices were contrary to those accepted by Barelwis. Some Muslims came to the conclusion and even articulated the position, that the only solution was to have separate mosques. For example, one Abdul Raoof wrote to the *Leader* in March 1983 that "with both the groups pointing their goals in different directions, there is only one solution if peace is to prevail among the Muslim community and that is to have separate mosques."[17] This is exactly what happened. Barelwis challenged the status quo and used their numerical superiority to oust the traditionally dominant trading elites from several mosques. Examples include, Verulam and Lodge Grove where trading elites were ousted, sometimes after lengthy court cases. The response of tabligh-aligned trading elites was to build their own mosques a short distance away even though population numbers did not warrant a second mosque. Examples include Verulam, Westville, and Mallinson Road where each tradition has its own mosque so that it can carry out its practices.

ISLAMIC COUNCIL OF SOUTH AFRICA (ICSA)

The formation of the Islamic Council of South Africa (ICSA), in November 1975 marked an attempt to unite Muslims on a national level. It was formed by Dr Inamullah Khan of the World Muslim Congress and Abdul Muhsin Al-Shaykh of Saudi Arabia, when 109 organizations met during a visit to South Africa. The first office-bearers of ICSA included, Advocate A. B. Mahomed (President), Mawlana Ansari (Vice-President), and Advocate Bawa (Secretary General).[18] Of the major Muslim bodies, the Transvaal Jamiat did not join because it held the view that only ulema, not professionals, could speak for Muslims.[19] To placate ulema from Natal and the Cape, ICSA gave them the power to veto any decision of the Judicial Committee. There were too many differences between the members. For example, ulema condemned the translation of the Qur'an by Muhammad Asad, a convert to Islam who adopted a liberal position, while educated Muslims welcomed it. This led to the MYM and Arabic Circle withdrawing from ICSA.[20] Political differences also led to a split. When the government created separate parliaments for Indians and Coloureds in 1983, ICSA rejected the proposals. The Juma Musjid Trust and Sydenham Muslim Association, whose respective chairmen, Aboobakr Ismail and Abdullah Khan were in favor of participating, withdrew from ICSA.[21] From the mid-1980s, ICSA was an empty shell. Its message and orientation did not sit well with traditional ulema. For example, when Bawa was president, he appealed to Indian Muslims "to increase their sensitivity to the situation and condition of the Black community ... quicken your conscience to help them in every way possible; be just in your dealings with them and build bridges of understanding ..."[22] This was the kind of message that Indian Muslims did not want to hear. There was minimal contact between them and African Muslims who were mainly cleaners and *Bhangi's* (callers to prayer) in mosques. By the 1990s, the balance of power was shifting to Islamic institutions controlled by the ulema, and to issues that were more pedantic. Though it continues to exist, ICSA enjoys minimal support among Indian Muslims.

ISLAMIC PROPAGATION CENTRE (IPC)

This period was also witness to cracks in the relationship between Hindus and Muslims as a result of the activities of Ahmed Deedat. He had formed the IPC in 1957 to counteract the propaganda of Christian missionaries who, he asserted, were claiming that Muslims were anti-Christ, Muslims worshiped Muhammad, and Islam was a danger to South Africa and so on.[23] Initially, both Hindus and Muslims supported the IPC because its attack was against Christianity. Hindus supported this crusade for two reasons. First, because the majority of Christians were white and any attack on whites was welcomed during the apartheid era. Second, even a cursory reading of newspapers during the 1970s and early 1980s showed the fear and concern among Hindu leaders regarding the conversion of Hindus to Christianity. Newspaper headlines such as "Christian exploitation of Hindus could lead to a religious war"[24] and "Conversions worry SA Hindus" were common.[25] Hindus welcomed Deedat's denigration of Christianity. This changed in 1986, when the IPC produced the video, *From Hinduism to Islam*. P. D. Persadh, General Secretary of the South African Hindu Maha Sabha, "viewed the present conflict with dismay ... Surely Islamic teachings are not intended to ridicule and build enmity."[26] The Sabha's appeal to the IPC to withdraw the video was unsuccessful as were the attempts of Hindu leaders to get the Government Publications Board to ban the video. Many Muslims also criticized the tape. For Example, Bawa of ICSA, "deplored attempts by any group to degrade the religious practices of any other community."[27] Notwithstanding this, there was tension between Muslims and Hindus. For example, at a meeting at UDW in 1986, Hindu students "heckled and booed Muslims in the audience, who then walked out."[28] In another incident, Hindus in Avoca, a suburb of Durban, circulated pamphlets to boycott a pharmacy owned by a Muslim, Mr Hassen.[29]

MUSLIMS AND APARTHEID

When it came to power in 1948, the NP was determined to entrench racial and ethnic identities by establishing 'nations.' Apartheid legislation restricted contact between Indians and those defined as African, Coloured, or white in all areas of life. The NIC did engage in cross-race protest with the ANC during the 1950s but this ended with the banning of the ANC and PAC in 1960.[30] Ironically, the continued existence of the Natal 'Indian' Congress perpetuated racial divisions of resistance and reinforced racial identities.[31] The legal position of Indians changed in 1961 when they were granted the status of permanent residents. A Department of Indian Affairs was established, and the government attempted to incorporate Indians politically by appointing Indian advisory bodies. The South African Indian Council, comprising of nominated members, was inaugurated in 1968. Local Affairs Committees were also established, to advice municipalities and local authorities on 'Indian matters.' In 1983, the Tricameral Dispensation introduced a separate parliament for Indians. The reaction of Indian Muslims to apartheid, like Indians, generally ranged from vigorous opposition to active cooperation with the regime. Muslims such as A. Joosub and A. M. Moolla participated in these structures, while the likes of Farouk Meer and Jerry Coovadia were active members of the United Democratic Front (1983), which had been established to coordinate opposition to apartheid. While the NIC joined the nonracial United Democratic Front during the 1980s to oppose participation in government-created ethnic structures,[32] the ideology of nonracialism did not extend to the masses. The racial exclusivity of Indians continued until the release of Nelson Mandela in February 1990, the unbanning of political organizations, multiparty negotiations, and ultimately, South Africa's first democratically-elected government in 27 April 1994. While it is dangerous to generalize, it can be safely argued that unlike the Cape, the Muslim experience in Durban has been a much depoliticized one and, in fact, that they largely avoided the turbulent 1980s. This differs from the more radical expression of Islam in the Cape during the apartheid years. Cape Muslims, influenced by the 1979 Islamic Revolution in Iran, formed the Pan-Africanist 'Qibla' under Ahmed Cassiem, which popularized the slogan — "One solution, Islamic Revolution." Qibla provided the revolutionary fervor that made Muslims a feared force amongst the police and the armed forces.[33]

POST-1994: TURNING TO THE CORE? [34]

The changes that were taking place during the 1970s and 1980s, particularly the growing influence of institutional Islam and ulema, has also had an impact on Islamic practices. The nonracial democracy has opened the society and clearly does not support an Islamic worldview; on the contrary, the new ANC government has legalized abortion, prostitution, pornography, and so on. All this has to be seen in the context of the government's affirmative action policy and African Renaissance agenda. The result of these external changes and growing influence of conservative tendencies from within is that large numbers of Muslims are changing their behavior in a number of areas. There is a staggering increase, for example, in the number of women who cover their face. The requirement to cover the face is contested within local Islamic tradition.[35] The veil is seen by the Ulema as a pivotal aspect of the drive to prevent transgression of gender norms. Muslim women venture far more in public spaces than their predecessors of a generation ago, appearing regularly in places where nudity and other un-Islamic practices are the norm, such as holiday resorts and the beach. According to the census of the total number of 24,842 Muslims in formal employment in Durban in 1996, 7900 (32%) were women. This is a relatively high percentage, considering that prior to the 1980s, there were few women in formal employment and that the census does not account for the large number of women in informal work such as dressmaking, cooking, babysitting, and religious teaching. The result of this drive to re-establish gender norms, will be a reversal of the trend in the 1970s and 1980s whereby Muslim women acquired education and went out to work.

There is far greater concern with observing religious 'regulations' concerning food consumption;[36] the number of Muslims going annually to Saudi Arabia for pilgrimage has increased, from an average of 4,000 per annum at the beginning of the 1990s to 8,758 in 1998;[37] there has been a concerted and successful effort to root out televisions from Muslim homes; Muslims are marrying younger and eliminating lavish ceremonies; there is a de-westernization in the way of dressing and a return to 'authentic' Islamic dress amongst many men who have taken to wearing Arab garb, short hair, shaved moustache, and long beards; many Muslims have given up insurance, including personal and car insurance, medical aid, and have turned to Islamic banks such as the Al-Baraka Bank; there is dramatic growth in Muslim and Islamic schools; while standardization of the syllabus has meant that madrassas are disseminating a rigorous knowledge of Islamic rituals, beliefs, values, and practices to children from a young age. The new Islamic lifestyle is behavioral in perspective as it based on conduct and social action. There is an almost complete lack of theological debate. 'Truth' is synonymous with the Ulema, and to question the Ulema means questioning the truth. Another conspicuous feature of the new Islam is self-reformation. The trend whereby individuals become attached to Shaykhs (Spiritual Mentors) is becoming extremely popular. The turn to mysticism is not self-conscious, as many respondents did not realize that these practices are part of Sufism. Like other aspects of the Islamic revival, these practices are a source of tension because some Ulema feel that they were not carried out by the Prophet and should therefore have no place in Islamic tradition.

In seeking to introduce new and tighter Islamic codes in the public and private domains, Indian Muslims are using the new freedoms of a secular state to create space for themselves and are thereby redefining for themselves the kind of Muslims they want to be. An inward-looking Indian Muslim community is developing, with an understanding that the constitution can be used to struggle for specific needs and rights. Oliver Roy regards this as the creation of 'liberated zones,' that is, forming spaces where the ideals of a future society can prevail. In "liberated zones, no counter-power is established, no counter-state." Instead, there prevails the "idea of later spreading the principles on which it is founded to the whole of society" (1996: 80). This did not imply animosity to the state. This differs from the Cape where Muslims have rallied in large numbers around issues of crime, drugs, the U.S. bombing of Iraq, and the visit by Tony Blair. Attempts by PAGAD to form a chapter in Durban under Rashid Suleman failed to muster support. The two Islamic parties that contested the 1994 elections, the Cape-based Islamic party under Abdullah Gamieldien, and the Africa Muslim Party under Imtiaz Sooliman, failed to gain a seat. In 1999, the Africa Moral Party contested the election without success (*Al-Qalam*, May 1999). The new Islam does not have a proselytizing aspect to it. It is based largely on self-reformation, while contact and integration with non-Indian Africans, white, and Coloured Muslims is largely nonexistent. While many Muslim intellectuals and professionals are concerned about the new conservatism, their problem is one of relevance because the shapers of opinion among the majority of Indian Muslims are formally trained Ulema. The influence of intellectuals is marginal and they are confined outside mosques.

CONCLUSION: CHANGING DISCOURSES, BOUNDARIES, AND IDENTITIES

Islamic and Muslim societies are often viewed as "one global, timeless and cultural system." On the contrary, Muslims and Muslim societies are "complex and sociologically diverse" (Roy, 1994: vii). As our study shows, there are multiple Islamic voices and multiple Islamic traditions. There has been continuous re-interpretation and re-definition of Islamic tenets, which is often contested. These debates have centered on what it means to be a Muslim, what Islam is about, and how the Qur'an and hadith should regulate ones life. This has not been confined to modernists but is integral to all traditions. While these traditions have been transforming, they have not lost their status of normativity. The majority of Muslims, and particularly the Barelwi and Deobandi traditions, continue to view Islam as a unique and timeless whole that is the sum total of divinely-ordained beliefs. The identities of Indian Muslims have been constantly shifting since they first arrived in South Africa in 1860. For the most part, the dominant identity in relation to outsiders was 'Indian' in a situation where race played a central role in defining existence. This is changing in post-apartheid South Africa where many Muslims seem to be retreating to an Islamic identity that is superseding ancestry, descent, and language. This needs to be understood in the wider sociopolitical context of African majority rule in South Africa, globalization, and Muslim fears. Muslims are constructing boundaries around various points of contact — between men and women, Muslims and non-Muslims, Muslims and the state, Islam and secularism, and so on. The interpretation of institutional Islam in the Deobandi/Barelwi tradition, which is conservative and strict, is becoming more hegemonic. The attempt to forge a "Muslim identity" is difficult because of deep differences of tradition. However, while it would be incorrect to suggest that a homogeneous Islam is emerging, there is greater tolerance for the perspectives of others. The violent altercations between Barelwis and Deobandis, for example, have subsided, while the rise of Sufi Islam is one example, where a middle ground has been found.

Endnotes

1. Details were kindly supplied by Professor Tom Bennett and Professor Joy Brain who are compiling an inventory of every indentured Indian. This figure is an approximation as it is made up of those who listed their caste as Muslim, castes that were entirely Muslim, and names that suggested that the immigrants were Muslims. Of 130,000 immigrants analyzed, there were 7874 Muslims, comprising of 4958 males, 2418 females, 233 girls, and 248 boys.

2. Following complaints by returning Indians about their treatment, a Protector of Indian Immigrants was appointed in 1874. Indentured Indians could lodge their complaints with him. In practice, he was powerless since he was an employee of the Whites.
3. Deeds of Transfer Constituting the Juma Musjid Sunat Jamat Anjuman Islam, Durban, 25 November 1893.
4. Deeds Constituting the Surti Anjuman Juma Musjid, 16.1.1899
5. *Gazetteer*, 1899: 56. Muin-ud-din was one of the *panj pir* (five pirs) who are considered the five great Chisti Shaykhs; the other four being Nasir al-din, Nizam al-din, Farid al-din, and Qutb al-din. Muslims from the Chisti sufi order from all over India visited Ajmer from the fourteenth century, even though this was a dangerous undertaking because of the terrain and danger of armed robbery. Most of these pilgrims came dressed in pilgrim garb (ihram-i-ziyarat) and a few even professed bay'at at the grave even though the saint was dead (Digby, 1983: 97).
6. *Gazetteer* of the Bombay Presidency, Musalmans and Parsis Vol. IX, Part II. (Bombay: Government Central Press, 1899), 61.
7. SAR, BNS 902 A/1675, 8 May 1926, Stanger Madrassa to Principal Immigration Officer.
8. Indian Views, 7 November 1934. The thirteen Mawlanas were Abdul Rehman Ansari, Pietermaritzburg; Ahmed Mukhtar Siddiqui of Durban; Mahomed Abdul Kadir Afriki of Durban; Abdus Samad of Durban; Sayyed-ul-Haq of Verulam; Mohamed Yousuf of Umzinto; Sayed Serfuddin of Durban; Abdul Karrim of South Coast junction; Hazrath-ud-Deen of Stanger; Sayed Abdul Kadir of Durban; Abdul Vahed Punjabi of Durban; Mohamed Abdul Aleem Siddiqui of Durban; and Suleman Mohammed Kafletvi of Durban.
9. SAR, BNS 902 A/1675, 8 May 1926, Stanger Madrassa to Principal Immigration Officer.
10. SAR, BNS 902 21/A/461, 26 May 1919, Principal Immigration Officer (Natal) to PIO (Durban).
11. SAR, BNS 902 21/A/461, 26 November 1917, Principal Immigration Officer (Natal) to PIO (Durban).
12. SAR, BNS 902 21/A/461, 18 June 1917, E. M. Paruk to Minister of Interior.
13. NAR, 3/DBN, 4/1/4/1093, D. E. Khan to Town Clerk, 3rd October 1949.
14. NAR, 3/DBN, 4/1/4/281, Sergeant Graham to Chief Constable, 7 November 1949. The seven were A. E. Shaikh of 339 Pine Street; A. M. Moolla of Lockhat Brothers; S. M. Lockhat of Lockhat Brothers; I. A. Kajee of 37 Albert Street; M. A. Lockhat of Commercial Road; E. I. Haffejee of the Natal Muslim Council; and the Mawlana (High Priest) of the Grey Street Mosque.
15. NAR, 3/DBN, 4/1/4/281, Natal Muslim Council to Chief Constable, 10 July 1949. The letter was signed by E. Haffejee, C. A. Kajee, C. Asmal, H. Badah, and A. Motala.
16. Pamphlet issued in March 1980. A kitaab is a book and this refers to the practice of Tablighi's to read extracts from the works of Mawlana Zakariyya of India.

17. "Leader," 4 March 1983. This is not the real name of the writer of the letter because Sufee, Mawlana of the Westville Soofie Mosque, was an opponent of the Tabligh's.
18. ICSA, First Annual Report by the Secretary-General (I. M. Bawa), 26 November 1976.
19. Interview with Ebrahim Bawa, 20 January 2000.
20. Interview with Ebrahim Bawa, 20 January 2000.
21. "Mercury," 7 June 1983.
22. *Post*, 6 July 1983.
23. *Mahida, History of Muslims*, 80.
24. *Sunday Times*, 30 September 1979.
25. *Sunday Times*, 2 May 1982.
26. *Post*, 4 May 1986.
27. *Sunday Tribune*, 20 April 1986.
28. *Post*, 18 May 1986.
29. *Sunday Tribune*, 11 May 1986.
30. (Gerhart 1978, 107).
31. Vawda and Singh.
32. The United Democratic Front (UDF), based on the principles of the Freedom Charter, was launched on 20 August 1983 to protest against the tri-cameral dispensation. It included trade unions, religious bodies, student organizations, and civic associations. The formation of the UDF marked another attempt to reinstate the heritage of nonracialism. The NIC's vigorous anti-election programme included mass and local rallies as well as house-to-house visits. This resulted in low voter registration and turnout.
33. F. Esack, "Three Strands in the South African struggle for justice," in *Third World Quarterly*, 10, 2: 473–498, 486.
34. For a detailed examination of this period, see Vahed, G. "Changing Islamic Traditions and Emerging Identities in South Africa," *Journal of Muslim Minority Affairs*. Vol. 20, No. 1, April 2000: 43–73.
35. The Jamiat, for example, ruled that "due to the immorality of the times … it is compulsory for a female to cover her face which is the focus of her beauty. This would accord a woman a 'degree of respect, honor and dignity and of being in charge of her body.' "The Sunni Jamiat, on the other hand, whose support base is amongst working-class Muslims, does not compel women to cover their faces.
36. Muslims cannot consume pork or alcohol while other animals have to be slaughtered in a prescribed manner.
37. Figures supplied by Farid Choonara, Chariman, Hajj, and Umrah Council, 19 August 1999.

Bibliography

Abbas, Rizvi S. A. *A History of Sufism in India, Vol. One*. New Delhi: Munshiram Manorharlal Publishers, 1978.

Ahmed, Akbar S. *Postmodernism and Islam. Predicament and Promise.* London: Routledge, 1992.
Alexander, R. "Progress of Arabs and Indians in the Borough during the past Twenty years." Natal Archives, GH 1589, 21 February 1885.
Anderson, B. *Imagined Communities. Reflections on the Origin and Spread of Nationalism.* London: Verso, 1983.
Anwarul Haq, M. *The Faith Movement of Mawlana Muhammad Ilyas.* London, 1972.
Bawa, I. M. *First Annual Report of the Islamic Council of South Africa.* 1976.
Bayly, S. *Saints, Goddesses, and Kings. Muslims and Christians in South Indian Society 1700–1900.* Cambridge: Cambridge University Press, 1989.
Bhana, S. "Indianness Reconfigured, 1944–1960: The Natal Indian Congress in South Africa," *Comparative Studies of South Asia, Africa, and the Middle East,* XVII, 2 (1997): 100–107.
———. *Gandhi's Legacy. The Natal Indian Congress, 1894–1994.* Pietermaritzburg: University of Natal Press, 1997.
———. *Indentured Indian Emigrants to Natal, 1860–1902. A Study Based on Ships Lists.* New Delhi: Promilla, 1991.
Bhana, S. and J. Brain. *Setting Down Roots. Indian Migrants in South Africa, 1860–1911.* Cape Town: David Philips, 1984.
Bhayat, H. I. "Arabic Study Circle." BA (Hons.), University of Durban-Westville, 1992.
Brijlal, P. "Demographic Profile," in A. J. Arkin et al. *The Indian South Africans: A Contemporary Profile.* Durban: Owen Burgess Publishers, 1989.
Bugwandeen, D. I. *A People on Trial for Breaching Racism: The Struggle for Land and Housing of the Indian People of Natal, 1940–1946.* Durban: Madiba Publications, 1991.
Buijs, G. "The influence of migration on ethnic identity: An historical analysis of the disappearance of caste among Indian South Africans," Paper presented at conference on "Ethnicity, Society, and Conflict in Natal," University of Natal, Pietermaritzburg, September 1992.
Da Costa, Y. and A. Davids, eds. *Pages from Cape Muslim History.* Pietermaritzburg: Shuter and Shooter, 1994.
Davids, A. *The Mosques of Bo-Kaap: A Social history of Islam at the Cape.* Cape Town: South African Institute of Arabic and Islamic Research, 1980.
Davies, R. J. "The Growth of the Durban Metropolitan Area," *South African Geographical Journal.* December 1963.
Digby, S. "Early Pilgrimages to the Graves of Mu'in al-din Sijzi and Other Indian Chishti Shaykhs," in *Islamic Society and Culture: Essays in Honour of Professor Aziz Ahmed,* edited by M. Israel and N. K. Wagle. New Delhi: Manohar, (1983): 95–100.
Edwards, I. and T. Nuttall. "Seizing the Moment: the January 1949 Riots, Proletarian Populism, and the Structures of African urban Life in Durban during the 1940s." Paper presented at the History Workshop, University of Witwatersrand, 6–10 February 1990.

Eickelman, Dale F. "Mass Education and the religious imagination in contemporary Arab societies," in *American Ethnologist*, 19, 4 (1992): 643–655.

Esposito, John L. *Political Islam. Revolution, Radicalism, or Reform?* London: Lynne Rienner Publishers, 1997.

Essack, F. "Three Strands in the South African Struggle for Justice," in *Third World Quarterly*, 10, 2 (1980): 473–498.

Freund, B. *Insiders and Outsiders.* Pietermaritzburg: University of Natal Press, 1995.

Gazatteer of the Bombay Presidency, Musalmans, and Parsis. Vol. IX, part II., 1899. Bombay: Government Central Press.

Henning, C. G. *The Indentured Indian in Natal.* New Delhi: Promilla & Co, 1993.

Hiralal, K. "The Natal Indian Trader — A Struggle for Survival." MA Dissertation, University of Durban-Westville, 1991.

Hiskett, M. *The Course of Islam in Africa. Islamic Surveys 15*, Edinburgh: Edinburgh University Press, 1994.

Jamal, R. C. "A Study of the West Street Mosque in Durban." BA Hons. Thesis, University of Durban-Westville, 1987.

Jeppie, M. S. "Historical Process and the Constitution of Subjects: I. D. du Plessis and the reinvention of the Malay." BA Hons. Thesis, University of Cape Town, 1987.

Jeppe, S. "Leadership and Loyalties: The Imams of Nineteenth Century Colonial Cape Town, South Africa," *Journal of Religion in Africa.* XXVI, 2 (1996): 139–162.

———. "Politics and Identities in South Africa: Reflections on the 1994 Tri-Centenary Celebrations in South Africa." 12th Annual Conference of the American Council for the Study of Islamic Societies, Villanova University, Philadelphia, 1995.

Khan, A. 'Homeland, Motherland: Authenticity, Legitimacy, and Ideologies of Place among Muslims in Trinidad,' in *Nation and Migration. The Politics of Space in the South Asian Diaspora*, edited by P van der Veer. Philadelphia: University of Pennsylvania Press, 1995.

Kramer, G. "On Difference and Understanding: The Use and Abuse of the Study of Islam," in *Allgemeine Themen*, 57–60.

Kuper, H. *Indian People in South Africa.* Pietermaritzburg: University of Natal Press, 1960.

Lee, R. "Foreword," in M. Arkoun, *Rethinking Islam. Common Questions, Uncommon Answers.* Translated and Edited by Robert D. Lee. Oxford: Westview Press, 1994.

Mahida, E. M. *History of Muslims in South Africa: A Chronology.* Durban: Arabic Study Circle, 1993.

Meer, F. *Portrait of Indian South Africans.* Durban: Avon Press, 1969.

Metcalf, B. D. *Islamic Revival in British India: Deoband, 1860–1900.* New Jersey: Princeton University Press, 1982.

Moosa, E. " 'Worlds Apart:' The Tabligh Jamat Under Apartheid 1963-1993," *Journal for Islamic Studies,* Vol. 17 (1997): 28–48.

Naidoo, M. "Education," in A. J. Arkin et al. *The Indian South Africans: A Contemporary Profile*. Durban: Owen Burgess Publishers, 1989.

Pachai, B. *International Aspects of the South African Indian Question*. Cape Town: Struik, 1971.

Padayachee, V. and R. Morrell. "Indian Merchants and Dukawallahs in the Natal Economy, c.1875-1914," *Journal of Southern African Studies* 17, 1 (1991): 1–28.

Podbrey, P. *White Girl in Search of the Party*. Pietermaritzburg: Hadeda Books, 1993.

Robinson, F. "Religious Change and the Self in Muslim South Asia since 1800," *South Asia*, XX (1) (1997): 1–15.

———. "Islam and Muslim society in South Asia." *Contributions to Indian Sociology*. 17, 2 (1983): 185-203.

Roy, Olivier. *The Failure of Political Islam*. Harvard: Harvard University Press, 1996.

Sanyal, U. *Devotional Islam and Politics in British India: Ahmed Riza Khan and His Movement, 1870–1920*. Delhi: Oxford, 1996.

Schell, Robert C. H. 'Islam in Southern Africa, 1652-1998,' in Nehemia Levitzon and Randall Pouwells, *The History of Islam in Africa*. Oxford: James Currey, (2000): 327-348.

Soofie, Shah Mohamed Saeid and Shah Abdul Aziz Soofie. *Hazrath Soofie Saheb and His Khanqaha*. Durban: Impress Web, 1999.

South African Institute of Race Relations. *The Indian Population of South Africa*. Johannesburg: South African Institute of Race Relations, 1946.

Sulliman, E. A Historical Study of the largest Mosque in the Southern Hemisphere, namely the Juma Musjid. BA Hons., University of Durban-Westville, 1985.

Swan, M. *Gandhi: The South African Experience*. Johannesburg: Ravan, 1985.

Sykes, P. "An analysis of Income and Expenditure of a sample of Indian families in the Clairwood area of Durban." *The South African Journal of Economics*, 1941.

Tayal, M. "Indian Indentured labour in Natal, 1860-1911," *Indian Economic and Social History Review*, XIV, 4 (1977): 519–549.

Tayob, A. *Islamic Resurgence in South Africa: The Muslim Youth Movement*. Cape Town: University of Cape Town Press, 1995.

———. *Islam in South Africa. Mosques, Imams, and Sermons*. Gainesville: University of Florida Press. University of Natal, 1952. *The Durban Housing Survey*. Durban: University of Natal, 1999.

Vahed, G. H. "Changing Islamic Traditions and Emerging Identities in South Africa," *Journal of Muslim Minority Affairs*, 20, 1 (2000): 43–73.

Vawda, S. and Wragg Singh Commission of 1885. *Documents of Indentured Labour: Natal 1851–1917*. Edited by Y. S. Meer. Durban: Institute for Black Research, 1980.

Interviews

I. M. Bawa, 20 January 2000.

Mr G. M. R., 22 April 1999 and 4 May 1999. Mr G. M. R. is a Gujarati-speaking male, born in Durban in 1913.

POLITICAL ISLAM AND AFRICAN POLITICS

6

Afrabia: Evolutionary Convergence between Africa and the Arab World

ALI A. MAZRUI

By far, the most ambitious idea floating in the new era of African-Arab relations is whether the whole of Africa and the whole of the Arab world are two regions in the process of merging into one. Out of this speculative discourse has emerged the concept of *Afrabia* — the interaction and fusion between Africanity and Arab identity.

Two tendencies have stimulated new thinking about African-Arab relations. One tendency, which is negative but potentially unifying, is the war on terrorism. The other is the deepening of relationships between Africa and the Middle East.

The new international terrorism may have its roots in injustices perpetrated against such Arab people as Palestinians and Iraqis, but the primary theater of contestation is blurring the distinction between the Middle East and the African continent.[1] In order to kill twelve Americans in Nairobi, in August 1998, over two hundred Kenyans died in a terrorist attack on the United States Embassy in Nairobi. In 2002, a suicide bomber in Mombasa, Kenya, attacked the Israeli-owned and Israeli-patronized, Paradise Hotel. Three times as many Kenyans as Israelis died. African countries like Uganda, South Africa, Tanzania, and Kenya have been under American pressure to pass antiterrorist legislation — partly intended to control their own Muslim populations and partly targeted at potential Al-Qaeda infiltrators. Uganda, Tanzania, and others have already capitulated to American pressure.

Independent of the war on terror, Islam as a cultural and political force has also been deepening relationships between Africa and the Middle East. Intellectual revival is not only in the Western idiom; it is also in the idiom of African cultures and African Islam. The hot political debates about the

Shari'a (Islamic Law) in Nigeria constitute part of the trend of cultural integration between Africa and the Middle East.

The new legitimation of Muammar al- Gadaffi, as an African Elder Statesman, has contributed to the birth of no less a new institution than the African Union. In my own face-to-face conversations with the Libyan leader, I have sometimes been startled by how much more Pan-Africanist than Pan-Arabic he has recently become. At least, for the time being, Gadaffi is out-Africanizing the legacy of Gamal Abdel Nasser.

The fourth force, which may be merging Africa with the Middle East is political economy. Africa's oil producers need a joint partnership with the bigger oil producers of the Middle East. In the area of aid and trade between Africa and the Middle East, the volumes may have gone down since the 1980s; however, most indications seem to promise a future expansion of economic relations between Africa and the Middle East.[2] In the Gulf countries of the United Arab Emirates and the Sultanate of Oman, the concept of *Afrabia* has begun to be examined on higher echelons. Let us look more closely at this concept in the light of the revival of both intellectual discourse and new approaches to Pan-Africanism.

WHO ARE THE AFRABIANS?

It was, initially, Trans-Saharan Pan-Africanism, which gave birth to the idea of *Afrabia*. The first postcolonial waves of Pan-Africanists, like Nkrumah, believed that the Sahara Desert was a bridge rather than a divide.

The concept of *Afrabia* not only now connotes an interaction between Africanity and Arab identity; it is also seen as a process of fusion between the two. While the principle of *Afrabia* recognizes that Africa and the Arab world are overlapping categories, it goes on to prophesy that these two regions are in the historic process of becoming one.

But who are the *Afrabians?* There are, in reality, at least four categories. Cultural *Afrabians* are those whose culture and way of life have been deeply Arabized, falling short of their being linguistically Arabs. Most Somali, Hausa, and some Waswahili are cultural Afrabians in that sense. Their mother tongue is not Arabic but much of the rest of their culture bears the stamp of Arab and Islamic impact.

Ideological *Afrabians* are those who intellectually believe in solidarity between Arabs and Africans, or at least between Arab Africa and black Africa. Historically, such ideological *Afrabian* leaders have included Kwame Nkrumah, the founder president of Ghana; Gamal Abdel Nasser, arguably the greatest Egyptian of the twentieth century; and Sékou Touré, the founding father of postcolonial Guinea (Conakry). Such leaders refused to recognize the Sahara Desert as a divide and insisted on visualizing it as a historic bridge.

Geographical *Afrabians* are those Arabs and Berbers whose countries are members of both the African Union and the Arab League. Some of the countries are overwhelmingly Arab, such as Egypt and Tunisia, while others are only marginally Arab, such as Mauritania, Somalia, and the Comoro Islands.

As for Genealogical *Afrabians*, they are those who are biologically descended from both Arabs and Black Africans. In North Africa, these include Anwar al-Sadat, former President of Egypt; he concluded a peace treaty with Israel and was assassinated in 1982, consequently. Anwar al-Sadat's mother was Black. He was politically criticized for many things, but almost never for being racially mixed.

Genealogical *Afrabians* in sub-Saharan Africa include Salim Ahmed Salim, the longest serving Secretary-General of the Organization of African Unity (OAU) — which is now called African Union (AU). Genealogical *Afrabians* also include the Mazrui clan scattered across Coastal Kenya and Coastal Tanzania. It should be noted that Northern Sudanese qualify as *Afrabians* by both geographical and genealogical criteria.

These four sub-categories of *Afrabians* provide some of the evidence that Africa and the Arab world are two geographical regions, which are in the slow historic process of becoming one.

However, the merger of the Arab world with Africa is a slow integration across generations. What is more urgent is cooperation based on reconciliation in the immediate future. Tensions in places like Darfur, in Sudan, make such short-term accord more difficult. Nevertheless, let us examine African-Arab relations with two models of historic reconciliation involving other societies. The Anglo-American model traces the transition from hostility to fraternity in the relations between the people of Britain and those of the United States from the late eighteenth century to the two World Wars. Are there lessons to be learnt which are relevant for relations between Arabs and Africans, historically?

The second model of reconciliation traces the transition from enmity to friendship between the United States and Japan from 1941 to this new century. Are there other lessons to be learnt in this Americo-Japanese model, which are also pertinent for African-Arab relations in historical perspective? Let us look at these two models of reconciliation more closely.

It was, of course, in 1776 that the Americans started their rebellion against the British Empire. It became the American war of independence. For at least a century, the British were a people the Americans loved most to hate. This included one additional war between the Americans and the British in 1812.

Today, Great Britain is perhaps the closest ally of the United States — arguably closer than even Israel and Canada are to Washington. The wounds of 1776 and 1812 between the Americans and the British have more than just healed. A new and deeper sense of shared identity has been forged.

In 1964, a revolution occurred in Zanzibar against a government that was perceived as Arab led and a monarchy that was perceived as Omani. Bitter bloodletting and venomous hatred occurred between Swahilized Arabs, on one side, and Arabized Waswahili, on the other. *Arabophobia* in parts of East Africa reached new depths. *Afrophobia* in parts of the Arab world was also unmistakable. In reality, it took about a century for the Americans and the British to stop hating each other and longer still for them to become close friends.

In relations between Africans and Arabs, will we also have to wait for a century for the wounds of the past to heal? Is the model between the United States and Britain — in which forgiveness was very slow but when it came was very deep — relevant? Or, is it the model between Japan and the United States that is relevant? In 1941, Japan committed treachery and bombed Pearl Harbor without declaring war on the United States. President Franklin Roosevelt described it as "a day that will live in infamy." Americans had good reason to hate the Japanese.

In August 1945, the United States dropped atomic bombs on Hiroshima and Nagasaki. The Japanese became the first physical casualties of the nuclear age — massacred and, in many cases, maimed for generations. The Japanese had good reason to hate the Americans, just as many Black Sudanese of Darfur may deeply resent their Arab neighbors.

Yet, within less than a single generation, the United States and Japan became great political allies and monumental trading partners. Forgiveness between the Americans and Japanese had been quick — but was it shallow? Forgiveness between Britain and the United States had been slow — but was it deep?

Forgiveness between the Arabs and Africans may be somewhere between the U.S.-British model (slow but deep) and the U.S.-Japanese model (quick but shallow). African-Arab reconciliation may be slower than the Anglo-American fraternity and significantly deeper than the Americo-Japanese reconciliation. But Afro-Arab reconciliation involves not only memories of the Zanzibar revolution but, even more fundamentally, memories of Arab involvement in the slave trade in Africa. Can the pain of the past be forgotten?

Global trends in the New Global Order are dictating speed in African-Arab reconciliation and integration. Historical continuities and geographical contiguities may lend greater depth to the future relationship between Africa and the Arab world. However, conscious steps need to be taken in pursuit of any new forms of solidarity. Forgiving the past is one thing; forging a new future is a bigger imperative.

The ideological walls separating Indo-China from the rest of South-East Asia have been falling. The ideological walls separating Eastern Europe from Western Europe have now collapsed. The economic walls separating the United States, Mexico, and Canada are also coming down. Will the walls separating Africa and the Arab world also come down — as part of the New World Order?

It is arguable that some of the walls separating Africans from Arabs are as artificial as the divisions that separated Slavs from Germans in Europe. There has been much discussion about the artificiality of the Sahara Desert, as a divide between Arab Africa and Black Africa. Even more artificial is the Red Sea as a divide. Now that we are examining the New World Order, should we not re-evaluate these old frontiers and re-define our identities?

AFRABIA: BETWEEN GEOGRAPHY AND CULTURE

The French once examined their special relationship with Africa and came up with the concept of *Eurafrica* as a basis of special cooperation. We, in turn, should examine the even older special relationship between Africa and the Arab world and call it *Afrabia*.

After all, the majority of the Arab people are now in the African continent. The bulk of Arab lands are located in Africa. As we have observed, there are more Muslims in Nigeria than there are Muslims in any Arab country, including Egypt. In other words, the Muslim population of Nigeria is larger than the Muslim population of Egypt. The African continent, as a whole, is in the process of becoming the first continent in the world with an absolute Muslim majority.

However, *Afrabia* is not just a case of the spread of languages and the solidarity of religion. Whole new ethnic communities have been created by this dynamic. The emergence of Cushitic groups, like the Somali in the Horn of Africa, is one case in point. Oman, Yemen, and Saudi Arabia were also instrumental in helping to give birth to whole new ethnic groups on the Eastern seaboard of Africa. Swahili culture and the Swahili city-states captured a whole epoch in African history and legacy. Oman is central to the modern history of the Swahili heritage.

The brave peoples of Eritrea are also a reluctant bridge of *Afrabia*. Even the Berbers of North Africa are a special case of *Afrabia*. The very name 'Africa' probably originated in a Berber language, and was initially used to refer to what is now Tunisia. The continent got its name from what is now 'Arab Africa.' Is there a stronger argument for *Afrabia?*

Then there have been the migrations and movements of populations between Africa and Arabia across the centuries. There is evidence of Arab settlements on the East African coast and in the Horn of Africa well before the birth of the Prophet Muhammad. Moreover, the fact that the first great muezzin of Islam was Bilal is evidence that there was an African presence in Mecca and Medina before Islam. Bilal was there before he was converted — a symbol of an older Arabian link with Africa. *Afrabia* is a pre-*Hijjra* phenomenon.

Islam itself is almost as old in Africa as it is in Arabia. In Ethiopia, Muslims came to seek religious asylum during the Prophet Muhammad's early days, when he and his followers were persecuted in Mecca. Archeological excavations in Eastern Africa have discovered remains of mosques that go back to the earliest decades of Islam. Islam, as a factor in *Afrabia,* does indeed go back some fourteen centuries!

There is the impact of language on *Afrabia*. The language with the largest number of individual speakers in the African continent is still Arabic. The most influential indigenous African languages are Swahili (Kiswahili) in East Africa and Hausa in West Africa, both of them profoundly influenced by both Arabic and Islam — a manifestation of *Afrabia.*

Linguistic links between Africa and Arabia are, in fact, much older than Islam. Everybody is aware that Arabic is a Semitic language; however, not as many people realize that so is Amharic, the dominant indigenous language of Ethiopia. Indeed, historians are divided as to whether Semitic languages originated in Africa before they crossed the Red Sea or originated in the Arabian Peninsula and later crossed over to Africa. The very uncertainties themselves are part of the reality of *Afrabia.*

In the New World of globalization, two processes are under way — centrifugal and centripetal — each seeking to redefine the nation-state. Centrifugal forces create fragmentation and separatism. The most dramatic examples have been the disintegration of the Soviet Union. Centripetal forces create bigger economic and political communities. The year 1992 was intended to witness deeper economic integration of the European Community, probably followed by the admission of more member states before the end of the twentieth century. The new century has witnessed further European expansion.

In the Arab world, the most serious cases of internal centrifugal fragmentation within countries are in Iraq, Lebanon, and the Sudan. Saddam Hussein's Iraq faced central oppression and ethnic separatism. The Kurds and the Shiites were often up in arms, sometimes literally; Lebanon has not yet healed its sectarian divisions; and the Sudan is torn not only by the civil war in the South but also by new religious and political tensions in the Northwest.

Centrifugal fragmentation in Africa includes not only the Sudan, but also ethnic separatism in Ethiopia, Liberia, Somalia, Senegal and, with lesser intensity, Nigeria. In addition to national centrifugal tendencies, there are wider regional forces of fragmentation in both Africa and the Arab world. The Gulf crisis of 1990–91 was one of the most divisive events in recent Arab history. One unthinkable scenario occurred in August 1990, when one Arab country completely swallowed up another — the brief conquest of Kuwait by Iraq. The other unthinkable scenario occurred in 1991, when Arab bombs and Arab missiles bombed fellow Arab cities. The wounds of division have yet to heal in the Arab world. Ironically, the continuing American-led war in Iraq is helping to heal inter-Arab wounds.

Africa did not enter the 1990s as deeply divided at the regional level as the Arab world did. But Africa's economic situation since the 1990s has been particularly severe, and the political will to pursue African unity fluctuated between the Organization of African Unity and the new African Union. Two happy developments in Africa of the 1990s have had the unintended consequences of diluting Pan-African commitment. The end of political apartheid in 1994 was, from almost every point of view, good news for Africa and the human race. But the struggle against apartheid had for so long been a great unifying force in Africa — at least as compelling as the struggle against Zionism has been in the Arab world. While Zionism is still powerful and defiant, political apartheid has crumbled; though economic apartheid is still intact. Pan-Africanism may have to pay a price for its own success. The end of apartheid could have deprived Pan-Africanism of a major unifying force. Fortunately, Black-led post-apartheid South Africa is now a leader in Pan-African movements.

The other happy trend in Africa since the 1990s has been the struggle for greater democracy — from Dar-es-Salaam to Dakar, from Lusaka to Lagos, from Algiers to Kinshasa. African rulers have been called upon to become more accountable. While the pro-democracy movement in Africa has been an exciting development, it has focused the minds of citizens on domestic issues in each country rather than continental issues of unification. The regional effect of democratic activism has, on the whole, been centrifugal — at least in the short run.

However, while Africa and the Arab world are each still internally divided in terms of contemporary politics, the forces of history and geography cross-culturally link the two overlapping regions. Indeed, there was a time when, what we now call the Arabian Peninsula was part and parcel of Africa — physically. It is to these geophysical lessons of *Afrabia* that we must now turn.

BLACK CONTINENT, RED SEA?

A central thesis of this section of the paper is that the Red Sea has no right to divide Africa from Arabia. Where then is Africa? What is Africa? How sensible are its boundaries?

Islands can be very far from Africa and still be regarded part of Africa, provided they are not too near another major landmass, but a peninsula can be arbitrarily dis-Africanized. Madagascar is separated from the African continent by the 500-mile wide Mozambique Channel. Greater Yemen, on the other hand, is separated from Djibouti by only a stone's throw. Yet, Madagascar is politically part of Africa while Greater Yemen is not.

Much of the postcolonial African scholarship has addressed itself to the artificiality of the boundaries of contemporary African states. However, little attention has been paid to the artificiality of the boundaries of the African continent itself. Why should North Africa end on the Red Sea when Eastern Africa does not end on the Mozambique Channel? Why should Antananarivo (also called Tananarive) be an African capital when Aden is not?

There has been discussion in Africa as to whether the Sahara desert is a chasm or a link. Continental Pan-Africanism asserts that the Sahara desert is a sea of communication rather than a chasm of separation. Yet there are some who would argue that North Africa is not 'really Africa.' Why? Is it because it is more like Arabia?

In that case, why not push the boundary of North Africa further east to include Arabia? Why not refuse to recognize the Red Sea as a chasm, just as the Continental Pan-Africanists have refused to concede such a role to the Sahara Desert? Why not assert that the African continent ends neither on the southern extremity of the Sahara nor on the western shore of the Red Sea? Should not Africa move northwards to the Mediterranean and Northeastwards to the Persian Gulf? Alternatively, should this new concept be called *Afrabia?*

The most redundant sea in African history may well be the Red Sea. This thin line of ocean has been deemed more relevant for defining where

Africa ends than all the evidence of geology, geography, history, and culture. The northeastern boundary of Africa has been defined by a strip of water in the teeth of massive ecological and cultural evidence to the contrary.[3] The problem goes back three to five million years ago when three cracks emerged on the east side of Africa. As Colin McEvedy put it:

> One crack broke Arabia away, creating the Gulf of Aden and the Red Sea, and reducing the area of contact between Africa and Asia to the Isthmus of Suez.[4]

Before the parting of the Red Sea, there was the parting of Africa to create the Red Sea as a divide. Three cracks had occurred on the African crust — yet only the one which has resulted in a sea was permitted to dis-Africanize what lay beyond the sea. The other two cracks resulted in 'rift valleys,' straight-sided trenches averaging thirty miles across. The eastern and western rifts left the African continent intact, but the emergence of a strip of water called the Red Sea has resulted in the geological secession of Arabia.

However, what a geological crack had once put asunder, the forces of geography, history, and culture have been trying to bind together again ever since. Who are the Amhara of Ethiopia, if not a people probably descended from South Arabians? What is Amharic but a Semitic language? What is a Semitic language, if not a branch of the Afro-Asian family of languages? Was the Semitic parental language born in Africa and then crossed the Red Sea? On the other hand, was it from the Arabian Peninsula originally and then descended upon such people as the Amhara, Tigre, and Hausa in Africa? How much of a bridge between Arabia and Africa are the Somali? All these are lingo-cultural questions, which raise the issue of whether the geological secession of Arabia three to five million years ago has been in the process of being neutralized by *Afrabia* — the intimate cultural integration between Arabia, the Horn, and the rest of Africa.

In the linguistic field, it is certainly no longer easy to determine where African indigenous languages end and 'Semitic' trends begin. There was a time when both Hamites and Semites were regarded as alien to Africa. In due course, Hamites were regarded as a fictitious category and the people represented by the term, the Tutsi — accepted as indisputably African. What about the Semites? They have undoubtedly existed in world history. But, like Moses on the run from the Pharaoh, are they 'Africans' who crossed the Red Sea — or are the Semites originally 'Arabians' who penetrated Africa? These agonizing problems of identity would be partially solved overnight if the Arabian Peninsula was part of Africa or if a new solidarity of *Afrabia* took root.

ON CULTURE AND CONTINENT

The cultural effort to re-integrate Arabia with Africa, after the geological divide five million years ago, previously reached a new phase with the birth and expansion of Islam. The Arab conquest of North Africa was a process of overcoming the divisiveness of the Red Sea.

Twin processes were set in motion in North Africa — Islamization, a religious conversion to the creed of Muhammad; and Arabization, a linguistic assimilation into the language of the Arabs. In time, the great majority of North Africans saw themselves as Arabs no less than the inhabitants of the Arabian Peninsula. In short, the Islamization and Arabization of North Africa were once again cultural countervailing forces, trying to outweigh the geological separatism perpetrated by the birth of the Red Sea millennia earlier. North Africans have been cast in a dilemma; are they as African as the people to the south of them? What has yet to be raised is whether the Arabs, east of the Red Sea are as African as the Arabs, north of the Sahara.

But if the Red Sea could be ignored in determining the northeastern limits of Africa, why cannot the Mediterranean also be ignored as an outer northern limit? There was indeed a time when North Africa was in fact regarded as an extension of Europe. This goes back to the days of Carthage, of Hellenistic colonization and, later, of the Roman Empire. The concept of 'Europe' was at best in the making at that time. In the words of historians R. R. Palmer and Joel Colton:

> There was really no Europe in ancient times. In the Roman Empire we may see a Mediterranean world, or even a West and an East in the Latin and Greek portions; but the West included parts of Africa as well as Europe...[5]

Even as late as the seventeenth century, the idea that the landmass south of the Mediterranean was something distinct from the landmass north of it, was a proposition still difficult to comprehend. The great American Africanist, Melville Herskovits, has pointed out how the Geographer Royal of France, writing in 1656, described Africa as "a peninsula so large that it comprises the third part, and this the most southerly, of our continent."[6]

The old proposition that North Africa was the southern part of Europe had its last desperate fling in the modern world in France's attempt to keep Algeria as part of France. The desperate myth that Algeria was the southern portion of France tore the French nation apart in the 1950s, created the crisis which brought Charles de Gaulle to power in 1958, and maintained tensions between the Right and the Left in France until Algeria's independence in 1962, with an additional aftermath of bitterness in the trail of Charles de Gaulle's career.

This effort to maintain Algeria as a southern extension of a European power took place at a time when, in other respects, North Africa had become a western extension of Arabia. From the seventh century onwards, Arabization and Islamization had been transforming North Africa's identity. Because Africa's border was deemed the Red Sea, the Arabs became a 'bicontinental' people — impossible to label as either 'African' or 'Asian.' Indeed, the majority of the Arab people by the twentieth century were located west of the Red Sea (i.e., in Africa 'proper'), although the majority of the Arab states were east of the Red Sea (deemed as Western Asia).

The Arabic language has, as we indicated, many more speakers in the present African continent than in the Arabian Peninsula, and Arabic has indeed become the most important single language in the present African continent in terms of speakers. The case for regarding Arabia as part of Africa is now much stronger than for regarding North Africa as part of Europe. Islamization and Arabization have redefined the identity of North Africans more fundamentally than either Gallicization or Anglicization has done.

In spite of the proximity of the Rock of Gibraltar to Africa, the Mediterranean Sea is a more convincing line of demarcation between Africa and Europe than the Red Sea can claim to be a divide between Africa and Asia.

All boundaries are, of course, artificial. But some boundaries are more artificial than others are. *Afrabia* has at least two millennia of linguistic and religious history to give it geocultural reality.

AFRABIA AND GLOBAL APARTHEID

One wider trend worth watching is the emergence of global apartheid. The white world is closing ranks, in spite of the disintegration of the Soviet Union and Yugoslavia. Pan-Europeanism is reaching new levels of solidarity from the Urals to the Pyrenees Mountains. The European Union now has twenty-seven members. Originally, only half a dozen European states had signed the Treaty of Rome in 1958.

In North America, a new mega-economy is emerging — encompassing the United States, Canada, and possibly Mexico. There are dreams of wider hemispheric integration. But when you look closely at this new world order, two disturbing tendencies emerge. Arabs and Muslims are disproportionately the frontline military victims of the new order. Blacks are disproportionately the frontline economic victims of the emerging global apartheid. The military victimization of Muslims includes:

- Invading and occupying Iraq (2003–to the present).

- Subsidizing Israeli's brutal occupation of Gaza (now under Palestinian control) and the West Bank.
- Permitting nuclearization of Israel but attempting to veto nuclear power in the Muslim world (Pakistan squeezed through though).
- Subsidizing Israel's military capability in the region.
- U.S. bombing of Beirut, under Ronald Reagan.
- U.S. bombing of Tripoli and Benghazi in Libya, under President Ronald Reagan.
- Shooting down of an Iranian civilian aircraft in the Gulf and killing all onboard, under Reagan.
- Senior Bush's decision to save time rather than lives in the 1990–1991 Gulf crisis — leading to the loss of hundreds of thousands of lives.
- Potential American strikes against Iran and Syria.

Two thirds of the casualties of U.S. military activity since the Vietnam War have been Muslims, amounting upwards to a million lives. The Muslim victims have been primarily Palestinians, Iraqis, Lebanese, Libyans, Iranians, and others.

If Muslims have been frontline military victims, Blacks have been frontline economic victims of the new world order:

- Many years of Western support for incompetent and corrupt African regimes.
- The negative consequences of economic structural adjustment under the IMF and World Bank in the 1990s.
- The injustices of the wider world of commodity prices against fragile African economies.
- The huge Black underclass in the United States, adding AIDS and DRUGS to poverty, crime, and social maladjustment.
- The rise of racism and *Islamophobia* in Europe (France, Germany, Belgium).
- The U.S. Supreme Court's move to the Right, hurting gains in civil rights and minority advances.

The relationship between the West and Afrabia is not without a silver lining here and there. Particularly dramatic has been the improved relations between the United States and Libya, following Libya's renunciation of weapons of mass destruction. Nevertheless, this new world order runs the risk of creating a disproportionate number of more dead Muslims. It also runs the risk of perpetuating a disproportionate number of more poor Blacks.

Afrabia is potentially part of the answer. Reconciliation between Arabs and Africans will continue to be needed, hopefully not as slow as the reconciliation between Britain and the U.S. after their 1776 and 1812 confrontations. The Afro-Arab *entente* will also hopefully not be as shallow as the cordiality between Japan and the United States. Africans and Arabs need to learn the lessons of speed from Japan and the U.S. and the lessons of deeper fraternity from the older experience of Britain and the United States.

We have had Arab institutions ostensibly designed to help Africa — the Arab Bank for African Development. We have not had African institutions designed to help poorer Arabs outside Africa. The innovations needed would break the mould of Arabs always as donors and Africans always as supplicants for foreign help. *Afrabian* institutions would pool the resources of both relatively wealthy Arabs and relatively wealthy Africans and target those resources to the needs of the poor in both Africa and the Arab world. *Afrabian* institutions would be under the joint control of both Arabs and Africans. At last, it would be conceivable for African money to help poor Arab countries like Yemen or even Palestine, just as Arab money has sometimes helped even relatively well-endowed African countries like Zaire (now Democratic Republic of the Congo).

Will such experimentation have to wait for the moment when majority rule in South Africa is fully consolidated? Will the first foreign aid from Blacks to Arabs have to come from a truly post-apartheid South Africa? That is at least one scenario. As South Africa gets more liberated and stabilized, there will be a need for a new summit meeting of Arab and African Heads of State and Governments to take genuine stock of 'the New Global Order.' It is to be hoped that high on that agenda, for an Afro-Arab summit, will be the creation of new and innovative *Afrabian* mechanisms of cooperation in this era of globalization. As the Afro-Arab past is forgotten, a new Afro-Arab future can thus be forged. It can be part of the defense against the dangers of global apartheid.

CONCLUSION

We live in an age when people's perception of themselves can be deeply influenced by the continent or region that they associate themselves with. Until the 1950s, the official policy of the government of Emperor Haile Selassie was to emphasize that Ethiopia was part of the Middle East rather than part of Africa. Yet, it was the Emperor himself who initiated the policy of re-Africanizing Ethiopia as the rest of Africa approached independence. Ethiopian self-perceptions are being slowly Africanized ever since.

Yet cultural similarities between Ethiopia and the rest of Black Africa are not any greater than cultural similarities between North Africa and the Arabian Peninsula. Nevertheless, a European decision to make Africa end at the Red Sea has decisively dis-Africanized the Arabian Peninsula and made the natives there see themselves as west Asians, rather than North Africans.[7]

Before the parting of the Red Sea, there was the parting of Africa to create the Red Sea. Several million years ago, the crust of Africa cracked and the Red Sea was born. As we indicated, this thin strip of water helped to seal the identity of whole generations of people living on both sides of it.

Yet, cultural change has been struggling to heal the geological rift between Africa and Arabia. Did the Semites originate to the east or the west of the Red Sea? Are upper Ethiopians originally south Arabians? Has Islam rendered the Red Sea a culturally irrelevant boundary? Has the Arabic language made the boundary anachronistic? Is it time that the tyranny of the sea, as a definer of identity, was at least moderated if not overthrown? We have sought to demonstrate that Africa and the Arab world have in any case been slowly merging into one vast region.

In any case, the tyranny of the sea is in part a tyranny of European geographical prejudices. Just as European mapmakers could decree that, on the map, Europe was above Africa instead of below (an arbitrary decision in relation to the cosmos) those mapmakers could also dictate that Africa ended at the Red Sea instead of the 'Persian Gulf.' Is it not time that this dual tyranny of the sea and Eurocentric geography was forced to sink to the bottom?

The most difficult people to convince may well turn out to be the inhabitants of the Arabian Peninsula. They have grown to be proud of being 'the Arabs of Asia' rather than 'the Arabs of Africa.' They are not eager to be members of the new African Union even if it were led by Libya. Will they at least embrace the concept of *Afrabia*?

Yet, if Emperor Haile Selassie could initiate the re-Africanization of Ethiopia and Gamal Abdel Nasser could inaugurate the re-Africanization of Egypt, prospects for a reconsideration of the identity of the Arabian Peninsula may not be entirely bleak. In the New Global Order it is not only Europe which is experiencing the collapse of artificial walls of disunity. It is not just the United States, Mexico, and Canada that will create a megacommunity. It is not just South East Asia which will learn to re-admit Indo-China to the fold. Also momentous, in its historical possibilities, is the likely emergence of *Afrabia* — linking languages, religions, and identities across both the Sahara Desert and the Red Sea in a historical fusion of Arabism and Africanity in the New World Order.

However, will *Afrabia* be a case of rich Arabs in a union with poor Africans? Actually, there are rich countries in Africa, poor countries in the Arab world, and vice versa. Africa's mineral resources are more varied than those of the Arab world, but African countries like Congo (Kinshasa) have been more economically mismanaged than almost any country in the Arab world.

Afrabia of the future will include post-apartheid South Africa — richer and more industrialized than almost any other society in either Africa or the Arab world. The *Afrabia* of the future may economically be led by the oil-rich and the mineral-rich economies but in a new order, equity and fairness will count as much between societies as they have sometimes done within enlightened individual countries. Relentlessly Africa and the Arab world continue their historic march towards merger — their historic destiny of integration.

Endnotes

1. According to Joseph A. D'Agostino (2001), among the 25 nations (they include Afghanistan, Algeria, Bahrain, Djibouti, Egypt, Eritrea, Indonesia, Iran, Iraq, Jordan, Kuwait, Lebanon, Libya, Malaysia, Morocco, Oman, Pakistan, Qatar, Saudi Arabia, Somalia, Sudan, Syria, Tunisia, the United Arab Emirates, and Yemen) classified by the U. S. State Department as where Al-Qaeda operates, are nine African countries (Algeria, Djibouti, Egypt, Eritrea, Libya, Morocco, Somalia, Sudan, and Tunisia. (Joseph A. D'Agostino, "7,000 Men Recently Entered from Al-Qaeda 'Watch' Countries," *Human Events Online*, Week of December 17, 2001).
2. According to the United Nations Economic Commission for Africa, financial aid from Arab countries to Africa increased from $0.1 billion in 1970 to $0.3 billion in 1999. ("Economic Report on Africa 2002: Tracking Performance and Progress," Overview Section. United Nations Economic Commission for Africa. http://www.uneca.org/era2002/index.htm).
3. The issue of whether the Red Sea is a legitimate boundary of Africa is also discussed in Mazrui, *The Africans: A Triple Heritage* (London: BBC Publications and Boston: Little, Brown Press, 1986) Chapter 1.
4. C. McEvedy, *The Penguin Atlas of African History* (Harmondsworth, Middlesex: Penguin Books, 1980).
5. See R. R. Palmer in collaboration with Joe Colton, *A History of the Modern World* (New York: Knopf, 1962) 2nd edition, p. 13.
6. See Merville Herskovits' contribution to Wellesley College, *Symposium on Africa* (Wellesley College, Massachusetts, 1960) p. 16.
7. This question also features in Ali A. Mazrui's television series, *The Africans: A Triple Heritage* (London: British Broadcasting Corporation and Washington, D.C.: WETA, Public Broadcasting System, 1986), Programme No. 1 "The Nature of a Continent."

7

Ethnoreligious Pluralism and Democratization in Nigeria: The Politics of the Shari'a

SIRAJ ABDULKARIM BARAU

Two main issues continue to generate international, political, and media attention in Nigeria today — the transition to democracy and the implementation of the Shari'a. While the federal government in Nigeria is stepping up efforts to make democracy acceptable and establish its roots, an increasing number of Muslim States are expanding and implementing the Shari'a in the North. The latter has created a stalemate between Muslim and Christian groups that has potentially diminished some crises, especially in the Niger delta, by creating a bigger national 'crisis' hence putting Nigeria's fragile democracy under great stress.

This chapter attempts to study the resurgence of Shari'a in democratic Nigeria. Here, we explore the following questions: Is there a linkage between the Shari'a's implementation and the now emerging democratic political dispensation? If the implementation of Shari'a is not politically motivated, is it a manifestation of a renewed awareness of Muslim self-identity? Considering issues like gender, democracy, globalization, and information revolution, have Muslims taken note of their current legal status under the Shari'a and the implication this has on Nigeria's socioeconomic dynamism? Does this centuries old 'excessive legalism' have something to do with *taqlid* (strict imitation) and the closing of the door of *ijtihad* (effort to issue new ruling)? If so, why have they not been dispelled? Is it want of effort or have Muslims succumbed to intellectual imperialism and decay?

For Islam to be relevant, for all time and for all people, it has to be a flexible and adaptable religion. According to the *hadith* of the Prophet, wisdom (knowledge, etc) is the lost property of a Muslim; wherever he sees it, he picks it. That knowledge gave Islam the ability to synthesize; but, are Muslims living up to that challenge?

In Nigeria, it should be noted upfront, the violent opposition to the Shari'a has traditionally come mainly from the northern minority Christians. These people have had a long history of political opposition to especially the Hausa-Fulani aristocrats. Does the violence therefore have more to do with the ethnicization of Christianity, which spawns 'ethnic cleansing' of Muslims, or is it because of the complex and historical problem of using Christianity as a vehicle of political protest? In a country with two main contending religions and over two hundred ethnic groups, would a lasting solution be found in federalism or confederation, or in the understanding and harnessing of the positive roles of differences in religion and ethnicity, not to mention the defeat of the fear and mistrust of the 'other' in democratic and accountable good governance?

NIGERIA: AN OVERVIEW

Nigeria is on the west coast of the African continent. It covers an area of 923,768 square kilometers and has a population of at least one hundred and twenty million people. The country is both an oil producer and exporter, in addition to possessing other types of mineral resources. It is the sixth leading member of the Organization of Petroleum Exporting Countries (OPEC); but probably more strategic and enduring is agriculture that has since independence been ignored by the successive leaders.

Nigeria is, in addition, an influential leader of the Economic Community of the West African States (ECOWAS) — an emerging leader in sub-Saharan Africa and is now increasingly becoming a recognized member of the international community.

Nigeria has at least two hundred ethnic groups, with some having a long history of culture, administration, and civilization. There are sixteen main ethnic groups in Nigeria — Hausa, Yoruba, Igbo, Fulani, Kanuri, Ibibio, Tiv, Ijaw, Edo, Annang, Nupe, Urhobo, Igala, Idoma, Igbirra, and Gwari. However, Nigeria's three main regions — northern, southern, and eastern, which dominate the country's politics and governance are, on the other hand, dominated by the country's three main ethnic groups — the Hausa-Fulani,[1] the Yoruba, and the Igbo, respectively.

The Hausas are overwhelmingly Muslim and generally farmers. For centuries, they have traded across the Sahara with their neighbors and lived in towns and villages. Islam brought them unity, administration, and civilization, especially after the reformative movement of Ousmane Dan Fodio.[2] The movement by the Shehu transformed the practice of Islam, from a court religion to a way of life, through the Shari'a that governed the state and the people. The Shehu succeeded in establishing the Sokoto Caliphate in 1807, through preaching and teaching tenets of Islam. According to historians, the triumvirate scholars[3] of the caliphate wrote at least four hundred books on religious rites and statecraft. The colonialists met and defeated this Caliphate in 1903 — thanks to their superior arms.

The expansionist nature of Islam, coupled with the Muslims' strong opposition to colonialism, motivated the colonialists and Christian missionaries to create the Middle Belt in the North. Historians note that the missionaries and colonial administrators deliberately created the Middle Belt, after discarding a plan for direct military action for complete control of Islam in the North (Hiskett, 1984). The aim was essentially to halt the advance of Islam to the South, by converting to Christianity the northern minority tribes inhabiting this Belt. The strongest opposition to the Shari'a today comes from this Belt.

The Yoruba share a common language and ancestry. They live in a forest zone and are generally farmers. In Yorubaland, Islam preceded Christianity, which came later with European missionaries; but now, the two faiths have almost equal numbers of adherents (Lubeck, 1988).

The Igbos lived in decentralized village communities of rain forest farmers and were ruled by elders and family heads prior to the coming of the colonialists. They became united through common markets, exogamous marriages, and traditional religion. Though Islam also came to Igboland before Christianity, today this region is overwhelmingly Christian.

POSTINDEPENDENCE: POLITICAL DEVELOPMENT OR POLITICAL DECAY?

Prior to independence when political parties were formed to contest, each region had its own party. The Northern People Congress (NPC) dominated in the Northern region, the National Council of Nigerian Citizens (NCNC) had a commanding presence in the Eastern region, while the Western region saw the ascendancy of the Action Group (AG). Virtually all these regional, and to some extent tribal, parties only effectively met at the federal level. The three regions were ruled autonomously of each other by the colonialists and, later, by these parties.

The British parliamentary system, prevalent at the time, saw Nnamdi Azikiwe of the NCNC come to power as the President of the First Republic while Abubakar Tafawa Balewa of the NPC, became the Prime Minister in a coalition of the two parties. The Action group became the opposition party.

The three political parties — NPC, NCNC, and AG — failed to emerge as truly national parties precisely because they were regionally and tribally based. The inherited colonial regionalization set the pace for tribal, regional, and even religious politics that continue to influence Nigeria's politics to date.

Nigeria's first and controversial military coup, in January 1966, was seen to be tribally and religiously influenced. The coup was engineered by junior officers of whom all "but one, (Major Ademoyega — a Yoruba), were Igbo. Nineteen of the other twenty-three active participants were also from the same tribe" (Luckham, 1971). "The pattern of the killings seemed selective in regional and tribal terms" (Ibid.), which further made the exercise to be seen as partial because the victims were either northerners or in alliance with the North. Examples of those killed included the Prime Minister, Abubakar Tafawa Balewa; the Premier of the Northern region, Ahmadu Bello; and S. L. Akintola, Premier of the Western region. Akintola was seen as being backed by the North to counter the opposition of Awolowo. Akintola was a Baptist but was "persuaded to convert to Islam by the Sardauna"[4] (Basri, 1994). The coup therefore succeeded in extending and establishing tribal and religious animosity from Nigeria's politicians to the military.

The January coup left a legacy of shock and mistrust among the soldiers, especially the northern officers. When the coup brought in General Aguiyi-Ironsi, an Igbo Christian, as head of state, the situation became increasingly restive. It therefore took few by surprise when, in July the same year, another coup occurred. This coup, led by the northern officers, saw General Yakubu Gowon, a Christian from the north, come to power. The major events of Gowon's nine-year rule were a civil war, which started in July 1967 and came to an end on 15 January 1970 with the defeat of the secessionists and the national reconciliation program that followed. The war was an attempt by leaders of the Eastern Region, led by Colonel Odumegwu Ojukwu, the Military Governor, to secede from the Federal Republic of Nigeria and form the Republic of Biafra. Ojukwu portrayed the war as the liberation of Christians from Muslim domination, adding tribal and religious undertones to get international support and sympathy (Cronje, 1972; Ifejika, 1969).

The Gowon regime undertook national reconciliation, emphasizing a 'no victor nor vanquished' policy. The regime also dismembered the regions, creating twelve states out of them. However, the tribal factor was to play its role because leading politicians like Awolowo and Azikiwe advocated for the states to be created along ethnic and linguistic affiliations (Amoda, 1972).

Considering the danger that tribalism posed to the country's future, in 1973 the regime introduced the compulsory one-year National Youth Service Corps (NYSC) program for graduating Nigerian students from universities and similar tertiary institutions in and outside the country. The graduating corps members were usually posted to a state in the country other than that of their ethnic origin.

General Murtala Ramat Mohammed, a Hausa Muslim from the North, came to power in a bloodless coup in July 1975. Gowon's regime was accused of corruption and indiscipline. The Murtala regime started with a mass dismissal of all allegedly corrupt civil servants. Within six months in office, additional states were created, a transition program worked out, a new federal capital located, and a Constituent Assembly — charged with the task of creating a new constitution — put in place.

Barely six months in office, there was an abortive coup, although the head of state — General Murtala Mohammed, was killed. It was alleged that the northern Christian minority in the army engineered the attempted coup, as an act of retaliation for Gowon's killing. Most of the coup planners were arrested, tried, and executed, further entrenching tribal and religious hostilities in the military — not only between northern and southern officers but also between officers from the far North and the Middle Belt. General Olusegun Obasanjo, who then was deputy to General Murtala Mohammed, took the mantle of leadership. He completed the transition program by handing power over to an elected civilian administration. This was on October 1, 1979.

The Second Republic then came into being through multiparty politics and a change from the British parliamentary to the American presidential system. The system was adopted to accommodate Nigeria's ethnic diversity. Despite this, the three main parties, and especially their leadership, betrayed traces of the first regional and tribal parties, and the election results reflected these biases. The thesis that, "no matter into how many states the original three [regions] have been subdivided, the tripartite regionalization effected by the colonizer with its imposed ranking has provided the basis for identity, conflict, and order in independent Nigeria" (Gboyega, 1997), seemed to hold. The National Party of Nigeria (NPN), whose base was the North, was linked with the NPC. The Unity Party of Nigeria (UPN) was strongest in the West and looked in all respects identical to the AG. The Nigerian People's Party was similarly in many aspects like the NCNC.

Alhaji Shehu Shagari was declared the elected Executive President of Nigeria after his runner-up, Awolowo of the UPN, challenged the election all the way up to the Supreme Court of Nigeria. However, the NPN failed to acquire the requisite number of seats in the National Assembly and therefore had to go into alliance with the NPP — a reflection of the First Republic. The Shagari regime was accused of financial recklessness and institutionalizing corruption (Ekwe-Ekwe, 1985). The regime was accused of reckless expenditure of the country's foreign reserve worth billion dollars (Momoh, ud). Activities of the regime at the new federal capital (Abuja), import and export licenses, and at the Ministry of Works and Housing left Nigerians feeling that the regime 'presided over the most serious economic crises that Nigeria had faced in twenty years' (Ekwe-Ekwe, op. cit.). However, to its credit, the regime gave a sense of belonging to all Nigerians because the party was truly national than the others were. During the Second Republic, there was no serious tribal conflict because it seemed more inclusive, with members from almost all the tribes thus reflecting its motto — One Nation, One Destiny. In the first and second elections, the party formed governments in some states, indeed in all the former regions.

The military however came back to power in December 31, 1983, when it toppled the Shehu Shagari's regime and installed General Muhammadu Buhari as Head of state. The Buhari administration was clearly 'too tough' for a 'loose' Nigeria. The regime sought to use coercion to check corruption and indiscipline. Implicated politicians at all levels, and especially those in the previous government, were tried and subsequently jailed. The press and other sectors were not left out either. Everyone was under a kind of 'siege.' Even though these measures seemed to have started making Nigerians disciplined and there might have been a brighter future for Nigeria, the regime was seen to be too authoritarian and its measures too draconian. However, regarding the measures taken, there was dissension within the military leadership. This led to a palace coup, which brought General Ibrahim Badamasi Babangida to power on August 27, 1985.

The Babangida regime ascended to power with promises of reform and respect for human rights. Various Commissions and Bureaux were formed. The economy was re-structured, and a transition to a democratically elected civilian government was worked out. The regime came up with another constitution, the Constituent Assembly alone, after the work of the Constitution Drafting Committee which had worked for over a year, finalized the draft constitution and submitted it to the Armed Forces Ruling Council for ratification.

When thirteen political associations submitted applications to the National Electoral Commission (NEC) for registration, only six were approved. However, the military, in its wisdom, disqualified all and created two parties — the Social Democratic Party (SDP) and the National

Republican Convention (NRC). The central government funded the building of the political parties' offices, from local government headquarters to the federal capital. Mobilization fees alone, given by the government for the registration of voters and administrative expenses, amounted to three hundred and sixty million American dollars. (Nigerian Interpreter Magazine, 1990).

The transition program succeeded in eliminating Nigeria's experienced and credible politicians. Of significance in the role of religion in politics, two Muslims — Adamu Ciroma and Shehu Yar'adua, who were emerging as the flag bearers of their respective parties, NRC and SDP, were disqualified at the request of Christian politicians. After a new process, the military-led government endorsed the late Moshood Abiola, a Yoruba Muslim from the South, on the ticket of the SDP and Bashir Tofa, a Hausa Muslim from the North on the NRC ticket, to contest the presidential election. Both candidates were known to be friends of the then military president, General Ibrahim Babangida.

The presidential election was held on June 12, 1993. Initial results showed that Abiola was winning. However, for reasons that to date remain obscure, the military government annulled the election. This singular act by the military, headed by a Muslim from the North, raised the tribal and religious tension in Nigerian politics to the highest level; not only between Muslims and Christians, but also between the Muslims in the North and their counterparts in the South. The tensions reached a secessionist level when the Yoruba's most influential *Oba* (Chief), the Ooni of Ife, remarked: "Our son won and you [Babangida] refused to declare him as the winner. There is no cogent reason for doing so. Yorubas will go on their own. (The African Guardian, 1993).

Further complicating the situation, both the 18th Sultan of Sokoto and the President General of the Supreme Council for Islamic Affairs (SCIA), Alhaji Ibrahim Dasuki, who was officially recognized as the leader of Muslims in Nigeria, called on Abiola to regard the unfolding scenario as an act of God.

The atmosphere became tense, especially when it became clear that General Babangida wanted to continue holding on to power. He even tried to manage the transition program. However, the pressure was unbearable and he had to 'step aside.' He left an Interim National Government (ING) headed by Ernest Shonekan, a Yoruba Christian from Abiola's home state. The ING's brief was to conduct another presidential election, since all other posts had been filled and were functioning. However, the pro-Abiola and other pro-democracy groups refused to recognize the ING and continued to call for the recognition of the election results and for Abiola to be sworn-in as president. A High Court ruling further weakened the ING when it was declared an illegitimate government. The country was drifting into lawlessness when General Sani Abacha took over.

The new military regime proscribed the two parties and all other democratic institutions. It also made clear its intention to allow for more than two political parties to be formed by the politicians themselves. In addition, it promised to come up with a more indigenous political system. In other words, Nigeria was going back to square one and Babangida's eight-year transition program turned out to be a colossal waste of resources and time for the country.

The Abacha administration turned out to be another fraud. Some of Nigeria's credible politicians were not only banned, but also killed or imprisoned. The top military officers crudely diverted the nation's resources to their personal accounts, a fact that came to light after the death of General Abacha.

Clearly, from the foregoing review, Nigeria was mismanaged in the name of governance especially by the immediate last two regimes, which played with the destiny of the country and flagrantly misused, mismanaged, and stole its resources with the support of some of the civil servants and politicians. They, thus, sowed the seeds of mistrust that Nigerians harbor toward members of the armed forces and politicians alike.

The military-led government only succeeded in corrupting and polarizing Nigeria's political and military groups along ethnic and religious lines. It was during Babangida's administration that an abortive coup occurred, which principally sought to excise the Muslim states from the federation. The leader of the attempted coup broadcast its aim on federal radio[5] hence bringing the military into religious politics.

The politicians could, it appeared, resolve the tribal polarization much easily, given their experience, than religiously triggered problems. This is because all civilian elections had cut across tribal lines. Consider, for example, the recent election of Shehu Musa 'Yar'adua. Not only did he qualify in the SDP primaries, he was also overwhelmingly voted for, in the southern states — beating the 'sons of the soils.' The election was, however, annulled by the Babangida administration just as he had previously annulled the elections that saw Abiola triumph, despite the overwhelming support that the latter had received in the North.[6] A further example demonstrating that ethnicity, which was least of Nigeria's problems, was in the 1999 election of the President Obasanjo. While President Obasanjo, a Yoruba, was overwhelmingly rejected by the Yoruba Southwestern states, the northern and Southeastern states overwhelmingly voted for him. (Y. B. Usman and Alkasum Abba, 2000).

The religious polarization is what I therefore consider as a more serious matter of concern, although in a religiously plural society such as Nigeria a solution to this problem could have been easily found. Religion is certainly a weapon of mobilization within the military or civilians, especially against members of another faith. It was unlikely that some members of the Nigerian Army, whose singular responsibility was the defense of Nigeria's borders, would attempt a coup only to excise some Muslim states from Nigeria. However, Muslims claimed that the erosion of Islamic values in Nigeria was a function of the Christianization of the country. Nigeria's new identity, according to a historian, looked "as if it were a non-Muslim country. The Symbols and trappings of state; the style of diplomacy; the direction of foreign policy; the political, legal, economic, and education systems; the structure of the working week; are all seen to be based on Western secular, albeit once, Christian model." (Clarke, op. cit.)

This new culture has made Nigerian Christians to oppose public policies with Islamic connotations. For example, Nigeria's membership in the Organization of the Islamic Conference (OIC) became one such case during the Babangida administration. While the OIC has African states with Christian majorities, such as Cameroon and Uganda, the Christians in Nigeria opposed it, sometimes through violent means. It took the country's enormous resources and time to control violence. Nigeria's diplomatic relations with the Vatican City, clearly more religious than that with the OIC which is an economic and development forum, has not softened the Christians.

Another serious matter of concern is the series of massacres of Muslims living in the Middle Belt, especially during communal clashes between Muslims and Christians, which occurred more regularly during the Babangida regime. As if these were not enough problems, there was the resurgence of the Shari'a that has now created a stalemate and challenged Nigeria's fragile democracy.

Will democratic leaders be able to surmount this hurdle and create a Nigeria belonging to happy and confident Nigerians? With forty years of 'political independence,' Nigeria does not seem to have established any credible political culture. If anything, decay, insecurity, and mistrust at the highest levels of the government have sadly been triumphant. However, despite this negative view of religion as one of Nigeria's twin-problems, religion can be a positive force for political development. (Philips Quarles van Ufford and Matthew Schoffeleers, 1988.)

THE RESURGENCE OF SHARI'A IN A DEMOCRATIC NIGERIA

Nigeria has been fragile, unable to create a nation, notwithstanding her more than forty years of 'political independence.' Nigeria's economic development and political growth has indisputably been stifled by corruption and ethnic as well as religious polarization.

Earlier in this paper, we argued that politicians could easily handle ethnically influenced problems. What, however, would test their skills is resolving the Shari'a stalemate. For different reasons in the past, be they political or religious or both, different groups had emerged in the Middle Belt and in the South but who now, incensed by the Shari'a's implementation, look more resolved in calling for an immediate restructuring of the Nigerian polity. They threaten that if this is not done, the country might be violently dismembered. Some of these groups include the Oodua Development Council (ODC), the Yoruba Leaders Forum (YLF), both in the Southwest; the Ohaneze Ndigbo in the Southeast; and the Middle Belt Progressive Movement (MBPM). In a recent meeting, the Fifth Pan-Yoruba National Congress resolved, among other things, that:

> The Congress notes with delight that the Ohaneze Ndigbo of the South-East, the Union of Niger Delta/South-South zone Governors and substantial elements of the Middle Belt had in the last one year come to the realization that the campaign for national restructuring is the correct path towards national stability. Congress, hereby, asks President Obasanjo as an elected Nigerian ruler, to urgently give effect to the genuine desire and aspiration of the majority of Nigerians by facilitating the convocation of a Sovereign National Conference so that the national question on equity, justice, fairness, revenue allocation, formula, and resource control, as well as devolution of power parameters can be discussed and resolved once and for all. (Resolutions of the Fifth Pan-Yoruba Congress, held in September 2000)

The North, on the other hand, formed the Arewa Consultative Forum (ACF) essentially to challenge what it perceived as deliberate marginalization of the North by the Obasanjo government, which the North elected to power. This is not to overlook the more youthful and violent groups, found in their respective regions, like Oodua People's Congress, Bakassi Boys and the Muslim/northern response, and the Arewa People's Congress.

The Muslims, using the democratic freedom and institutions, mobilized support for Shari'a, believing it would solve their social problems. However, the implementation of Shari'a triggered violent clashes between Christians and Muslims in Kaduna and a few other places in the country.

Thousands of people died, property worth billions of Nigerian Naira was destroyed, and an army of refugees was produced. The Southwest, the traditional hotbed of opposition to the North, was peaceful on the Shari'a issue, for Islam and Christianity live in a sort of equilibrium. In fact, almost every other home in this region has adherents of two somewhat divergent faiths living in harmony. Another reason as to why the Southwest was relatively peaceful may be due to the strong tribal consciousness of the Yoruba people. As a Yoruba scholar observed, "To the Yoruba Muslims in recent years, both Islam and ethnic identity count." (Abubakre, 1992)

The clashes had further hardened the positions of the adherents of both faiths. However, more dangerous were the accusations from especially the Muslims that the Army and police had taken sides when they were brought in to quell the disturbances. What then is the future of democracy in a corporate Nigeria, if the forces of law and order cannot be trusted by a significant part of the country?

The Muslims continue to argue that the Shari'a did not cause the Kaduna disturbances. To prove their case, they cited the chronic disturbances in the Belt.[7] These disturbances, they claim, were mainly instigated by the frustration created by a complex combination of ethnic, economic, and political demands than religious differences.

What is in the Shari'a that was causing Nigeria, its leaders, and its people acrimony? How did it affect the Christians? How was its implementation possible in a multiethnic and a multireligious environment in the twenty-first century?

William Wallis, of the *Financial Times,* reported during the launching ceremony of Shari'a in Kano, in June 2000, that "hundreds of thousands of Muslims [gathered] in the event was by far the largest show of support for a movement that is sweeping across the largely Muslim north of Nigeria ..." (Financial Times, June 22, 2000.) What was it about the Shari'a that attracted Muslims from far and near whenever it was launched, but further strained the relationship between Muslims and Christians? The Shari'a, it is argued,

> is an all-inclusive body of legislation that contains many principles, elements, doctrines, theories, rules, and maxims pertaining to all human aspects of life. Such principles and theories are, Muslims believe, capable of meeting the different challenges and requirements of individuals and groups in the present as well as in the future. (Al-Buraey, 1988)

Another view holds that the Shari'a is generally meant to "establish communal benefits and facilitate life ... criteria for prohibition [in Shari'a] is avoiding harm, while the criteria for allowance is facilitating (communal) benefit" (The Middle Path magazine, March 2000). The Shari'a, therefore, is mainly interested in facilitating a good life for all humans, free from harm, both in this world and beyond. The Shari'a principally seeks to preserve and protect for humankind their religion, life, family, intellect, and property.

For the Muslims in the North, therefore, the Shari'a was seen as a liberator that would save them from corrupt leaders. A former Minister wrote while in office that Nigeria's foreign debt, totaling to about thirty billion dollars by 1992, could be settled by 'fewer than half a dozen of our countrymen' (Momoh, ibid.). In essence, his message was that the Shari'a is what Nigeria needs in order to root out networks of corruption and corrupt leaders, who have seemed to overwhelm and circumvent Nigeria's existing legal system. Jika argued, for example, that:

> The honest fact is that the upsurge of clamor for Shari'a was induced from a lower level (the masses). While Sani Yerima can claim credit for igniting the demand, the staying power of the issue is the masses, who have lost confidence in the current system. The loss stems from the failure of Northerners who, while holding on to power for 35 years, have made little or no impact on the lives of their people. No education, no empowerment. The masses now see in the Shari'a, a final solution to their problems ... (Vanguard Viewpoint, gamji.com, September 2000)

This ideal hope attached to the Shari'a was what the masses believed and gave it their support for a change. There was a combination of belief and nostalgia that made Muslims overwhelmed by the Shari'a. During the time of the Prophet, when a woman from a famous family was caught stealing, someone requested the Prophet to intervene. The Prophet was so upset that he called the people and declared that the people in the past used to punish the weak but free the strong and powerful, even when found guilty. The Prophet had even sworn that if his daughter, Fatima, were to steal and was found guilty he would cut off her hand. His immediate successor, Caliph Abu Bakar, declared that the strong and the rich were the weakest before him until he collected from them what was due for the poor and the weak. Also, the weak and poor were the strongest before him until he gave them what was their due. In the recent past, the Muslims in the North remembered the position of Shari'a in the Sokoto Caliphate and many years earlier in the Kanem-Borno Empire.[8]

The leadership of the Caliphate "entrusted each office of state, and even the trade and guilds, to those capable of discharging them to the best interest of the community..." as part of the Shari'a. The abject poverty in the North, and corruption in Nigeria as a whole, was such that parents could not afford to feed their children three meals a day or attend to their educational needs, despite Nigeria's oil wealth. On the other hand, the people saw the arrogant display of wealth by a few people and their children whose parents might have been in government, no matter how brief. The majority who never resorted to criminal activities, by virtue of being deprived, gave their support to the Shari'a, believing that, since Islam stands for the protection of the weak, the oppressed would demand that "the root of oppressors and lovers of ill gotten luxury be completely cut off ..." (Sulaiman, 1988).

HISTORY OF SHARI'A IN NIGERIA

In the *Financial Times* article, referred to above, the author observed that "the Shari'a code has been a part of life in northern Nigeria for over 200 years. But since the British conquered the Sokoto Caliphate, at the turn of the twentieth century, it has been restricted largely to customary law." In the one hundred years of the life of the Sokoto Caliphate, the Shari'a was the source of law for the private and public spheres of life. It was therefore able to shape the behavior of the Muslims and made Islam the source of culture in the North. It was this century-old re-orientation that made Islam's position of influence in the Muslim North significantly different compared with its influence in other regions. During negotiations with the triumphant colonial forces, in 1903, the main preoccupation of the leaders of the Caliphate was negotiating for the freedom to practice religion without interference by the new masters. Therefore, the Shari'a continued during the colonial period. But later on, both the *hudud* (capital punishment) and other aspects of public life were gradually abolished.[9]

The Penal Code was introduced in the First Republic when the regions were autonomous. On the eve of independence, the Northern region was made to work out a synthesized law to replace the Shari'a by amalgamating the Indian Legal Code, Common Law, and Muslim Personal Law (the Penal Code for the independent North). In practice, the lower courts were told that they were administering the Shari'a without the *hudud*.

In the military regimes, the status quo remained virtually unchanged. Further, when the states were created, the Nigerian legal system recognized three types of law at the state level and only one at the federal level. The Common Law existed at both the state and federal levels. There was, in addition, the Shari'a Law in states with a Muslim majority that concerned itself with private matters or Customary Law derived from traditional African religion in most of the states in the South. Both the Shari'a Court of Appeal and Customary courts also existed in the federal capital. Thus, Nigeria's legal system recognized three sets of laws even though only the Common Law reigned supreme at the federal level.

During the periods of transition to democracy in 1977–78 and 1987–88, then under military regimes, new constitutions were to be made by the respective Constituent Assemblies; but the Shari'a debates created stalemate. Muslim members of the respective Assemblies wanted the Shari'a included in the constitution at state and federal levels, while Christian-led members, on the other hand, opposed this move. They insisted it was an ominous move towards the Islamization of the country — a plan to make Nigeria Islamic that Muslims had been committed to since the time of Sheikh Ousmane Dan Fodio (Clarke, op. cit.). However, using a more academic tone, the Christians argued that with the introduction of the Shari'a at the federal level, two parallel systems of law in one country would be introduced. This, they argued, would cause chaos in a country where Muslims and Christians were interdependent. The Christians were obsessed that the Shari'a was "more a religious [set of laws] than a set of laws meant to regulate the conduct of society." (Newswatch Magazine, 1988) The Christians further felt that "the implementation of Shari'a at the federal level would amount to imposing Islam as a state religion in Nigeria." (Ibid.) The debate was so intense, and the situation became so tense, that, in 1977–78, the Muslim group walked out. In the 1977–78 and 1987–88 constitutional debates, the military saved corporate Nigeria, by intervening to give the Shari'a its private status at state level, which Muslims had never been satisfied with. However, it needs to be understood that there was demand for the Shari'a prior to the 1977–78 debate. The Muslim Students' Society of Nigeria (MSSN),[10] the oldest, widest, and very influential organization, established in 1954, started the campaign for the Shari'a in the second decade of its existence. When Nigeria gained independence and was struggling to establish democracy, the MSSN enshrined in its constitution "to establish an Islamic *Ummah* governed by the principles and rules of the Shari'a." (Barau, 1996)

The return to the status quo that limited the Shari'a to personal status, dealing with matters of inheritance and divorce, was accepted by the Christians only after the military intervened. However, the recent expansion now gives the Shari'a a wider scope to include criminal offences that could attract capital punishment, where Christians allege they could be victims. Christian opposition to Islam and the Shari'a increased, insisting that the whole exercise was unconstitutional.

The present Shari'a-related conflict came to the fore when the Zamfara State Governor, in the Northwestern part of Nigeria, expanded the Shari'a's jurisdiction to include criminal offences. While there might have been some other political reasons that made the pioneer governor to expand the

Shari'a, the people of the state have now accepted it as their program. Clearly, under intense, extreme, and sustained pressure from their respective people about eight more state governors in the North, after some were even scolded by the people, reluctantly expanded the Shari'a's jurisdiction — even though that was not part of their electioneering promises.

During the recent campaign, the Muslims claimed that the processes followed were democratic and constitutional because bills proclaiming Shari'a were passed by the affected states' Houses of Assembly and signed by their respective governors into law. Muslims referred to the sections of the constitution that allowed states to create courts and assign jurisdiction to them and to the sections granting the respective Houses of Assembly the power to promulgate laws for the peace, security, and good governance of their states. A professor of law saw the implementation of the Shari'a as constitutional since the respective states were not declaring Islam as the State Religion, which section 10 of the constitution clearly prohibited (Yadudu, 2000).

Whatever the right constitutional interpretation might be, and important as it were, this is not the subject of this paper. We are here concerned with how the conflict could affect Nigeria's fragile democracy. The position of the Christians was clear and mirrored a sentiment expressed by an eminent jurist: "Shari'a is the very last straw which appears to have broken the back of the camel [meaning the corporate existence of Nigeria]." (Dr. Aguda, gamji.com, 27/9/00). The Muslim leadership denied the Christians' claims that the opposition that sparked crises in different parts of the country was triggered by the implementation of the Shari'a. The official leader of the Muslims in Nigeria, Sultan Muhammadu Maccido, said that "since Muslims have a right to embrace it [Shari'a] . . . [the] root causes of the crises should be looked for somewhere else' (Ibid.).

Where then is the future of the Shari'a in a democratic society? Can Nigeria's fragile democracy survive the Shari'a imbroglio and create for Nigeria the confidence it requires for stability?

THE SHARI'A AND DEMOCRATIC VALUES

Our utopian secondary school definition of democracy is "a rule of the people, for the people, and by the people." At various stages, there have been different studies about democracy in non-Western societies.[11] It was initially seen as a simple theory of transplanting democracy from the West to non-Western societies with little or no concern of the countries' peculiar situations. These peculiar conditions could range from poverty, corruption, religious, or ethnic values.

The nature of democracy in countries other than those in the West was later given some attention. It was acknowledged that "... the nature of democracy is diversifying as it proliferates and is conditioned by cultural and political differences and varying stages of economic and social development," (Inoguchi, Newman, and Keane (Eds) 1998).

In this regard, the Muslim societies were not left out in an effort to find the best way they could be democratized. These were efforts by intellectuals and activists to justify Islam as inherently democratic or even using democratic procedures to establish a government by the activists.[12]

Earlier, in this paper, we noted that as multiethnic and a multireligious country as Nigeria is, democracy is well suited to endure its stability. However, how does democracy face and synthesize the multifarious demands, including the challenges of implementing the Shari'a among other pressing challenges? Considering that democracy needs grassroots anchorage for its stability, it needs to accept the role of religions in the society. After all, religion is a significant form of identity which if not understood can endanger democracy.

On the other hand, followers of different religions and democratic institutions themselves must understand that a clash-free society may not exist. "It is only when incommensurable ideas and practices clash that democracy is threatened." (Ibid.) What is important therefore is the understanding and respect for each other's opinions or values and emphasizing the positive aspects, while also accommodating some unavoidable differences. When religious leaders inspire confidence and are enlightened about the advantages of democracy, they can be positively used to enthrone a viable democracy. A Christian leader emphasized the power of religion and of religious leaders, when he observed that:

> Let us make no mistake. Political leaders can respond to New World realities only as religious leaders re-define that world, and this re-defines what acting responsibly within that world means ... We in religion have the power to legitimate or de-legitimate secular rule. (Raines, 1986)

It is the contention of this paper that the fear of the 'other' had developed and became a reality with the corrupt misrule that Nigerians were subjected to by the military leadership especially in the recent past. The basic amenities of life never existed and hope was dashed. Nigerians believed that to 'make it in life,' one required a relative or a friend at the top. It was not a matter of education, hard work, or honesty. Leadership, therefore, became a matter of 'life and death' because of the corrupt benefits derived from it.

Given the country's condition of underdevelopment, power offers the opportunity of a lifetime to rise above the general poverty and squalor (dirty and unpleasant place) that pervades the entire society. It provides a rare opportunity to acquire wealth and prestige, to place one in a position to distribute benefits in the form of jobs, contracts, scholarship, gifts of money, and so on to ones relatives and political allies. (Towards ..., 1987).

The leadership of the Abacha regime not only profited his family members and friends, but also drained the country's coffers. On the other hand, if leadership, as defined by the Shari'a, was seen as a public service guided by the principle of justice and accountability, it would not have been that appealing to be clamored for. It is hoped that the new anticorruption commission that was recently sworn-in, will do what has been the dream of Nigerians.[13] However, an independent and respected judiciary, where the rule of law is upheld is key to its success. It could be remembered that the Murtala regime had a similar commission backed by a decree in 1975 (Oyediran, 1975). Had Nigeria succeeded from that time forward to curb corruption, it might have been a different country today. From the First Republic the Premier of the North, though himself Muslim, is till today positively remembered by Muslims and Christians for his selfless service to both Muslims and Christians.

If the socioeconomic aspects of the Shari'a were implemented, and people saw the economic benefits and corrupt leaders were jailed, the opposition to it would have probably diminished. The only memory associated with the Shari'a by especially those that do not know it, and who are also the majority, is the Alkali courts. When both Christians and Muslims were tried in these courts, the record did not provide a positive picture of the Shari'a.

Muslims must demonstrate that the Shari'a affects only them. They must also demonstrate that the Shari'a is flexible and adaptable. "Legal Rulings change with time, place, circumstances, and custom" (Qardawi, 1998) The fact that, Islam is interested in winning souls not defeating them, the Shari'a advocates must make it imperative to show the humane nature of the Shari'a so as to dispel fear and mistrust. To quote Qardawi again,

> The Shari'a, in its basis for judgment, concerns people and life. For the Shari'a is just, merciful, useful, and wise. Every judgment that deviates from justice to oppression, from mercy to ruthlessness, from usefulness to corruption, and from wisdom to folly, notwithstanding the different interpretations of it, is definitely not Shari'a oriented. (Ibid.)

Apart from the Christian misunderstanding or opposition of the Shari'a, there were the Muslim clerics, for example Alfas in Lagos state, who claimed, "in all our Mosques, the application of Shari'a has been in force all along, as our fathers have been applying them." The Council of Chief Imams and Ulamau registered their opposition to what they call politicized application of Shari'a and came with this conclusion:

> That this council affirms that any attempt to use the Shari'a to create any form of unrest and instability from any source in our state is not acceptable to us. This is because we are daily praying for the peace, unity, progress, and stability of this great country of ours. We pray that the present federal government will succeed in her endeavor to achieve all these in the name of Allah. (The Guardian, July 30, 2000).

Did the Council of Chief Imams and Ulamau of Lagos state not know what their Muslim counterparts in the North were doing? Was their fear of a political implementation of the Shari'a to do with a different perception of Islam? However, another view regarding the implementation of the Shari'a came from Ibrahim Zakzaky. Malam Zakzaky was a renowned figure in the struggle for Islam in Nigeria since his student days. He formed an Islamic movement and was imprisoned on a number of occasions. He has a different view with regards to this type of Shari'a implementation. In a paper he presented on the application of Shari'a in our time, he says:

> Those thinking of applying the Shari'a in any society should think first of making the state and government of the society Islamic. The Shari'a is meant to be applied by an Islamic government in an Islamic environment. The adoption of Shari'a in an un-Islamic system of government is not a step towards realization of that goal. (Zakzaky, 1999).

Zakzaky was not alone in expressing fear on this type of Shari'a implementation and especially in emphasizing its criminal aspect while overlooking its socioeconomic and political dimensions. However, from the remarks of Yadudu, the comprehensive implementation of the Shari'a as advocated by Zakzaky and others appeared to be the type that is unconstitutional. This is because it is tantamount to declaring a State Religion. If Muslims oppose this type of implementation of the Shari'a, this indicates the hurdles ahead in resolving this stalemate in peaceful and acceptable ways. Trust and confidence are the cornerstone of any relationship and it is through them that peace could be cultivated — or is it not?

Endnotes

1. The Hausa and Fulani are distinct tribes but with their mass acceptance of Islam and intermarriages, their interests were seen to be one, especially by the southern press and Christian scholars.

2. Sheikh Ousmane Dan Fodio was the leader of the movement that brought the Sokoto Caliphate. The movement was essentially reformative and made Islam and its culture very strong in the North. There are a number of masters and doctorate studies on the movement and its principal actors. See especially, Ibrahim Suleiman, *A Revolution in History: The Jihad of Usman Danfodio* (Mansell Publishers, 1986); also by the same author, *The Islamic State and the Challenge of History: Ideals Policies and Operation of the Sokoto Caliphate* (Mansell Publishers, 1986); Usman M. Bugaje, *The Sakkwato Model: A Study of the Origin Development and Fruition of the Jihad of Uthman b. Fodye (1754-1817)* (Published by Muslim Enlightenment Committee, Sokoto, n.d.).
3. They were Shehu Usman, his brother Abdullahi dan Fodio, and his son Muhammad Bello.
4. 'Sardauna' was a traditional title in the Sokoto Emirate Council.
5. It was an abortive coup led by Gideon Orkar that almost caused pandemonium in the country but for the timely defeat of the copyists (unimaginative imitators).
6. The primaries of Shehu 'Yar'dua and Adamu Ciroma that was annulled by the military claiming it was corrupt was clearly part of the military's leadership hidden agenda. The primaries election of Abiola and Tofa that was later upheld was not free from corrupt practices. See Abubakar Siddique Mohammed, 'The June 12 Presidential Election was neither Free nor Fair' (Centre for Development Research and Training, 2000).
7. Long before the Shari'a issue, at least ten disturbances had occurred in the Belt. See Yusuf Bala, *Usman and Alkasum Abba: The Misrepresentation of Nigeria* (Vanguard Printers and Publishers Ltd, Kaduna, 2000); Hadiza Nuhu (Mrs), *Religious Crises in Northern Nigeria: An Appraisal* (Kano, Nigeria, April, 1993); Bashir Isyaku, *The Kafanchan Carnage* (Ramadan 1411, April 1991); and Matthew Hassan Kukah, *Religion Politics and Power in Northern Nigeria* (Spectrum Books Limited, Ibadan, 1993).
8. On Kanem-Borno Empire see, Nur Alkali, "The Kanem-Bornu Empire under the Sayfawa: A Study of Origin, Growth and Collapse of a Dynasty" (Unpublished Ph.D. Thesis, Ahmadu Bello University, Zaria, Nigeria, 1978); Y. B. Usman and Nur Alkali eds., *Studies on the History of Pre-Colonial Borno* (N.N.P.C., Zaria, 1979).
9. For details see A. H. Yadudu, "We Need a New Legal System," in *On the Political Future of Nigeria,* ed. Ibrahim Suleiman and Siraj Abdulkarim, (Hudahuda Publishing Company, Zana, 1988).
10. The MSSN has about thirty million members with branches in the country's institutions of learning from secondary schools to tertiary. For details on the Society see Barau, Siraj Abdulkarim, "The Changing Role of Islam in Post-independent Nigeria: The Case of the Muslim Students' Society of Nigeria [MSSN]." (Unpublished Ph.D. Thesis, Institute of African and Asian Studies, University of Khartoum, 1996).

11. There are many literatures on the subject by political theorists, but see for example a book that summarized these approaches; Robert Pinkney, *Democracy in the Third World* (Open University Press, Buckingham, 1993).
12. The writings of Rashid Ghanoushi, an intellectual and activist, demonstrate the argument in favor of democracy and the need for the participation of activists in democratic election to bring Islamic change; see his, "The Participation of Islamists in a Non-Islamic Government" in *Power-Sharing Islam?* ed. Azzam Tamimi (Liberty for Muslim World Publications, London, 1993) and, "Islamic Movements: Self-criticism and Reconsideration" in *Middle East Affairs* (Winter Spring, 1997). Islamists had participated in democratic elections in Turkey, Algeria, Sudan, Kuwait, etc., and were becoming widespread.
13. It took the regime one and a half years to get the Commission sworn in while anticorruption was one of its cardinal programmes in a four-year term.

References

Abubakre, R. Deremi. 1992. "Religion, Culture, and Politics among the Yoruba Muslims" in *Religion and Peace in Multifaith Nigeria*, ed. Jacob K. Olupona. Ile-Ife, Obafemi Awolowo University, 1992.

Al-Buraey, Muhammad A. 1985. *Administrative Development: An Islamic Perspective*. Kegan Paul International Limited, New York.

Alkali, Nur. 1978. "Kanem-Borno Empire under the Sayfawa: A Study of the Origin, Growth, and Collapse of a Dynasty." Unpublished Ph.D. Thesis, Ahmadu Bello University, Zaria, Nigeria.

Barau, Siraj Abdulkarim. 1996. "The Changing Role of Islam in Post-Independent Nigeria: The Role of the Muslim Students Society of Nigeria." Unpublished Ph.D. Thesis, Institute of African Asian Studies, University of Khartoum.

"Shari'a in Nigeria." 2000. Contribution to a Symposium held under the auspices of the Royal African Society, London, (July).

Basri, Ghazali. 1994. *Nigeria and Shari'a: Aspirations and Apprehensions*. The Islamic Foundation, Leicester.

Bugaje, Usman M. *The Sakkwato Model: A Study of the Origin, Development, and Fruition of the Jihad of Usman b. Fodye (1754–1817)*. Muslim Enlightenment Committee, Sokoto, u.d.

Clarke, Peter B. 1988. "Islamic Reform in Contemporary Nigeria" in *Third World Quarterly*. Vol. 10, No. 2, (April).

Cronje, Suzanne. 1972. *The World and Nigeria: The Diplomatic History of the Biafra War 1967–70*. Sidgwick and Jackson Limited.

Ekwe-Ekwe, Herbert. 1985. "The Nigerian Plight: Shagari to Buhari" in *Third World Quarterly*. Vol. 7, No. 3, (July).

El-Affendi, Abdelwahab. 1991. *Who Needs an Islamic State?* Grey Seal Books, London.

Gboyega, Alex. 1997. "Nigeria: Conflict Unresolved" in *Governance as Conflict Management: Politics and Violence in West Africa*, ed. I. William Zartman. The Brookings Institution.

Ghannoushi, Rashid. 1993. "The Participation of Islamists in a Non-Islamic Government" in *Power-Sharing Islam?* ed. Azzam Tamimi. Liberty for Muslim World Publications, London.

"Islamic Movements: Self-criticism and Reconsideration" in *Middle East Affairs.* (winter-spring 1997).

Hiskett, Mervyn. 1984. *The Development of Islam in West Africa.* Longman Group, London.

Inoguchi, Takashi; Edward Newman; and John Keane (eds.). 1998. *The Changing Nature of Democracy.* United Nations University Press, Japan.

Isyaku, Bashir. 1991. *The Kafanchan Carnage.* Ramadan, 1411, (April).

Kamali, Mohammad Hashim. 1999. "Social Justice: A Comparative Analysis of Western Philosophy and the Shari'a" in *ISLAMICA.* Vol. 3, No. 1 (summer).

Khan, Mohammed A. Muqtedar. 1999. "Second-Generation Islamists and the Future of the Islamic Movements: A Response to Shaykh Rashid Ghannoushi" in *ISLAMICA.* Vol. 3, No. 1 (summer).

Kukah, Matthew Hassan. 1993. *Religion Politics and Power in Northern Nigeria.* Spectrum Books Limited, Ibadan.

Ling, Trevor. 1982. *A History of Religion East and West.* Macmillan Press, London.

Lubeck, Paul. 1988. "Islamic Political Movements in Northern Nigeria: The Problem of Class Analysis" in *Islam Politics and Social Movements,* ed. Edward Burke III and Ira M. Papidus. University of California Press, Berkeley.

Mazrui, Ali A. 1988. "African Islam and Competitive Religion: Between Revivalism and Expansion" in *Third World Quarterly.* Vol. 10, No. 2 (April).

Mohammed, Abubakar Siddique. 1999. "Human Living Conditions and Reforms of Legal Systems: The Talakawa and the Issue of the Shari'a in Contemporary Nigeria" (Paper prepared for presentation at the Conference on Shari'a and the Constitutional Process held at Kongo Conference Hotel, Zaria, Nigeria (17-18 November).

Murphy, Richard W. and F. Gregory Gause III. "Democracy and US Policy in the Muslim Middle East." In author's possession.

"The June 12 Presidential Election was neither Free nor Fair." Centre for Democratic Development Research and Training.

Momoh, Prince Tony. *Letter to My Countrymen: Whose Cause?* Federal Ministry of Information. Undated.

Nnoli, Okwudiba. 1994. *Ethnicity and Democracy in Africa: Intervening Variables.* Centre for Advanced Social Science.

Nuhu, Hadiza (Mrs). 1993. *Religious Crises in Northern Nigeria: An Appraisal.* Kano, Nigeria (April).

Nwanko, Arthur A. and Samuel U. Ifejika. 1969. *The Making of a Nation: BIAFRA.* Hurst & Company, London.

Osaghae, Eghosa. 1994. *Ethnicity and its Management in Africa: The Democratization Link.* Centre for Advanced Social Science.

Oyediran, O. 1978. *Survey of Nigerian Affairs 1975.* Published for the Nigerian Institute of International Affairs by Oxford University Press, Nigeria.

Paya, Ali. 2000. "Democracy in Iran" in *CSD Bulletin*. Vol. 7, No. 2 (summer).
Qardawi, Yusuf. 1998. *State in Islam*. El-Falah for Translation Publishing and Distribution, Cairo.
The Sunnah. 1998. *A Source of Civilization*. El-Falah for Translation Publishing and Distribution, Cairo.
Raines, John C. 1986. "The Nation, State, and Social Order in the Perspective of Christianity" in *Trialogue of the Abrahamic Faiths* ed. Isma'il R. al-Faruqi. International Institute of Islamic Thought, Herndon.
"Resolutions of the Fifth Pan-Yoruba Congress" (September 2000).
Sanusi, Sanusi Lamido. "Shari'a and the Woman Question" (gamji.com, May 11, 2000).
Suleiman, Ibrahim. 1991. *An Islamic Political System for Nigeria*. The Islamic Study Group of Nigeria, Lagos.
A Revolution in History: The Jihad of Usman Danfodio. Mansell Publishers, London, 1986.
The Islamic State and the Challenge of History: Ideals Policies and Operation of the Sokoto Caliphate. 1986. Mansell Publishers, London.
Tamimi, Azzam. Ed. 1993. "Democracy in Islamic Political Thought" (October 1998) ed. *Power-Sharing Islam*. Liberty for Muslim World Publications, London.
Government of Nigeria. 1958. Report of the Commission Appointed to Enquire into the Fears of Minorities and the Means of Allying Them. Her Majesty's Stationery Office, London, July.
Tessler, Mark and Merilyn Grobschmidt. "Democracy in the Arab World and the Arab-Israeli Conflict." In author's possession.
Towards the Right Path for Nigeria. 1987. The Fellowship of Churches of Christ, TEKAN Owe Press Ltd, Jos.
Ufford, Philip Quarles van and Matthew Schoffeleers. Eds. 1988. *Religion & Development: Towards an integrated approach*. Free University, Netherlands.
Usman, Yusuf Bala and Alkasum Abba. 2000. *The Misrepresentation of Nigeria*. Vanguard Printers and Publishers Ltd, Kaduna. Nur Alkali. Ed. 1979. *Studies on the History of Pre-Colonial Borno*. N.N.P.C., Zaria.
Yadudu, A. H. 1988. "We Need a New Legal System" in *On the Political Future of Nigeria*, ed. Ibrahim Suleiman and Siraj Abdulkarim. Hudahuda Publishing Company, Zaria.
———. "The Shari'a Debate in Nigeria: Time for Reflections." In author's possession.
Wright, Robin. 1991. "Islam's New Political Face." *Current History*, (January).
Zakzaky, Malam Ibrahim. 1999. "Application of Shari'a in the Contemporary World: Lessons from some Muslim Countries." A Paper presented to the National Conference on the Application of Shari'a, Jointly Organized by the Department of Islamic Law, Faculty of Law, Bayero University, and Ramnan Law Consult, Kano at Bayero University, Kano from 1-3 December.

Newspapers and Magazines

The African Guardian Magazine (Lagos, Nigeria)
Ethnic & Religious Rights Magazine (Quarterly Publication of Human Rights Monitor)
The Guardian Newspaper (Lagos, Nigeria)
The Guardian Newspaper (London)
The Middle Path Magazine (London)
The Vanguard Newspaper (Lagos, Nigeria)
The Tempo (Lagos, Nigeria)

8

Structuring Islam and the Culture of Democratization: The Case of Niger

ABDOULAYE SOUNAYE

The story of Islam in Niger can legitimately assert the characters of an African Islam, the contents of which are made up from two sources of values, that of the *Qur'an hadith* and the indigenous African values and practices. Islam, as a social fact, is thus characterized, in general, by particular contextual dynamics.[1] Before 1991, the year the National Conference[2] took place, Islam was officially represented by only one organization in Niger's civil society.

From then, a remarkable and continuous dynamism determines structures created on behalf of Islam and for the spread of Islamic ideology. For example, from 1991 to 1999, more than 40 new Islamic organizations were created. The new sociopolitical context is the principal reason of this tendency in a country where, habitually, even though Islam is the main religion, founding Islamic structures neither were the people's concern nor permitted by authorities.

Today, as we observe the phenomenon, some questions should be asked. For example, is this Islamic resurgence simply a transitory phenomenon? What is the aim of such a profusion of Islamic organizations? What role(s) do they play as civil society organizations? How do they voice political concerns as the state is undergoing radical political change?

Depending on the approach, many reasons may explain the change in the sociopolitical status of religion in Niger. The search for real independence is among the main reasons for structuring the Islamic sphere. Before the democratization era, especially under Seyni Kountché (1974–1987) and Ali Saibou (1987–1991), the government had total control over the religious sphere in general. With the advent of democracy, the Islamic structures called for purity in Islam and more consideration for Niger's social and cultural identity.

In the context of democratization and modernization, the debate on secularism and women's condition became the main issue that motivated Islamic associations. Particularly striking is the fact that these organizations reacted to what they regarded as an offense to the Nigerien Islamic culture. It is thus interesting to show how they utilized democratization and the freedom of speech as vehicles to imprint the 'authentic' mark of Islam on the society. Under such circumstances, religion became a key factor in understanding Niger's society, especially when religious actors undertook the task of redefining sociopolitical relationships by freeing themselves from government tutelage.

This chapter argues that Islamic activism in Niger seeks a moral refoundation of the state and by so doing, ridding Niger of the monopoly of the French and western-oriented elite and their push for secularism.

CONTEXT

The global context, which is very often characterized by competition and even a conflicting relationship between Islam and Western sources of values, has a considerable impact on the Islamic renewal in Niger. There are very few Western countries where Islam has not (yet) become synonymous with a burden (Kilani: 1993; Ramadan: 1996; Ramadan et Neirynck: 1999) and a source of conflicts. Many authors have already drawn attention to this condition in European political debate.

For the student of Islam in Africa, it is certainly worth noticing the geographical situation of Niger. Niger is surrounded by three countries, in which Islamic practices are pronounced and take on a clear political agenda. To the Northwest lies Algeria, where a very violent Islamist movement has developed. Despite the military repression, Islam remains highly politicized. Today, however, there is no evidence of direct relationship between the vectors of this Algerian Islamist effervescence and the activism of Islamic organizations in Niger.

Libya, to the Northeast, is also involved in a religious instrumentalization, though very different from the Algerian model. Through Islam, Muammar al-Gadaffi seems to have found an ideology that contributes to his fight against Western imperialism and the affirmation of another view on world order. Regarding Niger, his well-known support for Islam goes back to the 1970s. Since then, the Libyan leader has invested hundreds of millions into building mosques and *madrassas* (bilingual schools that use French and Arabic).

Lastly, to the south lies Nigeria, the country in sub-Saharan Africa most affected by religious upheavals. There too, Islam has become a phenomenon with great political stakes, particularly in the Northern part of the country where several states are already under formal Islamic legislation. Today, there is hardly need to say that the religious dynamism of the *big neighbor* also has a significant impact on Niger.

INFLUENCE: THE SPECIAL CASE OF NIGERIA

The relationship between Nigeria and Niger is exceptional in West Africa, particularly the economic ties. The two countries share one of the longest borders[3] in West Africa. However, because the two countries have been subject to different colonial systems, their cultural similarities differ from their political and institutional systems. The northern part of Nigeria and the southern part of Niger share the Hausa people — a people mostly Islamized today, but whose conversion increased sharply from the end of the nineteenth century to the beginning of the twentieth century. Sheikh Ousmane Dan Fodio's jihad played an important role in establishing Islam as a principal source of values in Hausaland.

Despite their different colonial histories and the development of specific postcolonial political systems, the influence of Islam in the social life remains very significant on both sides of the border. Islam is almost perceived as *the* natural religion of the region.

In Nigeria, Islam, which arose in the political arena in the 1980s, is now the state religion in the northern part of the federation. The recurrence of the Islamist issue seems to support the thesis that predicted the political conversion of the religious movements that spread out in the early eighties.

Obviously, facing the growth of Islamic activism in Niger, especially in the areas close to Nigeria, one cannot help asking about the impact the multiple Nigerian Islamic centers of the early eighties had had on Nigerien Islamic organizations. This is important in analyzing Islam's dynamism in Niger, in particular because northern Nigeria has represented and still represents a place of higher education for many Nigeriens, having reached a certain level in their Qur'anic education. Kanem, Borno, as well as Sokoto and Zaria were important places, where students from many parts of Niger often pursued their Qur'anic studies and earned Islamic degrees. E. Grégoire, for example, describing the emergence of the *Izala* reformist's movement in Maradi, asserts:

> Traveling to improve their knowledge of the Qur'an, marabouts from Maradi would spend time in the British-controlled cities of northern Nigeria. Kano, Zaria, Sokoto, and Maiduguri were highly regarded as centres of Qur'anic study. (Grégoire, 1993: 108).

Meanwhile, northern Nigeria is known to be an area of religious militancy that has developed violent reaction to authorities (Coulon, 1993). Given the fact that a significant number of students from Niger are trained there, it may be assumed, that they take back with them the ideals of the tradition they are trained in and try to institute them, especially when democracy and the freedom of speech make it possible. To some authorities in Niger, marabouts coming from Nigeria, find in Niger a land to be conquered. For example, the *Préfet de Maradi* (Prefect of Maradi),[4] the high regional authority, following Islamists' demonstrations which culminated in 1997, argued as follows: "our *intégristes* [French word for fundamentalist] are inspired by the Gentleman from Nigeria who is their spiritual leader. They just carry out his orders, aiming at extending their movement, their ideology."[5] A significant portion of people, especially civil authorities and the intellectual class, share the feeling that Niger's Islamists, in particular those that settled in Maradi, have strong connections with Nigerian Islamists.

Some of my interviewees in Niamey[6] and Maradi[7] view the Arab countries[8] as a source of support and funding for Islamic organizations. The Islamist groups, according to these informants, receive significant financial support from Arab countries through local businesspersons. Economic leaders have built large mosques with funds donated by Arab countries, including Kuwait and Saudi Arabia.

Although the influence of Nigeria in Niger is obvious, as far as religion and state relations are concerned, structurally, each country remains a distinct case. In Nigeria, Islam has permeated the political arena so much that it has been one of the main political issues for about twenty years. In contrast, in Niger, Islam had never been a serious political issue before democratization. In the meantime, while Islam was under government control in Niger, particularly with AIN[9] during Kountché's military regime, in Nigeria, Islam was quite autonomous vis-à-vis political authorities. As Miles (1994) argues, that is one of the main reasons Niger has never experienced religious uprisings akin to those frequently observed in Nigeria.[10] It appears that Niger's relative homogeneity stands in contrast to Nigerian pluralism.[11]

DEMOCRACY AND ISLAMIC REVIVAL IN NIGER

In Niger, the wind of democratization that swept up the political field and put an end to monopartism, had an impact on all the sectors of social life. The multiplication of Islamic structures came out of this new political philosophy.[12] As democratic change is spreading and freedom of speech instituted, the new Islamic organizations, stripped of anything likely to betray the Islamic principles, criticize the variations in Islam (mainly indigenous African oral practices). They point out the political ties of the single organization[13] that has so far spoken on behalf of Islam and Nigerien Muslims. The call for an authentic Islam lies, first, on a reforming process that principally means the *return to the letter of Islam*. This is the position strongly publicized by *Adini-Islam*, one of the leading organizations in the religious sphere. Additionally, most of the new organizations tend to reject the *archaism* in the methods[14] of the organization that had spoken so far for Islam. In this specific context, the associational mode represents a strategy to countervail power and in the meantime to get and reinforce freedom of speech.[15] It is interesting to note the role played by the media in providing these organizations with more visibility.[16]

Among the external signs of Islamic revival, one must mention the numerous mosques recently built. For example, in the early eighties, Niamey had just one big mosque for Friday prayers and another for the prayers of *Eid*. However, today, more than forty major mosques bloom in the capital; this is not because of the increase in Muslim population, but especially because of Islamic militancy and the desire for many associations to define themselves apart from the traditional clerics. As a result, each group aims at owning its place of prayer and sermon. In Zinder as well as in Niamey or Maradi, the *Yan Izala*,[17] in fighting the Islamic establishment, managed to get their own mosques. Mosques then acquired etiquette and became marked places where people were most likely associated to the group or association running the mosque. In the meantime, for the adepts, the mosque became one of the venues most frequently used for formal or informal gatherings. Gradually, mosques became symbolically loaded as they were also used for new and various reasons.

In terms of dress, the use of *Hijab* by women[18] and modest clothes for men, with pants hardly exceeding the tibia, became visible and were also encouraged by militants. The very thick beard is also one of the esthetical manifestations common to these groups. Similarly, shifting prayer timings (many new mosques call to *Az'zouhour* — the second of the five daily prayers — 30 to 45 minutes before the usual time) and newspapers (*As Salam, Iqra*, etc.) testify to the changes in Islamic practices. It is not surprising that the government, seeking support from these groups, proclaimed as a holiday (since 1997) the first day of the Muslim calendar, *Al-Mouharam*. Additionally, the introduction of new didactic means into the Qur'anic schools in order for students to master Arabic (use of desks, new handbooks, etc.), initiatives taken to build Islamic high schools, are other aspects that strengthen Islam and its militancy in the democratization era. These aspects confirm, in Niger too, the *Islamic identities' inflation* (Coulon analyzes) in northern Nigeria.

In short, the substance of the revival is expressed in a venture for purification, an internal process that preaches the return to Islam strictly and literally founded on the Qur'an, avoiding and fighting against the traditional maraboutic interpretations, very often based on religious leaders' interests. This call for a return to the letter of the holy book is conceived as the cornerstone of the reformist movement.

DEVELOPMENT OF ISLAMIC STRUCTURES

One of the main features in the development of the new Islamic organizations resides in the competing views on Islam, either in brotherhoods or in sects. Consequently, it generates distinctions that impact the social and the political capital of this religion. In the course of this reorganization and conquest, distinctions such as conservative Islam/reformist Islam, elitist Islam/popular Islam, brotherhoods/associations, pure Islam[19]/syncretic Islam were used. The categorization in itself contributes in depicting the divisions among Islamic organizations. To illustrate the intensity of this opposition, especially in Niamey, one should note the violence in which the competition may culminate, as it was the case on August 27, 1993 when Issa Doumbaye, member of the *Izala*[20] sect, was assassinated. In fact, the *Préfet Président de la Communauté Urbaine*, the local administrative authority, had to intervene frequently in order to settle growing and violent oppositions between Islamic leaders and groups.[21]

The development of Islamic associations is one manifestation of the sectarian divisions of Islam. Associations and Islamic groups are founded not exclusively to defend Islam, but also to convey views on this religion, depending on the Islamic tradition[22] the group follows. To the traditional and initial *tarikha*,[23] *tidjaniya* and *khadiriya* associations are added. These new organizations, even though they have not wiped out the old ones, spread out remarkably in the society, particularly in urban areas where they are most active.

The most prominent example of opposition in the fight for legitimacy is the one that focuses on practices of Islam maintained by the brotherhoods. Contradictory to the *Sunna* of the Prophet, the discourse of *Izala* — based on an overt criticism of the confreric practices — views aristocracy and innovation, as irrelevant. For *Izala*, Islam in the hands of the brotherhoods secretes a system of rules, which betrays the social model recommended by Islam. E. Grégoire sees in the discourse of *Yan Izala* a disagreement with traditional brotherhoods, which is not just doctrinal. As he remarks:

> It also reaches out into practices (the scheduling and length of daily prayers, distinct places of worship etc.,). In this respect, the Izala movement, like Wahhabism in Mali, can be said to be fundamentally opposed to the religious practices of the marabouts. Its followers criticize marabouts for their power and occult practices, for their quackery and for dealing in amulets and charms (still used in Maradi for obtaining success in work, business, or love and for healing purposes). They condemn the marabouts as parasites living on society through such heathen practices. (Grégoire: 1993, 112).

Leaders of brotherhoods, argues the *Izala* movement, set a system that reinforces their power upon the organization with no real consideration of the principles of Islam. Therefore, instead of backing the brotherhoods' institution of a power system, this sect prefers being a simple sect that finds in associations and mosques,[24] forums for "revealing and communicating the true message of Islam."[25] Not only do they think religion should not become a power for the *Sheikh*, but they argue that the principles enacted by the Qur'an must take precedence over all, in particular over the customary law.[26] In this context, the association becomes a place where "authentic Islamic identity is affirmed" and an efficient way to win the competition for recognition.

In Niger, and apparently in Northern Nigeria, *Izala* association is the principal organization to have called into question the classical social configuration of Islam. Two reasons explain its growing impact on the society — first, Izala calls for a fight against the practices developed by marabouts, who are traditionally the only experts of the Qur'an; secondly, the desire to overcome the ignorance of the holy texts and the linguistic barrier. Consequently, the movement founded an approach that combines initiation to reading and writing in Arabic.[27] In addition, its criticisms of the practices and the social behaviors ended up in the progressive abandonment of ostentation in ceremonies, in particular within the circle of its militants. For example, celebrations with dances and tom-toms in occasions such as ceremonies and marriages are progressively being replaced by gatherings for *fatiah* or Qur'an readings.[28]

However, it seems likely to me that *Izala* itself ended up in brotherhoods as we can see in many parts of Niamey,[29] where *izala* gatherings have developed and consists, most of the time, of men around 30 years old concerned with their Muslim identity.

ISSUES AT STAKE: IDENTITY AND NATIONAL POLICY

In order to have the government take into account the major religion of the country, especially in making decisions that affect the society, Islamic structures[30] seem to agree on coordinating their efforts. In many ways, their real objective is to eliminate the common enemy — westernization — to the benefit of the cultural influence of Islam, its political valorization against 'imported ideologies.' According to Islamic structures such as *Adin-Islam*, *AJMN*, Niger national policy should simply be based on the principles of Qur'an. Their claim is that the government policy is not in conformity with people's expectations, as far as it does not always meet their real needs. That is the reason these structures have regularly intervened to express Islam's point of view and to require that it be taken into account, in particular, when the issue affects society, women, and family.[31]

ISLAMIC ASSOCIATIONS AND SECULARISM

Secularity is a concept not only variously valued, but which often remains the crux of the conflicting relations between authorities and religious organizations, in particular, those that support an extremism that rejects any submission to a secular command. During the foundation of the Nigerien democracy, the National Conference tried to set the State free from direct influence of the power and views of the religious groups.[32] At the end of several long debates, the term *laïcité* itself was withdrawn from the *Third Republic's* Constitution Project, after a strenuous opposition from Islamic associations' delegates. Most religious leaders contend that secularity represents an underground crusade against Islam. They argued that the inclusion and the adoption of secularity in a fundamental law such as the Constitution, in a country like Niger, would simply contradict the sociocultural reality of the country and betray the aspirations of Nigeriens.

The solution to the problem, or what was regarded as such, was a compromise that withdrew the term from the Constitution but maintained its substance and philosophy.[33] Instead of resolving a fundamental problem, delegates to the National Conference proposed a purely formal, terminological solution. It is worth noting that Niger's democracy derives from the French model which, in fact, theoretically puts religion as a nondetermining element in politics. Secularity becomes the law and foundation of democracy, especially in delineating firmly the division between State and religion.[34]

From the perspective of Islamic militants, it appears that the principal concern of the participants to the National Conference of 1991 was the search for another political model rather than a model relevant to Niger. In this debate, they seemed to be more realistic when they pointed out that what often lays out in the text has no historical or cultural basis in Niger.[35]

For religious leaders, since Islam is one of the Nigerien cultural foundations, there is no reason for secularity in the country. They view Islam as political, social, and moral therapy, the result of which would be social well-being.[36] This view on the society re-introduces the key question of the philosophical basis of both political action and the orientation of the national policy. For many, this basis should necessarily draw its inspiration from Islam, because it conceives society in the way it satisfies moral needs.[37]

Secularity, or at least its assertion in the official addresses, is presented as one of the conditions in the modernization and the stability of Niger. Those against this view contend that Islamist protests are defending the identity and the authenticity of Nigerien society. Their key argument is the high percentage of Muslims among the population. If Niger is up to 98 percent Muslim, how can the State remain secular and its administration legitimate?

However, generally speaking, the Islamist discourse that criticizes the separation between State and religion is not wholly accepted. For example, political leaders claim it is antidemocratic to legalize associations, which under their own constitution are normally apolitical.[38] During a visit in the 'stronghold of the Islamist groups,'[39] the then President of the Republic[40] had to intervene in the debate and make clear the position of his administration. For him, contrary to Islamists' expectations, Niger Republic will remain secular, respecting democracy and the separation between State and religion. He concluded that he would never accept any attempt against Islam or on any other religion, in consideration to his oath.[41]

The practice of the separation of State and religion remains often ambiguous on the part of authorities themselves. In fact, Islam is present in all important public ceremonies and above all, in the national media.[42] It appears, in the Nigerien context, that the State practices overflow its constitutional nonconfessionality. Abdou Moumouni University of Niamey sociologist, Souley Adji, remarked in 1992, "Niger became a sort of Islamic republic wrapped in secularism."[43]

The Islamic structures, thus, stand for a means to imprint on the State, a new orientation and to shape its dominant ideology. We must note that they have gradually acquired a capability to pressure the state, as various episodes[44] to their relationship with authorities since 1991 can testify. Despite their contradictions, the Islamic structures share a common element in their standpoint and in their concept of society; they consider Islam as the ideological framework that should rule the country.

From a comparative perspective, one may clearly see that the relationships between the political and the Islamic spheres in Niger do not appear in the same way they are generally described in a country like Sénégal. In Sénégal, although the sociocultural characteristics are similar to those of Niger, it seems that Islam became such an integral part of politics that coming to power without a pact with the confreric order is not a consideration (Magassouba: 1985); even though, in Niger too, religion is becoming a slippery political floor. The leaders of religious organizations[45] are quite aware of this development, especially when they recognize that no political party, expecting to run the country, could have acts such as the ratification of CEDAW.[46] In this perspective, if the military head of State — Wanké, decided to ratify the Convention, it is only because staying in power was not his concern. Apparently, no political party is out to revive the question of the *Family Code*[47] either. In fact, the violent demonstrations have dissuaded more than one politician from confronting the issue. Even though the debate on the *Islamic Republic* remains a political taboo, Islam in Niger is objectively an essential factor in politics. For example, the display of one's obedience to Islam in a clear way has become a requirement that no one running for presidency could ignore.[48] To illustrate, in 1992 a grouping of four organizations (AIN, ANASI, ARCI, and ANAUSI) demanded the 'islamity' of the three most important personalities of the State — the President of the Republic, the National Assembly President, and the Prime Minister (Garçon: 1998).

During the *Fourth Republic* (1996–1999), the head of State, Ibrahim Maïnassara Baré,[49] facing persistent rumors and allegations, had to give the proof of his *muslimity*; he started attending prayers at the main mosque in Niamey, went to the *Oumra* in Saudi Arabia, assisted and paid frequent visits to Islamic leaders; in addition, he paid particular attention to Islamic authorities[50] some of who became his advisers.

So far, this ambiguity on the side of Nigerien authorities has become one of the features that best tell the power and the importance gained by Islamic organizations, as political groups and with potential opposition.

POINTS OF CONTROVERSY

THE FIMA

Beyond the controversies that fuel the political debate, there is actually a criticism of the orientation of the national policy. The regimes that have run the country for a decade, are considered by the Islamist militants, as mere agents in the implementation of Western values. In this role, authorities are said to contribute to the introduction of Western values, which are not only against the interests of the Nigerien society, but especially and essentially, against Islam. What authorities and civil society's organizations called modernization,[51] the Islamic associations interpreted as perversion and an anti-Islam operation. Such a view on governance explains the 'counter-crusade' and the legitimization of the violence to which Islamist militants resort against what they consider as cultural and moral aggression. This was the case in November 2000, when Islamists violently demonstrated in Maradi and Niamey against the *FIMA (Festival International de la Mode Africaine)*.

Although the first edition of this festival was held in 1998 in the North of the country, far from the Islamists contestation centers, it did not escape vehement criticisms from Islamists leaders. For the second edition, in November 2000, it was regarded as the repetition of a heinous crime rejected by Islamic morals. In sermons, especially on private radio stations, the Islamic leaders depicted the festival as an international fair of nudism and homosexuality in a Muslim country. The Islamists reactions that followed the sermons were to burn the 'signs of Satan' — bars, Clubs, kiosks of PMU (*Pari Mutuel Urbain*) and even a Protestant Church — and ransack houses of prostitutes.

At the same time, for the government and the promoter of the festival, the event represents an opportunity to promote tourism and to develop the country. The government's reaction was to arrest about eighty of the demonstrators and to ban seven of the main Islamic associations: Adin-Islam (*Association pour la Diffusion de l'Islam au Niger*), ARCI (*Association pour le Rayonnement de la Culture Islamique*), AEMUN (*Association des Etudiants Musulmans de l'Université de Niamey*), AJMN (*Association des Jeunes Musulmans du Niger*), ANECEM (*Association Nigérienne pour l'Enseignement Coranique et l'Education Musulmane*), ANVIEC (*Association Nigérienne de la Vie de l'Islam pour l'Enseignement Coranique*), and LIICIA (*Ligue Internationale des Intellectuels de la Culture Islamique et Arabe*). Many of the demonstrators are still in prison.

When the issue of the political status of Islam is put in the social sphere, one finds a debate on the identity of Nigerien society as a whole.

THE CEDAW[52]

For the majority of Islamic associations, the CEDAW represents an attempt to re-introduce the *Code de la Famille* that was almost unanimously rejected. Among eleven Muslim leaders that we interviewed, nine see no difference between the two initiatives and accuse government of disregarding them in favor of the donors and international institutions.

In a TV address to Islamic associations protesting the ratification of the CEDAW, the spokesman of *Conseil de Réconciliation Nationale* argued, "The State cannot be blocked or taken hostage by some individuals' desiderata."[53] These words illustrate the strained relations between Islamic associations and authorities, which were intensified by the debate over the CEDAW ratification. Associations accused the government of 'prostitution' and 'treason' in order to obtain funds from international institutions.

Obviously, the reactions from these associations have finally determined the 'reservations' that the government had to carry in the ratification of the convention. Once again, women's status seems to have been the crux source of protest to this ratification, as the 'reservations' essentially relate to articles concerning women directly.[54]

According to Islamic structures, the assertion of the need for gender equality is reserved for women and human rights associations, which are considered the agents of Western ideology. Islamic associations, especially those that gather well-read men, viewed the activism of human rights and women's organization as an importation of Western values.[55] The consequence is a questioning of the nature of the Nigerien society, which is fundamentally and deeply Muslim.[56] The principle constantly held is that women cannot have more than what the Qur'an allows to them. The argument goes on to assert that the Qur'an has solved the problem of her status, her place, and her rights in the society. Therefore, the defenders of the Islamic values conclude that in rejecting the Western approach of women promotion, they do nothing but defend women.[57]

As a teacher of Moufida Islamic High School in Maradi puts it, the Islam, which their actions preach and convey, is not against women's promotion at all; rather, it defends and gives recognition and respect to their rights. However, Islam could not accept the denial of the "Qur'anic code and its replacement by foreign principles and ideas." From this point of view, he explained, it is normal that people rise against decisions made by authorities. Here is an allusion to the Islamic distrust for the great importance attached by authorities to associations propagating women's promotion.[58]

Thus, what Islamic activism seeks is a moral re-foundation of the state, and by so doing, ridding Niger of the monopoly of the French and western-oriented elite. The debate is then taken to an arena that concerns immediately the 'fabric' of the political elite. Rapidly, the preoccupation turned into the search for ways to impact State policies and to substitute to the external determinations those that adhere to the religious identity of the Nigerien society.[59]

CONCLUSION

Analyzing the re-structuring trend, we observe that the associative mode is the strategy found by the Islamic militancy to get into the debate on the philosophical basis of the society, and even to impose its views on the State. Such a strategy seems to have been developed to thwart the tendency of "the exit of religion" (Kilani: 1998) from the political debate. Thus, it testifies to the extraordinary vitality of the religious structures, which finally, have a capacity to pressure the government. The case of Niger illustrates how a political re-foundation has spurred an extraordinary re-organization of the religious sphere.

Many people I interviewed, seemed to focus on an economic approach of the history of the Nigerien society and its political life. They relate the Islamic activism to a crisis whose origins reside in the increasingly frequent destitution of the citizen. Thus, the phenomenon is said to derive from the economic crisis that affects all the sectors of social life, including the religious.

But, it is important to fully understand the sociopolitical demonstrations of this Islamic revival. Upon closer examination, far from being a momentary and surface phenomenon, it seems that the Islamist militancy testifies existential distresses, either individual or collective, which characterizes social life. In addition, it reveals a sociopolitical dynamism highly unsuspected and generally not very well perceived by descriptions of the internal logic of African societies. Looking at the phenomenon from a global perspective, it stands for a symbolic system of language in the political modernity of the society.

It is interesting to note the taboo maintained around the religiosity of the State and the form of governance. Most of the time, for the current authorities, the question of the relationship between religion and State is ignored. If not, they take refuge behind a theoretician attitude that recalls the separation between State and religion, as the Nigerien Constitution puts it. In a certain way, the discourse and the attitudes carried and adopted in the process of structuring the Islamic sphere, re-introduce the question of legitimacy, not only to that of authorities — as *Shiite* militants in Maradi pointed it out — but to that of the Nigerien Constitution itself.

Islamic associations that emerge from the process of democratization play the role of 'deconstructing' the discourse of modernization, refuting its opportunity and its philosophy as exposed in Nigerien contemporary political situation through secularism. Their ambition is to implement a political change in favor of Islam.

A decade of democratic experiment in Niger makes it possible to note how animated the relations between Islamic associations and authorities remain. This is not surprising in a context where the dominant constitutional hue remains secularization. However, the question is, for how long. Apparently, the next stage of the Islamist discourse will be that of Shari'a. As we know, Northern Nigeria's success in implementing Islamic law opposes the federal constitutional mood. For Niger's Islamic associations, this represents enough evidence that very soon, in Niger too, Islamic law will rule, if democracy is founded on people's will and power, rather than on an immense masquerade.

Endnotes

1. Of course, this situation is not specific to Niger. Kilani writes in his presentation of a collective book: "les manières d'être musulman varient très significativement en fonction des situations historiques et culturelles auxquelles le message coranique s'est adapté et qu'il a façonnées à son tour," *Islam et changement social, sous la direction de Mondher KILANI*, ed. Payot (Lausanne, 1998).
2. The National Conference that took place in 1991 was considered the starting point of the democratization process of the country.
3. More than 1000 km.
4. Central part of southern Niger.
5. Lieutenant-colonel Mallam Oubandawaki, Préfect of Maradi, in Sahel Dimanche October 18, 1996/no. 696.
6. March–December 2000 and February–March 2001.
7. May 2000 and February 2001.
8. The strategy of the Islamic expansion seems to be founded on big traders because of their influence on the society.
9. AIN *(Association Islamique du Niger)* was the very first Islamic organization created under Kountché's regime in 1974, just a few months after his arrival.
10. "Given Nigerian religious pluralism, this freedom has given rise — especially in recent years — to conflict as yet inexperienced in Nigerien Hausaland." Ibid. p. 252.
11. "Whatever the root cause or causes, Nigerian Hausa society is experiencing heightened politicization of religious identity to an extent unknown in Niger. Colonial boundaries, which made Niger as religiously homogeneous as Nigeria pluralistic, bear indirect responsibility." Ibid. p. 255.
12. According to analysts, behind this expansion and agitation of associations, there is certainly the aiming of a right to speak, but also a way of seeking gifts and assistance from Arab countries.
13. AIN *(Association Islamique du Niger)*.
14. This is the reason ANASI *(Association Nigérienne pour l'Appel et la Solidarité Islamique)* thinks of a 'contextualization' which will use also French language in spreading the divine message over an intellectual class that doesn't speak

Arabic. Taking the same principle, they justify their relations with authorities saying, "we should not leave the Chief alone, in the hands of bad advisers" (H. F.).
15. One can see with the monopoly of AIN, how Seyni Kountché's regime had a very effective control on the religious field.
16. In Maradi, after violent demonstrations against the FIMA (*Festival International de la Mode Africaine*), inhabitants did not hesitate to qualify a radio in the town, "radio mille collines," name of these media which encouraged with hatred and ethnic elimination in Rwanda.
17. In Hausa, members of the sect *Izala*.
18. Wearing the veil is no more an extraordinary thing, especially in urban areas such as Maradi, Zinder, Niamey, or Tahoua.
19. To achieve the goal of purity in Islamic practices, implementing an approach that focuses on mastering Arabic — the language of the divine message, has become a priority.
20. This term refers to the motto of the sect: izalat'ul bida'a waqqamat'ul Sunna (literally: rejecting any innovation and maintenance of the tradition (of the Prophet)).
21. The opposition is primarily expressed through radio programs and public sermons.
22. However, leaders that we interviewed during our field research mentioned also that marabouts created associations not because they had a message different from that of the others to communicate, but because they simply wanted to have their own association.
23. Brotherhoods.
24. It is rare to find a town in Niger where *Izala* do not have their own mosque. In few large towns, they have up to several, like in Niamey, Maradi, and Zinder.
25. This student required anonymity.
26. Therefore, they are opposed to the traditional system of local chiefs, which is not founded on the Islamic law.
27. As is noticed in most of the schools created about ten years ago.
28. But, one should not fail to mention that this abandonment of ostentation in ceremonies coincided with a very difficult economic context in Niger.
29. Lazaret, Boukoki, or Talladjé.
30. Such as AJMN (*Association des Jeunes Musulmans du Niger*), ANAUSI (*Association Nigérienne pour l'Appel, l'Unité et la Solidarité Islamique*), Adin-Islam (*Association pour la Diffusion de l'Islam au Niger*), Jamiyat Nasirat Din (*Association féminine Islamique*).
31. We reconsider these aspects further.
32. As is known in West Africa, Islamic groups have developed a close relationship with Authorities, especially through various brotherhoods (*Tidjaniya, Khadriya, Mouride, Layenne*).
33. In fact, the term *laïc* was replaced by *non-confessionnel*.
34. The Fourth Constitution (*Quatrième République*), for example, put the separation of religion and State as one of its two fundamental principles.

Moreover, it specifies that the Republic *"respects and protects all beliefs"* and *"no religion, no belief can neither assume the right of the political power nor interfere in the government affairs,"* articles 4 and 8, and both the Third (1992) and the Fifth (1999) Constitutions adopted the same principle.

35. The Constitution of *Troisième République* was deeply inspired by the French Constitutional model, especially with its semi-presidential system.
36. In an interview with the newspaper *As Salam*, one of the leaders of ANASI, Sheikh Yousouf Hassane Diallo, reveals the necessary relation between Islam and the development: "There is no true development without reference to God and his commands." In Niger, the context of social and political instability helps Islamic organizations claim that Islamic morals represent the solution to the corruption of authorities and politics.
37. Westernization, that the Islamic structures criticize in the national policy, is often compared to the negation of any morals.
38. Interview with Bello Tiousso, Garba leader of UDP-Amintchi (*Union pour la Démocratie et le Progrès*) in Jeune Afrique (no. 1749, 14–20 July, 1994): "I think that associations which do not recognize secularity should not be legalized. Democracy also has its disadvantages, because it supports demagogy."
39. This is how most of the media speak about Maradi.
40. Mamadou Tandja, President, elected in November 1999.
41. Mamadou Tandja is the first president to take oath on the Qur'an Niger. This is an innovation introduced in the current Constitution that says any elected president will take oath according to his religion. No reference like this could be found before.
42. As an illustration, let's note that public television and public radio, main marks of the character of the State, start and finish their programs reciting Qur'an.
43. Newspaper, *Le Républicain*, no. 27 January 2, 1992.
44. For example, the issues of Family Code, Family Planning, Women's Promotion.
45. For example, H. F. from ANASI.
46. CEDAW, *Convention pour l'Elimination de toutes les formes de Discrimination à l'Egard des Femmes* (Convention on the Elimination of all forms of Discrimination against Women) ratified in August 1999, by the Government lead by Commandant Daouda Mallam Wanké.
47. In 1992, in reaction to the claim of feminist associations for adoption of the Family Code, violent demonstrators ransacked and burned the local offices of AFN (*Association des Femmes du Niger*) in Zinder and Maradi. I will present the issues of the Family Code and the CEDAW in coming paragraphs.
48. M. G., a militant of Adin-Islam, an association banned in November 2000 after violent demonstrations against the International Festival of African Fashion (FIMA), talking about authorities said, "they arrested and imprisoned our marabouts; we await them the elections and at that time, we will ask them the question: what have you done for Islam?"

49. He overthrew in 1996, Mahamane Ousmane — President, democratically elected in 1993 with the elections that followed the National Conference and the first democratic Transition.
50. Several of them received 'four-wheel drive' cars and many were sent in Hajj to Mecca.
51. It's a matter of law, in particular in its social aspects (promotion of gender, setting a code that will regulate household).
52. Convention on the Elimination of Discrimination of all forms against Women (*CEDEF in French: Convention pour l'Elimination de toutes les formes de Discrimination à l'Egard des Femme*) ratified in August 1999, by the Government lead by Commandant Daouda Mallam Wanké.
53. It should be said that few associations openly called with prayers and fast for the curse of the persons responsible for the ratification, especially the head of the State — Commandant Daouda Mallam Wanké.
54. One of the objections says, "the Government of the Republic of Niger issues reserves on subparagraphs D and F of article 2 related to appropriate decisions to repeal any habit and practice which constitutes a discrimination against woman; in particular as regards succession," *Le Sahel*, 24 (Août, 1999).
55. The Chair of *Cercle des Travailleurs Musulmans* (CTMM) rejects all the programs related to the so-called promotion of women describing them as dangerous for an Islamic Nigerien society. He adds that, *by using this concept, people encourage with women, exhibitionism which is rejected by Islamic morals.*
56. Obviously, the Islamic structures do not have completely the same views on the subject. Whereas AIN and ANASI, in spite of their criticisms, find some interests in what was called 'occidentalization' (westernization), Adin-Islam and AJMN reject all the process for nonconformity and innovation in the Islamic law.
57. In particular *the Project of Family Code*. This is the view of associations such as ANASI, Adin-Islam, and AJMN.
58. Let's note that women's associations were the main contributors elaborating the *Projet de Code de la Famille*. They also had a great influence on the ratification of the CEDAW.
59. But the problem here resides in the notion of 'identity of Nigerien society.' When Islamic organizations resort to the 'identity of the Nigerien society' a question often posed is: if the current system derived from colonization, does it mean that Nigerien identity was, or even is, strictly and only Islamic? This point suggests looking also at the diverse sources of values that shaped Nigerien state and society.

References

Bayart, J-F, Ed. 1993. *Religion et modernité politique en Afrique Noire*. Paris: Kharthala

Bayart, J-F, A. Mbembe, and C. Toulabor. 1992. *Le Politique par le bas en Afrique Noire*. Paris: Kharthala.

Bratton, M. and Nicholas van de Walle. 1997. *Democratic Experiments in Africa.* Cambridge: Cambridge University Press.

Capitant, R. 1972. *Démocratie et participation politique.* Paris: Bordas.

Coulon, C. 1983. *Les musulmans et le pouvoir en Afrique noire.* Paris: Kharthala.

———. 1993. "Les itinéraires de l'Islam au Nord Nigeria" in *BAYARD Religion et Modernité Politique en Afrique Noire.* Paris: Kharthala.

Decoudras, P. M. 1994. "Niger: Démocratisation réussie, avenir en suspens," in *L'Afrique politique: vue sur la démocratie à marée basse.* Paris : Kharthala/ CEAN.

Garçon, L. 1998. *Etude de l'évolution des pratiques de l'Islam au Niger.* Niamey: bureau de l'ambassade du Canada au Niger.

Glew, R. S. 1996. "Islamic Associations in Niger;" in *Islam et Sociétés au Sud du Sahara, Cahiers annuels pluridisciplinaires,* no. 10. Paris.

Grégoire, E. 1993. "Islam and the Identity of Merchants in Maradi (Niger)," in L. Brenner (ed.), *Muslim Identity and Social Change in sub-Saharan Africa.* Bloomington and Indianapolis: Indiana University Press.

Hachimou, I. 1992. *La pratique de l'Islam à la Cité Universitaire de Niamey,* Niamey: FLSH.

Jansen, G. H. 1979. *Militant Islam.* New York: Harper and Row Publishers.

Kilani, M. 1988. "Islam et économie de la dépense: une approche anthropologique" in *Revue Européenne des Sciences Sociales,* xxvi, no. 82.

———. 1998. *Islam et changement social.* Lausanne: Payot.

Magassouba, M. 1985. *L'Islam au Sénégal: demain les mollahs?* Paris: Kharthala.

Robinson, P. T. 1994. "Democratization: Understanding the Relationship between Regime Change and the Culture of Politics," in *African Studies Review* Vol. 37, no. 1.

Sounaye, A. 2000. "Emergence de l'Islamisme au Niger?" in *Orange Light,* Dakar. March 2000 issue.

Triaud, J-L. 1982. "l'Islam en République du Niger," in *Le Mois en Afrique.* Nos. 192–193.

Usman, Y. B. 1987. *The manipulation of Religion in Nigeria (1977–1987).* Kaduna: Vanguard Printers.

Villalón, Leonardo. "The Moral and the Political in African Democratization: The *Code de la Famille* in Niger's Troubled Transition," *Democratization,* vol. 3, no. 2 (summer 1996) pp. 41–68.

- *L'Afrique politique: Démocratisation: arrêts sur images.* Paris: Kharthala/CEAN 1996.

- *Politique Africaine.* Paris: Kharthala: no. 32, no. 45, no. 47.

Ministère du Dévelopement Social, République du Niger. 1992. *Projet de Code de la Famille.* Niamey.

9

Globalization and the Assertive Ummah: The Case of Islam in Kenya

GIMODE A. EDWIN

This chapter outlines trends in the fortunes and developments of the Kenyan Muslim community as a significant social category at the end of the twentieth and at the dawn of the twenty-first century. It specifically focuses on the trends in leadership in response to the fast-changing global and local circumstances and the strategies employed by the *Ummah* to re-negotiate its identity afresh in the light of a new political dispensation characterized by emphasis on a citizen-centered government.

THE UMMAH: BEFORE 1990

Today, the highest concentration of Muslims in Kenya is in Coast Province among the Waswahili, Arabs, Mijikenda and Somali, Boran, and related groups in the Northeastern districts of the country. Muslims are also found in significant numbers in cosmopolitan Nairobi and other urban areas. In addition, there are believers among virtually all ethnic groups but not in large numbers. Accurate statistics are hard to establish, as the issue has been rather emotive. It is reasonable, however, to estimate the Muslim population, in Kenya, as varying between a fifth and a quarter of the national population.

Islam is no newcomer to Eastern Africa. Along the Coast, Islamic culture has thrived for over a millennium. Thus, although most of the East Africans today profess Christianity, the latter is a latecomer, whose activities essentially cover the twentieth century. Christianity, coming simultaneously with the British colonial rule, was perceived by Muslims as the colonizer's religion. Consequently, for Muslims, the twentieth was a period characterized by a clash between two cultural systems in which they came to perceive themselves as an entity subjected to deliberate discrimination and marginalization by both the colonial and the postcolonial state in Kenya.

Up to 1990, these sentiments were strong but suppressed. A major explanation for this is often attributed to a lack of leadership that would defend and articulate the position of the *Ummah*. For the first seventy years of the century, the *Ummah* was heavily disadvantaged because of historical factors and religious conviction. The leadership was made up of the *sheikhs* and *imams,* whose worldview was strictly unitary. For them, it was against the spirit of Islam to separate life into spiritual and temporal departments. The mosque, for this 'old generation leadership,' was the center of social life. Those who took to secular education did so because of parents who realized the need to change with the times or by virtue of their own self-drive, but not at the encouragement of the religious leadership.

However, 1973 was a turning point in the history of the leadership of the *Ummah*. In this year, the Supreme Council of Kenya Muslims (SUPKEM) was formed. This was largely in response to the formation of the Uganda Muslim Supreme Council in neighboring Uganda. By law, it became the supreme organ to collate and articulate issues concerning the Muslims in the public domain. Other Muslim fora were to be affiliated with and to speak through SUPKEM (Mwakimako, 1995: 225).

To most young and educated Muslims, however, the performance of SUPKEM in the 1970s and 1980s remained suspect. Many believed it was being infiltrated and controlled by the government. An alternative channel of expression expected to speak for and on behalf of the *Ummah,* was through the elected political leadership. They were to reinforce the efforts of SUPKEM. In most cases, however, these politicians were perceived by most Muslims as being on the government payroll and, hence, not ready to effectively represent the community. On most controversial issues the leadership would come out divided, leaving the community weak.

A good example was the 1989 controversy concerning the identity and citizenship of the Kenyan-Somali ethnic group. According to the government, the incessant *militia* fighting in Somalia had led to an influx of many refugees into Kenya. Some of these refugees came with dangerous weapons and added to the crime and insecurity in the country. Consequently, there was need to thoroughly vet the Somalis in order to authenticate true Kenyan citizens from foreigners. The Somali found these procedures humiliating, as they were not directed toward any other ethnic group in Kenya (*Weekly Review*, November 17, 1989). They were expected to produce birth certificates, of both parents and grandparents, before getting national identity cards.

SUPKEM came strongly against this. It argued that this was aggression against Islam. Yet it was Maalim Mohammed, the only Muslim cabinet minister at the time, who led the Muslim politicians in supporting and defending the government action. In fact, the politicians took to task the Chairman of SUPKEM, Sheikh Ali Abdullah El-Maawy, and the Secretary General, Ahmed Khalif, for opposing the government. They masterminded the suspension of the two from their positions and replaced them with their deputies.

It was in such a state of division and weakness that the *Ummah* witnessed the dawn of the 1990s. However, things were to change shortly, as new forms of leadership came to the fore.

THE 1990s AND THE DAWN OF NEW LEADERSHIP

The dawn of the 1990s proved to be a defining moment in the history of the *Ummah,* in general, and its leadership in particular. The Muslims became increasingly conscious of their significance in the Kenyan society. It dawned on them that they were the single largest social category in Kenya, and so the biggest single stakeholder in the country's present and future (*Daily Nation,* November 24, 1994). Yet, politically, they were a significant minority.

This consciousness was part and parcel of a global Islamic renaissance, starting in the 1970s and maturing in the 1990s. There were several factors behind this. First was the Iranian Islamic Revolution (1978–80), which saw the downfall of the Shah. It brought to the fore the question of politics in religion and concentrated on issues like social justice and equity (Haynes, 1993: 1). This revolution gave Muslims worldwide, a revival of the passion for their religion and culture and a desire to re-negotiate and establish an assertive identity wherever they were. Kenya was no exception.

Then, in 1989, the *Iron Curtain* came down sending communism into recession. Muslims interpreted this as divine victory over atheism. However, it also made them brace themselves up against Westernism that was assuming unfettered global claims in economics and in culture. Westernization thus elicited a dialectic that unlocked a breathtaking and diverse resurgence of a powerful Islamic ideology, stretching from Africa's West Coast to the Pacific Rim (Shadid, 1996).

In December 1991, the Islamic Salvation Front (FIS) won the first multiparty election in Algeria. It humiliated secular parties, by becoming the first Islamic party in the Arab world to be democratically elected (*Weekly Review,* January 10, 1992). There was an anticlimax, when the victory was canceled. The terror that followed is history. What is important, however, is that the Muslim world felt victorious and revived. It was not surprising that the Islamic Party of Kenya (IPK) was formed fast on the heels of the FIS victory.

Apart from these international developments, there had been a silent transformation among the youths in the Kenyan *Ummah*. While the origin of this silent transformation is traceable to the time of independence, it gained momentum in the 1970s and matured in the 1980s. There emerged a young educated *ulema* trained in the Islamic citadels of learning in the Arab world and who proved, with time, to be far better educated than their classical predecessors. They had a heightened consciousness of belonging to a global and powerful religion (Bakari, 1995: 248). Combining secular and religious education, they commanded a better global perspective of social and intellectual issues. Contemporary global issues did not bewilder them.

In addition to the new *ulema*, the new generation of Muslims has recognized that they have a dual heritage. They have been educated in both the Islamic academy and the Western secular academy. They are familiar with the sociopolitical and economic trends of the contemporary world. They are also capable of addressing the needs of the *Ummah* in the idiom of the 'adversary,' ensuring better survival without betraying their faith.

This 'young' Muslim leadership has not sought refuge to any exclusive entity. It is realistic in outlook, not nostalgic about the past, and its agenda is different from that of the elders of yesteryears. The Somali element of the leadership does not think in terms of greater Somalia, because the latter collapsed as a state in the early 1990s and virtually ceased to be an exemplar of Islamic aspirations. Neither does it think strictly in terms of *Mwambao*, or coastal regionalism, a notion so popular around the time of independence. This, it recognized, is not realistic because the *Ummah* now covers the whole country. In any case, there is no sultan of Zanzibar to look to (Wandati, O. I. 1999).

Instead, the young Muslim leadership has led the *Ummah* to realize that a Kenyan Muslim is a Kenyan citizen just as much as the non-Muslims are. It seeks to influence events for the common good of all Kenyans, both Muslim and non-Muslim. This new generation of leadership has been preoccupied with two agenda, simultaneously. First, it has spoken vigorously against the discrimination and marginalization of the community. Second, it has carried out a severe self-censure of the community and told the *Ummah,* in no unspecific terms, to change and move with the times, negotiating an assertive identity in the affairs of the state as an antidote to marginalization. This, it argues, is the only antidote to Muslim consignment to the margins in the Kenyan public affairs.

This leadership is diverse. It includes the 'young' or modern *ulema* represented in people like Sheikh Ali Shee, who has served as Chairman of the Council of Imams and Preachers of Kenya; and Sheikh Hammad Kassim, who is the Chief Kadhi of Kenya. The latter holds a bachelor's degree in physics and masters in Islamic theology. It also includes full-fledged scholars, in their own right. In this category are, among others, Professor Ali Mazrui, internationally renowned political scientist, Kenya; Mohammed Hyder, retired professor of zoology, University of Nairobi; and Mohammed Bakari, former professor of linguistics at the University of Nairobi who now teaches at Fatih University, Istanbul, Turkey. There is also a myriad of party and pressure group activists who have ensured that the *Ummah* fully participates in the deconstruction of the erstwhile monolithic political structures. The sequel illustrates specific sites of struggle, where the new leadership is compelled to articulate the position of the *Ummah* and to shape the direction of Kenyan politics.

THE ROLE OF THE UMMAH IN THE 'SECOND LIBERATION'

A most sensational instrument used in articulating aspirations of the *Ummah* in the 1990s was the Islamic Party of Kenya (IPK). The origins of the IPK were extremely humble. In January 1992, a number of students at Kenyatta University met to discuss the destiny of the Muslim community in a fast-changing society. They had witnessed the formation of many pressure groups, which were formed on the basis of different interests, e.g., welfare, ethnicity, etc. (Chikombe, O. I. 1997).

The youths presented the idea of a Muslim forum to the elders of Nairobi South 'C' Mosque. The latter remained reticent and re-affirmed their loyalty to the government of the ruling party, Kenya African National Union (KANU). However, word of the newly formed caucus spread fast to the coastal town of Mombasa and attracted many. Shortly after, the group picked interim officials, transformed itself into a political party and embraced as its agenda the welfare of the Kenyan Muslim community. The officials of the newly formed political party included Omar Mwinyi, a school head teacher in Mombasa (Chairman); Abdulrahman Wandati (Secretary-General); and Sheikh Ali Shee, the then Imam of the imposing Jamia Mosque in Nairobi (Member).

At the outset, the party looked like nothing more than a fringe political grouping of "... little consequence to the country's political set up" (*Weekly Review*, January 24, 1992). Within six months, however, it had transformed itself into a formidable political force. Its registration became the major bone of contention between the Muslim community and the state for almost four years. The victory of the Islamic Salvation Front (FIS) in Algeria clearly gave them a much-needed inspiration. However, what seriously gave the IPK the initial drive was the tactless manner in which an overbearing government handled a freelance Muslim preacher, Sheikh Khalid Balala. In his thirties, Balala was a graduate of Comparative Religion from Madina University, Saudi Arabia. On May 19, 1992, the police arrested Balala, together with seven other preachers at *Mwembe Tayari* — an open market in Mombasa town — for allegedly uttering statements against the head of state. Balala was handcuffed and led away together with his friends. This act of unwitting humiliation immediately spawned a hero for the *Ummah* and a monster for the government. The crowd in attendance closed on the law enforcers and began chanting antigovernment slogans to the chorus of *"Allah Akbar" (Weekly Review*, May 22, 1992).

This degenerated into a full-scale riot. Vehicles were overturned and/or set ablaze, while buildings were stoned. Running battles with the law enforcers went into the night, as barricades were constructed on the roads, with protestors demanding that IPK be registered. The 'no nonsense' General Service Unit (GSU) indiscriminately set on members of the public. They pursued some of the demonstrators into the nearby *Kwa Shibu* mosque, from where they were arrested. The following day witnessed more violence in the otherwise normally peaceful Mombasa streets. Later in the week, when Balala was released on bond, there was further rioting. He (Balala) was smoothly transformed into a popular activist, demanding the registration of IPK. The most important thing about the May riots was that they gave the Muslim agenda a definitive form in the changing Kenyan politics and brought IPK into prominence.

The subsequent role that Balala played in IPK and the leadership of the *Ummah*, during the rest of the 1990s, is however a rather lackluster story. He constantly began to preach about the need for change though violence. He hijacked the leadership of the party to the chagrin of the officials and began issuing statements on its behalf without consultation. His growing ambition for leadership was punctuated by loose talking that depicted IPK and the *Ummah* in negative light. For instance, in July 1992, Balala announced that he was about to declare total war on the government, having allegedly made arrangements for financial and political support from Islamic states to get the IPK registered (*Weekly Review,* July 10, 1992).

This made teachers of some six *Quranic* schools to accuse Balala of aspiring to be an Islamic leader and a spokesman for all Kenyan Muslims. In fact, they alleged that he was serving his 'foreign masters.' They blamed him for the fracas that had rocked Mombasa, which had resulted in three deaths.

They posed the question, "who gave him the mandate to speak for us?" (*Weekly Review*, July 10, 1992).

In September 1993, Balala greatly offended the Muslim community by planting rowdy youths in the *Maulidi* procession in Lamu. They disrupted it, turning it into a violent demonstration against the government. He congratulated the youth for fighting against 'injustice.' On another occasion, he boasted at a public rally that he was one of the most feared activists in the country and that whenever he spoke, President Moi panicked (*Weekly Reviews*, June 16, 1992). On the same occasion, he called on all the Kenyan opposition parties to fight the government. He went on to announce the formation of what he called the Defense Council of Kenya (DCK), a supposedly military wing of the IPK.

He antagonized both the government and the *Ummah* by announcing that he was receiving funding from Sudan, to set up sister Islamic parties in Tanzania and the whole of East-Central Africa; claims that President El Bashir of Sudan dismissed. This and other pronouncements made Balala lose touch with the real agenda of the *Ummah* and failed to fit in the reconfiguration of Kenyan politics.

Balala's predilections aside, the sudden emergence of IPK was received with approval from all shades of the Muslim community. However, it assumed greater significance when highly respected Muslim intellectuals entered the fray to articulate its agenda and to urge its registration. They argued that it was the most viable vehicle to express the agenda of *Ummah*.

In July 1991, Professor Ali A. Mazrui had kicked off the debate on the 'second liberation' in Kenya. At a press conference in Nairobi, he made the first carefully articulated statement on the need for Kenyans to adopt political pluralism. For him, Kenya had been in the vanguard of the first (nationalist) liberation in Africa. It was not fitting, he argued, that she should be the last in the second struggle for political pluralism. "Kenya," argued Mazrui, "should not become the 'dragship' which pulls the democratic fleet behind." (*Weekly Review*, August 2, 1991).

Mazrui combined the struggle to de-center the powers of single party politics with a desire to see the *Ummah* take its rightful place in the emerging re-configuration of Kenyan politics. In some statements, he seemed to go to extremes in the quest for this. Following the May riots of 1992, Mazrui stated that Kenya was tottering on the brink of an Islamic uprising, a black *intifadah,* unless the government urgently addressed the unique problems of the *Ummah* (*Society,* June 29, 1992). He argued that the community had been treated as a social, political, and economic liability by the Kenyan state. This could only be reversed, he insisted, by the Kenyan state allowing the registration of IPK, of which he saw no problem because religious based parties were not inimical to the democratic process as long as they adhered to the democratic principles. (*Weekly Review*, June 12, 1992).

Then, with time, Mazrui seemed to go farther than just asking for equality. His utterances pointed to the creation of a near-exclusive Muslim entity similar to the Islamic entities governed by the Shari'a in Nigeria. He, for instance, came to urge that Muslims would not be comfortable so long as they were under a secular constitution. They needed to exercise their own law over themselves (*Sunday Nation*, February 14, 1993). He stated that because of deliberate government policies of marginalization, Muslims did not have any avenue for upward mobility. The unemployment rate at the Coast was twice the national average. Muslims at the Coast had suffered repression and discrimination to the point of being regarded as "... marginal and peripheral third class citizens" (*Society*, June 29, 1992).

Mazrui pointed out the linkage between equitable distribution of the national economic resources and democracy. In his words, he argued, "some people are losing control of their best land and their richest resources to citizens of other regions. If no answer is found to these tendencies of internal colonization, no democracy should expect to be stable." (*Kenya Times*, September 3, 1992). He was to moderate this view while contributing to the Constitutional Review Commission later in 2001, emphasizing more on equity and justice for all Kenyans.

Another scholar to speak prominently on the IPK was Professor Mohamed Bakari. He pointed out that many democracies all over the world had religious-based parties. For him, what mattered was the manifesto of the party. In fact, he found the IPK agenda sound because it was oriented towards the elimination of injustice, alleviation of poverty, and protection of human rights (*Weekly Review*, June 5, 1992). The emergence of the IPK and the May riots were, for him, a turning point in the history of the *Ummah*. They brought to the fore the injustices Muslims had suffered for many years and gave them a new perception of themselves. He urged Muslims to stand for their rights and to completely break the stereotype of docility and unquestioning submission.

Professor Mohammed Hyder considered the emergence of the IPK as critical in the history of the *Ummah*. For him, the clamor for registration was not the issue. Rather, IPK symbolized the underlying aspirations of the Kenyan Muslim. It was a turning point, giving Muslims a new identity. For long, they had been "... trampled upon and counted on to absorb the impact of it all without batting an eyelid." (*Weekly Review*, October 2, 1992). He decried the fact that years after independence there had been no Muslim in senior government positions. In his words:

It goes against all the laws of statistics and certainly has no mathematical basis. It certainly follows the laws of political mathematics rather than those of Euclidean mathematics (Ibid).

Consequently, he argued that IPK was a viable avenue for political expression and should not be driven underground. Instead, the state should grasp the IPK nettle.

In the final analysis, the government stuck to its guns and refused to register IPK. The officials entered a working arrangement with the FORD-Kenya party so that the party candidates would run on the latter's ticket for the December 1992 general elections. Two of them made it in Mombasa — Professor Rashid Mzee, in Kisauni constituency and Salim Mwavumo, in Likoni. KANU's Shariff Nassir, separated by seven votes, narrowly beat Omar Mwinyi, the IPK Chairman, in the Mvita constituency.

One thing remained clear, however. Because of the activities of the IPK, the government became sensitized to the importance of the *Ummah*. Never again would the *Ummah* be taken for granted in Kenyan politics. The many concessions that the community came to win in the 1990s were perceived to be a result of the militant IPK campaign of the early 1990s.

THE SUPKEM AND MUSLIM POLITICIANS LEARNING TO BITE

IPK may not have been registered for the 1992 elections and after. However, it had transformed the Muslim self-perception. Even those Muslims in government came to learn to censure the government and to speak for the *Ummah*. This was especially the case in 1993.

Worthy of special mention here is Maalim Mohammed, the first Muslim ever in the Kenyan Cabinet (appointed 1983). He had earlier served the government with unflinching loyalty. In 1989, during the controversial screening of Somali citizens, he had led the Muslim members of parliament in supporting the government move. Mohammed seems to have decided that 1993 was his year of making up for his past lackadaisical performance. Immediately after the election and the formation of government by his party, KANU, he began a series of stinging comments that left the government ridiculed and embarrassed. His theme was the marginalization of the Muslim community.

He pointed out that the Muslims had overwhelmingly voted for KANU and President Moi, whereby four fifths of the seats in Muslim strongholds went to the party. Yet, the reward they received was "a slap in the face." Their support was not reflected in the post-election appointments in the civil service and government. This, to him, had to change. "What we are asking for is not big jobs, but simple basic rights and equal opportunities" (*Weekly Review*, February 26, 1993).

Mohammed chose this time to revisit Moi's *Madaraka* (Independence) day speech of June 1992. In this speech, Moi had alluded to the emergence of the IPK radicalism in negative terms. He had made statements to the effect that Muslims had been slave traders and that IPK activities were reviving these bitter memories (*Kenya Times,* June 2, 1992). Mohammed pointed out that this was a terrible slur to the *Ummah.*

IPK rose, he explained, due to frustrations the community had been subjected to. He warned that despite denial of registration, the party was growing in popularity especially if the government did not reward them sufficiently after the election, as it seemed the case then. If this was not forthcoming, he warned, the community was ready to dump KANU and shop around for another political party.

Because of playing the gadfly against the government, Mohammed was moved from the prestigious docket of Minister in the Office of the President to that of Culture and Social Services. This did not deter him. In July 1993, he made the strongest criticism of the government yet from official circles. He reiterated his threat that the *Ummah* would think of ways of salvaging its position. He said:

> We are an important community in this country and we should be taken as such. The community might be forced to chart out a course of action to remedy the situation (*Weekly Review*, July 9, 1993).

The SUPKEM officials responded by supporting Mohammed's sentiments. Ahmed Khalif, the Secretary-General, provided backup, saying that the KANU government was no longer a threat. For him, "... they need us more than we need them" *(Weekly Review*, February 26, 1993). The Chairman of the council, Ghafur el-Busaidy, simply dismissed government appointments as contemptuous to the *Ummah.* What is worth noting here is that the Moi regime had kept giving concessions to the *Ummah* as a mechanism of trying to appease them.

The years between 1994 and 1997 were quieter in the *Ummah*-State relationship. Yet they ultimately proved to have been just a lull before the storm. The tail end of 1997 exploded into an imbroglio that left the relations seriously strained ahead of the December 1997 general elections. The bone of contention was the arrest of ten foreigners whom SUPKEM described as Islamic scholars and nongovernmental organization workers. The government threatened to deport them. They were employees of *Al-Haramain*, a Riyadh based Muslim NGO with operations in Garissa, Isiolo, and Dadaab areas in Northeastern province which are overwhelmingly Muslim.

What is significant here is that SUPKEM put up a strong fight against the government. It brought to the fore the motive of discrimination and marginalization. The action was described as "... an aggression against Islam," a terrorizing of the entire Muslim community by the state. On behalf of SUPKEM, Yusuf Murabwa issued a hard-hitting statement. He said:

> We will not tolerate the constant practice by the government of arresting our scholars on flimsy grounds. This is outright provocation (*Sunday Nation,* November 9, 1997).

He warned that Muslims might decide to vote *en bloc* in the election against those "... harassing and intimidating our scholars and elect those who will respect our rights" (Ibid). On its part, the government maintained that the suspects were foreigners, unlawfully working and living in Kenya and so must be deported. They were Algerian, Sudanese, Pakistani, and Ethiopian *(Daily Nation,* November 14, 1997). The point, however, is that whether the suspects were criminals or not, the government was forced to slow down on repatriating them, fearing of badly losing the December elections in the *Ummah*-dominated areas.

NAIROBI BOMB BLAST AND FRESH CHALLENGE TO UMMAH-STATE RELATIONS

The imbroglio surrounding the *Al-Harramin* Islamic NGO at the end of 1997 was nothing compared to the controversy between the state and the *Ummah* in the second half of 1998. On Friday, August 7, a massive mid-morning bomb blast rocked the city of Nairobi. It was exploded at the basement of the American embassy building in the city-center. This was simultaneous with another blast in the American embassy building in Dar-es-Salaam, Tanzania.

In the case of the Nairobi blast, buildings within a radius of seven hundred and fifty meters were badly shattered, with glass doors and windows broken. While the strong embassy building was badly damaged, it withstood the blast (*Sunday Nation,* August 9, 1998). Over two hundred and fifty people died, while over five thousand were maimed in a scene described by the media as a "... scene from hell" (*Daily Nation,* August 12, 1998).

The prime suspect was Arabian tycoon and self-confessed terrorist, dedicated to fighting the United States of America, Osama bin Laden. He had been linked to the 1995–96 Saudi bombings in which 240 U.S. servicemen were killed. A number of suspects were arrested and later charged in the United States of America.

For the purposes of this chapter, what is significant is that, at the local level, the relationship between the state and the *Ummah* took a turn for the worst. At the same time, the incident assumed international proportions, the criminalization and demonization of Islam by America was re-enacted on the Kenyan scene. It proved to be probably the toughest challenge to the *Ummah*, in general, and to its leadership in particular.

In the first place, President Moi made a statement that greatly antagonized the *Ummah*. He said that if the perpetrators had been Christians, they would not have committed the heinous act. To the Muslims, this was equating Islam with terrorism (*Daily Nation*, August 13, 1998).

This was especially offensive because Muslims, at both national and international levels, had condemned the act. The Chairman of the Imams Council of Kenya, Sheikh Ali Shee, had condemned the action and invoked *Allah's* curse on the perpetrators. Mombasa Muslims had condemned it as "blind terror unleashed on defenseless victims." At the international level, the Muslim world equally condemned it and expressed solidarity with the Kenyans. These countries included Sudan, Egypt, and Kuwait. The latter two went an extra mile by sending specialized medical personnel, together with medicines.

What stunned the Muslim community most, however, was that just after a month the government announced that it was giving five international Islamic NGOs a week to wind up. These organizations were Help Africa People (mentioned by the suspects as playing a central role in the bomb project); Mercy Relief International; the Riyadh based Al-Haramain (already implicated in the 1997 controversy); International Islamic Relief Organization; and Abdul Aziz al Ibrahim Foundation (*Daily Nation*, September 9, 1998). All these NGOs worked in the poverty-stricken North Eastern province, while some had offices in Nairobi.

The National NGO's coordinator announced the closure of their operations in the following terms.

> Our investigations reveal that the activities of the organizations are inconsistent with the reasons for which they were registered. They are supposed to work toward improving the welfare of Kenyans but instead they are endangering their lives, which we cannot allow to persist (Ibid).

The stage had been set for a bitter confrontation. The *Ummah* was unanimous in denouncing the decision by the government. In the following weeks, different Muslim leaders, especially the officials of SUPKEM, made some of the harshest statements against the government. The latter had apparently matured into a forceful mouthpiece of the *Ummah* interests.

Ghafur el-Busaidy, Chairman of SUPKEM, said that the *Ummah* would no longer accept any more of the state persecution. They found the government action "... provocative, discriminatory, vindictive, anti-Muslim, anti-Islam, and a continuation of harassment, persecution, and intimidation that Muslims had been subjected to." (Daily *Nation*, September 10, 1998). He argued that Muslims were targets of the state apparatus and did not enjoy "... the rights and freedoms other Kenyans enjoy." For him, the incident was proof that the marginalization of Muslims was not coincidental but deliberately designed and implemented (Ibid).

SUPKEM instructed imams countrywide to start preparations for the *gunut* (special) prayers until the government came to its senses and until justice prevailed. They were also to organize demonstrations throughout the country. In addition to SUPKEM, some of the strongest Muslim supporters of the government, for once questioned its actions. Mohammed Yusuf Haji, one of Moi's closest allies and former Provincial Commissioner, asked the government to reconsider its stand. It was also then that Alhaji Abdullahi Kiptanui, a Muslim leader from Moi's ethnic Kalenjin group, lay aside his sycophancy and pointed out that the de-registration of the NGOs had caused untold suffering to hundreds of widows, orphans, destitute, and youths. He led a demonstration in Nakuru town, the provincial Headquarters of the expansive Rift Valley Province and Moi's backyard (*Daily Nation*, October 3, 1998).

On its part, the Imams Council called on all Muslim KANU members of parliament to resign and be re-elected on an opposition ticket. The Chairman of the Council, Ali Shee, argued that the ban of the aforementioned NGOs was an insult to the *Ummah*, so soon after it overwhelmingly voted for KANU and for Moi (*Daily Nation*, September 20, 1988).

A GLOBAL INTERPRETATION OF THE BOMB BLAST

What made the bomb blast crisis more complicated was that Muslims, allegedly targeting American interests, perpetrated it. This dimension brought to the fore, on Kenyan land, what Muslims worldwide had come to regard as the criminalization of Islam by the Western world. For the Kenyan *Ummah*, the Nairobi bomb blast was merely a *casus belli* to pursue this objective.

To Muslim scholars the collapse of historical socialism, in 1989, made the West to turn to Islam as the next greatest ideological enemy, depicting it as the greatest danger to world peace. According to Hyder, the West has "... a morbid and almost fatalistic fear of Islam as perhaps the greatest threat to Western civilization ..." (Hyder, 1995: 279). He protests the distortion of Islam by the West, which equates the faith with fundamentalism and fundamentalism with militancy and militancy with terrorism (Ibid). He explains that fundamentalism is not fanaticism, but a strict practice of one's faith. At the same time, Islam cannot be violent because by its very definition it is "... submission to the will of *Allah* and peace" (Ibid).

Writing in the same vein, Ould-Mey states that the end of the Cold War and the establishment of the Western-led New World Order (NWO) left Islam as the target *par excellence* for the West. After the retreat of the Soviet Union, there was every effort to make Islamic fundamentalism the 'new evil' of post-Cold War era (Ould-Mey, 1994: 328). Accordingly, the Islamic world is "perceived by many Americans as the new focus of evil in the aftermath of communism" (R. Falk, quoted in Ould-Mey P.327).

It is within this international context that the crisis of the bomb blast in the last quarter of 1998 has to be properly conceived. The Muslims believed that the move by the government to ban the NGOs was not independent. It was a directive from Washington. This greatly offended them, and the leaders were duty-bound to lead the way in resisting it. Shortly after the blast and the subsequent arrival of the FBI in Nairobi, the focus of investigation was on Muslim suspects. This made El-Busaidy, the chairman of SUPKEM, to caution the government against the possibility of being dictated to by the USA (*Daily Nation*, August 13, 1998). With the ban of the NGOs, however, and the arrests of Muslims, the acrimony between the state and *Ummah* reached a new high. Minister Maalim Mohammed, together with twelve members of parliament, asked the government not to cave-in to U.S. pressure or else they would reconsider their political stand (*Daily Nation*, September 15, 1998).

To SUPKEM, the American connection in what the *Ummah* was experiencing was obvious. The Secretary-General, Khalif, put it in these words: "... it is almost certain that since the bomb blast ... the U.S. has endeavored to drive a wedge between the Kenyan government and the Muslim community" (*Daily Nation*, September 26, 1998).

All shades of the Muslim leadership accused Moi's government of engaging in an ideological warfare of another country, placing Kenya at the center of a religious conflict that she was not a party to (*Daily Nation*, October 3, 1998). They accused the government of abandoning its responsibility by allowing the FBI to take charge of the security of a sovereign state. They were particularly incensed with the FBI habit of invading their mosques, homes, social, and work places in pursuit of suspects — without warrants of arrest. The *Ummah* perceived this as part and parcel of "... a wider scheme fronted by the USA to criminalize Islam and wage an unjust war against the faith" (*Daily Nation*, September 26, 1998).

At the beginning of October, however, the conflict experienced a sharp diminuendo. On the eve of October 2, when Muslims were set to carry out demonstrations countrywide, President Moi decided on a *détente* and summoned the *Ummah* leadership to State House, in Nairobi. These were mainly national SUPKEM officials and members of parliament. He invited them supposedly to "... examine Muslim grievances" (*Daily Nation*, October 3, 1998). Consequently, the leaders called off the demonstrations at the last minute. At the meeting, Moi promised to look into problems facing Muslims. He promised that those who were innocent in the NGOs controversy would not be penalized.

For the rest of the *Ummah*, however, this amounted to a depressing anticlimax. They had been set for a showdown with the state. There arose a serious division in the *Ummah*. It took the shape of the rank versus file. The ordinary Muslims regarded their leaders as having sold out to the government. A Nairobi branch SUPKEM official, Alhaji Baricha Ali, denounced his seniors as traitors. For him, they were more loyal to the KANU government than to the *Ummah*. The imams joined in condemning of the calling-off of the demonstrations. They especially blamed SUPKEM and questioned its suitability as the *Ummah's* main mouthpiece. They called for the appointment of a *Mufti* (religious scholar) who would be their legal spokesperson in future.

Maalim Farah, a bitter critic of Moi, accused the SUPKEM leadership of conspiring with State House. For him, these leaders, as usual, had never been serious. Rather, they had been yearning to be "... addressed by the president the way one looks forward to going on a pilgrimage to Mecca" (Ibid). Gradually, however, the acrimony died down. Moi, in his characteristic way, de-steamed the crusade. He ensured that 1999 dawned on a peaceful note with the Ummah.

THE UMMAH LEADERSHIP AND THE CONSTITUTIONAL REVIEW, 1997–2005

Beginning in 1997, one of the outstanding topical issues in Kenyan politics was the review of the Constitution. This is the one site where the Muslim leadership laid intriguingly sound strategies in order to maximize benefits for the *Ummah*. The question of reviewing the constitution had remained thorny since the re-introduction of political pluralism in 1992. After the general elections of that year, the opposition argued that President Moi and KANU won because, as it stood, the constitution favored them. Hence, there was need to radically amend it, not overhaul it, so that he could not manipulate it to stay in power.

Many pressure groups and civil society bodies mushroomed to press for this. The Muslims were not left behind in this either. What especially sensitized them to become seriously involved in staking their claims was an event that took place in 1997, ahead of the general elections. Parties were asked to nominate a specific number of people from whom the President was to appoint an Electoral Commission, which would oversee the election. Of the lists submitted from all the parties, there was not a single Muslim.

This prompted Professor Rashid Mzee, Member of Parliament for Kisauni in Mombasa, to revisit the motive of marginalization in the house. He was surprised that not even the opposition parties found a Muslim worth nominating (*Daily Nation*, October 30, 1997). This spurred the Muslims to form as many pressure groups as possible if they had to make an impact on the political processes, and especially on the impending constitutional review. Such groups included Muslims for Human Rights (MUHURI), Muslim Youth of Kenya (MYK), the Muslim Consultative Council (MCC), and the Council of Imams and Preachers of Kenya (CIPK). SUPKEM was to remain the main mouthpiece of the *Ummah* and to coordinate the rest. Of these, the one that has become a household name in the review debate and process is the Muslim Consultative Council (MCC). The MCC was formed in July 1997. It was to be constituted by the Muslim religious, professional, and political leaders. They were to work out modalities of effectively involving the *Ummah* in the constitutional reforms, with the aim of effectively creating space for the Muslim agenda.

In a word, the MCC was to articulate the Muslim position on the constitutional review. It was to collate their views and to make recommendations. The interim officials were — Chairman, Sheikh Farouk Adam; Executive Director, Adbulrahman Wandati; Convenor, Salah Ul-Deeh (*Daily Nation*, November 24, 1997). Initially, the MCC was meant to synthesize the Muslim views and demands and to channel them to the Inter-Parties Parliamentary Group (IPPG) of 1997. The latter was the initial parliamentary organ, charged with the task of harmonizing constitutional changes. It was to focus on preparing a minimum level playing ground for all the parties before the December 1997 election. The MCC, however, outlasted the IPPG and remained an adroit articulator of the Muslim view into the first decade of the twenty-first century.

The argument was that the Muslim community perceived itself as the biggest single social category. Consequently, for them, it was the biggest single stakeholder in the country's present and the future (Ibid). The MCC was mandated to negotiate afresh the status of the Muslim constituency in the Kenyan body politic. It was to work to try and reverse part of the impact of the historical dynamics that were perceived to have made the community 'second-class' citizens. It was to press for a constitution, guaranteeing them self-governance in their personal affairs. This would ensure that "... our interests are best protected by those who are conversant with the *shari'a* and have interests of the *Ummah* at heart" (Ibid).

Over time, Muslims had learnt that being exclusivist was counterproductive. Hence, while the MCC was to speak for the *Ummah*, it was not to be exclusivist in totality. It was to cooperate with the other stakeholders in pursuance of an equitable and just order and to work for the realization of a peaceful constitutional change in Kenya (*East African Standard*, July 8, 1997).

By the end of the century, however, there was still a stalemate in the modalities of reviewing the constitution. President Moi and KANU, together with the National Development Party (NDP) and the Kenya National Congress (KNC) argued that only parliament could legally review the constitution. Together, the members of these parties came up with a parliamentary select committee to work out the modalities of the review. On the other hand, the rest of the opposition parties, together with leaders of various religious persuasions and groups that described themselves as civil society, argued for what they described as a people-driven constitutional review. As a result of the *impasse,* the later groups congregated at Ufangamano House in December 1999, to form a rival committee. It came to be described as the *Ufungamano Initiative*. It is here that both SUPKEM and the MCC sent their representatives.

It was in this general state of *impasse* on the Kenyan political scene, that the twentieth century closed and the twenty-first century dawned. However, the *Ummah* leaders made sure that whichever structure the review framework would take they were amply represented. For instance, when the twelve-member committee for the Ufungamano Initiative was picked to form a merger with the Raila-led parliamentary team, five were Muslims (*East African Standards*, April 7, 2001). On the other hand, the deputy chairman of the Parliamentary Initiative Commission, Prof. Idha Salim, was a Muslim.

The fact of the matter is that ultimately, when an Act of Parliament established the Constitution of Kenya Review Commission (CKRC), a third of the commissioners were Muslims. Idha Salim remained the Vice-Chairman, deputizing Prof. Yash Pal Ghai, a Kenyan citizen of Asian origin, teaching law at the University of Hong Kong.

The Muslim contribution did not just come suddenly among the commissioners but came especially from Muslim intellectuals and professionals who advise the commissioners. Ali A. Mazrui made crucial interventions in shaping both the agenda of the *Ummah* and the direction of the constitutional review as a whole. In the month of July 2001, Mazrui visited his homeland and delivered a crucial public lecture at the Jamia Mosque in the heart of Nairobi. In this lecture, attended by Yash Pal Ghai, Chairman of the Review Commission, Mazrui urged the Kenyan Muslims to be bold enough to aim for senior offices in the state (*Sunday Standard, July 22, 2001*) and negotiate for vice-presidency, if not the presidency.

A month later, Mazrui was officially invited by the Review Commission to come back home and give a public lecture on the theme of making an ethnic-proof constitution in an ethnic-prone body politic. This lecture was delivered at the amphitheatre of the Kenyatta International Conference Center on August 23. In his address, Mazrui articulated the various dimensions of making a fair constitution. He addressed the questions of ethnicity and religion, gender, unitary versus pluralist systems, fair distribution of economic resources, freedom of expression, etc. In this lecture, he suggested to the commission that a constitution that was to be fair to all the Kenyans should involve devolution of the executive powers to the provinces and to apply affirmative action to cushion vulnerable sectors of society on the basis of gender, religion, and physical disability.

The exit of Moi's quarter century control of Kenya, in December 2002, witnessed also the exit of KANU and the entry of Mwai Kibaki, as the third president of Kenya, sponsored by the National Rainbow Coalition (NARC). By 2005, Kibaki's administration had proved to be a big disappointment to Kenyans, especially in regard to the lack of political will to complete the review of the constitution. Kibaki had campaigned on a platform of delivering the constitution within a hundred days of being sworn in. It became clear that once in power he did not wish to change structures, but rather to exercise the near absolute powers that Moi had enjoyed.

In this saga, the position of the *Ummah* has remained steadfast, together with other progressive forces, on realizing a constitution that devolves power. At the same time, the *Ummah* was firm in its commitment to ensuring that the Kadhi's courts would be enshrined in the republican constitution.

CONCLUSION

This paper has attempted to give an outline of the changing patterns in the leadership and fortunes of the *Ummah*. These changes have been most characteristic in the last decade of the twentieth century and are set to go on for some time to come, as the future of Kenyan politics is revised, to provide space for Muslim involvement. It has demonstrated that this process is determined by interplay of both international and local factors. At the dawn of the twenty-first century, Muslims have made significant strides in staking claims to their rightful place in a fast changing Kenyan society. They have worked out strategies that harmonize their demands and maximize their benefits, in addition to influencing the total Kenya body politic.

The *Ummah*, in Kenya, has positioned itself in strategic positions — both in government and outside government — to play a role that cannot be ignored in any meaningful balance of power in future. The *Ummah* leadership has been flexible. It makes its demands while at the same time supporting the government when this suits it. It has allied with the Christian rank and file and the civil society when it has been necessary to prune the powers of the state. It has openly stated its position when the government attempts to downplay the role of the *Ummah*. The full potential of this positioning of the *Ummah* will only be realized as time unfolds.

Bibliography

Aina, T. A. *Globalisation and Social Policy in Africa: Issues and Research Directions*. Dakar: CODESRIA Working paper Series, 6/96, 1997.

Ake, C. *Is Africa Democratising?* Port Harcourt: CASS, 1996.

Bakari, M. "Muslims and Politics of Change in Kenya," in *Islam in Kenya*, edited by Bakari and Yahya. Nairobi: MEWA Publications, pp. 234–251, 1995.

Central Bank of Kenya. 1991.

Gallardo, H. 1997. "Globalisation and Social Movements in Latin America: A Conceptual Approach," in *Social Movements: Challenges and Dilemmas*, edited by Batista. Geneva: World Council of Churches, pp. 63–75.

Haynes, J. 1993. *Religions in Third World Politics*. Buckingham, Philadelphia: Open University Press.

Huntington, S. P. 1996. *The Clash of Civilizations and the Remaking of World Order*. New York: Touchstone.

Hyder, M. 1992. "President Moi and the IPK Nettle," in *Weekly Review*, October 2, 1992.

———. 1995. "Islamic University of Kenya: Is there a case for it?" in *Islam in Kenya*, edited by Bakari and Yahya. Nairobi: MEWA Publications, pp. 278–293.

Ling, L. H. M. 1999. "Sex Machine Global: Global Hypermasculinity and Images of the Asian Woman in Modernity," in *Positions. East Asia Cultures Critique*. 7.2 Duhe University Press, pp. 277–306.

Mittelman, J. H. 1994. "The Globalisation Challenge: Surviving at the Margins," in *Third World Quarterly*, vol. 15, no. 3, pp. 427–443.

Mwakimako, H. 1995. "Muslim NGOs and Community Development: The Kenyan Experience," in *Islam in Kenya* edited by Bakari and Yahya. Nairobi: MEWA Publications, pp. 224–233.

Ould-Mey, M. 1994. "Global Adjustment: Implications for peripheral States," in *Third World Quarterly*, vol. 15, no. 2, pp. 319–336.

Said, A. S. 1995. "An Outline History of Islam in Nyanza," in *Islam in Kenya*, edited by Bakari and Yahya. Nairobi: MEWA Publications.

Shadid, A. 1996. "Muslims Seek New Identity," in *Daily Nation*, December 3, 1996.

Shiva, V. 1997. "Democracy in the Age of Globalisation," in *Social Movements: Challenges and Dilemmas*, edited by Batista. Geneva: World Council of Churches, pp. 134–141.

UNRISD. 1996–1997. *Social Development Research: UNRISD ACTIVITIES*, Geneva.

Yahya, S. S. 1995. "The Uses and Abuses of Wakf," in *Islam in Kenya*, edited by Bakari and Yahya. Nairobi: MEWA Publications.

The Press

Daily Nation, October 30, 1997. Nairobi: Nation Media Group
Daily Nation, November 14, 1997. Nairobi: Nation Media Group
Daily Nation, November 24, 1997. Nairobi: Nation Media Group
Daily Nation, August 12, 1998. Nairobi: Nation Media Group
Daily Nation, August 13, 1998. Nairobi: Nation Media Group
Daily Nation, September 9, 1998. Nairobi: Nation Media Group
Daily Nation, September 10, 1998. Nairobi: Nation Media Group
Daily Nation, September 15, 1998. Nairobi: Nation Media Group
Daily Nation, September 20, 1998. Nairobi: Nation Media Group
Daily Nation, September 26, 1998. Nairobi: Nation Media Group
Daily Nation, October 3, 1998. Nairobi: Nation Media Group
East African Standard, July 8, 1997. Nairobi: The Standard Ltd.
Kenya Times, June 2, 1997. Nairobi: Kenya Times Media Trust.
Kenya Times, June 13, 1997. Nairobi: Kenya Times Media Trust.
Society Magazine, June 29, 1992. Nairobi.
Sunday Nation, February 14, 1993. Nairobi: Nation Media Group Ltd.
Sunday Nation, November 9, 1997. Nairobi: Nation Media Group Ltd.
Sunday Standard, July 22, 2001. Nairobi: The Standard Ltd.
Weekly Review, August 9, 1998: Nairobi: Stellagraphic.
Weekly Review, January 10, 1992: Nairobi: Stellagraphic.
Weekly Review, January 24, 1992: Nairobi: Stellagraphic.
Weekly Review, May 22, 1992: Nairobi: Stellagraphic.
Weekly Review, June 5, 1992: Nairobi: Stellagraphic.
Weekly Review, June 12, 1992: Nairobi: Stellagraphic.
Weekly Review, June 16, 1992: Nairobi: Stellagraphic.

Weekly Review, July 10, 1992: Nairobi: Stellagraphic.
Weekly Review, October 2, 1992: Nairobi: Stellagraphic.
Weekly Review, February 26, 1993: Nairobi: Stellagraphic.

Oral Sources

Chikombe, Musa, *Oral Interview*, May 12, 1999.
Wandati, Abdulrahman, Executive Director of the Muslim Consultative Council (MCC).
Oral Interview, June 23, 1999.

ISLAM AND COMPARATIVE CULTURE

10

Islam and Acculturation in East Africa's Experience

ALI A. MAZRUI

Officers of Jomo Kenyatta University of Agriculture and Technology are engaged, at the Kenyan Coast, in exploring special relationships with Coastal institutions. These explorations have eventually culminated in the establishment of the first university at the Kenyan Coast — Pwani University College, a constituent college of Kenyatta University.

The Coast was the first region of Kenya to be literate. People were writing and reading in Coastal towns hundreds of years before other Kenyan languages had a word for the pen or a concept of paper. And yet, since independence, six public universities have been established in Kenya — and not a single one at the Coast until 2007.

Because the Coast was the first part of Kenya to become literate, the oldest body of recorded literature in Kenya is from the Coast. Poems like *Al-Inkishafi* and *Utenzi wa Mwana Kupona* go back to hundreds of years. The Swahili language has been a written language at least since the fourteenth century of the Christian era, though, of course, the language has been evolving these last six to seven hundred years, and has changed extensively.

Because the Coast was the first area of Kenya to become literate, the earliest written documentation for Kenya's history has come disproportionately from Coastal archives — exchange of letters, written discourses about war and peace between Coastal cities, and memoranda by Chroniclers.

Because the Coastal people were the first in literacy in Kenya, they were the first to adjudicate on the basis of written law, especially the *Shari'a* in Islam. Hence, the long duration of Kadhi's Courts in Kenya's history. Kadhi's courts, or their variants in Islamic jurisprudence, are a thousand years old in Kenya. There were Kadhi's courts in Kenya hundreds of years before the United States created its exceptionally powerful Supreme Court. There were Kadhi's courts in Kenya long before England had its Magna Carta. British colonial rule stripped Kadhi's courts of their jurisdiction in criminal cases and of their powers in most commercial and economic disputes. But the British were sensitive enough to create a Triple Heritage of Law — indigenous customary law, Islamic personal and social law, and a more wide-ranging legacy of British jurisprudence in criminal and other legal domains.

Nor should Islam at the Kenya Coast be regarded as a heritage of only Muslim people. The Islamic religion is primarily an inheritance of Muslims, but Islamic culture is interwoven with African culture and has become part and parcel of the national legacy of Kenya. Many Kenyans who are not Muslims, and who may not even speak Kiswahili, may nevertheless use the words *dini* for religion, *malaika* for angel, and *dunia* for world in their own ethnic languages.

> Islam is too big a force in African history to be monopolized only by Muslims.
> Winds of the world give answer,
> They are whimpering to and fro,
> Who would know of Islam
> Who only Muslims know?

A Muslim who knows only about fellow Muslims and Islamic studies, has yet to learn about the influence of Islam in other civilizations. Who would know about Islam, who only Muslims know?

Many Kenyans speaking the English language may not realize that they are using Arabic-derived words when they say such English words as the following: Algebra zero [sufr], tariff [taarifa], admiral [al-amir], and (surprisingly) alcohol [al-quhl].

Non-Muslim places which bear Arabic-derived names include Gibraltar [Jabal Tar — the Rock of Tar] and, of course, Sahara [Arabic word for desert]. Even the name 'Africa' is, in all probability, originally Tunisian, though derived from a Tunisian Berber language rather than from Arabic.

What all this means is that much of African thought and conceptualization is already the product of a dialogue between African civilization, Islam and the legacy of Arabic.

Islam arrived into Eastern Africa while the Prophet Muhammad was still alive. But Islam's first African landing space was not Mombasa or Tanga, but a part of Ethiopia. Persecuted Muslims from Arabia arrived in

Abyssinia in quest of asylum during the Prophet of Islam's own lifetime.[1] It is because of that factor that some have argued that the Hegira from Arabia to Africa was almost as holy, and in a few respects almost as symbolic, as the Prophet's own Hegira from Mecca to Medina. Uthman bin Affan, who later became Caliph, was among the refugees into Abyssinia. With the African Hegira (migration for asylum), a seed was being planted which, by the end of the twentieth century, had turned Africa into the first continent to have an absolute Muslim majority.

Not long after the death of the prophet Muhammad, Islam got to the part of Eastern Africa that is now the Swahili Coast. Mosques were being built in this part of East Africa, before they were constructed in parts of what is now the Middle East. Islam in Mombasa is older than Islam in Istanbul and the rest of Turkey. It may be older than Islam in Islamabad and the rest of Pakistan. Is it older than Islam in parts of what is now the Arab world itself? Certainly; Islam probably penetrated parts of the Maghreb in North Africa such as Morocco later than Mombasa, though much of this is in the arena of historical calculation rather than confirmation.[2]

Before long, the arrival of Islam in Mombasa and Coastal Tanzania affected diverse areas of the cultural experience of the people.[3] Marriage and kinship relations were changed profoundly, as were the rules of inheritance and succession. African indigenous norms were often in competition with the Islamic rules. In some cases, syncretism was the result; in some cases the indigenous norms still had an edge; but, increasingly, the Afro-Oriental phase of Swahili history witnessed the gradual pre-colonial triumph of the Islamic rules of marriage, kinship, inheritance, and succession.

The arrival of Islam along East Africa's Coast also had a profound impact on dress culture. The concept of nakedness was completely redefined for both men and women, with practical consequences for forms of attire for each gender. The kanzu entered the scene for men (the long outer garment, usually white), which subsequently became religion-neutral in Uganda, where both Christians and Muslims accepted it as a kind of national dress. (In Kenya the kanzu was still associated with Muslims.)[4]

In Mombasa and the Tanzanian Coast the womenfolk developed the black buibui for outdoor use, intended not only to veil their faces but also to deny shape to their bodies.[5] Muslim women of Zanzibar wore the buibui, only out of doors, when they visited relatives or went grocery shopping.[6] The shapelessness of the garment was part of Islam's quest for female modesty in public places. "In public do not emphasize the curves. Conscience begins with avoidance of temptation." This is a strong Islamic premise.[7] It profoundly affected dress culture on the Swahili Coast during the Afro-Oriental phase.

The arrival of Islam among the Swahili also affected architecture, initially with the minaret and the architectural culture of the mosque. The homes of the Swahili people increasingly felt the influence of Islamic conceptions of gender segregation, the courtyard, the use of tiles and clay in construction, and the place of prayer for women and with the ablution washroom attached to many homes.[8]

It often makes better sense to think of the impact of *Islamic languages* on African verbal culture than to refer to the impact of Arabic alone. Many words in Kiswahili or Somali, which appear to be of Arabic derivation, may in fact be originally Persian or Turkish.[9]

Swahili words like *Serikali* (government), *tajiri* (rich person), *bandari* (harbor or port), and *bakhshish* (gratuity or tip) may appear Arabic in derivation but may have been originally Persian or Turkish. Alternatively, they may have come into East African languages by culture-contact with the Shirazi (Persians of Zanzibar) or in contact with the Ottoman Turks.

There is a hidden linguistic architecture in Kiswahili, which sometimes creates a remarkable symmetry between Islamic words and indigenous [Bantu] words. Let us explore such symmetries of cross-linguistic vocabulary.

LINGUISTIC ARCHITECTURE

From Islamic Languages *(Arabic, Persian, or Turkish)*	From African Indigenous Languages *(Bantu and Others)*
Politics: *Siasa*	Economics: *Uchumi*
East: *Mashariki*	North: *Kusini*
West: *Magharibi*	South: *Kaskazini*
Freedom: *Uhuru*	Slavery: *Utumwa*
Uncle (paternal): *Ammi*	Uncle (maternal): *Mjomba*
Angels: *Malaika*	God: *Mungu*
The past: *Zamani*	The Future: *Mbeleni*
Teacher: *Mwalimu*	Student: *Mwanafunzi*
Fish: *Samaki*	Flesh or meat: *Nyama*
Sugar: *Sukari*	Salt: *Chumvi*
Earth: *Ardhi*	Sky: *Mbingu*
Pen: *Kalamu*	Ink: *Wino*
Book: *Kitabu*	Print: *Chapa*
Minister: *Waziri*	King: *Mfalme*
President: *Raisi*	Parliament: *Bunge*

THE CLOCK, THE CALENDAR, AND THE ALPHABET

Islam arrived in East Africa with new disciplines, previously unknown, south of the Sahara, besides Ethiopia. There was first the discipline of the clock. Of course, all cultures know about time, but not all cultures are guided by the clock. Before Islam arrived, most ethnic cultures in Eastern Africa knew almost nothing about watches and clocks. The cultures had broad ideas about early morning, mid-morning, noon, afternoon, and evening. But the precision of keeping an appointment at, say, 12:15 was an alien experience.

The arrival of Islam, introduced into East African 'tribal' life not only the actual mechanical pieces, but also concepts like a 24-hour day and 60 minutes of each hour. Words for hour, minute, and clock in several East African languages are based on the Arabic words for those temporal phenomena. In Kiswahili, the word for both hour and clock is *saa*, the word for minute is *dakika,* and the word for time itself is *wakati* — all of them Arabic-derived. Other East African languages, like Luganda, have variants of those Swahili loan words.

Islam also introduced time-specific routines into East African cultures. Formal Islamic prayers are within fixed time limits. Muslims may not be punctual in their appointments with each other, but it is a sin to keep God waiting. Among Islamized Africans it is not unusual to see a worshipper praying by the roadside, to make sure that the time for the mid-day prayer (*dhuhr*) is not overtaken by the time for the mid-afternoon prayer (*asr*). A devout Muslim should try hard not to keep God waiting.

Related to this discipline of the clock, Islam also brought into East Africa the discipline of the calendar.[10] The lunar month was a familiar unit of time locally, but the solar year was regarded as less exact, except in terms of rainy and dry seasons. The idea that a year consisted of twelve months was quite alien before Islam arrived in Eastern Africa, except for Ethiopia and the lower Nile Valley. In some cultures, a year was only nine months — like a pregnancy.

Islam and the Arabic language have also impacted the vocabulary of the march of time in some East African languages. The word for the past in Kiswahili and related languages is *zamani,* the word for history is *tarehe* — both of them loaned from Arabic.

In addition to the twin disciplines of the clock and the calendar, Islam also introduced the discipline of numerals into indigenous East African languages. The word for ten is indeed Bantu (*kumi*) in Kiswahili, but all subsequent units of ten are usually borrowed from Arabic (twenty, thirty, forty, up to a thousand — *ishirini, thalathini, arubaini* onwards to *mia* for a hundred and *alifu* for a thousand).[11]

The European impact on East African vocabulary for counting does not begin until the millions. We then proceed to billions and trillions, all of them of European derivation.

In addition to this discipline of numerals, Islam also brought into East Africa the discipline of literacy. Outside Ethiopia and the northern Nile Valley, the earliest forms of literacy in Africa's 'tribal' cultures were based on the Arabic alphabet. Kiswahili was written in the Arabic alphabet for at least six hundred years before the Latin alphabet overtook it in the twentieth century.[12] Arabothography was the initial foundation of literacy in most of Eastern Africa (as indeed in most of West Africa).

It is worth remembering that the impact of the Arabic alphabet was not always directly from the Arabic language. Among the Shirazi in Zanzibar, Arabothography came indirectly from the Persian language. Some parts of Eastern Africa were first acquainted with the Arabic alphabet by the Ottoman legacy. The Turkish language used the Arabic alphabet until the revolution of Mustapha Kemal Ataturk in the years between the two World Wars. Alphabetically, Turkey went Roman in the wake of the Ataturk revolution. But, before that, the Turkish language had bequeathed Arabothography to other cultures through Ottoman influence.

GENDER: BETWEEN AFRICANITY AND ISLAM

In addition to the disciplines of the clock, the calendar, the numerals, and the letters, has Islam also introduced into Eastern Africa a new discipline of gender in East African cultures? Indigenous cultures in East Africa gave more roles to women than Islam did, while Islam gave more rights to women than indigenous culture had.

The gender discipline of Islam in Eastern Africa had, on the whole, been negative. Under Islamic influence, the roles of women in Eastern Africa have become more restricted as compared with indigenous culture. But the rights of women in inheritance have improved under Islam than under indigenous traditions. Women own more under Islam than under native customary law. But what about the role of women in the wider Islamic experience? East Africans should pay attention to trends in the wider Muslim world.

Although the Prophet Muhammad's widow, Ayesha, set the precedent of Muslim women in combat roles on the battlefield, there is general consensus among Muslim jurists that killing women or children is beyond the pale.[13]

This has to be seen in the context of three varieties of sexism evident in human behavior, not uniquely Islamic. Benevolent sexism is a form of gender discrimination, which selectively favors the otherwise disadvantaged gender. For example, when in 1912 the captain of the *Titanic* decided that the limited space on the lifeboats was to be reserved for women and children, that was a form of benevolent sexism with which most cultures would agree; the safety of women and children came first.[14]

Most cultures would also agree that while women may have a duty to die for their faith or for their country, women do not have a duty to kill for their faith or their country. Even in the West, drafting women for direct combat has been culturally repugnant. Forcing women to go and kill has tended to be avoided in most cultures, including Western and Islamic.[15]

In spite of Ayesha's role in the Battle of the Camel, benevolence in Islam has spared women obligatory combat roles. East African Muslim women have similarly been demilitarized, except perhaps in Somalia from time to time.

In addition to benevolent sexism, there is benign sexism. This benign sexism is of differentiation rather than of discrimination. A policy of different dress codes for men and women has been part of the sexism of differentiation in Islam.[16] There are different rules of modesty for males and females. In most cultures women are expected to cover more of their bodies than men.[17] The Swahili *buibui* is part of the local female dress code.

In addition to benevolent sexism and benign sexism, there is the third version, which is malignant sexism. This is the kind of gender discrimination which results in sexual exploitation, economic marginalization, cultural subordination, or political disempowerment.

Although many Muslim countries are guilty of such versions of malignant sexism, there are paradoxes in the Muslim world. In no Muslim country are women more liberated than women are in the United States, but in some Muslim countries women have been more empowered than women have been in the United States.

Right now two Muslim countries, outside Africa, have women as heads of state or heads of government. Indonesia, the largest Muslim country in population, has a woman as President — Megawati Sukarnoputri. In Bangladesh, both the Head of Government and the leader of the Opposition have been women. Sheikh Hasina Wajed and Begum Khaleda Zia have alternated in political power for more than a decade.

Two other Muslim countries, outside Africa, have had a woman chief executive at the top of the political process. Benazir Bhutto was Prime Minister of Pakistan twice. And Tansu Ciller has been Prime Minister of Turkey.

All these cases of Muslim women at the top have occurred long before the United States has had a woman president or Germany a woman Chancellor or Italy a woman Prime Minister or Russia a woman President. But Asian Muslims have been ahead of Africans in this empowerment.

While serving as heads of government, such Muslim women in those countries have been *de facto* Commanders-in-Chief. Were they continuing in the tradition of the Prophet's widow Ayesha in the middle of the Battle of the Camel, way back in the first century of the Hegira calendar, the seventh century of the Christian era?

Have any of these Muslim women in power had to contend with terrorism by fellow Muslims? Bangladesh has not had conflicts, coups, and assassinations over the years, and neither have Sheikh Hasina Wajed (in power) nor Begum Khaleda Zia had to fight terrorism.

On the other hand, Megawati Sukarnoputri in Indonesia was under enormous pressure to act against Islamic militants, especially after the devastating bombings by terrorists in the resort town of Bali.[18]

Muslims are not unique in resorting to terrorism in a bid to redress wrongs perpetrated against them. But terrorism, by Muslims, gets far more publicity as a rule than terrorism by others. What all cultures and all religions are being forced to scrutinize more closely than ever, are the detailed ethics of terrorism. Eastern Africa is caught up in the crossfire between Middle Eastern militancy and the American war on terror.

In Eastern Africa, Uganda has led the way in the political empowerment of women. It was a Muslim President of Uganda, Field Marshall Idi Amin, who appointed the first woman Foreign Minister in Eastern Africa. This was two decades before Bill Clinton appointed the first woman Secretary of State in American history.

But although appointed by a Muslim Head of State, Foreign Minister Elizabeth Bagaya of Uganda was not herself a Muslim. President Yoweri Museveni has since carried female empowerment in Uganda even further. Uganda under Museveni has known a woman Vice-President long before the United States has had one. Yet, once again, the highest-ranking Ugandan women have not yet been Muslims. In Eastern Africa as a whole, the political empowerment of Muslim women still has a long way to go, though military regimes have sometimes opened more doors to women than have civilian governments.

The headquarters of Islam in Kenya is the Coast, where Kadhi's courts have existed for a thousand years. It would be an act of cultural cleansing and religious bigotry to abolish the courts at this late hour.

THE PRICE TAG OF THE KENYA COAST

What is distinctive about the Coast of Kenya? What does the Coast bring to the national heritage which is uniquely Coastal?[19]

First, the Coast brings to the national table the national language of Kiswahili — the most successful indigenous language on the African continent.[20] This linguistic legacy was not forged just by the Waswahili, it was also shaped and influenced by all Coastal peoples, the Giriama and the Digo, the Taita, as well as the Mijikenda. In the Kenyan context, the Coast is the fountainhead of the national language.

Secondly, the Coast offers its natural features for sport — the splendor of its beaches. Thirdly, the exceptional utility of its harbors has made it the gateway to the outside world for centuries. Without Kilindini Harbor the economies of Kenya, Uganda, and elsewhere would be in serious trouble. Without the beaches of Malindi and other Coastal playgrounds, Kenya's tourist industry would diminish.[21] Without Kilindini, Kenya's economy would shrink. No other part of Kenya can claim to make similar contributions to Kenya's economy.

The fourth area of uniqueness of the Kenya Coast is its historicity. Of course all parts of Kenya have a history, but there is something about the history of the Coast which is captured not only in the oral tradition, but also in stone, in written documents hundreds of years old, in the ruins of ancient cities like Gedi, and in the living continuities of ancient city states like Lamu.[22] No other part of Kenya brings this kind of legacy to the national heritage.

Fifthly, the Coast is unique in Kenya in being the fountainhead of Islam — Islam as a faith, as a culture, and as a civilization. In the Kenya Coast the *muezzin* was calling Muslim believers to prayers hundreds of years before the Protestant Reformation in Europe. It is arguable that Islam in Kenya is older than it is in some areas of the Middle East. No other part of Kenya brings the Islamic legacy as decisively to Kenya's national heritage as the Coast does.

What do noncoastal Kenyans feel about this five-sided distinctiveness of the Coast? Perhaps the nation has come to value the national language, Kiswahili. Perhaps the nation appreciates its great dependence on Kilindini Harbor. But is there a tendency to take the Coast for granted?

Moreover, the least appreciated of the Coast's five contributions to the national heritage is Islam. And yet, Islam is also part of the ancestry of the national language, Kiswahili — which was born out of a meeting of two civilizations, African and Islamic.

Islam is also part of the historicity of the Coast, from the Swahili city-states to the fluctuating fortunes of Fort Jesus across the centuries.

In short, of the five aspects of uniqueness that the Coast brings to the national banquet, three aspects are profoundly influenced by Islam — language, history, and religion. Can Kenya afford to despise Islam and still save the other four legacies of the Coast — language, national gateway, tourist playground, and monumental historicity?

The Waswahili are still by far the most gifted users of the national language, Kiswahili. And the Waswahili are, in their great majority, Muslims. A repressed Swahili community is unlikely to be a major agent for enriching the national language.

Although the proportion of Muslims in the population of Tanzania is larger than the proportion of Muslims in Kenya's population, the proportion of non-Muslim experts of Kiswahili in Tanzania is paradoxically also larger than the proportion of non-Muslim Swahilists in Kenya.[23] Julius Nyerere, for example, was not a Muslim. But he also happened to be one of the most brilliant users of the Swahili language in Tanzania. He even translated William Shakespeare into powerful Kiswahili.[24]

Compared with Tanzania, Kenya has a smaller percentage of Muslims. But for the enrichment of its national language, Kenya is in reality more dependent on Muslim Swahilists than Tanzania is. In Kenya, to repress the Waswahili is to impoverish the Swahili language.

In Kenya, to repress the Muslims is also to detract from the special historicity of the Coast. For much of what is distinctive about the history of the Coast, is the profound interaction between the African people here and the Islamic culture. For more than a thousand years, the Kenya coast has not only been a part of the history of Africa but has, simultaneously, been part of the history of Islam worldwide.

What about the Coast as a gateway into and out of East Africa? What about the Coast as a tourist playground? How would the repression of Islam affect those? The last thing any patriotic citizen would want is a situation where there is so much discontent among the local people of the Coast that it begins to show; first in escalating social deviancy, then in escalating crime, and finally in escalating rebellion and rioting. Joblessness corrupts; absolute joblessness corrupts absolutely. If the Coast were to become ungovernable, Kilindini's Harbor would be endangered, the railway artery would be at risk, the peaceful beaches would be in turmoil, and the historic sites could be a nightmare. The Coast is too valuable to Kenya to be taken for granted.

KENYA AND PAX AMERICANA

Since September 11, 2001, the Kenyan authorities have been so eager to please the Americans that they are tempted to repatriate their own Kenyan citizens to the United States on the slightest encouragement. Fortunately, the American Embassy in Nairobi is sometimes more cautious.

President Moi of Kenya marched in sympathy with the victims of September 11. The Muslims of Kenya marched against the American bombing of Afghanistan in 2002. President Moi asked, "Why didn't the Kenyan Muslims march when Nairobi was bombed by terrorists in August of 1998?" The Kenyan Muslims turned the tables on their President, "Why didn't President Moi lead a march when Nairobi was bombed in August 1998?"[25]

The President of Tanzania declared a day of mourning for the victims of September 11 in the United States. His critics retorted that they did not remember a day of public mourning in Tanzania when 800,000 Rwandans were killed in the genocide of 1994. Africans grieve when Americans are massacred, but do we grieve as much when Africans are massacred? As *The Economist* has put it, "When terrorists murder Westerners in Africa, a much larger number of Africans usually die too."[26]

There is some anxiety that September 11 and its aftermath may exacerbate tensions not only between pro-Western and anti-Western schools of thought in this continent, but also between Christians and Muslims in Africa. A demonstration by Nigerian Muslims in Kano against the American war in Afghanistan provoked stone throwing by Nigerian Christians in Kano, which flared up into communal riots.[27] Churches and mosques were soon being burnt. President Olusegun Obasanjo had to rush to Kano to contain the tensions before they spilled over into sectarian riots all over Nigeria.

The United States' efforts to unite African governments against terrorism may be dividing African people among themselves — a coalition of elites resulting in a contestation at the grassroots.

The pressure on many African governments to enact new legislation against terrorism may pose newer threats to civil liberties in Africa just at the time when democratization is gathering momentum in some African states.[28] Nor must we forget that if America's own democracy decays, it makes it easier for Africa's own dictators to justify their own tyranny.[29]

In November 2002, there was another remarkable terrorist act in Mombasa on the same day as the suicide bombing of the Paradise Hotel. This was the attempted shooting down of an Israeli airliner with over two hundred tourists on board. A surface-to-air missile seems to have been used in an attempt to blow up the Israeli plane.³⁰ The global media presented this as a wholly new threat to civilian aviation. In fact, this attempt to shoot down a civilian plane was not new even in Africa. Sub-Saharan Africa had a 1978 precedent at the level of national terrorism. North Africa was accused of a similar destruction of a civilian airline in 1988 at the level of international terrorism. The sub-Saharan precedent was the shooting down of a civilian government airliner by Zimbabwe liberation forces in 1978, in which about 50 people died.³¹ Among those who survived on the ground, Joshua Nkomo's forces killed or attempted to kill several of them. NEWSWEEK carried a photograph of Joshua Nkomo and Robert Mugabe raising their glasses. The caption of the photograph was, "We shot it down!" It was not clear whether the photograph was not an old one, dug up by NEWSWEEK and taken long before the shooting down of the plane.

But there is no doubt that Joshua Nkomo accepted 'credit' for shooting down the plane; he caused an uproar when he chuckled over the incident in a BBC interview. This was all part of anti-colonial terrorism at the national level of the politics of Rhodesia/Zimbabwe.

Less clear-cut was whether Libya was really responsible for the bombing of the Pan American flight 103 over Lockerbie, Scotland, in 1988. The fact that a Scottish court has convicted one Libyan has still left many doubts about the nature of the evidence. But if Libya was indeed responsible for the bomb which destroyed Pan American flight 103, it was North African participation in terrorism at the international level.³²

Libya itself had been a victim of trigger-happy Israelis. A 727 Libyan airliner was shot down by Israel in February 1973, killing 108 innocent civilian passengers of all ages — young and old, men and women.³³ A country like Israel was in a position to say "Oops! Sorry! My mistake!" And Israel was bound to get away with it.

Similarly, an American warship in the Persian Gulf shot down a Persian airliner with 292 civilian passengers on board. This was in July 1988. Again, like Israel, the United States was in a position to cry out "Oops! I didn't mean that! Would you like some dollars to cheer you up?" Apparently, nobody was court marshaled in the United States. The incident was simply described as a "regrettable defense action" or "an unfortunate and tragic error."³⁴

The Soviet Union was less hypocritical in its war games. It deliberately shot down a South Korean civilian airline in 1982 over the Sakhalin Island — insisting that the civilian plane was being used for spying.³⁵ Over 290 civilian lives were lost.

The powerful have been playing war games with civilian airlines in the past and never got punished. The powerless resort to similar games — either to end white rule in Zimbabwe or to end Israeli occupation of Palestine or to tame the mighty power of the United States.

The city of Mombasa is over a thousand years old. Because historically it had a superb natural harbor, it was fought over many times — by the Arabs, by the Portuguese, by the Zanzibaris, by the Mazrui, by the British, and by others. Indeed, there was a time when the city of Mombasa was called *Mvita*, the Isle of War. To the present day the Swahili dialect of Mombasa is called *Ki-mvita*.

In ancient days, war in Mombasa was fought with swords, spears, and later, cannonballs. It was against this background that these Coastal people coined the proverb, *"Ndovu wawili wakipigana,ziumiazo na nyasi."* [When two elephants fight, it is the grass that suffers]. In the twentieth century, a companion concept evolved — not always suitable for polite society: *"Ndovu wawili wakitombana,ziumiazo ni nyasi."* [When two elephants copulate, it is still the grass that suffers].

Since the attack on the Israeli hotel, *The Paradise*, in November 2002, has Mombasa reverted to its ancient identity of *Mvita*, the Isle of War? Are we also back to the older proverb: "When two elephants fight, the grass suffers?" Or, are we really confronting an entirely different phenomenon? Is this really a case of the single elephant, the United States, with its protégé, Israel? Has the singularity of the beast created an entirely different jungle game — *"Ndovu mmoja akicheeza ngoma, maumivu ni nyasi"* ["When a single elephant does a war dance, the grass feels the pain"]? Economically, as well as in terms of security, the anguish of Mombasa may have only just begun. The shadows of September 11, the repercussions of the Arab-Israeli conflict, the postcolonial local discrimination against Muslims, and the reincarnation of *Mvita* have tragically converged on this historic African seaport on the Indian Ocean. Speedy action is needed to restore the sense of dignity of the Coast and of Muslim Kenyans before Kenyan Islam is radicalized into a new Black *Intifadah*.

CONCLUSION

No one would like to see such a Coastal nightmare. That is why the Provincial Commissioner, at the Coast, was compelled at that time to speak to Muslim and other Coastal leaders. That is why President Moi probably regretted his provocative remarks in his 1992 *Madaraka* Day Speech, alleging a link between Islam and slavery in Kenya. That is why there is hope. No one wants to witness a prolonged Black *Intifadah* in Kenya. Four forms of tension can be devastating for Kenya — tension between so-called 'tribes,' hostility between regions, violent prejudice between races, and explosive distrust between religions.

Right now, Kenya is indeed experiencing tension between 'tribes' and hostility between regions. From time to time, Kenya has also experienced violent prejudice between races, ranging from the Mau Mau war in the 1950s to more recent economic riots against Asian merchants. But, until now, Kenya has basically avoided domestic sectarian violence — enmity and local brutality on the basis of religion. It would be utterly tragic if the authorities in Kenya allowed the situation at the Coast and the American war on terror, to set the stage for sectarian confrontations between local Muslims and the government administrators. A trigger for a Black *Intifidah* could be excessive compliance with American counterterrorism.

When the forty-first President of the United States, George H. W. Bush, was confronted with the violent situation in Los Angeles, he promptly invited African-American leaders to Washington, D.C. for consultations about how to ensure that the American system not only worked but was also seen to work fairly and justly. The Black leaders met President Bush at the White House and the President later went to Los Angeles to see for himself.

Should President Moi have gone to the riots at the Coast of Kenya and talked to the local people himself? Should President Moi have toured the disturbed areas of the Western province and the Rift Valley? Should President Daniel Arap Moi also have invited Muslim leaders to State House to discuss how best to ensure that in the future, misunderstandings between the Government, police, and the Muslims did not recur? Did President Moi miss too many opportunities of reconciliation?

We should remember that when the Indian Prime Minister, Indira Gandhi ordered the invasion of the Golden Temple of the Sikhs, she created so much hatred at such a violation of the temple's sacredness that she later lost her life as a result; a Sikh killed her.

The Muslim population of Kenya is proportionately more than ten times the percentage of the Sikh population in India. Fortunately, the Muslim population of Kenya is not in the least interested in starting a terrorist indigenous movement in the country. On the contrary, until the 1990s, Muslims in Kenya were among the most law-abiding and docile of citizens. Is the American campaign against terrorism in danger of activating religious resistance?

I, personally, hope that Kenyan Muslims will become less docile and more assertive of their rights. But I still want Muslims to be law-abiding. But I would also like the police to be law-abiding. After all, the Rodney

King riots in Los Angeles were a protest against policemen who broke the law. Kenya police are not always law-abiding either.

Let us not create conditions, which will give rise to a Black Coastal *Intifadah* in our beloved country. If it can be avoided, let us not have Muslim women dance before the President, if this would fuel fundamentalist rage. On the other hand, let us end the near Christian monopoly of religious programs on the electronic media. Let us end this electronic theocracy. Let us restore more Muslim programs, which used to exist under Jomo Kenyatta. Let us also give due recognition to African indigenous religions on state occasions like *Madaraka* Day. Let us not violate places of worship the way the Mombasa police violated the sanctity of a mosque, as well as the civil rights of the worshippers in the 1990s.

Above all, let us end conditions of regional, ethnic, and religious discrimination for either local or American reasons. As far as the Kenya Coast is concerned, social justice and religious respect are the only ways of averting a militant black *intifadah* in the years ahead.

The British were Christianized nearly fifteen hundred years before the first Kenyan became a Christian. The British had no difficulty accommodating Kadhi's Courts for half a century of British rule. Jomo Kenyatta had no difficulty accommodating Kadhi's Courts either. Why should more recent Christians be more intolerant than long-established Christian nations like Britain? If Eastern Africa was the original Garden of Eden, let it now become an Eden of tolerance as well as of ancestry.

Endnotes

1. For discussion of this journey, see W. Montgomery Watt, *Muhammad at Mecca* (Oxford: Clarendon Press, 1953) pp. 101–117.
2. Some estimates put the arrival of Islam in Egypt at 640 A.D., and on the Atlantic coast of Morocco in 711 A.D.; see Falola, *Key Events in African History*, pp. 83–84.
3. See, for example, R. L. Pouwels, *Horn and Crescent: Cultural Change and Traditional Islam on the East African Coast, 1800–1900* (Cambridge University Press, 1987).
4. For a related, extended discussion on clothing in Zanzibar, see Laura Fair, *Pastimes and Politics: Culture, Community, and Identity in Post-Abolition Urban Zanzibar, 1890-1945* (Athens, OH and Oxford, IK: Ohio University Press and James Currey, 2001) pp. 64–85.
5. For a discussion on the buibui, see Ntarangwi, *Gender, Performance & Identity*, (Trenton, New Jersey, and Asmara, Eritrea: Africa World Press, 2003) pp. 123–127.
6. Consult Fair, *Pastimes and Politics*, pp. 85–96.

7. One explication of the Islamic attitudes towards modesty in dress may be found in Murtaza Mutahhari, *The Islamic Modes Dress*, 2nd ed., translated by Laleh Bakhtiar (Albuquerque, NM: Abjad, 1989).
8. Some of the architectural impact of Islam is discussed in Ntarangwi, *Gender, Performance & Identity*, p. 55.
9. Relatedly, consult Ali A. Mazrui and Pio Zirimu, "The Secularization of an Afro-Islamic Language: Church, State and Marketplace in the Spread of Kiswahili," in *The Power of Babel: Language and Governance in the African Experience*, ed. Ali A. Mazrui and Alamin A. Mazrui (Oxford, Nairobi, Kampala, Cape Town, Chicago: James Currey, E.A.E.P., Fountain, David Philip, and the University of Chicago Press, 1998) pp. 169–171.
10. For a brief introduction to the Islamic calendar, consult LeRoy E. Doggett "The Calendar," in *General Editor, The History of Science and Religion in the Western Tradition: An Encyclopedia*, Gary B. Ferngren (New York: Garland Publishing, 2002) p. 324.
11. A fascinating account of the history and transmission of numbers may be found in Georges Ifrah, *The Universal History of Numbers: From Prehistory to the Invention of Computers*, translated by David Bellos, et al. (New York: J. Wiley, 2000).
12. This may have to do with the German colonialists' fear of the Islamic element of Kiswahili; consult Ali A. Mazrui and Alamin M. Mazrui, *Swahili State and Society: The Political Economy of an African Language* (Nairobi and London: East African Educational Publishers and J. Currey, 1995) pp. 38–40.
13. On Ayesha's role and the precedents it offered Muslim women, see Denise A. Spellber, "Political Action and Public Example: Aisha and the Battle of the Camel," in *Women in Middle Eastern History: Shifting Boundaries in Sex and Gender*, ed. Nikkie Keddie and Beth Baron (New Haven, Ct: Yale University Press, 1999) pp. 45–57.
14. See Lisa C. Ikemoto, "Lessons from the Titanic," in *Mother Troubles: Rethinking Contemporary Maternal Dilemmas*, ed. Julia E. Hanigsberg and Sara Ruddick (Boston: Beacon Press, 1999) p. 4.
15. This changed certainly in Palestine with a number of female suicide bombers; for a detailed analysis of the suicide bombers' psychology, see Suzanne Goldberg, "Special report: A mission to murder: Inside the minds of the suicide bombers," *The Guardian* (London) (June 11, 2002) p. 4.
16. The Qur'anic verse, 24; 31, is cited for the Islamic custom of veiling in, for example, Fadwa El Guindi, *Veil: Modesty, Privacy and Resistance* (Oxford and New York: Berg, 1999) p. 85.
17. Relatedly, see *Dress and Gender: Making and Meaning in Cultural Contexts*, ed. Rught Barnes and Joanne B. Eicher (New York: Berg and St. Martin's Press, 1992).
18. Consult Anthony L. Smith, "Reluctant Partner: Indonesia," Asian Affairs: An American Review (summer 2003) Volume 30, Issue 2, pp. 142–150.
19. Relatedly, see Susan Kask and Martin Kenzer, "The Geo-Economics of Kenya," in *Kenya: The Land, the People, and the Nation*, Azevedo, p. 63; and

Mark Horton and John Middleton, *The Swahili: The Social Landscape of a Mercantile Society* (Oxford and Malden, MA: Blackwell, 2000).

20. Relatedly, consult Ali A. Mazrui and Pio Zirimu, "The Secularization of an Afro-Islamic Language: Church, State and Marketplace in the Spread of Kiswahili." In Ali A. Mazrui and Alamin A. Mazrui, *The Power of Babel: Language and Governance in the African Experience* (Oxford, Nairobi, Kampala, Cape Town, Chicago: James Currey, E.A.E.P., Fountain, David Philip, and the University of Chicago Press, 1998) pp. 169–171.

21. On the growth of tourism in the Kenyan economy, consult Martha Honey, *Ecotourism and Sustainable Development: Who Owns Paradise* (Washington, DC: Island Press, 1999) pp. 296–297.

22. For descriptions of contemporary Lamu and some other cities on the Swahili Coast, see Robert Caputo, "Swahili Coast," *National Geographic* (October 2001), Volume 200, Issue 4, pp. 104–139 and Horton and Middleton, *The Swahili: The Social Landscape of a Mercantile Society*, pp.115–139.

23. For the percentage of Muslims in Tanzania, see Oded, *Islam and Politics in Kenya*, p. 166.

24. Nyerere translated Julius Caesar and Merchant of Venice into Swahili.

25. See the report in *The Nation* (Kenya), October 21, 2000, reported in the Africa News Service on-line at <http://allafrica.com/eastafrica/>

26. "Now for Africa," *The Economist* (July 5, 2003) p. 9.

27. This was reported in *The Washington Post* (October 15, 2001), p. 9.

28. See V. Rich, "Africa's New Wind of Change," World Today, Volume 48, Number 7 (July 1992) pp. 116-119 and also Julius O. Ihonvbere, "On The Threshold of Another False Start? A Critical Evaluation of Pro-Democracy Movements in Africa," *Democracy and Democratization in Africa: Toward the 21st Century*, ed. E. Ike Udogu (Leiden and New York: E.J. Beill, 1997) pp. 125–142.

29. A Human Rights Watch report pointed out that country leaders were taking advantage of the antiterror campaign to suppress dissent and abuse human rights; see *The Washington Post* (January 18, 2002) p. 12.

30. Beth Potter, "No Vacation from Terror's Reach," *US News & World Report*, (December 9, 2002)

31. See Richard Hull, "Rhodesia in Crisis," *Current History* (March 1979), Volume 76, Number 445, p. 107.

32. Indeed, Libya has now taken responsibility for the Lockerbie bombing in an apparent bid to end sanctions; see *The Washington Post* (August 13, 2003) p. 17.

33. The plane was downed on February 21, 1973; see the report in *New York Times* (February 22, 1973), p. 8.

34. For discussion of the Iranian plane being downed by the USS Vincennes, see S. Shuger, "Why did the Navy shoot down 290 Civilians?" *Washington Monthly* (October 1988), Volume 20, Number 9, pp. 20–27.

35. Some still maintain the KAL plane was a spy plane; consult, for instance, *The New York Times*, (December 9, 1996) p. 12.

11

To Veil or not to Veil: Faces of Islam in Comparative Literature

ABD EL KADER CHEREF

"I came out of the darkness of the unknown into a world that was unprepared to accept me. My mother tried to get rid of me in the first months of her pregnancy with me. She tried and repeated the attempt. But she failed."[1]

This epigraph clearly echoes the Qur'anic verse about the pagan Arabs' (*Jahiliya*) treatment of baby girls, a practice largely condoned by traditional Arab idolatry:

"And when the female infant buried alive shall be questioned. For what sin she was killed?" (Sura 81, 8–9)

"And kill not your children for fear of poverty. We provide for them and for you. Surely, the killing of them is a great sin." (Sura 17, 31)

Devoted to the dynamics of contemporary Muslim communities in the Maghreb — Algeria, Morocco, and Tunisia — this chapter examines points of conflict involving Muslims who emphasize different aspects of Islamic religiosity (traditionalists) and Muslims who invoke Islam as a political agenda (Islamists). Specifically reading the Algerian novelist, Assia Djebar's *A Sister to Scheherazade* (1987), the Moroccan Leila Abouzeid's *Year of the Elephant* (1989), and the Tunisian Souad Hedri's *Vie et Agonie* (1978), we raise and examine a cluster of issues associated with gender relations and the representation of authority in the Maghreb.

These Maghrebi novels compel us to ask intricate questions about Islam and feminism. Are feminist or gender-conscious strategies pertinent to an Islamic non-Western community, particularly if feminism is regarded as a doctrine of Western origin? Alternatively, as Juliette Minces asks, can the evolution of the condition of women in the Arab world be evaluated through the same criteria as in the West? Is it not Eurocentric to put forward the lives of Western women as the only democratic, just, and forward-looking model?[2]

What is the connection between women's political and economic venture and women's liberation? What about the correlation of women and their communities? What are the circumstances that drive a Muslim woman to a new type of sensibility? What is the function of Islam in such a transformation? Is it a catalyst for change or resistance? Does authentic liberation signify greater participation in political fields, for instance? Are these narratives, feminist novels? What does the term feminism designate in non-Western cultures?

It appears to me that the most complex and controversial socio-ideological picture of these societies is the one that represents the complicated situation of women. And these novels ought to be considered as informative ideological documents that faithfully reflect historical reality.[3] For prose by its nature can permit a clearer representation, a more elaborate re-formulation and re-structuring of the world. Mimesis is tied to its essence.

Furthermore, I accept and develop the notion that all these writers expose sexism and sexist violence in their respective communities. My objective in selecting a particular generation of three novelists from three societies (Algeria, Morocco, and Tunisia) is to explore the similarities and contradictions inherent in them. Djebar, Abouzeid, and Hedri communicate across their countries within the same world of literary discourse. If they write about female autonomy and sexuality, domestic and national relations, these three female writers propose not only dissimilarities of character in their comprehension of women's possibilities but also a broadly different word-stock of emotion. The subjects that these novels broach are strikingly similar. In other words, these writers tackle issues of male rejection, women's subjugation, women's access to power and economic resources, women's legal and social standing, and the entire issue of the state and gender in the Maghreb.[4]

In the eyes of the Algerian government dignitaries, Assia Djebar is a 'Westernized' expatriate whose feminist books in French misrepresent women's conditions in Algeria. Undoubtedly, Djebar's novels are feminist and significantly analytical of women's condition in Algeria. Her fiction has "broached an area of interrogation ... that calls into question not only tradition, convention, and religion but the modern uses of power in post-independent North Africa as well."[5]

In the first part of this chapter, I offer a reading of *A Sister to Scheherazad* — a novel that considers Algerian women as subjects who personify contemporary Algeria's irreducibly conflicting identity, and which confronts the subjugation of women by articulating a sharp skepticism about feminism's potency to transform social relations in contemporary Algeria.

Trying to retrieve a Maghrebi authentic identity from a postcolonial predicament, *A Sister to Scheherazade* is a novel that poignantly presents itself as a "cluster of strangled cries"[6] written in "the language used formerly to entomb my people"[7] and one that no longer deals with the historical concerns of *Fantasia*. Yet, like Djebar's previous novel, *Fantasia* is narrated by an educated urban woman who has lived abroad with her husband and daughter. Besides, *A Sister to Scheherazade* is an exploration of two female existences in post-independent Algeria:

> Two women, two wives: Hajila and Isma ... a strange duet: (they) are not sisters, not even rivals, although ... they are both the wives of the same man — The Man — ... This man does not come between them but nevertheless does not turn them into accomplices. (1)

Like Leila Abouzeid's *Year of the Elephant* or Hedri's *Vie et Agonie*, rebellion against mores and family is one of the main subjects of the novel. Unlike the other women who are frequently confined to their 'apartments' having their deeds prescribed by society or by male authority, Hajila rebels against the asphyxiating restrictions implemented by her mother and her husband, who practically sequester her and supervise her every action in the name of shielding the family honor:

> "Around the house: high windowless walls surmounted by broken glass; around the village: every kind of natural protection, ditches, hedges of prickly pear; around the tent: a pack of half-wide dogs, but rendered even more impregnable than by the dogs — the whole vicinity has been 'sacralized' and cannot be violated without violating that most sacred of all concepts: *horma* — honor.[8]

What Hajila notices around her is a muffled atmosphere, where women mumble. The harem no longer exists. Nevertheless, its practices, the law of silence and invisibility, impose themselves. Woman's voice is suppressed and her space is restricted. The theme of confinement permeates the whole novel. Hajila ignores the joy of open space, as did the former nonconformist heroines such as Nadia and Dalila, but is constantly secluded and walled in. "Here, in this country, they annihilate you by shutting you up behind walls and windows hidden from view. No sooner do you set foot outside than you feel exposed." (80) Nevertheless, the author implies that if a woman's body

— and even her communication — is castigated by the veil and sequestration, her soul is in motion. It is possible that contemporary Algerian women will cross the boundary and "deliver themselves ... completely from the rapport of shadow maintained for centuries with their own bodies."⁹

In the passages dealing with Hajila, Isma sketches Hajila's advent from the prison of domesticity where her husband has sequestered her: a luxurious apartment with a "new kitchen that is like a tomb" (85). Here, the novel parallels *Fantasia* in expanding the female universe as a 'sarcophagus' from which women must emerge. Similar, to the implacable Berbers' descendants in *Fantasia,* these "anonymous women who remain hidden from sight" (79) must break the age-old silence.

Much of the account is arranged in an opposition between spaces of confinement and spaces of liberation, with Isma, the narrator, catapulting Hajila from the house to the streets, away from the fetters of her unhappy wedlock, from the shelter/prison of the veil into the sunlight, and from a "maternal cocoon"¹⁰ (152) to the wide world:

> You make your sudden decision to take off that veil! As if you wished to disappear ... or explode! ... You, the new woman, you who have just been transformed into another woman ... You tuck the *haik* (veil) under your arm; you walk on. You are surprised to find yourself walking so easily, at one fell swoop, out into the real world! (30-1)

Unquestionably, considering the sociopolitical situation in Algeria, the apprehensions articulated in Djebar's novel are corroborated by the national context. And because the circumstances are so strenuous and the stakes so high, it is crucial today to confirm "Algerian women as subjects in their own right."¹¹ This attempt embodies the construct of a macrocosmic web in which feminism's affiliation to other anti-imperialist struggles "can be defined within specific historical, geopolitical, and cultural contexts, and in which languages of revolt can challenge the hegemonic discourses, including those of first-world feminism."¹²

How is liberation achieved for Hajila in these circumstances? The narrator broaches the framework of the *Arabian Nights* ¹³ as a viable explanation:

> What if the sister had thus relaxed her guard and the sultan's bride for one night had been delivered up to the executioner? ... What if, at every present and future dawn, once or a thousand and one times, every sultan, every beggar, who is a prey to the ancestral fear that leads to violation, were still satisfying his need for a virgin's blood? (143)

Thanks to her sister's vigilance, the beloved storyteller could defer the death sentence. This is an illustration of a sisterly solidarity: two bridged destinies. If Dinarzade sleeps, Scheherazade is offered up as a sacrifice; i.e., if women fail to protect their 'sisters,' every woman becomes a sacrificial victim.

This plot summary may be considered as an elementary level of reading. Yet, I may venture to say that Hajila's environment is a closed one. It denotes a place "of women always in waiting;" "sad caged bird women" (131) living like captives in "that rarefied atmosphere of close confinement."[14] Besides, the muffled violence that runs through the novel is partly related to Hajila's ordeal. Lonely, neglected, battered, sequestered, first, by her mother and, later, by her husband, the young woman discovers and details a new universe that she has not perceived so far.

Djebar's writing has never been so articulate and so accurate in staging the ecstasy and rapture of being 'naked in the world outdoors.' (26) For in *Fantasia*, she equates the veiled woman to the sightless: "Render her invisible. Transform her into a being more blind than the blind."[15] Here, the relationship between blindness and corporeality is evident. We can see clearly that the visually impaired subject and the female are assigned to the same universe: one of corporeality, infirmity, and social marginality.

> You are 'going out' for the first time, Hajila. Your face completely hidden, leaving only one tiny gap exposed through which you peep to see where you are going ... The black triangle of your eye darts to right and left and to the right again, then ... 'O All-Highest! ... O gentle prophet! I stand still, I take a step forward, I glide through the air, I no longer feel the ground beneath my feet, I ... O, widows of Mohammed, come to my aid!' (19)

According to Frantz Fanon, the French-speaking West Indian psychiatrist and writer, who had fought alongside the Algerian freedom fighters during the Algerian war of liberation (1954–1962), attributes to the veil a "historic dynamism." Dream data reveals that the veiled woman is bewildered when she appears unveiled in public space, i.e., she has difficulty evaluating distances outdoors and to mark out her own silhouette: "The unveiled body seems to get away from itself, to go to pieces. There is an impression of being improperly dressed, even nude." Consequently, Fanon affirms that during the revolution, the Algerian female combatant in Western garments infiltrated the European precinct of the city "completely-nude," and thus had to "re-learn her body, re-install it in a totally revolutionary way."[16]

The disclosure accomplished by Fanon's essay, explicitly empowers the Algerian woman to "re-learn her body [and] re-install it in a totally revolutionary way." Furthermore, it institutes between Western and Third World feminisms a perimeter that most contemporary feminist activity is re-opening, both in politics and in scholarship.

Germaine Tillion, for instance, argues that "on the Muslim side of the Mediterranean," the veil forms not just an exotic outfit, "but a veritable border. On one side of this border, female societies stagnate; on the other side, there lives and progresses a national society which, by virtue of this fact, is but half a society."[17] Here, Tillion tackles the issue of women's correlation to nationalism in contemporary Maghrebi societies in terms that, today, hinder, as much as they promote feminist investigation of the question.

In placing the tradition-bound woman's universe in conflict with the modern State, and in emphasizing women's banishment from 'affirmative action' in Maghrebian societies, Tillion's conception represents a whole range of Western scholarship on women in post-independent Algeria. For instance, David Gordon affirms that years after independence,

> confused and economically ominous as the atmosphere was, the expectations of and for women were high. But the force of the legacy of centuries was soon to make itself felt. The gap between promise and reality, law and fact, was to widen.[18]

In fact, the promise of social justice for women was dropped right after independence in 1962. Thus, this democratic deficit by the country that had played an admirable role in anti-colonial wars caused an excruciating malaise.[19] The subordination of women to pseudo 'Islamic tradition,' and their subsequent exclusion from national life, was perceived by feminists to be a betrayal both of the women freedom fighters and of the Algerian Revolution itself. In this respect, Catherine Delcroix presented, in 1986, this issue in dichotomous terms. She affirms that,

> "in view of the Algerian women's higher level of education today, her under-representation can only foster frustration and obstruct the evolution of her personal status, and thus, of her emancipation."[20]

Delcroix argues that the electorate's traditionalist mentality is as accountable for women's exclusion as "the ideological system itself, which doesn't sufficiently mobilize the female population for fear of seeing a woman transgress her role as guardian of traditional values."[21] This argument echoes Tillion's identification of the veil as "a veritable border" splitting the nation because "the ideological system" prevents women from a significant participation in the country's development.

Thus, in cases where feminists in Muslim communities subject women's contention to class struggle or nationalism or anti-imperialism, it is fundamental to explore the post-revolutionary cultural changes. Conceding the nationalists' treachery of women in post-independent Algeria and underscoring the alliance of women's movements in the Third World, Nayereh Tohidi declares:

> Alone, a woman's movement can never transform the foundations of sexism and sexual oppression. Neither can a revolution, which seeks to transform class relationships, meet its goals if it does not incorporate the question of women's oppression. Specific demands of women must be incorporated into the national anti-imperialist movement and class struggle right from the beginning. The women's question should not be relegated to the days after the revolution.[22]

However, Peter R. Knauss's investigations of current male-female relations reveal that the state backed-up practices not only emasculate women but also "contain the social consequences of significant changes that have taken place in education and employment." This is done in the name of "patriarchy, which has become part of the warp and woof of Algerian political culture."[23] This is perceptible in the permanence of traditional social customs ordained by regressive interpretations of the *Shari'a* (Islamic law) and promoted by cynical political regimes ever since independence. These disempowering traditions have been confirmed in constrictive laws like the "Family Law" of 1984.[24]

Djebar's interest in the Algerian woman's body is in itself a rebellion against the harsh injunctions of 'Muslim society' that recommend the veiling of the female body, for it is considered a source of sacrilege, debauchery, and dishonor. The body is thus the locus of woman's alienation.[25] Furthermore, Djebar is perfectly conscious that a "woman's body is indeed problematic." Like many "modern feminist authors in the Arab World," she knows that if she wants to "achieve [her] right to literary speech, [she] must begin by re-conquering [her] body."[26]

Thus, Hajila brutally discovers that happiness is possible outside while being audaciously unveiled. For, on her way back from her parents' home, she notices in an ordinary public garden a scene that really overwhelms her:

> A woman with a pushchair has just sat down on one of the benches. She leans forward and picks up a baby :.. this unknown woman gives a peal of uninhibited laughter, her evident delight clearly legible on her face, which is framed by a halo of red hair. The baby wriggles, the woman laughs ... (27)

Opposing this spontaneous liberty and thrill, her mother's and her husband's speeches appear hollow and shallow. The mother is good at reciting plaintive litanies, and the husband acts like a rapist. Here, the novel examines the couple's sexual relationship — a daring issue in the Maghreb, when one considers the times and the culture for the discussion of sensual pleasures. This is reprehensible to the Muslim mentality. Tradition enjoins arranged marriages determined by family status and wealth, in which love as a catalyst is superfluous. Djebar ventures to electrify the Algerian temperament, though to the Western reader her articulation of sensuality might be considered trite.

> The husband would cough: the indication for you to bring him an ashtray. You would enter that bedroom. There was a new bed ... It was too high for you; like a throne? or a platform? You would lie down, next to that other body. Careful not to brush against anything. A hand would fondle your breasts in the darkness, and you would try to draw in your stomach to avoid his groping fingers ... You would hold your breath, lying quiet still, waiting, wide awake. A little later, you would get up in the dark and go to lie on the mattress on the carpet at the foot of the modern bed. (17)

This *locus classicus* explores the couple's vicissitudes and the falsehood on which their relationship sometimes lies, and the novel, as a whole, compels 'The Man' to comprehend his relationship with his woman. This, in Joan Monego's words, implies that "there are ties to be broken and bridges to be built."[27]

Djebar's contribution to Maghrebi literature undeniably lies in her examination of women's liberation and the relationship between husband and wife. In Monego's terms,

> She lays bare the conflicts that spring forth from a woman's immature soul and catch her in a struggle between affirming her independent existence or of finding that affirmation only by yielding her will to the authority of a man.[28]

Djebar intimates that women ought not to consider each other as potential foes, but must direct their attention to the fact that they share a common fate. According to Djebar, this is the *sine qua non* condition for women's salvation. *A Sister to Scheherezade* powerfully epitomizes a bonding between women, who wisely comprehend that their prisons are in the marrow of their bones. For even those unveiled women like Isma are entangled in invisible veils. Therefore, the question that one might ask is, how will the change for the Algerian woman be achieved? The author responds, "to talk among ourselves and to look; to look outside; to look beyond the walls and persons!"[29] This answer seems flimsy in comparison to the prevailing sociopolitical situation in Algeria. While she exhorts her heroines to progress with determination and audacity, she provides them with no pragmatic agenda to emancipate themselves. Her revelations of the circumstances that have maintained women in bondage will probably have no significant impact on most Algerians. As far as the Algerian woman is concerned, it seems that her emancipation is simply like an ebb and flow or, in Djebar's terms, "the past paralyzed in the present and the present midwife of the future."[30]

Confronting this question, Marie-Blanche Tahon castigates Djebar for her prudent method and her flimsy attitude as an expatriate intellectual whose existence is different from that of her heroines. Tahon explains the author's difficulty, as she understands it, "She is immediately suspected of wanting to deny the Arab-Islamic values, those of her people, in order to promote Western values, those of the occupier."[31] For Djebar had a bitter experience with the publication of her first novel, *La Soif* (1957) and since then has adopted a cautious strategy to women's emancipation. The sturdy bridges she means to build, and the bonding in affliction that she delineates, are moderately hinted at. However, her novels do not articulate fervent appeals to construct a new society. When Isma goes to the help of Hajila, she is not performing a militant act. She is simply achieving what Fedwa Malti-Douglas terms Homosociality.[32]

If her earlier novels delivered a daring call for a mutual comprehension and a true communication between the sexes, *A Sister to Scheherazade* reproduces no such aspiration. Djebar discards this issue in favor of a bonding between women. However, this alliance, whose objective is reciprocal empathy, is of ill omen for it foretells no affirmative changes other than those invoked in the narrative.

In *Veil of Shame*, Evelyne Accad says that Assia Djebar's fiction reflects:

> The exact path of women's liberation in Algeria, which stopped dead after independence. A reflection of her country's line of action, Assia Djebar's novels indicate a progression and a regression, because like Algeria's revolution, Djebar's was not a total and profound one. The rebellious rage voiced in the fifties and sixties has given way to a moderate whimper. The nationalistic spirit so necessary for the revolutionaries to oust the French colonizers became counter-revolutionary after the oppressor had been evicted, in that traditional laws were re-instituted which deprived women of the [meager] rights they had enjoyed under colonial rule.[33]

On the other hand, women's electoral backing for the Islamists stunned Algerian feminists. This backing had already been proclaimed in a rally when, for the first time in the nation's history, scores of veiled women marched in procession.[34] According to Aissa Khelladi,[35] these women marched in favor of 'Islamic womanhood' not because they were baffled, but because the Islamist parties' ethical and political agenda and appeal for social justice went to their hearts. Whereas for different reasons, (due to anti-Western grievances) they remained indifferent to "liberals' calls" for women's rights and liberation. And now that the regime rules the country with a rod of iron[36] and Algerian nationalism has become a tyrannical dogma in the hands of a myriad of corrupt government bureaucracy and a backward-looking 'elite,'[37] and when the "Islamists' power" challenges that of the 'government,' it is beside the point to construe Algerian fiction as a self-sufficient aesthetical discourse, especially if it involves political polemics in Algeria. We should, rather, substantiate literature's nexus to those movements of opposition that have surfaced after the October 1988 riots against unemployment and corruption.[38] These forces compelled the Army to amend the constitution and consent to the formation/legalization of political parties that were to take part in what proved to be a hapless electoral process.[39] And now that we have experienced the hardships of this postelectoral process, the subsequent civil war, and taken into account the tragic sociopolitical situation in Algeria, I can simply affirm that the anxieties manifested in Djebar's fiction are substantiated by the national context.

In contemporary Morocco, almost over fourteen centuries after the advent of Islam, women's condition is still dreadful. One of the novels published recently in Morocco conveys a version of self-reliance that is so circumscribed by a misogynistic system that it is hard to see as a 'feminist.' Leila Abouzeid's *Year of the Elephant: A Moroccan Woman's Journey Toward Independence* (1989), critiques the subjection of women and the constraints women negotiate daily in marriage or the nuclear family, and voices pessimism about the possibility of lifting these burdens. This work combines the aesthetic and the political, the formal and the ideological, the private and the public. The approach of inserting the story of a woman's physical and moral abuse in the frame of the Moroccan struggle for independence, which calls back a captivating moment in the country's and Moroccan women's history, compels Maghrebi and non-Maghrebi readers alike not to take women's harassment lightheartedly.[40]

While Abouzeid's divorced protagonist, Zahra, epitomizes a destitute woman in post-independence Morocco, she implicitly criticizes the socioeconomic changes and the corruption of the new rulers, those who have replaced the French colonizers. Zahra's opinions, emotions, and recollections show how history is individually experienced, how it is processed, and how it is verbalized and represented.

Zahra is almost homeless and unable to make both ends meet after being a heroine during the war of independence. Abouzeid conceives a protagonist of an earlier period because she wants to capitalize on both the symbolic significance bestowed upon women's role during the Resistance and to elude the accusation of writing autobiographically, i.e., writing only to broach her own preoccupations.

Year of the Elephant [41] is an "event in cross-cultural literary history."[42] It is the first novel by a Moroccan woman to be translated from Arabic into English. This work, through the tribulation of one impoverished working-class woman, discusses Morocco's struggle for independence and its consequence on the nation. Zahra's predicament synecdochically relates her decrepitude and personal pathos to the decrepitude and pathos of Morocco as it moves through its own labyrinthine history. And though it is in many ways similar to some male writers' fiction about men and women and the ways into which they interact, the outlook throughout is that of the woman.

The author is an offshoot of the newly independent Morocco, and symbolizes the generation that came to adulthood under a new despotic and misogynist regime. The post-revolution generation's society is antithetical to that of their parents. Consequently, *Year of the Elephant* broaches fundamental issues such as equal rights under the law, equal access to economic wealth, and legal protection from physical and moral abuse. According to the author, these questions are very important to post-independence Morocco.

Leila Abouzeid is unquestionably giving credit to common people for the accomplishment of the Moroccan independence. Zahra becomes one of the 'flocks' of cheap and insignificant humanity that made the difference in the undeclared war against French rule. We read that the protagonist has sold her olive trees, jewels, and "everything worth selling for the cause. Resistance took the place of emeralds and rubies in [her] life, and today [she] feel[s] only contempt for such trinkets." (20)

Such has been the case with the blacksmiths, the homemakers, the spice merchants, the rug merchants, and the lorry drivers. To those who very often viewed in the history books and the media as 'the rank and file,' or simply 'terrorists,' Abouzeid confers faces and names. We come to know Rahal, the tall and thin spice merchant with "an eastern-style turban" and "a sixth finger like a tumor on his left hand;" (28) Hajj Ali, the "husky and enduringly cheerful blacksmith whose skill at his craft fueled his happiness and glowed like live coals under the bellows of his forge," and "whose love for his work was matched only by his love for his country;" (31) Safia and Roukia, the women who hide fugitives in their store houses; Walter, the "very fair skinned" German guard "married to a Moroccan woman from Chtouka;" (43) the rug merchant with a Berber name, Moha ou Alla; Faqih, the one-legged veteran of Dien Bien Phu.

Year of the Elephant derives its force from a conflation of personal and public experience, a historiographical mode in which 'subjective' and 'objective' historical terms become inseparable. Such a historiographical narrative process occurs throughout the novel, ironizing both radical subjectivity and public objectivity by baffling the attempts of its readers to tell the difference between them. In this work, the interior dramas of individuals reflect the exteriorized patterns of behavior they create with one another.

From the very opening chapter of the narrative, the author stresses the magnanimity of the people: "I dedicate this book to all those women and men who put their lives in danger for the sake of Morocco and did not expect to be rewarded or thanked for it." (V) She suggests that the majority of Moroccans took part in the struggle, including the monarch himself, King Mohammed V. Because of his backing of the major Nationalist party, *Istiqlal* (Independence), he was deported by the French military authorities and thus became a national hero. Zahra vividly describes this circumstance:

> When they exiled him, a deep collective grief had fallen over the nation and I mourned with the rest of my compatriots ... Fantastic what effect he had on our hearts! His exile had wrapped him in a sacred cloak, and for his sake the people had joined the resistance, as if he had become an ideal or a principle. Had the French not exiled him, their presence in Morocco would have continued much longer; I'm certain of that. (50)

Historic events 'animate' but do not 'dominate' this text. Her discourse is set against the backdrop of Morocco's Resistance to French rule, and its backlash on Moroccan women in particular. The political contestation is present and withheld, displaced most often by the gender outlook of the narrator "because the story of a woman's selfhood is inseparable from her sense of community"[43] against which the ordinary events of the story take place: the childhood and matrimony of the female narrator, the missions of the underground movement in which she plays a very decisive part, the ultimate victory of nationalist forces, the new regime which has socially promoted Zahra's husband,[44] the change that benefitted "a handful of people," (54) her divorce and her re-evaluation of what independence actually means, "independence was the one almighty goal, the key to paradise." (12) *Year of the Elephant* opens with Zahra's divorce and her feeling of having been treated inequitably.

I come back to my hometown feeling shattered and helpless. He had simply sat down and said, "Your papers will be sent to you along with whatever the law provides." My papers? How worthless a woman is if she can be returned with a receipt like some store-bought object! How utterly worthless! Those few seconds destroyed the whole foundation of my being, annihilated everything I trusted. My jaw dropped as I stared at him. "Why?" "I haven't got a reason."(1)

Zahra is then confronted to a gloomy future since her husband, her source of support, has repudiated her, and the religious legislation that has determined her existence is found unsatisfactory. The narrator exploits this situation to comment on the urgency for revision of 'family law,' which has been in practice in the Maghreb since independence. It should be noted that 'family laws' accord with the dominant ideology of each Maghrebi state. Thus, Abouzeid, like Djebar before, hits Moroccan men with a double whammy; not only should they not engage in debauchery, but they ought to also take a tough look at their attitudes toward tradition, the past, and women.

"Whatever the law provides." And what is that? Expenses for a hundred days. That shows the extent of the law's regard for women. Throw them out on the street with a hundred days of expenses. (11)

Here, the author critiques that premise of man's 'superiority' over women, frequently debated on the basis of Qur'an 2: 228[45] and 4: 34.[46] This postulate is unfounded because it is based on an erroneous explication of the Scriptures. What the Qur'an enunciates on man's rank *vis-a-vis* the woman simply affects his function as head of the family, being the provider and protector. Concerning divorce, women have a say in the arrangement as it is revealed in the Qur'an 65: 1.[47]

While *Year of the Elephant* is not as virulent a novel as *Vie et Agonie* or *A Sister to Scheherazade*, its narrator, Zahra, epitomizes the valiant and candid wife who interferes with the conception of a traditional family and the vision of progressive post-independence nationalism. "These contemporary female cosmopolitans" — Abouzeid, Djebar, Hedri —

may be treacherous in ways that significantly complicate, and possibly even nullify, the traditional description of postcolonial cosmopolitans' betrayals of local politics or Third World nationalisms. Each, in different ways, engages in battle with patriarchal and parochial belief systems.[48]

About this, it might be interesting to refer to Mai Ghoussoub's article, "Feminism — or the Eternal Masculine — in the Arab World," which concentrates on the near impossibility of oppositional feminist politics in Muslim countries:

The bitter reality is that Arab feminism, in the modern sense of the term, exists as a force only in the student milieu of Europe and America, to which a privileged few can escape, and in a growing but still very modest academic literature. The double knot tied by the fatal connections in Arab culture and politics between definitions of femininity and religion, and religion and nationality, have all but throttled any major women's revolt so far. Every assertion of the second sex can be charged — in a virtually simultaneous register — with impiety to Islam and treason to the nation.[49]

What does Zahra do? Whom does she turn to? In a society where parents are traditionally the source of security for their children, whether they are single, divorced, widowed, or in economic difficulty, she cannot turn to her parents for they are dead. She returns to her hometown: "A dying town" that "is trying to fight off death with hope and miracles," whose alleys are peopled by "broad-shouldered young men [who] stand leaning against dilapidated walls." (53) It is here that she still owns property, an inheritance from her parents that consists of one room in a house. She recalls her grandmother's recommendation that "a woman has nothing but her husband and her property, and that husbands cannot be trusted." (13)

The forty-year-old Zahra, who is "haunted by bitterness," has been married for twenty years "without ever clearly seeing the man" (1) she married. She had not even seen him before her engagement. He noticed her instead at her grandfather's door watching a musical procession pass by and sent his parents to ask for her hand, basing his choice on her long hair and dark eyes. "And the family decided to marry [her] off without ever asking for [her] thoughts." (17)

Now weary, alienated, and broke, she comes back to her hometown, as a "stranger among strangers," feeling like a freed prisoner returning to prison. Then, Zahra goes to visit the *Sheikh* (literally a religious leader) of the local shrine, whom she had known as a child. She is so thrilled by the eloquence of the verse that she thinks it is addressed to her. His Qur'anic recitation, "so despondent were they that the earth, for all its vastness and their own souls, seemed to close in upon them,"[50] seems to voice out her own plight. For a Western feminist reader, this is amazing; women facing such an impasse would go to a 'shrink,' but would not be expected to go to a religious leader for assistance. Besides, she has been divorced not because she is self-reliant and intractable but, rather, for the antithetical reason — she is too conventional. For the protagonist declares: "I don't eat with a fork. I don't speak French. I don't sit with men. I don't go out to fancy dinners ... I'm nothing but an old coin fit only for the museum shelf. Their positions in society now call for modern women." (8–9) Later, she would assert, "These days my husband needs a wife who will offer cigarettes to his guests and help pave the road to the top for him by any means necessary." (54)

However, despite such cultural discrepancies, Zahra's quandary is the same to that of any woman, in any society, who is divorced, uneducated, and without financial resources. Apart from "a maintenance allowance for three months and ten days" (9) she is compelled to find a way to ensure her subsistence and accommodation. This is neither a facile, nor an attainable task. Zahra's life as a small town daughter, a guerilla combatant, and a homemaker has not provided her with any background she can use in the demanding marketplace. Her brother-in-law informs her, "These days you need a high school degree to get any work at all. Soon they'll require a college degree, and some day soon a college degree won't even get you a job sweeping streets." To this malevolent and sassy observation, Zahra retorts, "I just want a job that will earn me an honorable living; I don't care what it is." And she adds defiantly, "I'm not looking for a government position." (66)

Although her sister and brother-in-law attempt to take her in, she declines the invitation with the severity, "I'm not anyone's inheritance," (65) a powerful proclamation of emancipation. But her sister perseveres. "Clearly she expects that like other divorced women I will abide by custom and live with her." (65) Zahra revolts: "Do you have legal custody of me?" (66) A rebuttal that she knows will engender years of disaffection between the two sisters. But she has decided to make her own way.

By the end of the story, Zahra has developed a new freedom and balance within herself and dispelled her earliest resentfulness. She has started a new life, she informs her old friend the *Sheikh*, which "is constituted of work, faith, and other things that aren't so important. The important thing is that I remember God and concentrate on this idea of mine that we are only passing through this life to build a road to the next one." (68)

Obviously, the protagonist does not take any pride in the political achievement of her own country that is "wallowing in filth" (9) and where "misery flows through the air and mingles through our very breath." (10) This is, by itself, eloquent. This manifests a sense of disenchantment in a revolution that was the catalyst of the masses. "I ... entered the struggle and carried out missions for my homeland. But now, what does my homeland do for me. The struggle has come to nothing."(24) Though women energetically took part in the Resistance, they have neither been compensated with admittance to formal politics nor are their issues being taken into account. The narrator implicitly admits that there are no facile solutions to the predicament that is sadly gripping her newly-independent fellow citizens.

> In the beginning of the Resistance, we believed the struggle would wash away all spite and malice, just as we thought that Independence would relieve our cares and heal our sores like miracle cures sold in the market. In fact, we loaded Independence down with a burden it could not bear. (67)

In her discussion of the liberation of women in Morocco, Abouzeid has favored the national liberation discourse as a strategy to deal with women as part of the movement for political and economic decolonization. Yet, if we consider the significance of women's roles in the Moroccan struggle for independence, we are impressed by their humility. While women became more committed to Resistance and politics, their activities did not oppose the predominating gender expectations. They were normally ascribed the chores traditionally identified with women, like nursing, cooking, carrying weapons, and concealing guerilla fighters. They executed strategies conceived by others, but they did not take part in the decision-making discussions. As Judith E. Tucker observes, "Instead of introducing new roles for women, the old ones were imbued with new respect."[51] Besides, the emphasis on the solidarity of men and women in the struggle for decolonization, put off the crucial consideration of the discrepancies of power between men and women in the Moroccan society. Without the rectification of the latter, the prospect of radical transformations in the postcolonial societies will remain unrealized as it is accurately portrayed in *Year of the Elephant*.

It should be noted, though, that the narrator's disenchantment coupled with domestic violence first appeared at home when she discovered her husband's love affair with the secretary. When she vehemently asked him whether the "finance department" is paying the bills of the hotel that has been turned into a whorehouse, insinuating the corruption of the new regime, he slapped her.

> Holding my face with one hand, I pointed at him with the other and shouted with all my strength, as if addressing an imaginary crowd. "And we are waiting for reforms to come from the likes of these! You're more dangerous than the colonizers!" (55)

An accusation that expresses the malaise and fury these women are suffering from. They witness the failings of these men who are supposed to bring up the long-promised changes.

Unable to find a suitable job in a factory she finally accepts a position as a cleaner at the French Cultural Center, and realizes that "secretaries and office boys are running the country."(65) As other Moroccan women who have not been strangers to political activity, which is a significant contribution to the national liberation struggle in the Maghreb, she bitterly remembers the time when very few could carry out the missions she has bravely taken:

> I fastened my belt, slipped the pistols wrapped in cloth inside my blouse and recalled my grandfather speaking of Asma, who took food to the Prophet Mohammed and to her own father Abu Bakr, when they were hiding from their enemies in a cave during their flight from Mecca to Medina ... The comparison shook me and made me realize that the struggle has been the same down through the centuries, in that women, too, have always taken their part in it. (39)

This reminiscence clearly shows the protagonist's awareness of her Islamic heritage. She adopts as her role model one of the founding mothers of Islam, those women who joined in the early religious conquests and were part of the progressive *cadres* of Islamization. With those predecessors as her example, Zahra, like her secular sister Zhor Lazrak[52] or the Egyptian activist Zainab Al-Ghazali, regards her struggle as decisive for the survival of Islamic ethics and her achievement as redemptive. Furthermore, Zahra means "to preserve and to redefine for the given historical moment the cultural images which underwrite collective action ... of a people seeking to liberate themselves."[53]

The publication in French of *Vie et Agonie* (1978), has marked contemporary Tunisian literature. This piece of fiction signifies a sense of discouragement, if not resignation, with respect to women's situation in Tunisia. In other words, this novel pictures the backslide of Tunisian society and the imprisonment of its women. It also aims at reflecting and expressing women's challenges and aspirations vis-a-vis the ideology that prevails in post-independence Tunisia. However, when Tunisian women writers

> are not discussed solely in terms of their attention to the conjugal couple, they are nonetheless treated with a certain condescension because their writing is considered to be trite and to serve, at best, to demonstrate pregiven ideologies, especially anticolonial, democratic, and feminist ideologies. While it may be acknowledged that women's demonstrations of feminist ideologies are necessary and valuable, it is assumed that they are only marginally pertinent to literary activity per se, that is, the process of interrogating the conditions of possibility of meaning and disrupting the fixed meanings that underwrite the existing social order.[54]

In picturing the material and subjective reality of a woman in a Third-World country and advocating a feminist, sexual, and social liberation, it seems that Souad Hedri "casts doubt on the clear-cut opposition between, on the one hand, a [tradition] founded on the sacred, which muzzles and even asphyxiates women, and, on the other, a [European] culture founded on secularism and the rights of man, which liberate women."[55]

With respect to the global and regional contexts, the author is conscious that her role as an intellectual is not to enunciate the determination of the society (in the Gramscian sense) but, rather, "to struggle against the forms of power that transform [her] into its object and instrument in the sphere of 'knowledge,' 'truth,' 'consciousness,' and 'discourse,'" through a micropolitics that is cognizant of specificity and contingency.[56]

Nevertheless, while admitting the relevance of Gilles Deleuze's concept of micropolitics and Foucault's examination of the power/knowledge nexus[57] in validating the futility of trying to account for social strife within the structure of a single narrative, intellectuals such as Edward Said, Radha Radhakrishnan, and Gayatri Spivak question their proclamation that "the great narratives of emancipation are over." Said affirms that this declaration, however satisfactory at a particular level of representation, operates to deter any potential reaction from subordinate groups whose collective emancipatory discourses can, from this vantage point, only play into the hands of power.[58]

Spivak puts forward a related point when she contends in "Can the Subaltern speak?" that the prioritization of concrete experience by Foucault and Deleuze impedes

> the necessity of the difficult task of counterhegemonic ideological production ... It has helped positivist empiricism — the justifying foundation of advanced capitalist neocolonialism — to define its own arena as "concrete experience" "what actually happens." Indeed, the concrete experience, that is the guarantor of the political appeal of prisoners, soldiers, and schoolchildren, is disclosed through the concrete experience of the intellectual, the one who diagnoses the episteme.[59]

So when I probe Souad Hedri's protagonist, I notice that besides her incessant outings that outraged her parents, she starts smoking, a practice inconsistent with the Islamic culture of the region; Maghrebi tradition dissuades women from smoking. The act is considered exclusively to be a man's domain. Moreover, as Islam and Maghrebi culture do not conceive of a union out of marriage, Aida exhorts her sister to talk the matter over with Raouf. For "marriage is ideally the place where individual desire finds public sign and body."⁶⁰ After a premonitory vision, she decides to bring up the subject. He confesses that he is already engaged to a cousin of his. He claims that he has to respect his family's will. Arranged marriages between wealthy relatives are quite common within his social group. As often happens with endogamy, the objective is to keep the inheritance from alien hands.

> Ever since Raouf was a student, his parents had chosen for him the prettiest of his cousins. A juvenile love was born in the girl's heart. Raouf loved her keenly, without passion and desire. He was sensible and amused by the fiancee's furtive looks and half-smiles, more expressive than inflamed sermons. She was getting ready for the happy event for quite some time. Did he have the right to break such a tender heart?

Through this instance, the novel assumes the centrality of the family and society to the elaboration and enforcement of specific views of male and female behavior, as well as to the issue of how women and men should interact. However, the relevance of the family to the daily construction of gender roles and relations is never challenged. There is a tendency to assume the hegemony of a 'traditional' family, defined and regulated by Islamic law, which varies from class to class.

Although Hedri's narrative does not reconcile the groups who stand in conflict in the fiction by integrating them into a new communal whole, it does illustrate some of the means which can alleviate apprehensions about identity so that people reconcile themselves with the differences that both inhabit them and demarcate them from others.

With the protagonist's death, the author epitomizes the dead end that Tunisian women have reached. There has been a frustration about the fact that progressive personal status laws have not, on the whole, encouraged the change of negative attitudes toward women. This, combined with the rise of state conservatism,⁶¹ has been a fundamental catalyst responsible for the organization of an association and the publication of a periodical, *Nisa'a*.⁶² Both forums broached debates about the way in which personal experiences are also political experiences, a philosophy considered as a novelty in Tunisia and the rest of the Maghreb. They also underscored the importance of comprehending these experiences as part of a larger social and political preoccupation for development and democratization.

During its first year of publication, *Nisa'a*, similar to *Vie et Agonie*, discussed the issues of sexism, violence against women, sexuality, desegregation, and the conservative backlash against the 1956 Tunisian personal status law. Lately, there have emerged two other structures. One, the Tunis Association of African Women for Research, formed in 1989 to "highlight the role of women in development ... and create a favorable gender focused development."⁶³ The second was Women Democrats, which "works to integrate women in society and to build up a new society based on men and women working together."⁶⁴

If these women seem to be growing more straightforward in their critique of the current sociopolitical dispositions, I can hardly believe that their conceptions of gender relations have repercussions on all social groups. Yet, it appears that such an investigation has, at least, a substantial middle-class public. For one should bear in mind that there are still reticent voices that rise against women's emancipation:

> All revealed laws agree that a woman is weaker than a man, that she is his inferior in body and comprehension, and that 'men are superior to women.' Thus, men rightfully have supremacy over women ... and women's submission to men is part of God's order ... Women were created for men's earthly pleasures and in order to take care of domestic affairs; God did not create them to attempt to defeat the men, nor to give opinions or establish policies. If God had wanted to do so, He would have given women courage, intrepidity, chivalry, and gallant audacity, which is not the case. And if women wanted to behave like men and carry heavy burdens to be his equal ... would this not be a shirking of the duty assigned them by the Almighty?⁶⁵

This quotation powerfully configures a kind of orthodox misogyny in the Maghreb. It illustrates ongoing insults and hierarchicalization of women's status in the area. Based explicitly and systematically upon an ideal of patriarchal domination, which authorized women's subjugation, this quotation also reinforces my perception of the vulnerability of Tunisian women in a dangerous and unpredictable sociopolitical context.

One should bear in mind that the Qur'an provides women political rights, which they faithfully used during the prophet's lifetime, but the early Caliphs overlooked the rights. The Qur'an confers women the liberty to work — women in Islam are under a social and religious obligation to work, as no development is conceivable without women's participation in the work force.

Much more threatening than working outside the home, however, is women's interest in politics. This point is explicitly presented in a *Hadith* in Bukhari, which says that "those who entrust their affairs to a woman will never know prosperity!"⁶⁶ Not only this, *Hadith* is the singular evidence manipulated by those who want to ostracize women from public life and relegate them to the household; but it is so momentous that it is virtually preposterous to address the issue of women's political rights without mentioning it. For, there are still some authorities in Islam who in their endeavor to belittle women's role in Islamic history, assert that "Muslim women played no role in public affairs, despite all the rights that Islam gave them."⁶⁷ They seem to forget that neither have millions of men in the 'Arab World!'

The question that we may ask is to what extent can one re-interpret the sacrosanct texts? Be it Zahra's husband or any Muslim power structure, not only have the Scriptures always been manipulated, but also their application has always been a justification of the practice of power in Muslim societies. Since all authority from the seventh century on, was only scripturally validated, political groups and economic stakes prompted the devising of erroneous traditions. In this conjecture of political interests and tensions in post-independence Algeria, Morocco, and Tunisia, religious discourse has proliferated along with practices that have (thus far) confirmed specific privileges. In this respect, *Year of the Elephant* — as an idiosyncratic illustration — stands against the power's discourse and Abouzeid is articulating herself instead of serving as an echo chamber for the frenzy of the potentates. As Fatima Mernissi points out,

> those who read in the seventh-century texts, the necessity to deprive half of the Muslim population — women — of the exercise of their political rights, [are afraid of] democracy and the exercise by all citizens, whatever their sex, of their public rights.⁶⁸

Zahra becomes a self-reliant woman but in an inconsequential restricted way, that few feminists would idealize. Her experience undoubtedly does not correspond to that of most Western feminists. She is neither a Westernized woman nor a Western woman, but a Muslim Moroccan woman who finds contentment in Islam. For the narrator, Islam, truly comprehended, can be a catalyst for feminist change. Zahra is the result of a distinct tradition, a separate contingency. The author illustrates this discrepancy, in her fruitful endeavor to integrate her heroine's enfranchisement and its inherent difficulties to the broader question of national independence and its complexities. A woman's ordeal is a trope for the whole community. This is a conception that has more to do with Maghrebi views of the significance of the society than with Western notions of individualism. The narrative does not make a doctrinal assertion, no political 'mumbo jumbo,' but genuinely broaches in fictional form the tangible life condition of a real Muslim woman. As Barbara Harlow indicates, this narrative "analyzes the past, including the symbolic heritage, in order to open up the possibilities of the future."⁶⁹

Because political usefulness of a representation is the issue that is at stake here, the line separating culture from politics in feminist study must be revealed. As Rabia Abdelkrim-Chikh points out:

It is not so much a matter of consuming secularism as of producing women's identity articulated to a culture and a history, while simultaneously contributing to the deconstruction of all models and monopolies. This elaboration of women's identity, which must pass by way of equality without being fixed there, will make possible the birth of ... a world that will no longer destroy alterity by virtue of its inscription, solely within the abstract rights of 'man,' but will instead produce concrete plurality in which difference will not be discriminated against.[70]

Assia Djebar, Leila Abouzeid, and Souad Hedri are not producing texts about how Maghrebi women are victimized and 'spat upon,' their discourse is about Maghrebi women and their arrangements with men and women from their respective communities. These writers are simply depicting their reality from their vantage point.

Rather than suggesting, for instance, that the horrendous political atmosphere of Algeria, Morocco, and Tunisia is a consequence of an underdeveloped culture, Djebar, Aboueid, and Hedri assume that this hostile sociopolitical situation is the result of the authoritarian discourses of nationalism and patriarchy. *A Sister to Scheherazade, Year of the Elephant,* and *Vie et Agonie* explore the consequences that nationalist definitions have on their respective heroines, as individuals, and on the nation. Therefore, Hajila, Zahra, and Leila's dedication is to the family, rather than to the nation, and especially to the women in the family. The coherence and pathos in these novels powerfully highlight a bigger story — the moral despair that permeates the Maghreb. The careful and elaborate depiction of the self enables all these authors to examine family and national history as well as collective and individual experience.

The force of these three novels stems from their respective authors' talent to express the informative and sharp forms of knowledge, that political and personal dissatisfaction affect the postcolonial subjects. These narratives are used to form a bridge between the history with which the authors struggled and the history formed by their readers' encounters with the historical objects constituted by these texts. By doing so, they explore occult relations between individual and collective human experience, and thereby discover new ways to recount individual and collective history. In other words, their novels are, according to Bernard Bell, both "private and public linguistic enactments of human relationships reflecting ethical decisions inside and outside of the text."[71]

Rather than returning to ethnographic interpretations of literature and culture, the substantial work of scholars as different as Edward Said and Gayatri Spivak, reveals that the investigation of a given literature or culture must delve into the processes by which it is made up as an object of knowledge and the political stakes of those processes. I have argued that, rather than retracting from the historical demands pertinent to the Maghreb of their time, Djebar, Abouzeid, and Hedri have thrown all of their stamina, in these works, into helping their countries write themselves out of their evident interminable miseries.

"Life and history are put into writing, and then disassembled, and the fictions of family and nation are exposed in the process."[72] And these novelists, who deliberately intertwine history, Islam, politics, and reality, do not simplify those issues of authorial intention and the artwork's ideological significance. The protagonists' elaborated how cosmopolitan voices could be interpreted as the writers' own. Nevertheless, 'Western' or cosmopolitan, the philosophical tendency of these authors might be that they are concerned with an authentic feminist and social liberation.

I suppose that one of the predominant trends touching Maghrebi women is the surge of 'fundamentalism.' But if we are to evaluate accurately women's expectations in Muslim societies, we have to renounce simplistic *clichés* that show fundamentalism as a demonstration of regressive medieval archaism, and comprehend it on the contrary as a political manifesto about men and women enduring puzzling, intense changes influencing their economic and political identity — changes so penetrating and varied that they prompt profound fears. Yet, in both Algeria and Tunisia, and to a lesser degree in Morocco, 'Islamism' has appeared as an ideology distinguishing the social and political programs of the youthful generations of men and women from the older generation whose legitimacy they contest.

Frantz Fanon asked, "What does a black man want?"[73] In this paper, I have asked myself what these Maghrebi women want. Their fictional works are not art for art's sake or text for text's sake. Djebar, Abouzeid, and Hedri have wanted to communicate something very specific to the Muslim men and women of their societies. They have reminded them that women were militant partners with their men in the time of Muhammad and the early *Califat*, but later veiled ánd segregated in the tradition of underdeveloped Arab countries.

These three novelists are taking a stand against women's maltreatment in their respective Muslim communities, which, alas, condone these acts. They are simply reminding us that Islam is not what Muslims are doing to half of the society.

Endnotes
1. Fedwa Tuqan, *A Mountainous Journey: An Autobiography*, trans., Olive Kenny, (London: The Women's Press, 1990) p. 12.

2. Juliette Minces, *The House of Obedience*, (London: Zed Press, 1982), p. 25.
3. Gloria Wade-Gayles, *No Crystal Stair: Visions of Race and Sex in Black Women's Fiction* (New York: Pilgrim Press, 1984) argues that "fiction is often a mirror of reality," and that African-American women novelists create "an imaginary world that is strikingly similar to the real world," p. 56.
4. See Mounira Charrad, "State and Gender in the Maghrib," *Middle East Report*, No. 163 (March-April 1990) pp. 19-24.
5. Barbara Harlow, "Introduction," in Malek Alloula, *The Colonial Harem* (Minneapolis: University of Minnesota Press, 1986) p. xxi.
6. Assia Djebar, *Fantasia, an Algerian Cavalcade* (London: Quartet, 1985) p. 59.
7. Ibid., p. 215.
8. Germaine Tillion, *The Harem and Its Cousins*, quoted in Assia Djebar, *Scheherazade*, op. cit., p. 5.
9. "Se délivrent . . . tout à fait du rapport d'ombre entretenu des siècles durant avec leur propre corps." Assia Djebar, *Femmes d'Alger dans leur Appartement* (Paris: des femmes, 1980) p. 9.
10. Throughout this novel, Djebar delivers a strong critique of mothers who make themselves the instruments of repression.
11. Rabia Abdelkrim-Chikh, "Les enjeux Politiques et Symboliques de la Lutte des Femmes pour l'Egalite entre les Sexes en Algerie," *Peuples Mediterraneens* 48-9 (July-Dec. 1988): 276.
12. Winifred Woodhull, *Transfigurations of the Maghreb: Feminism, Decolonization, and Literatures*, (Minneapolis: University of Minnesota Press, 1993) p. 87.
13. "Little did Shahrazade know, when she stepped into the textual world of *The Thousand and One Nights* that she would one day become a pawn in this game of gender politics. Little did she know that she would engender (in both senses) modern texts that would recast her own story. Little did she know that her control of narration . . . would be used to argue in favor of the Arab woman's access to discourse." Fedwa Malti Douglas, *Woman's Body, Woman's Word: Gender and Discourse* in Arabo-Islamic Writing, (Princeton, NJ: Princeton University Press, 1991) p. 5.
14. Assia Djebar, *Femmes d'Alger*, op. cit., p. 171: "Femmes en attente toujours [dans] cette atmosphere rarefiee de la claustration."
15. Assia Djebar, *Fantasia*, op. cit., p. 138.
16. Frantz Fanon, "Algeria Unveiled," in *A Dying Colonialism*, (New York: Groove Press, 1967) p. 42. It should be mentioned, though, that at the beginning of the Algerian revolution, which lasted eight violent years (November 1954-July 1962), wearing the veil suggested women's loyalty to cultural traditions and their resistance to French aggression. Consequently, female combatants began concealing weapons and explosive devices under their veils. Later, Algerian women continued their guerrilla activity in Western dress, hiding bombs in their bags rather than in the folds of their veils.
17. Germaine Tillion, "Les Femmes et le Voile," in *Etudes Maghrébines: Mélange Charles-Andre Julien*, ed. Pierre Marthelot and Andre Raymond (Paris: P.U.F, 1964) p. 29.

18. David C. Gordon, *Women of Algeria*, (Cambridge, Mass.: Harvard University Press, 1968) p. 61.
19. Fadela M'rabet, *La Femme Algérienne, suivi de Les Algériennes*, (Paris: Maspero, 1969).
20. Catherine Delcroix, *Espoirs et Réalité de la Femme Arabe (Algérie, Egypte)*, (Paris: l'Harmattan, 1986) p. 39.
21. Ibid., p. 138-139.
22. Nayereh Tohidi, "Gender and Islamic Fundamentalism: Feminist Politics in Iran," in *Third World Women and the Politics of Feminism*, ed. Chandra Talpade Mohanty, et al., (Bloomington and Indianapolis: Indiana University Press, 1991) p. 260.
23. Peter R. Knauss, *The Persistence of Patriarchy: Class, Gender, and Ideology in Twentieth Century Algeria*, (New York: Praeger, 1987), p. 137–41.
24. In 1984, the most reactionary and cynical government of Colonel-President Chadli Benjedid concocted the notorious Code de la Famille (family law). Under this law, women remain legal minors; a woman's decision to marry must be authorized by a guardian; and it is tedious and disastrous for women to initiate divorce.
25. In *Le Corps dans la Tradition au Maghreb,* (Paris: Presses Universitaires de France, 1984) p. 23, Malek Chebel views corporeality in the Maghreb in dichotomous terms: "compared to the complete liberty of expression left to the male body, that of the young girl is very early submitted to a repertory of prohibitions . . . The young boy can roll around in all directions, raise his legs in the air, proceed to a complete uncovering of his body, and appreciate precociously its possibilties and its limits. The girl, in contrast, can neither lie down as she would probably have a tendency to do, imitating her little brother or creating original positions, nor raise her legs in the air, nor open her thighs, nor spread her knees when she is seated, nor jump if she is older."
26. Malti Douglas Fedwa, op. cit., p. 110.
27. Joan Phyllis Monego, *Maghrebian Literature in French*, (Boston: Twayne Publishers, 1984) p. 138.
28. Ibid., p. 143.
29. Assia Djebar, *Femmes d'Alger*, op. cit., p. 68: "Parler entre nous et regarder. Regarder dehors, regarder hors des murs et des prisons."
30. Assia Djebar, "Nous Boitons en Croyant Danser," *Jeune Afrique*, No. 351, (October 1, 1967), pp. 38–39: "Le passe paralyse dans le present et le present accoucheur d'avenir."
31. Marie Blanche Tahon, "Review of Femmes d'Alger dans leur Appartement," in *Ecriture Francaise dans le Monde, la Tribune des Francophones*, No. 5 (1981) p. 114.
32. Homosocial must be differentiated from homosexual. It is not a libidinous relationship, but rather a social relationship between two persons of the same gender. "There is a tendency in the West to interpret examples of homosociality as indexes of latent or overt homosexuality. But this is really a reflection of the obsessional relationship of Western culture with

homosexuality, and the culture's homophobia, since the later Middle Ages." Malti Douglas Fedwa, op. cit., p. 15.

33. Evelyne Accad, *Veil of Shame: The Role of Women in the Modern Fiction of North Africa and the Arab World*, (Sherbrooke, Quebec: Editions Naaman, 1978) p. 47.
34. The December 1989 impressive demonstration initiated by the Islamic League in commemoration of the "Islamic woman."
35. Aissa Khelladi, "L'homme est-il l'avenir de la femme?" *Ounoutha* (April 1991): 19.
36. I am indebted to Lahouari Addi, "Le Regime Algerien et ses Oppositions," *El-Watan*, (Nov. 23 1995).
37. "Dans l'Algerie independante, le Pouvoir politique ne s'est pratiquement jamais trouve en face d'intellectuels contestataires." Youcef Zirem, "Intellectuels Algeriens: La Sempiternelle Compromission," *La Nation 130*, (January 16-22, 1996) p. 21.
38. "Les evenements d'Octobre 1988 revelent precisement la manifestation de la conscience de soi d'une societe desirant s'affranchir d'un . . . assujettissement. . . vecu par tous comme le resultat d'une politique autoritaire." Sidi Mohamed Barkat, "Algerie: Vers L'Etat Islamique?" *Peuples Mediterreens* 52–53 (July–Dec. 1990): 74.
39. In the legislative elections of Dec. 27, 1991, the Islamic Salvation Front (FIS) obtained a majority of seats in the first round. This success, induced a military coup that overthrew Colonel-President Chadli Benjedid, called off the second round of elections, and incarcerated thousands of Algerians in concentration camps in the Sahara. Though it seemed that the FIS would not get the two-thirds majority indispensable to change the Algerian constitution, the Army, pretending that they were opposing the establishment of an Islamic state, feared that a FIS victory would spur the end of their privileges, the government's nepotism, and the Nomenklatura's bureaucratic inefficiency and corruption that have been tolerated ever since independence.
40. A comparable approach is evident in the Algerian Yamina Mechakra, *La Grotte Eclatee, 1979,* (Algiers: ENAL, 1986).
41. "Have you not seen how your Lord dealt with the owners of the elephants? Did he not make their plot go astray? And sent against them birds in flocks, striking them with stones. And made them like an empty field of stalks." Qur'an 105:5. Muhammad Taqi-Uddine Al-Hilali & Muhammad Muhsin Khan, *Interpretations of the Meanings of the Noble Qur'an in the English Language, 1993,* (Riyadh: Maktaba Dar-es-Salam, 1994) p. 968. Leila Abouzeid gives the Moroccan struggle weightiness in Islamic history by equating it to a decisive battle in early Islam, when alien tribes riding thirteen elephants marched on the shrine at Mecca. The battle of "Year of the Elephant," as it is recorded in the Holy Qur'an, was a victory, not because the Muslims outnumbered their enemy, but thanks to the backing of flocks of birds which miraculously "air-raided that army with small stones slightly bigger than a lentil seed . . . Such was the victory bestowed by Allah to the people of Mecca."

42. Elizabeth Fernea, "Introduction" to Leila Abouzeid, *Year of the Elephant*, (Austin: The University of Texas Press, 1989), p. xi.
43. Bernice Johnson Reagon and Susan Stanford Friedman, "Women's Autobiographical Selves: Theory and Practice," in *The Private Self: Theory and Practice of Women's Autobiographical Writings*, ed. Shari Benstock (Chapel Hill: University of North Carolina Press, 1988) p. 43.
44. Throughout the narrative, the name of the husband is witheld from the reader. It only appears for the first and the last time at the the end of the text. A similar technique is used in *A Sister to Scheherazade*.
45. ". . . And they (women) have rights (over their husbands) similar (to those of their husbands) over them . . . but men have a degree (of responsibility) over them. And Allah is All-Mighty, All-Wise." Muhammad Taqi-Uddine Al-Hilali & Muhammad Muhsin Khan, *Interpretations of the Meanings of the Noble Qur'an in the English Language*, op. cit., p. 56.
46. "Men are the protectors and maintainers of women . . . " Ibid., p. 130.
47. "When you divorce women . . . fear Allah your Lord, and turn them not out of their (husband's) homes, nor shall they (themselves) leave, except in case they are guilty of some moral turpitude. And those are the set limits of Allah. And whosoever transgresses the set limits of Allah, then indeed he has wronged himself." Op. cit., pp. 877–878.
48. Mia Carter, "Cosmopolitanism and Communion: Re-Negotiating Relations in Sara Suleri's Meatless Days," in Articulating the Global and the Local, ed. Ann Cvetkovich and Douglas Kellner, (Boulder: Westview Press, 1997).
49. Mai Ghoussoub, "Feminism — or the Eternal Masculine — in the Arab World," *New Left Review* 161 (Jan–Feb 1987): 17.
50. Holy Qur'an (9: 118).
51. Judith E. Tucker, ed., *Arab Women: Old Boundaries, New Frontiers*, (Bloomington: Indiana University Press, 1993), p. 42.
52. Sophie Bessis and Souhayr Belhassen, *Femmes du Maghreb: L'enjeu*, (Paris: J. C. Lattes, 1992), p. 70.
53. Barbara Harlow, Resistance Literature, (New York: Methuen, 1987), p. 82.
54. Winifred Woodhull, *Transfigurations of the Maghreb: Feminism, Decolonization and Literatures*, (Minneapolis: University of Minnesota Press, 1993) p. 78.
55. Rabia Abdelkrim-Chikh, "Les Femmes Exogames: Entre la Loi de Dieu et les Droits de l'Homme," *Annuaire de l'Afrique du Nord* 27 (1988): 237.
56. Radha Radhakrishnan, "Toward an Effective Intellectual: Foucault or Gramsci?" in *Intellectuals: Aesthetics, Politics, Academics*, ed. Bruce Robbins, (Minneapolis: University of Minnesota Press, 1990) p. 68.
57. Michel Foucault, "Intellectuals and Power," in *Language, Counter-Memory, Practice*, ed. Donald Bouchard, (Ithaka, N. Y.: Cornell University Press, 1980) p. 260.
58. Edward Said, "Foucault and the Imagination of Power," in *Foucault: A Critical Reader*, ed. David Couzens Hoy, (Oxford: Basil Blackwell, 1986) p. 153.

59. Gayatri Chakravorty Spivak, "Can the Subaltern Speak?" in *Marxism and the Interpretation of Culture*, ed. Cary Nelson and Lawrence Grossberg, (Urbana and Chicago: University of Illinois Press, 1988) p. 275.
60. What is being said about 16th-century England is relevant to 20th-century Tunisia. Terry Eagleton, *William Shakespeare*, (Oxford: Basil Blackwell, 1986) p. 21.
61. Despite the apparent freedom that Tunisian women witnessed during the reign of President Habib Bourguiba (1957–1992), the situation under Colonel-President Zine-Eddine Benali (1992–   ) is not encouraging.
62. Tahar al-Haddad, the first male advocate of the liberation of women in Tunisia, organized a Cultural Club in 1984, and in 1985 the women's magazine, Nisa'a came into existence.
63. Society for International Development, "Report on Middle East and North African Region: Tunis Symposium," 64th Governing Council Meeting, November 17–18, 1989, Document 1, p. 7. in *Arab Women: Old Boundaries, New Frontiers*, ed. Judth E. Tucker, (Bloomington: Indiana University Press, 1993).
64. Ibid., p. 8.
65. Muhammad Tal'at Harb, *Tarbiyat al-Mar'a wal-Hijab*, (Cairo: Matba'at al-Taraqqu, 1899) pp. 10–19; cf. Thomas Philipp, "Feminism and Nationalist Politics in Egypt," in *Women in the Muslim World*, ed. Lois Beck and Nikki Keddie, (Cambridge, Mass.: Harvard University Press, 1978) p. 279.
66. Al-Bukhari, Al Sahih, *Collection of Authentic Hadiths*, (Beirut: Dar al-Ma'rifa, 1978), Vol. 4, p. 226. Through a historical and methodological investigation of this Hadith, Fatima Mernissi has established that this is a "weak" Hadith. It alludes to a woman who had taken power among the Persians between AD 629 and 632. Fatima Mernissi, *The Veil and the Male Elite: A Feminist Interpretation of Women's Rights in Islam*, 1987, trans. Mary Jo Lakeland (Reading, Mass. : Addison-Wesley, 1991) pp. 49–50.
67. Muhammad 'Arafa, *The Rights of Women in Islam*, (n.p.: Al-Maktab al-Islami, 1980), p. 149.
68. Fatima Mernissi, op. cit., p. 21.
69. Barbara Harlow, op. cit., p. 82.
70. Rabia Abdelkrim-Chikh, "Les Enjeux politiques et symboliques de la lutte des femmes pour l'egalite entre les sexes en Algerie," *Peuples Mediterraneens* 48–49 (July–Dec. 1989): 277.
71. Bernard W. Bell, The Afro-American Novel and its Tradition, (Amherst: The University of Massachusetts Press, 1987) p. 339.
72. Mia Carter, op. cit., p. 25.
73. Frantz Fanon, *Black Skin, White Masks*, trans. Charles Lamm Markmann, (New York: Grove Press,1967) p. 10.

Bibliography

Abdelkrim-Chikh, Rabia. "Les enjeux Politiques et Symboliques de la Lutte des Femmespour l'Egalité entre les Sexes en Algérie." *Peuples Méditerranéens*, (July–Dec.), 1988.

———. "Les Femmes Exogames: Entre la Loi de Dieu et les Droits de l'Homme." *Annuaire de l'Afrique du Nord*, 27, 1988.

Abouzeid, Leila. *Year of the Elephant: A Moroccan Woman's Journey toward Independence*. Trans. Barbara Parmenter. Austin, Texas: Center for Middle Eastern Studies, 1989.

Accad, Evelyne. *Veil of Shame: The Role of Women in the Modern Fiction of North Africa and the Arab World*. Sherbrooke, Quebec: Editions Naaman, 1978.

Al-Bukhari. *Al Sahih*. (Collection of Authentic Hadiths) Beirut: Dar al-Ma'rifa, 1978.

'Arafa, Muhammad. *The Rights of Women in Islam*. n.p.: Al-Maktab al-Islami, 1980.

Barkat, Sidi Mohamed. "Algérie: Vers L'Etat Islamique?" *Peuples Méditerranéens* 52–53, 1990.

Bell, Bernard W. *The Afro-American Novel and its Tradition*. Amherst: The University of Massachusetts Press, 1987.

Bessis Sophie and Souhayr Belhassen. *Femmes du Maghreb: L'enjeu*. Paris: J.C. Lattes, 1992.

Carter, Mia "Cosmopolitanism and Communion: Re-Negotiating Relations in Sara Suleri's *Meatless Days*," in *Articulating the Global and the Local*. Edited by Ann Cvetkovich and Douglas Kellner. Boulder: Westview Press, 1997.

Charrad, Mounira. "State and Gender in the Maghrib." *Middle East Report*, 163, March-April, 1990.

Chebel, Malek. *Le Corps dans la Tradition au Maghreb*. Paris: Presses Universitaires de France 1984.

Delcroix, Catherine. *Espoirs et Réalité de la Femme Arabe (Algérie, Egypte)*. Paris: l'Harmattan, 1986.

Djebar, Assia. *A Sister to Scheherazade*. London: Quartet, 1987.

———. *Fantasia, an Algerian Cavalcade*. London: Quartet, 1985.

———. *Femmes d'Alger dans leur Appartement*. Paris: des femmes, 1980.

———. "Nous Boitons en Croyant Danser," *Jeune Afrique*, 351, 1967.

Eagleton, Terry. *William Shakespeare*. Oxford: Basil Blackwell, 1986.

Fanon, Frantz. "Algeria Unveiled," in *A Dying Colonialism*. New York: Groove Press, 1967.

Fanon, Frantz. *Black Skin, White Masks*. Trans. Charles Lamm Markmann. New York: Groove Press, 1967.

Foucault, Michel. "Intellectuals and power" in *Language, Counter-Memory, Practice*. Edited by Donald Richard. Ithaka, N.Y.: Cornell University Press, 1980.

Ghoussoub, Mai. "Feminism — or the Eternal Masculine — in the Arab World." *New Left Review*, 161, 1987.

Gordon, David C. *Women of Algeria*. Cambridge, Mass.: Harvard Universiy Press, 1968.

Harlow, Barbara. "Introduction" in Malek Alloula, *The Colonial Harem*. Minneapolis: University of Minnesota Press, 1986.

———. *Resistance Literature*. New York: Methuen, 1987.

Hedri, Souad. *Vie et Agonie*. Tunis: Editions Bouslama, 1978.

Khelladi, Aissa. "L'homme est-il l'avenir de la femme?" *Ounoutha.* April, 1991.
Knauss, Peter R. *The Persistence of Patriarchy: Class, Gender, and Ideology in Twentieth-Century Algeria.* New York: Praeger, 1987.
Ladner, Joyce. *Tomorrow's Tomorrow.* Garden City, N.Y.: Double-day & Co., 1971.
Mernissi, Fatima. *The Veil and the Male Elite: A Feminist Interpretation of Women's Rights in Islam.* Trans. Mary Jo Lakeland. Reading, Mass: Addison-Wesley, 1991.
Minces, Juliette. *The House of Obedience.* London: Zed Press, 1982.
Monego, Joan Phyllis. *Maghrebian Literature in French.* Boston: Twayne Publishers, 1984.
M'rabet, Fadela. *La Femme Algérienne, suivi de Les Algériennes.* Paris: Maspero, 1969.
Philipp, Thomas. "Feminism and Nationalist Politics in Egypt," in *Women in the Muslim World.* Edited by Lois Beck and Nikki Keddie. Cambridge, Mass.: Harvard University Press, 1978.
Radhakrishnan, Radha. "Toward an Effective Intellectual: Foucault or Gramsci?" in *Intellectuals: Aesthetics, Politics, Academics.* Edited by Bruce Robbins. Minneapolis: University of Minnesota Press, 1990.
Said, Edward. "Foucault and the Imagination of Power," in *Foucault: A Critical Reader.* Edited by David Couzens Hoy. Oxford: Basil Blackwell: 1986.
Spivak, C. Gayatri. "Can the Subaltern Speak?" in *Marxism and the Interpretation of Culture.* Edited by Cary Nelson and Lawrence Grossberg. Urbana and Chicago: University of Illinois Press, 1988.
Tahon, Marie Blanche. "Review of Femmes d'Alger dans leur Appartement," in *Ecriture Française dans le Monde, la Tribune des Francophones,* 5, 1981.
Taqi-Uddine Al-Hilali, Muhammad and Muhammad Muhsin Khan, *Interpretations of the Meanings of the Noble Qur'an in the English Language.* Riadh, Kingdom of Saudi Arabia: Maktaba Dar-es-Salam, 1994.
Tillion, Germaine. "Les Femmes et le Voile," in *Etudes Maghrébines: Mélange Charles-Andre Julien.* Edited by Pierre Marthelot & Andre Raymond. Paris: P. U. F, 1964.
Tohidi, Nayereh. "Gender and Islamic Fundamentalism: Feminist Politics in Iran" in *Third World Women and the Politics of Feminism.* Edited by Chandra Talpade Mohanty, et al. Bloomington and Indianapolis: Indiana University Press, 1991.
Tucker, Judith E. Ed., *Arab Women: Old Boundaries, New Frontiers.* Bloomington: Indiana University Press, 1993.
Tuqan, Fadwa. *A Mountainous Journey: An Autobiography.* Trans. Olive Kenny. London: The Women's Press, 1990.
Wade-Gayles, Gloria. *No Crystal Stair: Visions of Race and Sex in Black Women's Fiction.* New York: Pilgrim Press, 1984.
Woodhull, Winifred. *Transfigurations of the Maghreb: Feminism, Decolonization, and Literatures.* Minneapolis: University of Minnesota Press, 1993.
Zirem, Youcef. "Intellectuels Algériens: La Sempiternelle Compromission." *La Nation* 130, January 16–22, 1996.

12

Cultural Interaction and Comparative Architecture: The Colonial Experience in Francophone Africa

LIONE MOSHE

The administrative and strategic functions that colonial Dakar acquired, up to the beginning of the twentieth century, have transformed it into the dominant city that it is, in West Africa. Dakar served, from 1902, as the capital city of the *L'afrique Occidentale Française* (AOF), which contained eight colonies — Senegal, French Sudan, French Guinea, Ivory Coast, Dahomey, Upper Volta, Niger, and Mauritania. Its' harbor was turned into a commanding central port, which was connected to peanut plantations in the interior by a series of railroads. Both the European and African populations continued to grow. In spite of the re-iterative yellow fever epidemics, Dakar had more than forty thousand residents in 1914.[1]

Ironically, the establishment of the federal city at Dakar preceded the establishment of the city itself.[2] Since Dakar's urban morphology aimed to express French colonial intentions, in this part of the globe a conscious search was begun for an imperial building style which would suit these high purposes. The public design of the city's space was influenced not only by conceptualizing Dakar as a 'model' for French colonial cities, it was also tightly related to the contemporary official French doctrine of 'assimilation.' Accordingly, "the colonies could not be separated from the Republic and were subjected to the same rules."[3] After the French invasion of Algeria was complete in 1848, for instance, the country was proclaimed part of French territory in the geographical, political, and economical sense — just as Dakar was proclaimed a remote suburb of Paris at the colonial congress of 1889.[4]

The establishment of physical homogeneity between the metropolis and its colonies obliged Dakar's transformation into a French city, including all its inhabitants. The policy of assimilation was designed to create a global, unified community of "one hundred million Frenchmen." In reality, it served to justify colonization as a *mission civilisatrice*. It also represented a mixture between rationalistic and egalitarian beliefs — legacies of the French revolution in addition to a variety of orientalistic images. Consequently, the pre-colonial space of the French cities, and especially that of Dakar, underwent great change in the course of only a few decades. This change was guaranteed by strict urban legislation enforcing a grid of orthogonal, wide, paved streets with sideling trees.

The 'white city,' it was conceived, was to be introduced as a model for the natives, who would adapt its morphology and duplicate it in their living quarters.[5]

Rectangular houses, constructed with bricks or stone, symbolized the wealth and power of the dominant European group and their 'civilization.' The straw huts, on the other hand, were perceived as 'Negroes' dwellings — a symbol of barbarity and savagery. The straw huts were precarious dwellings. Apart from the constant danger of fires, they were also confiscated through/by various municipal laws which were designated to keep the poor local population away from the center of the colonial cities.[6]

These measures, used towards a total disposal of the African huts, frequently resembled military expeditions, especially after the first half of the nineteenth century when military troops were recruited by the colonial administration to implement this goal. Yet, the straw-hut landscape never disappeared from the West African cities.

This landscape did not fit well with the idealistic visions of the colonial governors, most of whom graduated from the prestigious metropolitan, *École Polytechnique* and *École des Ponts et Chaussées*. They understood very well that only a small portion of the local Muslim elite could afford to buy stones for building, which had to be imported from the Canary Islands. These governors, however, thought that living in the 'city'— a modern territory, was a privilege worth some monetary sacrifice. They strove to introduce 'labor' as a moral value. The minimal effort that was required to build a straw hut, with its locally available materials and its temporary manner, were deemed 'marginal' elements, not 'modern' ones.[7]

Consequently, the majority of the African population was transferred to newly-planned living quarters. The French, inspired by their experience in Northern Africa, named these enclaves in Western Africa *Médinas* or *les Médines*. The term Médina is synonymous with the term Casbah,[8] both referring to the medieval heart of the Muslim city. The meaning of the word in Arabic is 'town' or 'dwelling place.' Yet, in the colonial context, the term 'Médina' was used for the living quarters of the 'natives,' including both the old Muslim one and newly created African living quarters. The longstanding presence of the Muslim religion in the AOF's colonies was a perfect excuse for this practice.

Paradoxically, while the models of private habitations — like the 'house with the verandah' — were modified to meet the tropical climate, the colonial administration preferred to adapt the old metropolitan habit for its public buildings. Influenced by the third republic's building style, this formal habit was tied to the classical roots of the French culture. Hence, the Neo-Classical style was projected on to West African colonies, as well as other French colonies like Tunisia and Saigon. Greco-Roman, Renaissance, and even Victorian architectural elements were included in it.

Yet, alongside the many disadvantages in importing this alienated, extravagant, and expensive building style to West Africa, internal criticism from France itself toward the assimilationist policy grew massively. For moral, and especially practical, reasons, it was understood that some kind of collaboration between the colonizer and the colonized was essential. Hence, most of the advocates of the subsequent colonial doctrine, the 'association,' called for preservation of local cultures and their historical monuments. They believed that this aspect, with the addition of some social service buildings like schools and hospitals, could 'pacify' natives more effectively than military power.[9] As the French architect Joseph Marrast wrote, subsequent to his Moroccan-inspired design of Casablanca's courthouse in 1920, "we will conquer the natives' hearts and win their sympathy . . ."[10]

To be coherent, to function ideologically, and to legitimate themselves in relation to the native population, colonial policy designers began to look at African visual models for public building in Western Sudan. Unfortunately, they regarded the AOF's vernacular architecture as provisional. They were disappointed by its impermanent manner, mainly because of the extensive use of mud employed by the local builders. Any turn towards the historical past seemed to be impossible. They were also disappointed about its lack of monumentality in comparison to other French territories overseas, especially Northern Africa.[11]

The existence of a consolidated, monumental architectural style in North Africa testified to the power of the political entities that were conquered. At the same time, it made the colonial occupation seem more heroic and grandiose from the metropolitan viewpoint. Therefore, the invented architectural tradition, which was practiced by the colonial authorities for the North, could easily rely upon the existing formal repertoire of that region.

The eclectic, stylistic realizations were entitled 'neo-Moorish' or *Arabisances*. They have received much criticism in the postcolonial literature, mainly because of their being an 'invented tradition,' in Eric Hobsbawm's sense. That is a practice which tries to establish continuity with a proper historical past through formalization and ritualization. Simultaneously, this deliberate process immediately breaks any continuity with the past.[12]

The apparent absence in Western Sudan of local architecture, which deserved to be cited and re-invented, caused the French to project the neo-Moorish style there. Once again, the established presence of the Muslim religion in the AOF's colonies was a perfect excuse for this practice. One example, taken from a contemporary postcard, was a memorial to Senegal's sacrifice in World War I.[13] It was initiated in the 1920s at *place Prôtet*, Dakar. Some typical Islamic motifs, like the horseshoe arch and combinations of floral relics, can be identified.

These motifs were already well known to the French through their northern colonies. They were also documented and photographed by them, as another contemporary postcard from Algiers testifies.[14]

An international congress, held in 1931 at French initiative, was dedicated to colonial urbanism. Colonel Weithas spoke of the absence of native architecture in West Africa.[15] Similarly, a government representative from French Equatorial Africa proclaimed, "monuments for preservation are non-existent...old natives' cities do not exhibit any interest..."[16] On the other hand, not all the French colonial administrators shared those views. Many of them were extremely fascinated by the 'discovery' of the medieval Sudanese mud mosques on the Niger Delta and of houses of rich Muslim merchants at old cities like Djenné and Timbuktu.[17]

Sudanese architecture, which was built by African Muslims, quickly excited the French imagination. The starting point were the reports of the colonel, who erected his military camp in front of Djenné in April 1893.[18] His accounts reached the French mass media and prompted many geographical expeditions, accompanied by painters and photographers. Consequently, this architecture was found suitable for evaluation and preservation. Moreover, it earned the pure aesthetic admiration of contemporary architects, including those from the *École des beaux-arts* — the French academic fortress of artistic conservatism.

These architects studied the building techniques and the characteristics typical to this style, such as the projecting wood sticks, which served as buttresses to renew the mud exteriors every rainy season.

The French built *Polyclinique* at the beginning of the 1930s at *Avenue Blaise Diagne*, in Dakar.[19] It recalls motifs originated by mosque architecture. The visual forms were not just alienated from their social and cultural context, but were always carried out under external Eurocentric logic.

Forced concrete was usually in use for that invented building style. It was colored in ocher, to imply the mud bricks of the savanna. Moreover, these vernacular elements were always subjected to the formal canon of the *École des beaux-arts*, like the symmetrical principle. The zigzag decoration of the *Polyclinique*, its blind columns and the projecting drainpipes which recall the original wood sticks — all these elements were typical characteristics of the 'neo-Sudanese' style or *Style AOF*.

Ironically, the most memorable realizations of the 'neo-Sudanese' building style were not performed in West Africa but in Europe itself. About ten colonial and universal expositions were held in Europe between 1855 and 1937, most of them in Paris. They contained series of pavilions, each of which symbolized a different occupied country. The complex, as a whole, presented a miniature, of a unified, peaceable empire, of which the French dreamt but were never fortunate to wake up to.[20]

Every pavilion, promised by its erectors, was 'original' and 'authentic.' Yet, after two decades, the neo-Sudanese style was fixed and fossilized. It became a broad symbol of traditional Muslim architecture in French West Africa and a symbol of every West African pavilion in every colonial exposition, be it French, British, Belgian, or German. The next example was taken from AOF's section in the colonial exposition of 1931.[21] This section did not express each of the eight colonies as distinct. Instead, the various countries were lumped into a main building. The last comprised of a set of red stucco structures modeled after the *tata* or fortified palace and Muslim mosques of the upper Niger region, such as the Djenné mosque.[22]

The nature of the interface between traditional, Islamic, and French interests is apparent from the next example.[23] When it was decided that the mosque at Djenné would be rebuild in 1907, a revised francophone model was already at hand. Sponsored by the French government and funded with French francs, built under the direction of a French military engineer-administrator, it was acclaimed as "the most important monument of Sudanese art in our African empire."[24]

The internal logic of the neo-Sudanese style is explicit of the change in French colonial doctrine from 'assimilation' to 'association.' The visual culture, especially architecture and urbanism, was the most essential image of French ruling policy. It became a superficial expression of defensive rhetoric, rhetoric of pseudo-cooperation and conservation. The last was based on the orientalistic assumption that there is a basic difference between the West and the rest of the world.

However, many scholars noted the gap between glorious ideas concerning architecture and reality in the French colonies. Neo-Sudanese style remained an embryonic, indecisive phenomenon. It was an enterprise of very few people and manifested at the level of public building alone. Unlike the neo-Moorish style of North Africa, it never influenced other colonial cities outside the AOF and was left free to every available interpretation. It was fashionable in the years when the empire was apparently safe and the colonial city had gained public functions, which called for new emblems. The neo-Sudanese style vanished immediately after World War II and was replaced by the 'International Style.'[25]

The 'International Style,' also known as the 'Modern Movement in Architecture,' represented the contemporary European avant-garde. It was initiated in 1915, by the projects built in forced concrete by Auguste Perret in Casablanca and then by his disciple Le Corbusier in Algiers. This style advocated simple geometric forms, without any decoration. In this era, many African cities, without any consideration for their native setting and irrespective of their European background, began to acquire a vertical appearance due to the skyscrapers.[26]

The ex-colonized point of view in this context is worthy of some examination. In the first two decades after Senegal's independence in 1960, for example, a few realizations of neo-Sudanese style could be seen in Dakar. Equally, a conscious effort was begun, to search for an 'African' building style that would integrate tradition and modernity.

This future style was supposed to offer a new model under the previous neo-Sudanese style, which was now perceived as an anti-model. Needless to say, both styles were 'invented traditions.' "They come to us as they come to visit a zoological garden; to amuse and recreate themselves on Sunday afternoons," argued the first president of Senegal.[27]

This president, Léopold Sédar Senghor, who served as a minister in the French government and was also a well known poet and philosopher, was the main brain behind the 'new' proposed style. According to him, Africans must create one architectural style to symbolize Africa and one asymmetrical analogue, which will enounce African art, like the asymmetrical African sculpture. But his 'new' style was never realized, nor served as precedent to any 'Pan-African' building style.

In fact, its single expression can be noticed only in Senghor's private house in Dakar.[28] His house was built after his retirement in 1981. It was erected near the seashore of *Fann Résidence* and named by the local inhabitants *maison des dents* — "house of teeth." That is because it is composed of straggly, diagonal, asymmetrical, and non-regular architectural forms. These kinds of forms, in addition to the house's ocher color, recall the original model of the medieval mud mosques of Djenné and Timbuktu — as a response to the colonial architectural tradition of the French.

Endnotes

1. Jean Suret-Canale, *French Colonialism in Tropical Africa* (London, 1970) p. 308; Assane Seck, *Dakar: Métropole Ouest Africaine* (Dakar, 1970) pp. 483–485.
2. As was noted by Raymond F. Betts, "Dakar: Ville Impériale (1857–1960)," in *Colonial Cities: Essays on Urbanism in a Colonial Context*, ed. Ross, Robert, and Gerard J. Telkamp (Dordrecht, 1985) p. 204.
3. Raymond F. Betts, *Assimilation and Association in French Colonial Theory, 1890-1914* (New York & London, 1961) p. 13.
4. Ibid, pp. 31–32.
5. Alain Sinou, *Comptoirs et villes coloniales du Sénégal* (Paris, 1993) p. 300.
6. Ibid, pp. 158–159.
7. Ibid, pp. 164, 207–208.
8. Andrew F. Clark & L. Colvin Phillips, *Historical Dictionary of Senegal* (Metuchen & London, 1994, 1981) pp. 196–197.
9. Gwendolyn Wright, "Tradition in the Service of Modernity: Architecture and Urbanism in French Colonial Policy, 1900-1930," *Journal of Modern History*, 59, 2 (1987) p. 229.
10. Gwendolyn Wright, *The Politics of Design in French Colonial Urbanism* (Chicago, London, 1991) p.1.
11. Alain Sinou, *Comptoirs*, p. 334.
12. Eric Hobsbawm, "Introduction: Inventing Traditions," in *The Invention of Tradition*, ed. Eric Hobsbawm and Terence Ranger (Cambridge, 1983) pp. 1–2.
13. Dakar's Monument aux Morts 1914 - 1918 (now in Bel-Air); Archives de l'AOF, Sénégal, 4F1 84.
14. Algiers, detail from the great mosque, a French postcard from the beginning of the 20th century; Private collection.
15. E. Weithas, "Rapport général sur l'urbanisme en Afrique tropicale," dans: L'urbanisme aux colonies et dans les pays tropicaux, tome 1 (2 tomes), ed. Royer, Jean (1932) p. 114.
16. Le directeur des affaires économiques du gouvernement général, "L'urbanism en Afrique Équatoriale Française: considérations générales," dans: Royer, L'urbanisme, p. 158.
17. The city of Timbuktu, a French postcard from the beginning of the 20th century. In its center is situated Mosque Sankore (11th century); Archives de l'AOF, Sénégal, 4F1 1099.

18. Labelle Prussin, "The Image of African Architecture in France," in *Double Impact: France and Africa in the Age of Imperialism*, ed. G. Wesley Johnson (Westport, London, 1985) pp. 213, 215.
19. Institut d'Hygiène Sociale, Polyclinique de la Médina, the beginning of the 1930s; Private collection.
20. Raymond F. Betts, *France and Decolonization, 1900–1960* (New York, 1991) pp. 12–13.
21. The main AOF's pavilion, the Colonial Exposition of 1931; Patricia A. Morton, *Hybrid Modernities* (Cambridge, (Massachusetts) & London, 2000) Pl. 1.25.
22. Morton, pp. 41–42.
23. A photograph of the great mosque of Djenné after the French 'restoration'; Nnamdi Elleh, *African Architecture: Evolution and Transformation* (New York, 1996) fig. C. 55.
24. Prussin, "The Image," p. 226.
25. Raymond F. Betts, "Imperial Designs: French Colonial Architecture and Urban Planning in Sub-Saharan Africa," in *Double Impact*, ed. Johnson, pp. 198, 204.
26. John, Musgrove, "Modern Movement," in *The Dictionary of Art*, ed. Jane Turner (New York, Vol. 31, 1996) pp. 779–780; Françoise Choay, *Le Corbusier* (New York, 1960) pp. 9–11.
27. L. S. Senghor, "Standards critiques de l'art African," *African Arts*. 1, 1 (1967) p. 8.
28. A sketch of Senghor's house, 1981, Dakar (taking photos there was not permitted); Private collection.

13

Comparative Human Values: African and Islamic

ALI A. MAZRUI

In the Western worldview, rights and obligations are derived from principles of ethics. In the African worldview, pillars of wisdom govern rights and obligations. Ethics are measured by the criteria of right and wrong. Wisdom is measured by the criteria of degree of enlightenment.

If Western rights and obligations are based on ethics, and African rights and duties are based on wisdom, where do Islamic rights and obligations lie? The Islamic worldview is somewhere in-between the ethical imperatives of the West and the wisdom imperatives of the African code. Yet, ultimately, the Islamic code of conduct is rooted in faith as a measure of wisdom.

However, let us not be too rigid about these distinctions between ethics, wisdom, and faith. Instead, let us address the Islamic and the African codes of conduct on the basis of the Seven Pillars of Wisdom — independently of both Biblical origins of such pillars and the more recent legacy of Lawrence of Arabia.

The first pillar of wisdom is tolerance. Which of the values of Africa and Islam are supportive of tolerance? Both Africa and the Muslim world seem to be conflict prone. Does conflict not signify a breakdown in tolerance?

PILLARS OF A GLOBAL ETHIC

The behavior of every people is only partially determined by the moral standards of its culture. Some cultures are born intolerant, some become intolerant, and some have intolerance thrust upon them. How much of the violence in the Muslim world is native born and how much has been thrust upon Muslims?

There are currently three Muslim countries under military occupation — Iraq, Afghanistan, and Palestine. There are other Muslim populations forcefully and sometimes brutally integrated into wider state-systems. These include the Chechens under Russian occupation, the Kashmiris under Indian rule, and the ethnic Albanians in Kosovo under international trusteeship, with no hope of self-determination. In the last three years, at least two hundred thousand Muslims have been killed in Afghanistan, Iraq, Gujarat, Kashmir, Palestine, and Chechnya. In the period since the 1991 Gulf War, we may have to add a million more, killed by United Nations sanctions in Iraq and by Serbian brutalities in Bosnia, Kosovo and elsewhere, and by the merciless Israeli occupation of the West Bank and Gaza. Counting the number of dead in the world as a whole, since 1990, Muslims are a people more sinned against than sinning.

One of the most memorable verses of the Qur'an celebrates human diversity. Through the Qur'an, God addresses the human species as a whole. He says:

> O humankind! We have created you from a single pair of male and female, and made you into Nations and tribes that you may know each other [respectfully]. Verily the most honored among you in the sight of God is the most righteous among you. God is the most knowledgeable, the best informed. [Sura Hujurat 49, Verse 13]

> Yaa ayuha Nasu! Innaa khalaqnakum min dhakarin wa unthaa wa jaalnaa kum shu'uban wa qabaila li-taarafu. Inna akramakum i'nda 'llahi atqaakum. Inna'Allaha alimun khabir.

At the core of this Qur'anic verse is a celebration of human differentiation. Education is about understanding ourselves (auto-comprehension), about understanding other people (ultra-comprehension), and about understanding our environment (eco-comprehension). On issues of war and peace, friction versus friendship, conflict versus cooperation, and education are ultimately about how we relate to human diversity.

Let us be presumptuous and assert that God is on the side of creative diversity. Different religions have emphasized this fact in their different ways. Muslims believe that the Qur'an is the word of God, directly. In the Qur'an, God addresses humankind quite simply as follows: *"We have created you from a male and female, and made you into nations and tribes that you may know each other."* [Qur'an: Sura 49, Verse 13]

There is a lot in the wisdom code of Islam, which recommends forgiveness and compensation rather than revenge. In Sura 2 (*Surat el Baqara*), the Qur'an does not recommend turning the other cheek. It does allow for legitimate retaliation occasionally (*Al-Qisas*), if the retaliation is in pursuit of real justice. Nevertheless, the *surat* recommends compensation and forgiveness as a better alternative. [See Sura 2 and such verses as 178]. Indeed, the same *Surat* goes on to emphasize, "Kind words and the forgiving of faults are better than charity followed by injury." [Sura 2, verse 149]

And when the Prophet Muhammad conquered Mecca from the ruling *Quraysh*, he did not issue playing cards of the fifty most wanted *Quraysh*. He did not imprison thousands, as some conquerors have done. The Prophet Muhammad conquered Mecca, granted amnesty to all *Quraysh* who entered the sacred mosque for asylum or stayed peacefully in their homes or found their way to the home of the paramount *Quraysh* leader Abu Sufyan, Muhammad's former enemy.

As for the importance of asylum in Islam, it is captured in the origins of the Islamic calendar. The Islamic calendar does not begin from when the Prophet Muhammad was born (570 CE), or from when the Prophet Muhammad became a Prophet (610 CE), or when he died (632 CE). The *Hegira* from Mecca to Medina, in the *Miladiyya* year 622 CE, was a quest for religious refuge. The whole Islamic calendar is therefore a celebration of asylum.

In Africa's wisdom code, tolerance is partly captured in Africa's short memory of hate. While Islam recommends compensation and forgiveness as a better response than retaliation, Africanity recommends a return to normality without hate after each conflict. The Nigerian civil war of 1967–1970 ended without reprisals and without an African equivalent of the Nuremberg trials. Ian Smith unleashed a racial war on Zimbabwe and lived to sit in Zimbabwe's parliament and criticize the successor Black regime. Nelson Mandela lost twenty-seven of the best years of his life under a white racist regime and emerged ready to have afternoon tea with the widow of the architect of apartheid, Mrs. Verwoerd. Jomo Kenyatta was imprisoned by the British and denounced by a British Governor as a "leader unto darkness and death." He emerged from detention and turned Kenya towards a pro-Western orientation in which it has regrettably persisted. Kenyatta even published a book entitled *Suffering without Bitterness*.

Africans fight deeply and passionately, sometimes ruthlessly, in defense of either their identities or their values. But when the fighting is over, African cultures have a low level of hate retention. Potentially, this could be part of Africa's contribution to the principle of tolerance in the Global Ethic.

IN SEARCH OF ECONOMIC WISDOM

The second pillar of wisdom is the optimization of the economic well-being of the people. Traditional Islam is basically pro-profit but anti-interest. The oil wealth of the Muslim world challenges Muslim believers to find out where legitimate economic returns end and illegitimate usury and exploitation begin. Ancient laws of *zakat* (religious tax) and *sadaqah* (charity) may need to be transformed for the age of petroleum. However, the blessing of oil-wealth can also be the curse of vulnerability to the global strategy of the American Empire.

African economic wisdom goes back to the concept of *ujamaa* in Julius K. Nyerere's prescription for postcolonial Tanzania. While the West in the twentieth century had evolved the concept of the welfare state, Africans had evolved even earlier, the concept of the welfare tribe. Long before welfare socialism in Britain, Africa had developed a *de-facto* system of collective responsibility for orphans, for the infirm, for the aged, and for the needy. African communities had historically looked after their most vulnerable members.

From former German East Africa (Tanganyika), Julius K. Nyerere expanded this African sense of family (*ujamaa*) into the basis of modern socialist ethic of sharing. In the era of globalization, we go a step further and globalize *ujamaa* into a wisdom-pool for the human family as a whole.

RACE: BETWEEN AFRICANITY AND ISLAM

The third pillar of wisdom is social justice. It is a struggle to reduce ethnic and racial inequalities in a quest for a more humane equilibrium. If, in terms of political violence in the world, Muslims are a people more sinned against than sinning, Africans are similarly more sinned against than sinning in terms of racial prejudice and discrimination. Black people across the centuries have been humiliated, enslaved, colonized, castrated, marginalized, and spat upon. The tormentors of Black folks have sometimes been Muslims, sometimes Christians, sometimes others. Blacks have been racial victims par excellence.

The *Qur'an* tells Muslims that when confronting injustice, reparation is often better than revenge. However, Black people are only just beginning to mention the word 'reparations' for outright enslavement or for the obscenities of apartheid. In 1992, a summit meeting of the Organization of African Unity (OAU) appointed a group of eminent persons to explore the modalities and strategies for claiming reparations for Black enslavement. One of the biggest problems faced by this Reparations Committee was the relative lack of support from Africans themselves for the reparations crusade.

In terms of the Global Ethic, perhaps there should be reparations for Black people, just as there have been reparations for the Jewish people.

In the United States of America, former Secretary of State, Colin Powell and current Secretary of State, Condoleezza Rice symbolize a new kind of Black empowerment. These are descendants of slaves who have come to wield power among white people who had once enslaved their ancestors. In other words, one form of reparation is the empowerment of Black people in countries that had previously traded in slaves or practiced slavery.

One day, in the future, Africans and Arabs would need to negotiate what kind of reparation is feasible for the Arab slave trade. Among the factors that make the Arab slave trade a different system, is the Arab lineage system, which regards a child as Arab if the father is Arab regardless of who the mother is. Thus, *Sheikh* Saad Abdallah Salim al-Sabah has been Prime Minister of Kuwait though descended from a Black mother. Anwar Sadat was President of Egypt and was not faulted for having a Black mother.

In the Royal Houses of Kuwait and Saudi Arabia, where some of the princes have African mothers, which prince would pay reparations to which? A wholly different formula would have to be devised, if any reparations were to be negotiated in the future concerning the Arab slave trade.

As for the position of the Islamic religion on the race question, it is arguable that Islam is the most racially egalitarian of all three Abrahamic religions — Judaism, Christianity, and Islam. The *Qur'an* tells Muslims that they have been created into nations and tribes mainly so that they could know each other. Moreover, the Prophet Muhammad said to his followers more explicitly, "An Arab is not superior to a non-Arab or a red man to a black man, except through piety and virtue."

Islam, thus, brings to the Global Ethic a doctrine of racial egalitarianism, which goes back fourteen centuries. Where the historical record of Islam is less impressive is with regard to the fourth pillar of wisdom — equality between men and women. Let us turn to this issue of gender in the experience of both Muslims and Africans.

GENDER: BETWEEN AFRICANITY AND ISLAM

This has to be seen in the context of three varieties of sexism, evident in human behavior, not uniquely Islamic. Benevolent sexism is a form of gender discrimination, which selectively favors the otherwise disadvantaged gender. For example, when, in 1912, the captain of the *Titanic* decided that the limited space on the lifeboats was to be reserved for women and children that was a form of benevolent sexism with which most cultures would agree; the safety of women and children came first.

In addition to benevolent sexism, there is benign sexism. Benign sexism is sexism of differentiation rather than of discrimination. A policy of different dress codes for men and women has been part of the sexism of differentiation in Islam. There are different rules of modesty for males and females. In most cultures, women are expected to cover more of their bodies than men. The Swahili *buibui* is part of the local female dress code.

In addition to benevolent sexism and benign sexism, there is the third version — malignant sexism. This is the kind of gender discrimination which results in sexual exploitation, economic marginalization, cultural subordination, or political disempowerment. Although many Muslim countries are guilty of such versions of malignant sexism, there are paradoxes in the Muslim world. In no Muslim country are women more liberated than women are in the United States; but in some Muslim countries, women have been more empowered than women have been in the United States.

Indonesia, the largest Muslim country in population, had a woman as President until 2004. Her name is Megawati Sukarnoputri. In Bangladesh, both the Head of Government and the leader of the Opposition have been women. Sheikh Hasina Wajed and Begum Khaleda Zia have alternated in political power for more than a decade.

Two other Muslim countries, outside Africa, have had a woman chief executive at the top of the political process. The late Benazir Bhutto was Prime Minister of Pakistan twice. And Ms. Tansu Ciller has been Prime Minister of Turkey, a far cry from the political culture of the Ottoman Empire.

All these cases of Muslim women at the top have occurred long before the United States has had a woman president or Germany a woman Chancellor or Italy a woman Prime Minister or Russia a woman President. However, Asian Muslims have been ahead of Africans in this empowerment.

Women in Africa are custodians of fire (symbol of heat and light), custodians of water (symbol of life and cleanliness), and custodians of earth (dual fertility). Sons in both Africa and the Muslim world respect their mothers more than do sons in the West. However, husbands in Africa and the Muslim world respect their wives less than do husbands in the West.

THE ECOLOGICAL PILLAR OF WISDOM

Let us now turn to the environmental pillar of wisdom — the quest for ecological balance and the protection of Planet Earth against excessive exploitation and devastation. Muslims have often chosen green as the color of Islam, partly because green was associated with peace. However, from the middle of the twentieth century, environmental movements committed to keeping the hills and valleys of Planet Earth forever green, have adopted the green color too. In this ecological sense, we may indeed ask — How 'green' is Islam doctrinally and in practice, and how ecologically friendly is the African culture?

Environmentally, there is a remarkable contrast between the ancestral homeland of Islam and the ancestral core of sub-Saharan Africa. Islam was born in a region which was ecologically sparse and dry. Equatorial Africa, on the other hand, is a region of lush natural abundance, including equatorial forests. The Arabian Peninsula, as the birthplace of Islam, is a region of limited natural rainfall and limited water supply. Equatorial Africa, on the other hand, is a region of tropical downpours and some of the greatest rivers and lakes on the face of the earth.

It is in that sense that the dry geography of Islamic origins and the abundant geography of equatorial Africa have represented striking contrasts in the ecological heritage of Planet Earth.

There is a related paradox with regard to the geographical origins of Islam. The Arabian lands, which were so short of water during the Prophet Muhammad's time, were destined to become lands of abundant oil fourteen centuries later. Lands that once celebrated oases of water became lands that celebrated oases of oil. The greatest oil reserves were discovered beneath the ground where the Prophet and his companions once walked. A religion that taught its followers how to clean themselves with sand (*tayamam*) when they ran out of water later discovered God's petro-bounty beneath the sand.

Unlike Islam, Africa's traditional religion draws no sharp distinction about where the Creator ends and the created begins. More clearly in African religion, than in Islam, particular rivers and hills may be sacred, particular trees (like the baobab) may be worthy of awe.

Islam has profane animals (especially the pig) but no sacred animals (such as the cow in Hinduism). African traditional religions, on the other hand, have both sacred and profane animals. Indeed, some African ethnic and clan cultures have totems which identify with particular animals (e.g., the owl totem for a clan or a totem of the hippo or monkey).

There is concern for the rights of the leopard, the owl, and the rhino; the rights of fish in the rivers and oceans; the green rights of valleys and hills. These too are 'strangers in our midst,' deserving asylum.

Other environmentalists go further. They seem to share William Wordsworth's belief that Nature's grand design is predicated on joy and wonderment. The discordant note in Nature's grand design is man. In Wordsworth's words:

> Through primrose tufts in that green bower,
> The periwinkle trailed its wreaths,
> And it's my faith that every flower,
> Enjoys the air it breathes.
>
> The birds around me hopped and played,
> Their thoughts I cannot measure,
> But the least motion which they made,
> It seemed a thrill of pleasure.
>
> The budding twigs spread out their fans,
> To catch the breezy air,
> And I must think, do all I can,
> That there was pleasure there.
>
> If this belief from heavens be sent,
> If such be nature's holy plan,
> Have I not reason to lament,
> What man has made of man?[1]

Yes, the grand design is for joy and wonderment. The discordant note is Man, including postcolonial man in Africa.

The environmental revolution and the gender revolution are interlinked at various points. However, they are interconnected most poignantly through the issue of population and the whole culture of having and rearing children. It is to this area of convergence between gender, population, and environment that we must pay special attention.

Many African countries have been witnessing their population double every 20 years. Children under 15 years of age probably account for 45% of the population of Africa as compared with 37% in Asia and 40% in Latin America.

The Green movements of recent decades have also been inspired by the esthetics for conservation. The concept of 'endangered species' has been associated with deference to biodiversity, a deference that is rooted in the belief that a world with fewer species of animals and narrower range of plants is a world impoverished and less beautiful.

INTERFAITH RELATIONS: GAINS AND LOSSES

Islam attempted to lay the foundation of unity of the Abrahamic religions with the concept of *ahl al kitab* (People of the Book). The Crusades and the Nazi Holocaust sabotaged it.

Western sense of guilt over the Nazi Holocaust has, on the whole, helped improve relations between the Christians and Jews. However, Western appeasement of the Zionist movement has damaged relations between Muslims and Jews. About ten years separated two documents of momentous consequences for the Middle East. One was, indeed, the *Balfour Declaration* of 1917 about a Jewish home in Palestine. The other was Hitler's *Mein Kampf* of 1927. The Balfour Declaration was controversial, but was in the tradition of 'the British fudge.' Mein Kampf was a work of evil. However, in their vastly different ways, the two documents unleashed forces that favored the long-term aims of the Zionist movement. Israel was indeed created, and the world has never been the same since.

America's unquestioning and uncritical pro-Israeli policies are part of the problem but not the only one. Increasingly, in the course of the twentieth century, the United States became a new kind of empire. The new American Empire is an empire not of occupation but of control, not a land-hungry hegemon but a resource-hungry colossus.

Militarily, American power adds up to the military power of the next ten countries added together. In global reach, the United States has some degree of military presence in nearly one hundred countries already.

Relations between mainstream Christianity and Islam have become exceptionally cordial in the Western world. In fact, denominations like the Roman Catholic Church and the Anglican Church have never been more Muslim friendly than recently. Pope John Paul was strongly against the American-led war in Iraq in 2003, partly out of concern for the risk of damaging Christian-Muslim relations.

Prince Charles, the Prince of Wales, is a Patron of the Oxford Center for Islamic Studies. In 2004, he received a special award from the Sultan of Brunei for contributing to *Dialogue among Civilizations*. When he becomes King of England, Prince Charles would like to include *Defender of Faith* (i.e., all religions) rather than Defender of only the Church of England.

In 2004, I was awarded an Honorary Doctorate in Divinity not by a Muslim institution nor by a non-Muslim institution in a Muslim society, but by Lafayette College, in Pennsylvania, a primarily Christian and Euro-American institution of Presbyterian origins. The Governor of Pennsylvania was in attendance at the award of the doctorate.

As for relations between Christianity and Islam in Africa, both religions are expanding in numbers and growing in influence. However, can they co-exist peacefully? Christianity and Islam are divisive in Africa only if they reinforce prior ethnic and linguistic divisions.

In Nigeria, almost all Hausa are Muslims, almost all Igbo are Christians, and the Yoruba are split in the middle. Thus, Islam reinforces Hausa identity; Christianity reinforces Igbo identity; and Yoruba nationalism unites the Yoruba, regardless of religion.

Islam and Christianity divide Northern and Southern Sudan mainly because the two regions were already divided by even deeper cultural differences. The two regions had belonged to two different indigenous civilizations even before they were either Islamized or Christianized.

On the other hand, Muslims in Senegal repeatedly voted for a Christian president from 1960. For twenty years, Leopold Sedar Senghor, a Roman Catholic, was President of a country, which is over ninety percent Muslim. Leopold Senghor was succeeded, for another twenty years, by a Muslim president of Senegal. The Muslim president, Abdou Diauf, had a Roman Catholic First Lady. This degree of ecumenical democracy has not been achieved in the Western world. No Western democracy has ever elected either a Jew or Muslim for President. Joseph Lieberman, a distinguished Jewish Senator in the United States, trailed far behind in his bid for the Democratic presidential nomination in the 2003–2004 primaries.

As for the distinguished British Tory, Benjamin D'Israeli, there is general consensus that he would never have become Prime Minister of Great Britain in the nineteenth century had his dad, Isaac D'Israeli not quarreled with his Synagogue of Bevis Marks and then decided to have his children baptized as Christians. After all, not all Jews by religion until 1858 were allowed even to run for parliamentary elections in Britain, let alone become ministers.

On the other hand, Tanzania has had a religiously rotating presidency. Ali Hassan Mwinyi, a Muslim, succeeded Julius K. Nyerere, a Catholic; Benjamin Mkapa, a Christian, succeeded Ali Hassan Mwinyi; Jakaya Kikwete, Tanzania's incumbent President, is a Muslim. Will the next Tanzanian president be a Christian? The religious rotation may indeed continue, but who can be sure?

Nigeria has not yet developed a religiously rotating presidency. However, there are advocates of a regionally rotating Nigerian presidency, alternating between the north and the south. Such regional alternation could *de facto* be a religious alternation in the Nigerian presidency.

Africa had no religious wars before the arrival of Islam and Christianity. Now that Africa has embraced its own Islam and Christianity, the Africans are developing ecumenical attitudes to religion, which are far ahead of the rest of the world. The ecumenical spirit of Africa may be part of its contribution to the Global Ethic and to the sixth pillar of wisdom.

TOWARDS GREATER WISDOM: THE SEVENTH PILLAR

The seventh pillar of wisdom is a relentless quest for greater wisdom. An important part of this area of wisdom is the pursuit of creative synthesis. The synthesis may be between wisdom and knowledge, between religion and science, and between one culture and another. It is arguable that Islam was historically at its most creative when it was ready to learn mathematics from India, philosophy from ancient Greece, architecture from Persia, science from the Jews, and jurisprudence from the legacy of Rome.

Muslims believe that God's first words to the Prophet Muhammad were indeed about knowledge, and God's first command to the Prophet was the imperative *Iqra* (Read). The earliest *Qur'anic* verses linked biological sciences with the sciences of the mind.

Moreover, by proclaiming that all knowledge is ultimately from God, the earliest *Qur'anic* verses warned against the arrogance of pseudo-omniscience among humans. Science was morally accountable:

1. Read in the name of thy Lord who created;
2. Created the human person out of a mere clot of congealed blood;
3. Read and thy Lord is most bountiful;
4. He who taught by the pen;
5. Taught man that which he knew not.
6. Yet man does transgress all bounds.
7. In that he looketh upon himself.
8. Verily to the Lord is the final return.
    [Sura Iqra or Alaq, verses 1–8]

God "taught by the pen." In contemporary terms, 'the pen' could be extended to include teaching using the computer and the internet. God taught human beings "that which they knew not." Within the last one hundred years alone, this has included splitting the atom, landing a man on the moon, sending a spacecraft to Mars, discovering the human genome, cloning a sheep, and exploring cyberspace.[2]

The distinctive aspect of early Islam as a civilization was precisely this readiness to synthesize what was best from other cultures. Those early *Qur'anic* verses stressed that all real knowledge came from God, regardless of which *insaan* (human being) discovered it. Every successful scientific discovery helped to reveal more of God.

This early Muslim readiness to learn from other civilizations later declined. By the second half of the Ottoman era, in the eighteenth century, the Muslim world was getting to be scientifically marginal.

However, in South Asia, Pakistan has broken through the nuclear barrier and succeeded in giving the Muslim world its first nuclear power. In other respects, Malaysia had been the most successful Muslim-led country in the world. Yet, Prime Minister Mahathir Mohamad used his Swan song of retirement in 2003 to call upon fellow Muslims to close the knowledge gap between themselves and such adversaries as the Zionists.

THE CHINA CARD

Pakistan's nuclear program was apparently aided by China. Were the Pakistanis responding to a saying attributed to the Prophet Muhammad? *"Itlibil Ilama was lau bi Swiin."*

According to Ibn Abdul-Barr, the Prophet Muhammad had called upon his followers to pursue knowledge "even as far as China." Did Muhammad learn about China when he was a traveling salesman between Mecca and Damascus and beyond, on behalf of his wife Khadijah? Did the Prophet anticipate Samuel Huntington's worry, at the end of the twentieth century, about an emerging alliance between Islam and countries of the Confucian heritage?

As for Africa, its credentials for a global role in the twenty-first century are still in terms of natural resources and intrinsic cultural values, rather than in technological skills. However, African thinkers are in disagreement about the relationship between wisdom on one side and technical skills on the other. Philosophers of romantic gloriana emphasize the monumental achievements of Africa's past, ranging from the pyramids of Egypt to the brooding majesty of Great Zimbabwe. Without necessarily realizing it, such gloriana thinkers seem to share part of Betrand Russell's conviction that civilization is a child of the pursuit of luxury.

The greatest of Africa's postcolonial gloriana thinkers was Sheikh Anta Diop of Senegal, who emphasized ancient Egypt's pivotal role in the origins of world civilization as a whole. Diop saw the River Nile as the mother of the earliest human achievements.

The other major African school of civilizational theory has emphasized not the grand monuments of Africa's structural achievements, but the wisdom of being nontechnical. In the words of the Black poet, of Martinique, Aime Cesaire:

> Hooray for those who never invented anything!
> Hooray for those who never discovered anything;
> Hooray for joy, hooray for love;
> Hooray for the pain of incarnate tears ...
>
> Honor to those who have invented neither powder nor the compass;
> Those who have tamed neither gas nor electricity;
> Those who have explored neither the seas nor the skies ...

My negritude [my Blackness] is neither a tower nor a cathedral;
*It plunges into the deep red flesh of the soil.*³

The greatest African thinker of this simplifying school was also Senegalese. The late Leopold Sedar Senghor, who was President of Senegal from 1960 to 1980, was a philosopher and a poet as well as a statesman. Senghor argued that while Cartesian epistemology starts from the premise "I think, therefore I am," African epistemology starts from the vastly different source of self-awareness: "I *feel*, therefore I am." Senghor belonged to the philosophy of unscience, in contrast to his gloriana compatriot, Sheikh Anta Diop.⁴

As we seek to construct a Global Ethic based on seven pillars of wisdom, we need to listen to those two competing philosophies, about the relationship between expertise on one side and genuine wisdom on the other. We also need to listen to Africa's song of self-affirmation as captured in the following poetic prose:

> "We are a people of the day before yesterday and a people of the day after tomorrow. Long before slavery, we lived in one huge village called Africa, and then strangers came into our midst and took many of us away, scattering us to all the corners of the earth. Before those strangers came, our village was the world; we knew no other. But we are now spread out so widely that the Sun never sets on the descendants of Africa. The world is now our village, and we plan to make it more human between now and the day after tomorrow."⁵

Wisdom begins when we understand ourselves. Wisdom matures when we aspire to higher human standards. How we treat strangers in our midst is the ultimate humane standard. Let us do so guided by the Seven Pillars. As the book of Proverbs announced to the world, more than two thousand years ago, "Wisdom hath built a house; she has carved out her seven pillars." In our own modern ways, let us respond to those imperatives.

Endnotes

I am indebted to Thomas Uthup and Muhammad Yusuf Tamim for research and bibliographical assistance.

1. William Wordsworth, *Complete Poetical Works: Archive of Classic Poems.* <http://www.everypoet.com/Archive/Poetry/William_Wordswoth/William_Wordswoth_130.htm> February, 26, 2004.
2. These issues are discussed more fully in Ali A. Mazrui and Alamin M. Mazrui, "Islam and Civilization" chapter in *Dialogue of Civilizations: A New Peace Agenda*, ed. Majid Tehranian and David W. Chapell (New York: L. B. Tauris, 2002) pp. 139–160.
3. Aime Césaire, "Return to Native Land."

4. Leopold Sedar Senghor. See also Ali A. Mazrui and J. F. Ade Ajayi et al "Trends in Philosophy and Science in Africa," in *Africa Science,* ed. Ali A. Mazrui (1938); C. Wondjii, *UNESCO General History of Africa*, Vol. VIII (London: Heinemann Educational Books, 1993).
5. This African song of reaffirmation is paraphrased from programme 9 of Mazrui's television series, *The Africans: A Triple Heritage* (BBC/PBS and Nigeria's Television Authority), 1986.

Subject Index

Abrahamic religions, ix, x, xxii
    Africa giving asylum to, ix, x, xii
    Egypt as cradle of, x, xi
    North Africa as mother of, ix, *see also* North Africa
Afrabia and global apartheid, 119
    Afrabia as counter to global apartheid, 121
    Blacks economic victims of, 119, 120
    Muslims and Arabs as victims of, 119, 120
Afrabia creation of, 118, 119
Afrabia defined, 109, 113, 116
Afrabia led by oil rich countries, 123
Arabia view itself as part of Africa, 122
Afrabians types of, 111–114, 117
Africa:
    and China Card, 255, 256
    and September 11/2001, 22–25
    and World Bank, 28
    Arabization of, xii, xxiii
    between expertise and wisdom, 256
    caught in crossfire American/Middle-East conflict, 22–24, 26, 27
    centrifugal fragmentation, 115
    democracy struggle, 115
    economic fatwa, 28–29
    Francophone *see* Francophone Africa
    impact of Christianity and Islam on, xvii, xix, xx
    impact on Christianity, xvii
    impact on Muslim history, vii, ix, x, xi
    seven triads of, xxii–xxv
    impacted by Euro-Christianity, xvii
    impacted by European imperialism, xvii
    impacted by The Triple Heritage, xvii
    Pan-Africanism dilution of, 115
    Protestant revolution, 29
    reparations, 247, 248
    role in origin of world civilization, 255, 256
    short memory of hate, 246–247
    wisdom and technical skills, 255, 256
    wisdom of being non-technical, 255, 256
Africa-Arabia relationship *see also* Afrabia
    Arabic and Islamic influence, 118, 119
    caught in American/Middle-East conflict, 109
    forging reconciliation, 111–113
    influenced by war on terrorism, 109
    learn from Anglo-American relationship, 111
    learn from America-Japan relationship, 111
    linguistic binders, 117
    Middle-East, 109
    Red-Sea divide, 116–119
Africa: religious distribution
    Catholic, 4, 5
    conversions, 4, 13
    growth of, 7
    impact of, 7

influence of, 7
Islam, 4, 5
Indigenous, 4
North-South divide (Sudan, Nigeria), 22
Other (Hindu), 5
Former colonial power
Belgium, 7
France, 6
Other (Eritrea), 7
Portugal, 7
United Kingdom, 6
Regional distribution classification of, 8
East Africa, 6
Middle Africa, 6
North Africa, 5
Southern Africa, 6
West Africa, 5
African diaspora and African solidarity, xiv
African diaspora in Spain, xv–xvi
African ecumenical spirit, 18, 253, 254
African spirituality and scientific development, 28
Algerian revolution influence on French politics, 118, 119
Arabia-African pre-Islamic presence in, xiv–xxiv
Arabic:
as chosen language, xiii
impact on Africa, xviii
impact on African languages, xiii
impact on Hausa, xiii, xxv
impact on Kiswahili, xiii
spread of in Africa, xiii
Atlantic Slave Trade, xvi

Christianity:
as Afro-Western, xxi
distribution in Africa, 3, 4
impact on Africa, xvii
impact on African Islam, xvii

Christianity and Islam:
competitive relationship, xvii, xxv
conflictual relationship, xvii, xviii, xx, xxi, xxv
ecumenical relationship, xvii, xviii, xx, xxi, xxv
Christianity and Islam relations:
determinants of, xviii
doctrinal, xviii–xx
historical, xviii–xx
sociological, xviii–xx
Colonization impact on Christianity and Islam, xviii
Cultural revivalism:
rekindled by structural adjustment, 19–23, 27
rekindled by globalization, 19–23, 27–29
rekindled by tribalization, 19–23, 27–29

Dakar see Francophone Africa

East Africa:191
impact of Arabic on, 192, 193
Islamic cultural impact, 191–193
literacy impact, 194
political empowerment of women (Uganda), 196
sexism in and types of (benevolent, benign, malignant), 194–195
East African diaspora in Arabia, xiv–xvi
East African Islam see also Kenya Coast
Ecumenical spirit see African ecumenical spirit
Egypt:
as centre of African, Arab and Islamic cultures, xi
Islamization of, xi, xii
Ethiopia, x, xi, xii, xxiii
as refuge for early Islam, x, xi, xii, xxiii, 13, 17, 114, 190, 191

Subject Index

Francophone Africa: 236–243
  architecture cultural influence on, 236–243
  Dakar-building style, 237, 238, 239
  Dakar-establishment of, 236
  Dakar- French characteristic of, 236, 237, 238
  Dakar-French landscape, 237
  Dakar-impacted by Sudanese architecture, 239, 240, 241
  Dakar-International Style architecture, 241, 242
  Dakar-Islamic impact, 239, 242
  Dakar-neo-Moorish architecture, 239, 240

Global Ethic: African and Islamic, 244–257
  Seven pillars,
    of ecological balance, 249, 250, 251
    of economic wisdom, 247
    of gender equality, 248, 249
    of greater wisdom in Islam and Africa, 254, 255
    of interfaith relations, 251, 252, 253
    of race and social justice, 247
    of tolerance, 244–246
  China Card, 255, 256
Globalization and cultural revivalism *see* Cultural Revivalism

Hausa impact of Arabic on, xiii, xxv
Hausa impact of Islam on, xiii, xxv

Indirect rule:
  and Christianity, xix
  and Islam, xviii, xix
  genesis of shariacracy, 20, 21
  impact on Christian-Muslim relations, xix
Islam in Africa:
  and ancient African diaspora, xiv
  as Afro-Asian, xxi
  between revivalism and radicalization, 17, 19, 27
  distribution in Africa, 3, 4
  East African, xii, *see also* East Africa
  geographical expansion (by trade and other ways), 14–16
  impact on Africa, vii, viii, xvii
  impact on Egypt, xii
  impact on Hausa, xiii, xxv
  impact on North Africa, xii, 13, *see also* North Africa
  Kenya *see* Kenya Islam in
  Niger *see* Niger Islam in
  Northern Nigeria, 19, 20
  nuclearization of (Pakistan), 254, 255
  religious tolerance South Saharan, 19
  scientific spirit and creative synthesis, 254, 255
  Southern Africa, xii, 17, *see also* South Africa
  statistics, 17, 18
  Uganda, 19, *see also* Uganda
  West Africa *see* West Africa Islam in
Islam: literary view
  and feminism, 206, 207
  and the Magreb, 206
  as political agenda, 206, 214, 215, 225, 226
  traditionalist view, 206
  Country focus:
    Algeria (Assia Djebar's, *A Sister in Scheherazade*), 206–215
    rebellion against mores and family, 208–215
    role in Algerian revolution and politics, 210, 211, 212, 214, 215
    Women's condition (veiling), 206–214
  Morocco (Leila Abouzeid's, *Year of the Elephant*), 215–222
    rebellion against mores and

family, 208, 215–222
search for equality and liberation, 216, 221
Women's condition, 206, 215–222
Tunisia (Souad Hedri's, *Vie et Agonie*), 208, 222–225
rebellion against mores and family, 208, 222–225
Women's conditions, 222–225
Izala Sect, 152, 153

Kenya:
and Pax Americana, 199
and September 11/2001 exacerbating Christian-Muslim relations, 199–203
caught in American/Middle East conflict, 24, 25
Constitution of Kenya Review Commission, 172, 179–183
Ali A. Mazrui input, 179, 182
Muslim and Ummah response to, 180–183
Ufungamano Initiative, 181
Defence Council of Kenya, 171
Government action against Islamic NGOs, 176–178
Islam in, 165
Islamic Party of Kenya (IPK) and impact on the Ummah, 168–174
Muslim political marginalization, 173, 174
By KANU, 173, 174
Nairobi bomb blast (1998), 175–178
Somali status of, 166, 167
state of, 167, 168
statistics, 165
SUPKEM formation, 166–180
SUPKEM-Muslim political bite, 173–175
SUPKEM-Ummah relations, 176–180

Ummah (before 1990), 165
Ummah disadvantaged status, 166
Ummah (after 1990) and the second liberation, 169–173
Ali A. Mazrui view of, 171, 172
Mohamed Bakari view of, 172
Mohammed Hyder view of, 172
resurgence of, 168, 170, 173, 174
State relations, 173–183
young Muslim leadership and, 168–170
Kenya Coast: 189–205
Black Intifadah, 201–203
caught in American/Middle East conflict, 199–201
dependent on Muslim Swahilists, 198
distinctiveness of, 197
fountainhead of Islam, 197
gateway into and out of East Africa, 198
gender issues, 194–195
Islam influencing history, language and religion, 191, 198
Islamic culture interwoven with African and Arabic culture, 190, 191
Kadhi Court protection, 203
literacy in, 189
Madaraka Day (Moi speech), 201–203
need to restore it, 201
shariah legacy, 189, 190, 196, 197, 203
social justice, 203
Kiswahili impact on Africa, xiii, xiv, xxiv, xxv, 192, 193

Libya and Lockerbie plane bombing, 200

Monotheism origin of, ix, x, xi
Africa as its cradle, ix
Moors, xv, xvi

Subject Index

Muslim countries under female leadership, 195
Muslim Spain, xv

Niger: democracy and Islamic revival, 150, 151, 152, 159, 160
  Islam in, 147
    against Western gender views, 158
    call for authentic Islam, 151
    impact of Nigerian Islamic centres, 149, 150
    influenced by Islamic Associations, 152, 154
    influenced by neighbouring states, 148, 149
    Islam against westernization (FIMA and CEDAW), 156–158
    Islamic Associations vs secularism, 154, 155, 159, 160
    Islamic identity and national policy, 154–157
    Islamic impact on politics, 156, 159
    Islamic organizations–structural development of, 152–154
    Izala Sect influence on, 152, 153
    Nigeria sharing Islamic ties, 149
    protecting womens rights proscribed by the Quran, 157, 158
    resurgence of Islamic organizations, 147, 151–153, 159
    revival of, 151, 152
    State-moral re-foundation of, 148, 158
Nigeria:
  Christian-Muslim polarization, 131, 132
  Indirect rule, 20, 21
  Islamic expansion, 126
  Military coups, 127–132
  Muslim political role, 130
  Muslims view as Christian state, 132
  Northern Islam, 19, 20
  North-South religious divide, 20, 21
  overview of, 125
  political party regional distribution as source of conflict, 126–132
  religious landscape, 126
  Shari'a in see Shari'a see also Shariacracy
North Africa:
  Arabization of, xii, 13, 14
  European presence, xv, xvi
  Islamization of, xi, 13

Ottoman Empire, x

Re-tribalization caused by counter-terrorism, 23
Re-tribalization and globalization, 27–29
Re-tribalization as pre-condition for re-modernization, 29
Romantic gloriana, 255

Senegal religious tolerance, 18, 19
September 11/2001, 22–25 see also Africa and specific African countries
September 11/2001 affecting Christian-Muslim relations, 25, 27, 199–203
September 11/2001 compromising civil liberties, 25, 26
Shari'a: 124
  and democratic values, 138–141
  and Itjihad, 124
  as Muslim self-identity, 124
  Christian-Muslim conflict, 133, 134, 137
  Christian opposition to, 125, 126, 131, 132, 137, 138, 140
  history of, 133, 136–138
  Muslims deny Shari'a caused Kaduna conflict, 134, 135

Muslim's Student Society of Nigeria
  campaign for, 137, 142 (n10)
  politically motivated, 124, 140, 141
  resurgence in Nigeria, 124, 133–136
  save Muslims from corrupt rulers, 135
Shariacracy, 20, 21
Shariacracy and globalization, 20, 21
Slavery-Islamic view of, 248
Sokoto Caliphate, 126
South Africa:
  Islam and indentured Indians, 73, 74
  Islam in, 73
    Pre-Apartheid South Africa, 80–88
      Leadership-Ulema role, 85–86
      Leadership-trader role, 85–86
      Muslim community activity, 82, 83
      Muslim-Hindu trader unity, 81–82
      Muslim-Indian unity-cemented by African antagonism, 87–88
      Muslim Organizations (Natal Muslim Council), 83–88
      religious education, 82–83
      repatriation policy, 81
      socio-economic conditions, 80–81
    The Apartheid Period, 1948–1994
      Islam consolidated by residential segregation, 88–89
      Islamic revivalism, 89–90
        Arabic Study Circle, 90, 95
        Barelwi Islam, 93
        Deobandi Islam, 92–95
        Deobandi-Barelwi differences, 93–95
        Iqbal Study Group, 90–91
        Islamic Council of South Africa (ICSA), 95, 96
        Islamic Propagation Centre, 96, 97
        Jamiatul Ulama Natal, 92, 93
        leadership-Ulema role, 88–89
        leadership-trader role, 85, 88
        Muslim Youth Movement, 90–95
        Qibla Movement, 97, 98
        Tabligh Jamaat, 93
      Muslims and apartheid, 97, 98
      youth role of, 88–89,
    Post-Apartheid Period, 1994-
      conservatism in, 98, 99
      intellectuals marginalized, 99, 100
      leadership-Ulema role, 99
      perceived as 'Indian,' 79, 80, 87, 88, 100
      shifting boundaries, identity, and tolerance, 100
  Indian Muslims defined as Arabs, 73
  Muharram Festival promoting Indianness, 74–75, 79–80, 86–87
  Muslim class distinction, 73, 79
  Muslim-Hindu working class unity, 79
  race, class, religious and political distinctions, 78, 79, 87
  role of traders and mosques, 77

Soofie Saheb and working class Muslims, 75–76
Surtee-Memon distinction, 77
Spain Islam in, xv, xxiv
Sudan caught in American/Middle East conflict, 24
Sudan (Eastern) Islamization of, 17
Sudan, North-South divide coinciding with religious divide, 22
Sudan (Northern) Arabization and Islamization, 14, 22
Sudan (Southern) Arabization faster than Islamization, 14, 22

Tawheed, ix
The Triple Heritage, vii, xviii, xxiv
   and Africa, xvii
   and Christianity-Islam relations, xviii
Traditional religions distribution in Africa, 3, 4 *see also* Africa religious distribution

Uganda:
  Islam in
    caught in American/Middle East conflict, 26, 27
    Christianity rise and spread of, 48–50
    Christianity-Islamic confrontation, dialogue and tolerance, 47–50, 52, 54–62,
    Christian-Muslim attitude to other faiths, 63
    Church-survival of, 48
    Islam as State religion (Idi Amin), 54, 62
    Islam rise and spread of, 48–52, 62–63
    Islamic organizations, 55
    Muslim declining power of, 52–53
    Muslim political marginality, 53–55
    Muslim religious confrontation, 51
    Muslims suspicious of Christian education, 61–62
    North-South does not coincide with religious divide, 22
    religious pluralism in, 48
    religious tolerance in, 19

West Africa:
  Islam spread of, xii, 31–46
    Almoravids unifying West-North African markets, 42–43
    by Almoravid dynasty, 32–35
    by Arab cultural centres, 40, 41
    by Arabic language, 39–40
    by Jihad, 32–35, 39
    by military expeditions, 32
    by Muslim communities, 38–39
    by scholars and preachers, 37–38, 39
    by trade, 35–37, 39
    founding of schools, 41, 42
    on Africa-European economic relations, 42–43
    spread of Arab-Islamic culture, 39–41
West African diaspora in America, xvi, xxiv
Women as political leaders, 195
World Bank, 28

Zanzibari revolution, 112

Author Index

Abacha, General Sani, 131, 140
Abiola, Moshood, 130
Abouzeid, Leila, 206
Accad, Evelyne, 214
Ahmed bin Ibrahim, 49
Ahmed Mohammed Lockhat Wakuff (Trust), 83
Al-Azhar University, xi, xxv
Al-Bakri, 32, 34, 38
Al-Makkari Brothers, 37
Al Mùstadhir Billah, 35
Al-Qaeda, 22, 24
Amin, Idi, 19, 53, 54, 62
Amod, Aboobakr, 77
Arabic Study Circle, 90, 92, 95
Ashcroft, John, 26,
Association of Muslim Doctors (SA), xxi
Awolowo, O, 127
Azikiwe, N. 126, 127

Babangida, General Ibrahim, 129
Bakari, Mohamed, 172
Bakari II, xvi
Balala, Sheikh Khalid, 170
Balewa, Abubakar Tafawa, 127
Barau, Siraj Abdulkarim, 124
Baré, Ibrahim M. 156
Barelwi Islam, 89, 93, 94
Bawa, Advocate Ebrahim, 83, 84, 96
Bello, Ahmadu, 127
Bello, Muhammad, 17
Bhutto, Benazir, 195
Bilal, xiv, xxiv, 13
Bishop Taylor, 57

Boutchich, Brahim El Kadiri, 31
Buhari, Muhammadu, 129
Bush, George W. 26

Carew, Jan, xv
Cassiem, Ahmed, 97, 98
Cesaire, Aime, 255, 256
Cheref, Abd El Kader, 206
Church Missionary Society (Uganda), 49, 50
Ciller, Tansu, 195
Clinton, Bill, 24
Columbus, Christopher, xvi
Conable, Barber B. 27

Deedat, Ahmed, 96
Delcroix, Catherine, 211
Deobandi Islam, 89, 92, 93
Diauf, Abdou, 253
Diagne, Pathé, xvi
Diop, Sheikh Anta, 255, 256
Diouf, Abdou, 19
Djebar, Assia, 206

Edwin, Gimode A. 165
Emir Abù Bakr Ben Omar Lamtùni Jihad, 33, 34

Fanon, Frantz, 210, 211

Gaddafi, Muammar al, 110, 148
Ghai, Professor Yash Pal, 182
Ghoussoub, Mai, 218, 219
Gowon, Yakubu, 127

Hafiz Abu Bakr, 91
Hedri, Souad, 206
Houphouet-Boigny, Felix, 19
Hyder, Mohammed, 172, 173, 178

Ibn Abi Zaré, 34
Ibn Battùta, 38
Ibn Khaldun, 14, 31
Ibn Muhammad Ahmad, Abdullah, 17
Ibn Tachfine, Yoùssef (Jihad), 33, 34, 35, 37, 40
Ibn Umar, Abù Bakr, 40
Ibn Yassine, Abdùllah (Jihad), 32, 33
Iqbal Study Group, 90, 91
Islamic Council of South Africa (ICSA), 95, 96
Islamic Party of Kenya (IPK), 168–174
Islamic Propagation Centre (IPC), 96, 97
Ismail, E. H. 90

Jamiatul Ulama Natal, 92, 93
Jhaveri, Omar, 79
Joomal, A. S. K. 91

Kaba, Amadu Jacky, 3
Kajee, A. I. 83, 84
Kalouche, Fouad, viii
Karam, Abdelmonim, 31
Kenyatta, Jomo, 246
Khan, Advocate R. K. 82
Khan, Aga, 16,
Khan, Dr. Inamullah, 95
Khelladi, Aissa, 215
Kibaki, Mwai, 182
King Nuhu Kalema, 52
King Suuna, 49
Knauss, Peter R. 212
Kountché, Seyni, 147, 150

Lakhi, M. E. 81
League of Arab States, xii
Lord Lugard, 20, 21

Mall, Dr. Daud, 90, 92
Mandela, Nelson, 246
Marrast, Joseph, 238
Mazrui, Ali A. ix, 13, 109, 171, 172, 189, 244
Megawati, S. 195
Mernissi, Fatima, 226
Minces, Juliette, 206, 207
Mkapa, Benjamin W. 25, 253,
Mohammed, Murtala, 128
Moi, Daniel Arap., 24, 174, 176, 179, 199–202
Moolla, A. M. 83
Motala, M.A. 82
Moshe, Lione, 236
Museveni, Yoweri Kaguta, 54
Muslim Supreme Council (Uganda), 62
Muslim Youth Movement (SA), 91, 92, 95
Mutesa I, 49
Mwinyi, Ali Hassan, 253
Mwinyi, Omar, 169
Mzee, Rashid, 180

Naim Kaddah, 39, 40
Nasser, Gamal Abdel, 110, 122
Natal Indian Congress (NIC), 78
Natal Muslim Council, 83, 84, 86,
Ndyabahika, James, 47
Nkrumah, Kwame, 110
Nyerere, Julius K. 253

Obasanjo, Olusegun, 128, 131
Obote, Milton, 19
Osama bin Laden, 22, 175
Ostergard, Robert, viii
Ousmane Dan Fodio, xii, 16, 125, 126, 137

Paruk, E. M. 84, 85
Perret, Auguste, 241
Pharoah Akhenaton, ix, xxii
Pope, Alexander, 29
Powell, Colin, 248

Prince Charles, the Prince of Wales, 252
Pwani University College, 189
Qibla Movement, 97, 98

Red Sea, 116, 119, 122
Rice, Condoleezza, 248

Saibou, Ali, 147
Sadiq el Mahdi, 17
Said, Edward, 227, 228
Salim, Professor Idha, 181
Salim, Salim Ahmed, 111
Sebuharara, Ruzimah, viii
Seghatolislami, Tracia L., viii
Senghor, Leopold Sedar, 18, 241, 242, 253, 256
Sertima, Ivan van, xv
Shagari, Alhaji Shehu, 128
Sheikh Muhammad Ben Mani, 41
Society of African Missions (Uganda), 50
Songhai, Kingdom of, 35
Soofie Saheb, 75, 76,
Sounaye, Abdoulaye, 147

Spivak, Gayatri, 223, 227, 228
Sultan Ahmed Ben El Hadj, 40
Sultan, M. L. 82

Tabligh Jamaat, 93
Tahon, Marie-Blanche, 214
Tillion, Germaine, 211
Timbuktu, 40, 41
Tohidi, Nayereh, 212
Toler, Michael, viii
Touré, Sékou, 110

Uthman bin Affan, xi
Uthup, Thomas, viii

Vahed, Goolam, 73

Wajed, Sheikh Hasina, 195
Wallis, William, 134, 136
Wordsworth, William, 250, 251

Zakzaky, Ibrahim, 141
Zia, Begum Khaleda, 195